Praise for

THE REAL JANE AUSTEN

~~~

"Brilliantly illuminating . . . riveting. . . . Again and again . . . Byrne opens out Austen's story with a novelist's persistent probing of the evidence."

—Simon Callow, *The Guardian* (London)

"An excellent new biography . . . well researched and entertaining. . . . Byrne gives us a Jane Austen many readers may not recognize: a woman who enjoyed black humor and was well aware of the political scene of her time. Byrne uses artifacts from Austen's life as a starting point for her engaging chapters on the events that shaped Austen's worldview and inspired some of the most beloved scenes and characters in all of English literature."

—Bookreporter.com

"Paula Byrne's magnificent *The Real Jane Austen* explodes the old view of her subject. Her research is wide, deep, and meticulous. . . . A more vivid and memorable Jane Austen emerges than a relentlessly 'straight' old-fashioned narrative could deliver."

—*Times Literary Supplement* (London)

"A vivacious new portrait. . . . Byrne's Austen, as revealed through this archive of objects, emerges as a worldly woman, profoundly enmeshed in a wider world than she's often acknowledged to occupy. This is an Austen with a sense for the political as well as for the finer points of sensibility—and one who will be unfamiliar (though never unrecognizable) to many readers."

—*Publishers Weekly*

"Under Byrne's scrutiny, Austen's satirical and wickedly delicious wit, her worldly ways, and her confidence in her craft serve as an antithesis to the image of a staid, naive maiden living a simple country life. The result is a fresh behind-the-scenes look at an author who, for many, stands behind only Shakespeare as the greatest English writer."

—Shelf Awareness

"In *The Real Jane Austen*, Byrne's engaging prose and thoughtful, determined analysis of tangible objects from her life give us a picture of Austen as a vivid, vital woman committed to her career as a novelist, clear-eyed and part of the wider world. Well worth a read."

—*The Literary Omnivore*

"An eminently readable narrative."   —*Los Angeles Review of Books*

"Byrne takes a clever approach to scrutinizing the few facts that we know about Austen's life. . . . Byrne's aim is to show how these objects, many of them reproduced in her book in lush color plates, reveal a much more cosmopolitan awareness of the world than is commonly credited to Austen."

—Maureen Corrigan, NPR's *Fresh Air*

THE REAL
JANE AUSTEN

THE REAL
JANE AUSTEN

A Life in Small Things

Paula Byrne

HARPER  PERENNIAL

NEW YORK • LONDON • TORONTO • SYDNEY • NEW DELHI • AUCKLAND

HARPER PERENNIAL

First published in the United Kingdom in 2012 by HarperPress, an imprint of HarperCollins Publishers.

First U.S. hardcover published in 2013 by HarperCollins Publishers.

HarperCollins books may be purchased for educational, business, or sales promotional use. For information, please e-mail the Special Markets Department at SPsales@harpercollins.com.

Illustrations copyright © 2013 by Sara Mulvanny

Chapter openers designed by Vera Brice

An extension of this copyright page appears on pages 359–361.

FIRST HARPER PERENNIAL EDITION PUBLISHED 2014.

Library of Congress Cataloging-in-Publication Data has been applied for.

ISBN 978-0-06-199910-9 (pbk.)

HB 12.22.2021

For my very own Elinor (Ellie)

CONTENTS

CONTENTS

The room was most dear to her, and she would not have changed its furniture for the handsomest in the house, though what had been originally plain, had suffered all the ill-usage of children – and its greatest elegancies and ornaments were a faded footstool of Julia's work, too ill done for the drawing-room, three transparencies, made in a rage for transparencies, for the three lower panes of one window, where Tintern Abbey held its station between a cave in Italy, and a moonlight lake in Cumberland; a collection of family profiles, thought unworthy of being anywhere else, over the mantelpiece, and by their side, and pinned against the wall, a small sketch of a ship sent four years ago from the Mediterranean by William, with H.M.S. Antwerp at the bottom, in letters as tall as the main-mast.

Mansfield Park, VOL 1, CH. 16

[S]he seized the scrap of paper ... locked it up with the chain, as the dearest part of the gift. It was the only thing approaching to a letter which she had ever received from him; she might never receive another; it was impossible that she ever should receive another so perfectly gratifying in the occasion and the style. Two lines more prized had never fallen from the pen of the most distinguished author – never more completely blessed the researches of the fondest biographer. The enthusiasm of a woman's love is even beyond the biographer's.

Mansfield Park, VOL 2, CH. 9

AUTHOR'S NOTE

Each chapter begins with a description of the image that sets its theme, illustrated in plate sections throughout the book. Jane Austen's novels are quoted from the Oxford World's Classics editions, but references in the endnotes take the form of volume and chapter number, so as to make it possible to locate the relevant passage in other editions. So, for example, 1.8 means chapter 8 of volume 1 (*Persuasion* and *Northanger Abbey* were each originally published in two volumes, the other four completed novels each in three volumes). The irregular spellings in Austen's letters and youthful writings are retained (most famously, 'Love and Freindship', but also 'beleive', 'neice', 'Lime' for Lyme, 'Keen' for the actor Kean, and so on). The endnotes also acknowledge, at relevant points, the work of the many wonderful Jane Austen scholars on whom I have drawn.

In order to give readers an idea of monetary values – whether for the cost of a card of lace or the worth of Jane Austen's royalty cheque – I have given 2011 equivalents derived from the Bank of England's online historical inflation calculator (and with a dollar equivalent on the rough basis of $1.50 to a pound). It must, however, be remembered that these are merely indicative sums: over the centuries inflation has been much greater for some things than others.

PROLOGUE

Captain Harville's Carpentry

This is a watercolour of Lyme Regis on the southern coast of England. The cottages nestle on the hillside. An old stone breakwater leads down to the shoreline. A man and a woman are walking on the beach and a solitary figure is looking out to sea. A rowing boat is on its way out to a ship at anchor in the bay. The eye is drawn to an expansive view of sloping cliffs and open sky.[1]

Jane Austen loved the sea. The story goes that when her father announced in December 1800 that he was leaving his position as rector of the parish of Steventon and retiring to Bath, she was so shocked that she fainted. She reconciled herself to the move only when the family promised to take a holiday by the seaside every summer. In 1801 and 1802 they went to Sidmouth and Teignmouth in Devon. In 1803 and 1804 it was the turn of Lyme Regis.

'The young people were all wild to see Lyme.' When they arrive, in chapter eleven of *Persuasion*, Jane Austen describes the little seaside resort in the style of a tour guide: the pleasant bay, the new-fangled bathing machines, the famous Cobb, the beautiful line of cliffs stretching out to the east of the town, the charms of 'the immediate environs' – the high sweep of countryside around Charmouth, 'the woody varieties of the cheerful village of Up Lyme, and, above all, Pinny, with its green chasms between romantic rocks … a scene so wonderful and so lovely is exhibited, as may more than equal any of the resembling scenes of the far-famed Isle of Wight'.[2]

1

'These places must be visited, and visited again to make the worth of Lyme understood,' Jane Austen tells her readers. She had visited Lyme at least twice, on one occasion witnessing a fire that destroyed a number of houses. When she describes the place in her novel, she is visiting it yet again, this time in her imagination. Her description is the literary equivalent of the engravings of popular tourist sites that were readily obtainable in the burgeoning print market of the age – the Regency version of the picture postcard.

Jane Austen cared a great deal about accuracy. She wanted her novels to be true to life. When reading a draft of a novel by her niece Anna, she pointed out that it was an error to portray people in Dawlish gossiping about the news from Lyme: 'Lyme will not do. Lyme is towards 40 miles distance from Dawlish and would not be talked of there.'[3] Her novels were grounded in the real world. In order to create them, she drew upon the reality that she knew: the people, the places, the events. The celebrated fictional scene in which Louisa Musgrove nearly dies when being 'jumped' off the narrow steps of the Cobb is not based on a real incident, but it could not have been written if Jane Austen had not visited the real Lyme and memorized its topography.

The picturesque description of the romantic rocks of Lyme is not, however, her most common style. And in this case her passion for the sea perhaps led her to idealize the reality of the place. 'I was disappointed in Lime,' wrote her sister-in-law Mary to that niece Anna, 'as from your Aunt Janes Novel I had expected it a clean pretty place, whereas it was dirty and ugly.'[4]

The fall on the Cobb, the bad-tempered exchange at Box Hill, the escape across the ha-ha from the grounds of Sotherton, the road-traffic accident with which her final unfinished novel begins: outdoor scenes in Austen's novels are often dramatic excursions – involving misadventures, transgressions, arguments, misunderstandings, proposals – whereas her habitual location is indoors, within the world of polite, if barbed, conversation in drawing rooms and over dinner tables. Chapter eleven of *Persuasion* does not dwell for long on the seaside panorama. The narrative swiftly follows the visitors inside.

Not, however, into a great house of the kind that has become familiar in television and film adaptations of Austen's novels (in which the houses are nearly always bigger than they should be). 'Near the foot of an old pier of uncertain date'[5] on the seafront at Lyme there is a row of cottages. We enter a cramped but welcoming parlour. It is the home of Captain Harville, who has retired in poor health as the result of a severe wound incurred on naval service during the war that lasted for almost the whole of Jane Austen's adult life. This snug little dwelling-place will be revisited later, but for a first glimpse of Austen's art of minute observation consider a single detail:

> Captain Harville was no reader; but he had contrived excellent accommodations, and fashioned very pretty shelves, for a tolerable collection of well-bound volumes, the property of Captain Benwick. His lameness prevented him from taking much exercise; but a mind of usefulness and ingenuity seemed to furnish him with constant employment within. He drew, he varnished, he carpentered, he glued; he made toys for the children, he fashioned new netting-needles and pins with improvements; and if every thing else was done, sat down with his large fishing-net at one corner of the room.

Anne Elliot will soon engage Captain Benwick in conversation about books, debating the relative merits of the two most fashionable poets of the day, Sir Walter Scott and Lord Byron. She gently suggests that romantic poetry might not be the most healthy reading for a man with a broken heart such as Benwick – though she sees the irony of her admonitions to 'patience and resignation' in the light of her own broken heart.

But it is Captain Harville's carpentry that sticks in the mind: the prettily fashioned shelves, the varnish, the glue, the toys for the children. Jane Austen grew up in a house of books and reading, but she also came from a family that valued handiwork, the craft of making things, whether with needle or wood.

Captain Benwick reading poetry aloud while Captain Harville mends his net is a little image of how she imagined a secure home and a sense of belonging. Her family circle was a place of quick tongues, laughter and moving fingers, with a novel being read aloud and everyone busy at their needlework. Both her world and her novels can be brought alive through the texture of things, the life of objects.

* * *

Sketch of a Royal Navy ship by Jane Austen's
nephew, Captain Herbert Austen

In January 1852 Admiral Francis Austen received a letter from the daughter of the President of Harvard University. 'Since high critical authority has pronounced the delineations of character in the works of Jane Austen second only to those of Shakespeare,' Miss Quincy began, 'transatlantic admiration appears superfluous; yet it may not be uninteresting to her family to receive an assurance that the influence of her genius is extensively recognised in the American Republic.'[6] She was writing because she wanted an autograph of the great novelist.

The Admiral was more than obliging. He was delighted to hear that the 'celebrity' of his late sister's works had reached across the Atlantic. He sent not merely a signature but a whole Jane Austen letter. And he was happy to provide a character sketch of her. She was cheerful, not easily irritated, a little shy with strangers. Her natural reserve was sometimes misinterpreted as haughtiness. She was kind and funny, never failing to excite 'the mirth and hilarity of the party'. She loved children and they loved her: 'Her Nephews and Nieces of whom there were many could not have a greater treat than crouding around and listening to Aunt Jane's stories.'

Miss Susan Quincy shared the contents of the Jane Austen letter with her sister, who was 'quite carried off her feet' with excitement. The conclusion, they agreed, could only be that Admiral Austen was so charming that 'he must have been like Captain Wentworth when he was young'. Was Jane Austen's brother really the inspiration for the hero of *Persuasion*? Miss Quincy communicated her sister's response to the elderly Admiral. He replied that he was very flattered, but:

> I do not know whether in the character of Captain Wentworth the authoress meant in any degree to delineate that of her Brother. Perhaps she might, but I rather think parts of Captain Harville's were drawn from myself; at least the description of his domestic habits, tastes and occupations bear a considerable resemblance to mine.

Admiral Austen does not deny the possibility that there might be some element of himself – or of Jane's other naval brother, Charles – in the character of Captain Wentworth. But he positively celebrates the fact that Captain Harville's handiwork is his own.

When Francis Austen's baby was born in 1807, he cut out the patterns for the infant's night-clothes himself. On another occasion, according to his sister Jane, 'he made a very nice fringe for the drawing room curtains'. Like Harville, he 'turned silver' to make needles for fishing nets. When Jane Austen watched her young nephews passing the evenings by making nets in which to catch rabbits, she described them as sitting 'side by side, as any two Uncle Franks could do'.[7] Jane also remembered her brother Frank, as she always called him, making 'a very nice little butter-churn'.[8] He was skilled at turning wood.

There can be no doubt that Captain Harville's carpentry is both a compliment to Frank and a family joke. By acknowledging the allusion after Jane's death, Admiral Austen is giving her readers warrant to make connections between the people his sister knew and the characters she created. By implication, he is also licensing us to make links between her novels and the places she went to (and those she heard about), not to mention the historical events through which she lived.

Yet in the 'official' family biography of Jane Austen, it is stressed that hers was an enclosed, sequestered world and that the characters in her novels were always generic types, never based on real individuals. The ground for this reading of her was laid by her brother Henry in the brief 'Biographical Notice of the Author' which prefaces her posthumously published novels *Northanger Abbey* and *Persuasion*: 'Short and easy will be the task of the mere biographer. A life of usefulness, literature, and religion, was not by any means a life of event.' Furthermore, 'Her power of inventing characters seems to have been intuitive, and almost unlimited. She drew from nature; but, whatever may have been surmised to the contrary, never from individuals.'[9]

Henry's denial of eventfulness and of drawing 'from individuals' was of a piece with the desire of the clerical Austens to be discreet, decorous and reticent. That was the image of Jane Austen herself that the family wished to establish in the public domain. They reinforced it in the Victorian era by means of a memoir published in December 1869 by James Edward Austen-Leigh, son of another of her clergy brothers, James. Jane Austen was one of the wittiest of writers, but there are not many jokes in the official family record. Admiral Francis Austen was known for his lack of a sense of humour, but at least he manages to drop in a joke at the end of his second letter to Miss Quincy: 'I am not a *Vice* Admiral, having for the last 3 years attained the higher rank of Admiral. I wish I could believe that in the change of rank I had left every *vice* behind me.' Startlingly, here he seems to be remembering his sister's most questionable joke, concerning '*Rears*, and *Vices*' in the British navy. That was not the sort of subject to detain James Edward Austen-Leigh in his pious record of his aunt's allegedly quiet life.

The family memoir inaugurated the tradition of full-length Jane Austen biography. It proceeded from cradle to grave at uneventful pace and with provincial calm. In the century and a half since it was compiled, devoted scholars have gathered many more details about Austen's life. One hundred and sixty of her letters survive, as do the pocket books of family members, the diaries of acquaintances, the banking transactions of her father.[10] With the benefit of such mundane material, biography after biography has followed the pattern of James Edward and tracked Jane Austen's daily life from Steventon to Bath to Chawton to Winchester.[11]

This book is something different and more experimental. Rather than rehearsing all the known facts, this biography focuses on a variety of key moments, scenes and objects in both the life and work of Jane Austen. It does not begin where the official family record began, with the tracing of ancestry. It does not seek to foster the illusion that Austen knew little of the world. It recognizes the gaps in our knowledge as well as in the documentary evidence. Several thousand of her letters are lost or destroyed and for some crucial years we know hardly anything of her whereabouts.

In addition, this biography follows the lead of Frank Austen rather than Henry. It suggests that, like nearly all novelists, Jane Austen created her characters by mixing observation and imagination. She drew on people she knew and experiences she went through. Captain Harville is not a *portrait* of Frank, but the fictional character is brought alive and made memorable by the adoption of a particularly charming characteristic of a real individual: his fondness for carpentry. When Austen writes about ideas – the virtues and vices of the British navy, the case against the slave trade, the Evangelical movement – she does so by creating memorable characters, not by writing sermons. Her sympathy for abolition may be inferred not only from what she writes in her letters about the campaigner Thomas Clarkson but also from the pro-slavery associations of two of her most monstrous characters, Mrs Norris and Mrs Elton.

Jane Austen loved nothing more than to talk about people. She knew a great deal about the lives of her extended family, her friends and her slighter acquaintances. When we tell the stories of these people's lives, we suddenly see Austen on a much wider stage than that on which she is confined in the clerical brothers' version of her life. We are transported to the East Indies and the West, to the guillotine in revolutionary Paris, to a world where there is high-society scandal one moment and a petty case of shoplifting the next. This biography follows Austen on her travels, which were more extensive than is often recognized, and it sets her in contexts global as well as English, urban as well as rural, political and historical as well as social and domestic. These wider perspectives were of vital and still under-estimated importance to her creative life.

Kingsley Amis, a comic novelist who admired Austen enormously, once wrote that 'those who know my novels and me will also know that they are firmly unautobiographical, but at the same time every word of them inevitably says something about the kind of person I am'.[12] It is in this spirit that we should read the relationship between Jane Austen's novels and her world.

The opinions of her characters are not her own. The writings in which she exposes her true self most directly are her letters. When her devoted niece Fanny Knight died in 1882 (by which time she was Lady Knatchbull), Fanny's son Lord Brabourne came upon a treasure-trove: the original manuscript of *Lady Susan* 'in Jane Austen's own handwriting' and:

> a square box full of letters, fastened up carefully in separate packets, each of which was endorsed 'For Lady Knatchbull,' in the handwriting of my great-aunt, Cassandra Austen, and with which was a paper endorsed, in my mother's handwriting, 'Letters from my dear Aunt Jane Austen, and two from Aunt Cassandra after her decease,' which paper contained the letters written to my mother herself.[13]

These letters, Brabourne suggested, 'contain the confidential outpourings of Jane Austen's soul to her beloved sister, interspersed with many family and personal details which, doubtless, she would have told to no other human being'. With his mother's death, the time was ripe for their publication. The unique talent of '"the inimitable Jane" (as an old friend of mine used always to call her)' was, Brabourne argued, that she 'describes men and women exactly as men and women really are, and tells her tale of ordinary, everyday life with such truthful delineation, such bewitching simplicity, and, moreover, with such purity of style and language, as have rarely been equalled, and perhaps never surpassed'.

For this reason, what could be more fitting than the publication of 'the letters which show what her own "ordinary, everyday life" was, and which afford a picture of her such as no history written by another person could give so well'? 'It is certain', Brabourne triumphantly concluded, 'that I am now able to present to the public entirely new matter, from which may be gathered a fuller and more complete knowledge of Jane Austen and her "belongings" than could otherwise have been obtained.'[14]

All subsequent biographers have made extensive use of the letters. Nevertheless, a fresh reading of them reveals a number of hitherto neglected but significant details and connections, among them a crucial act of literary patronage, the momentous consequences of a will, and evidence of Austen's knowledge of the extraordinary story of the abolitionist judge Lord Mansfield's adoption of a black girl.

Lord Brabourne's view of his great-aunt as the inimitable novelist of 'ordinary, everyday life' had become a commonplace opinion by the late Victorian era. It is ultimately derived from the most important account of Austen's work written in her own lifetime: a long review-essay on the publication of *Emma*, also discussing *Sense and Sensibility* and *Pride and Prejudice*, by Sir Walter Scott, the most celebrated novelist in all Europe (though one who at this time was still publishing his fiction, like Austen herself, under the veil of anonymity). Scott's essay will be further discussed towards the end of this book, but its main thrust is indeed the high claim that Jane Austen was the first novelist in history to offer an accurate representation of 'the current of ordinary life'. She presents to the reader 'instead of the splendid scenes of an imaginary world, a correct and striking representation of that which is daily taking place around him'. Scott concludes that 'The author's knowledge of the world, and the peculiar tact with which she presents characters that the reader cannot fail to recognize, reminds us something of the merits of the Flemish school of painting. The subjects are not often elegant, and certainly never grand; but they are finished up to nature, and with a precision which delights the reader.'[15]

The 'correct and striking representation' of scenes from 'ordinary life', rendered with precision, tact and minute detail: this is indeed the essence of Austen's art, as it is of Dutch realism in painting. Vermeer creates the sense of a real world by means of an opened letter, a pearl earring, a latticed window, a jug and a tablecloth, a musical instrument. By the same account, objects play a key part in bringing alive Austen's fictional worlds.

My inspiration for the writing of this book came from two exquisite moments in *Mansfield Park*, quoted earlier as my epigraphs. First there is Fanny Price's little sitting room, made real by a few carefully chosen things.

Mounted on the window-panes are three pictures of romantic scenes – the ruin of Tintern Abbey, a wild cave in Italy and a moonlit lake in Wordsworth country – in the new and fashionable form of 'transparencies'. In *An Essay on Transparent Prints and Transparencies in General*, published in 1807, a certain Edward Orme claimed that he invented the medium by accident when he dropped some varnish on to the dark part of an engraving 'which afterwards being exposed again to light, the spot where the varnish had been spilt formed a light in the midst of shadow'.[16] Their presence hints at Fanny's romantic sensibility.

Over the mantelpiece hangs a collection of family 'profiles': this was another fashionable non-elite artistic medium, the silhouette, a form of portraiture that will be discussed in chapter one. The close-knit Austen family cherished their profiles and miniatures, the equivalent of framed photographs of loved ones in a modern home.

Beside the profiles, pinned against the wall by Fanny herself, is the thing that makes the room truly her own: 'a small sketch of a ship sent four years ago from the Mediterranean by William, with H.M.S. Antwerp at the bottom, in letters as tall as the main-mast'. Just as Jane Austen corresponded constantly with her brothers when they were away at sea, worrying about their survival in the face of war and weather, so Fanny stays close to her midshipman brother through his sketch on the wall. Though the action of the novel rarely leaves the confines of Mansfield Park, the objects transport the reader on to a wider stage.

In the second passage, Fanny invests all her seemingly unrequited love for Edmund in two other small objects: a scrap of paper and a simple gold chain. Small things in Jane Austen's world do not only evoke distant places. They can also be the bearers of big emotions. The intense emotions associated with love and death are often refracted through objects. Letters and tokens are of great importance in the novels: focus upon an object is often a signal to the reader that this is a key sequence in the emotional unfolding of the narrative. This biography is an attempt to write Austen's life according to the same principle. Following the example of Captain Harville's carpentry, each chapter begins with a real thing, some of them coming directly from her life, others evoked by her novels. These objects and images cast new light on Austen's life and her fictional characters, on the workings of her imagination and on the shaping of her incomparable fictional worlds.

The Family Profile

All the faces are turned towards the young boy. He is being passed to one of the two fashionably dressed women with powdered hair who are sitting at the table playing chess. The surrounding drapery makes the portrait resemble a theatrical scene. In the manner of actors well versed in the art of gesture, the figures are talking with their hands: the father's fingers rest on his son's shoulders, while the boy has his arms outstretched in supplication towards his new mother. Her hand remains on a chess piece, as if she has won a pawn. The master of the house leans on the back of the chair of the other woman, who is his sister. His relaxed pose bespeaks the casual assurance of proprietorship. The sister is pointing her finger at the boy, as if to say 'so this is the child who is coming to our great house'. The boy's birth-mother is absent.

The silhouette, dated 1783, is by William Wellings, one of the leading practitioners of this highly fashionable form of miniaturized portraiture. A plain black profile cut on card could be taken in a few minutes and cost as little as a shilling. Though sometimes known as 'poor men's miniatures', profiles were renowned for the accuracy of representation that they could achieve. 'No art approaches a well-made silhouette in truth,' wrote the influential physiognomist Johann Caspar Lavater. Jane Austen's nephew James Edward would become renowned within the family for his skill at the art. He could execute silhouettes without preliminary drawing, cutting them out directly with a special pair of scissors, 'the points ... an inch long, and the curved handles about three inches'.[1]

Silhouettes were known as 'shadows' or 'shades' or 'profiles'. Hence Austen's imagining of the 'collection of family profiles' in Fanny Price's sitting room in *Mansfield Park*. This one tells a story. To modern eyes, the starkly shaded medium seems particularly fitting because of the solemn nature of the subject: the handing over of a child from one family to another. It was commissioned by Thomas Knight, a wealthy but childless gentleman from the county of Kent, to commemorate his formal adoption of his nephew, Edward Austen, one of the elder brothers of the future novelist. It was not only the Wellings silhouette that commemorated the adoption. The Knights also had an oil painting commissioned. This painting hangs now in Chawton Cottage and shows a very handsome child with golden hair and bright hazel eyes. He is wearing a blue velvet suit.

In the family profile the father, to the left of the scene, is George Austen. The adoptive mother, receiving Edward, is Catherine Knight, who many years later became Jane Austen's only literary patron. Thomas Knight himself is to the right, standing over his sister Jane. In 1783, the boy Edward reached his sixteenth birthday, whereas the child in the silhouette appears to be rather younger. This suggests that Knight may have requested the artist to evoke the scene two or three years earlier when the boy first went to stay with the childless couple in the great house.

Little Neddy first met his wealthy uncle and aunt when he was twelve. In 1779 the newly married Knights visited their relatives at Steventon and took such a fancy to the golden-haired boy that they decided to bring him along with them on their honeymoon. It was quite common to do such a thing: George and Cassandra Austen took a boy called George Hastings with them on their own honeymoon tour. Genteel children generally had more freedom and independence than we might expect by today's standards: as a young girl, Jane Austen's sister Cassandra often visited her aunt and uncle Cooper in Bath.

In 1781 Thomas Knight inherited two large estates in Hampshire and Kent. By then, it was a matter of concern that he and his wife Catherine showed no sign of having children of their own. They needed a suitable boy to adopt and make their heir. Again, the practice was not unusual in the Georgian era, when the preservation of large estates was the key to wealth and status. So it was that young Edward Austen was taken away to Kent, first for extended visits during the summer months and eventually as a permanent arrangement. According to perhaps over-dramatic family tradition, George Austen hesitated, only for his wife to say, 'I think, my Dear, you had better oblige your cousins and let the Child go.' Mr Knight's coachman, who had come on horseback, had led a pony all the way from Godmersham in Kent. The boy rode it all the way back, about a hundred miles. Among the brothers and sisters he said goodbye to when he left home was Jane Austen, aged about five and a half.

It wasn't just boys who were transferred into wealthy families. Jane Austen knew at least two childless couples who adopted young girls and made them their heirs. There was Lord Mansfield, the great abolitionist judge, who adopted his niece Lady Elizabeth Murray. She became a neighbour of Edward Austen, and met Jane Austen on several occasions. And then there was a family called the Chutes in a big house near by, who adopted a girl called Caroline Wigget when she was three years old. So it should not come as a surprise that Jane Austen's novels show more than a passing interest in adoption. In *Mansfield Park* Fanny Price, considered a burden on her family, is sent to live with her wealthy cousins, the Bertrams. In *Emma*, Frank Churchill is adopted into the family of a rich but childless couple, and Jane Fairfax, an orphan, is brought up with the Dixons.

The case of Emma Watson in Jane Austen's incomplete novel *The Watsons* offers a striking reversal of the convention, whereby she has lived away from her birth family but is sent back to live with them. In *Emma*, Isabella Knightley exclaims against adoption, suggesting that it is unnatural: 'there is something so shocking in a child's being taken away from his parents and natural home! ... To give up one's child! I really never could think well of any body who proposed such a thing to any body else.'[2] But Jane Austen believed that the good fortune of one family member was the good fortune of all.

* * *

On a fine summer's day in 1782 a six-year-old girl was excitedly awaiting the return of her father in a hack chaise, the equivalent of a taxi cab, from the main stage-coach post in Andover, Hampshire. Her father was returning home with his elder daughter, who had been visiting relatives in Bath. Unable to contain her excitement at seeing her beloved sister, and with the promise of a ride home in the chaise, the six-year-old dragged her three-year-old brother Charles by the hand and they walked alone as far as New Down, a hamlet near Micheldever – some six miles away – to meet the chaise.[3]

The entrance hall of the big house at
Godmersham, where Edward Austen lived on
being adopted by his wealthy uncle

Jane Austen, the seventh child of the Reverend George Austen and his wife
Cassandra, née Leigh, was born in the Steventon village rectory on Saturday
16 December 1775, and baptized privately by her father on the morrow to
ensure that her soul would be saved should she die in her first few days. He
said that she looked very like her brother Henry, who was four, and would
be 'a plaything' for her sister Cassandra, who was nearly three.[4] Jane was
publicly christened the following April, on Good Friday. She had three
godparents: her great-aunt, also called Jane Austen, wife of Francis Austen of
Sevenoaks in Kent, a well-to-do relative; Samuel Cooke, a vicar from Surrey
who had graduated from Oxford and was related to a maternal cousin; and
a Mrs Musgrave from Oxfordshire, wife of another maternal cousin.

These are the bare facts of her birth, but the walk to meet the hack chaise is the first glimpse we have of her as a child. The vignette may suggest that she was bold and unafraid to take the lead. What it certainly indicates is how much she loved and missed her elder sister. It sets a pattern for the rest of her days. For most of her life, Jane Austen was under the same roof as Cassandra. When they were parted, with one of them visiting friends or relations, they wrote to each other almost daily. Infuriatingly, Cassandra's letters to Jane are lost and, to our eyes unforgivably, Cassandra destroyed far more of Jane's than she kept. But those which survive provide the best record we have of her inner life.

Jane Austen was brought up in a large and loving family, consisting mainly of boys. She was one of two girls in a family of eight, sandwiched between Frank, who was born in 1774, and the youngest, Charles, born 1779. These two would grow up to become her 'sailor brothers'. Frank was just twenty months older than Jane. Charles she described, quoting one of her favourite writers, Fanny Burney, as 'our own particular little brother'.[5] Her brothers were of immense importance to her throughout her life. The loss of nearly all her letters to them leaves the biggest gap in our knowledge of her. She wrote to Cassandra only when they were apart; she wrote to her brothers away on service almost all the time.

All the Austen children were nursed with a neighbouring family, the Littleworths, returning home when they were toddlers. One of them gave the family particular anxiety: George, the second son, born in 1766, was mentally incapacitated. He was epileptic and possibly deaf. In July 1770, his father wrote that the little boy was suffering from fits and showed no sign of improvement: 'God knows only how far it will come to pass, but for the best judgment I can form at present, we must not be too sanguine on this Head; be it as it may, we have this comfort, he cannot be a bad or a wicked child.'[6]

By December of that year George, now four, was living with foster parents. His mother wrote that he was still having fits. 'My poor little George is come to see me today. He seems pretty well, tho' he had a fit lately; it was near a twelve-month since he had one before, so [I] was in hopes they had left him, but must not flatter myself so now.'[7] The severity of his condition is apparent from a letter in which his godfather Tysoe Saul Hancock, Mr Austen's brother-in-law, mentions 'the case of my godson who must be provided for without the least hopes of his being able to assist himself'.[8]

Around the time this letter was written, Mrs Cassandra Austen told a relative that she could not visit Kent because of her domestic situation.[9] She was seven months pregnant and had four young boys all living at home: seven-year-old James, George six and with special needs, Edward just turned five, Henry seventeen months and recently back from being nursed in the village. There were servants to help, but it was necessary to manage both the household and its small plot of land, which had chickens and a cow. The Reverend George Austen was busy with his parish duties and business affairs. The following year he obtained the living of a second parish. In these circumstances, it was hardly surprising that a home was found for young George where he could be given more attention and assistance.[10]

Mrs Austen was no stranger to mental infirmity. Her younger 'imbecile brother' Tom had been placed under the care of a parish clerk, Francis Culham, at Monk Sherborne near Basingstoke. George was sent to join him there when it became clear that he was not improving. He lived with his uncle Tom and the Culhams for the rest of his life, surviving into his seventies. He died of dropsy (accumulation of bodily fluid, often caused by kidney failure) early in the reign of Queen Victoria, just over twenty years after his sister Jane's death. On his death certificate he was described as a 'gentleman'.

On Mrs Austen's death in 1827, some stocks that she owned were sold and the proceeds divided among her surviving children. Edward Knight, adopted into wealth, made his portion over to George to pay for his care. Some biographers have taken a censorious attitude towards the Austens for their treatment of George. Several have assumed that the family was ashamed and ill-prepared when it came to mental illness, exiling George for the sake of the other children. Others have argued to the contrary that a reference in Jane Austen's letters to 'talking with fingers' suggests that she might have been adept at sign language as a result of conversing with her allegedly deaf 'idiot' brother. We will never know whether or not she visited him at the Culhams'.

There were many private madhouses in the Georgian era, some of which had dark reputations for their inhumane treatment of the insane, Bedlam Hospital in London being the most infamous. The majority of the mentally ill were confined to workhouses, poorhouses and prison. By boarding out George with a family, the Austens saved him from this fate.

Jane Austen's life coincided with a period of new enlightenment in relation to madness and mental incapacity. King George III went mad and was treated, in a firm and well-publicized manner, by Dr Francis Willis at his asylum in Lincolnshire. The search for a cure for the King led to a shift in public attitudes towards the mentally infirm. By the end of the century, the Quaker William Tuke had founded The Retreat, an asylum in York that pioneered the humane treatment of the mentally ill. It provided a model for other institutions.[11]

Thanks to the madness of King George, which was witnessed at first hand by the novelist Fanny Burney, mental illness ceased to be an unmentionable topic of conversation in polite society. Jane Austen frequently joked about madness in her earliest writings. As an adult she made fun of her family's history of madness in relation to her niece Anna, who was hoping to marry, against her family's wishes: 'My dear Mrs Harrison, I shall say, I am afraid the young Man has some of your Family Madness – and though there often appears to be something of Madness in Anna too, I think she inherits more of it from her Mother's family than from ours.'[12] This is not entirely a joke: Jane Austen's mother's family, the Leighs of Stoneleigh, had a spectacular history of madness, and her attitude towards madness and mental illness shows a lack of embarrassment and sentiment perhaps because of her proximity to those affected by it. In addition to those in the immediate Austen family circle, her uncle Tom and her brother, Jane's cousin Eliza de Feuillide had a son called Hastings who had 'fits' and did not develop like other children.

The story of George Austen remains shadowy. As a little girl, Jane was especially close to two other brothers Frank and Charles. Frank, nicknamed 'Fly', was a small, burly boy, 'fearless of danger, braving pain'. He often got into trouble. Jane gives a lovely retrospective glimpse of his childhood self in a poem she wrote to celebrate the birth of his son:

> My dearest Frank, I wish you joy
> Of Mary's safety with a Boy …
> In him, in all his ways, may we
> Another Francis William see! –
> Thy infant days may he inherit,
> Thy warmth, nay insolence of spirit.[13]

Warmth, insolence, spirit: these were qualities that Jane Austen had herself and that she valued in Frank. At the same time, she had a soft spot for Charles, the baby of the family, who was sweet-tempered and affectionate, without the fiery nature of Fly. It is easy to see him being dragged along by Jane to meet Cassandra's coach. The affection in which she held her siblings is clear from the way that her novels are full of private jokes – a phenomenon that is common among large families, who so often have their own secret language.

It was not only because of the brothers that Steventon parsonage, the family home, was a household of boys. Jane Austen's father George took in scholars to supplement his rector's stipend, effectively running his own little boarding school. Over the years there were probably more than fifteen boys, who provided a network of contacts among prosperous local families. Many of them remained devoted to the Austens and among them were some potential suitors for the two girls. Jane's mother Cassandra seems to have been very popular with the schoolboys. She composed comic verses for them. She wrote a funny poem urging one reluctant schoolboy to return to school and his studies, rather than wasting his time dancing. Another boy complained to Mrs Austen that he felt left out because she hadn't written a special poem to him.

The first schoolboy to be taken on at Steventon, in 1773, was a five-year-old aristocrat, John Charles Wallop, Lord Lymington. He was the 'backward' and eccentric eldest son of Lord Portsmouth, who lived just ten miles away at Hurstbourne Park. A boy called William Vanderstegen was taken on later that same year. By 1779, the year that Jane Austen's mother Cassandra gave birth to her last child, there were four boys living at Steventon – Fulwar Craven Fowle, Frank Stuart, Gilbert East and a boy named Deane (either George or Henry). By 1781, the pupils included George Nibbs and Fulwar's brother Tom and possibly his brothers William and Charles. In later years, John Warren, Charles Fowle, Richard Buller, William Goodenough, Deacon Morrell and Francis Newnham attended the school. At least ten of the boys stayed four years or more. The Reverend George Austen only stopped teaching in 1795 when Jane was in her twentieth year.[14]

Lord Lymington stayed just a few months at Steventon. Mrs Austen found him 'good-tempered and orderly',[15] but his mother took him away on account of his very bad stammer, which grew worse as his behaviour became more erratic with the passage of years. Tales abounded of his eccentricities, including his habit of pinching servants, throwing them into hedges and playing other practical jokes. He once tried to hang a young boy from the bell tower of the village church. The young Lord Byron objected strongly to being pinched by Lord Portsmouth, threw a large shell at his head in retaliation (breaking a mirror) and, many years later in 1814, exacted cruel revenge by taking part in a devious plot to marry him off to a vicious woman who tortured him and beat him with a horsewhip. Jane Austen commented on this marriage to her sister Cassandra: 'And here is Lord Portsmouth married too to Miss Hanson!'[16] Whether or not she knew that Lord Byron gave away the bride is not known. Byron recorded in his journal that he 'tried not to laugh in the face of the suppliants' and 'rammed their left hands, by mistake, into one another'.[17]

Later, John Wallop became known as the Vampyre Earl for his supposed addiction to drinking the blood of his servants. He was eventually certified a lunatic. Despite all his tribulations, he never forgot the Austens and invited them to his annual ball at Hurstbourne Park. In 1800, just after his first marriage, Jane attended his ball and wrote a long vivid account to her sister. Cassandra had clearly made a favourable impression on the Earl over the years. Jane seems surprised by his interest: 'Lord Portsmouth surpassed the rest in his attentive recollection of you, enquired more into the length of your absence, and concluded by desiring to be "remembered to you when I wrote next".'[18] Our customary image of Jane Austen's family home does not usually make room for her fond memories of the lunatic Earl.

The other boys opened up a range of worldly contacts for the Austen family. William Vanderstegen was an only child, born almost twenty years after his parents married. His father was one of the first Commissioners of the Thames, deeply involved in a campaign to make the river more navigable. George Nibbs's father owned a plantation in the West Indies: we will meet him in a later chapter. Richard Buller, who stayed for five years, became a clergyman in Devon before dying at a sadly young age. His closeness to the Austens is apparent from a letter written by Jane to Cassandra in 1800, in which she gives the news that he has recently married: 'I have had a most affectionate letter from Buller; I was afraid he would oppress me by his felicity and his love for his Wife, but this is not the case; he calls her simply Anna without any angelic embellishments, for which I respect and wish him happy – and throughout the whole of his letter indeed he

Rear view of Steventon rectory: Jane Austen's
childhood home

seems more engrossed by his feelings towards our family, than towards her.'[19] The following year, they visited him in his Tudor vicarage in the little stone-built town of Colyton on the Devon coast.

Cassandra made an especially strong impression on another of her father's boarders, Tom Fowle. They became engaged and were due to be married before he died of yellow fever in the West Indies. This loss was a decisive factor in the development of Jane Austen's own life. George Austen clearly had no compunction about bringing up his daughters alongside a variety of unfamiliar young men, though no record survives of any romantic interest on Jane's part. The uproariously funny tales that she wrote as a young girl, full of violence, drunkenness, madness and suicide, suggest that she played more of a tomboyish role at Steventon than that of a young ingénue looking for love. She was more of a Catherine Morland – playing baseball,[20] rolling down the green slope at the back of the house, preferring cricket to dolls – than a boy-mad Isabella Thorpe chasing unsuspecting young men along the streets of Bath. There was indeed a green slope at the back of Steventon rectory, perfect for rolling.

* * *

Perhaps in part due to the need to house an ever-increasing number of boarders, George and Cassandra Austen decided to send their daughters away to school. At the age of seven, Jane Austen, together with her ten-year-old sister, was taken to Oxford by their cousin Jane Cooper. They were to be taught by a Mrs Cawley, a Cooper relation. Seven seems to us an early age for a young girl to be living away from her family, especially from such a warm, loving home, full of life and animation. It must have been a wrench to leave the safety and security of the family home for school in Oxford, though elder brother James Austen was studying there and showed the girls the sights of the city. The arrangement was similar to that in Steventon: it was a case of a family taking in pupils, not a formal school environment. Presumably George Austen had made the financial calculation that the income gained from sending his girls away and creating more space for boy boarders in the rectory would exceed the outlay required to keep them in Oxford.

According to family lore, Jane insisted on accompanying her sister to Oxford. Mrs Austen claimed that if 'Cassandra were going to have her head cut off, Jane would insist on sharing her fate'.[21] Hampshire to Oxford is about fifty miles, which the two young girls would have travelled in a stage-coach.

In September, Mrs Cawley moved her 'school' to Southampton, only for it to be struck by a typhus outbreak. The three girls fell ill, but Mrs Cawley failed to alert the family. It was Jane Cooper who wrote to her mother and told her the news. Mrs Austen and Mrs Cooper came immediately to take the girls home. Jane Austen was very ill and nearly died. They all made a full recovery, but Mrs Cooper caught the fever and died in October. One can only imagine the shock and distress of the family. Dr Cooper was heartbroken and devoted the rest of his years to bringing up his children Jane and Edward. To commemorate his beloved wife he sent Cassandra a 'ring representing a sprig of diamonds, with one emerald' and Jane was given a headband, which she wore to balls.[22]

The Southampton experience did not deter the Reverend and Mrs Austen from the idea of boarding school. Within a year, Jane and Cassandra, together with their now motherless cousin Jane Cooper, found themselves at a more formal establishment, this time in Reading, a prosperous trading town just over twenty miles from Steventon, on the main coaching routes from London to Oxford and the west country.

It was called the Abbey School and was run by Sarah Hackitt, who went by the name of Madame Latournelle, no doubt because female French teachers were the height of fashion. The school adjoined the remains of the ancient Abbey of Reading: 'the greater part of the house was encompassed by a beautiful old-fashioned garden, where the young ladies were allowed to wander under tall trees in hot summer evenings'.[23] The school was connected to an antique gateway, which looked out on the green and a marketplace beyond. Inside, new girls were received by the headmistress in a wainscoted parlour in which chenille tapestries depicting tombs and weeping willows were hung round the walls.

According to a family member, the school was a 'free and easy one ... In Cassandra and Jane's days the girls do not seem to have been kept very strictly, as they and their cousin, Jane Cooper, were allowed to accept an invitation to dine at an inn with their respective brothers, Edward Austen and Edward Cooper.'[24] As the family descendants noted, it all sounds rather like Mrs Goddard's school in *Emma*, which 'had an ample house and garden, gave the children plenty of wholesome food, let them run about a great deal in the summer, and in winter [she] dressed their chilblains with her own hands'.[25] Madame Latournelle always dressed in the same way and had a cork leg. She encouraged the arts, dancing and theatre in particular. It seems to have been a happy place, full of girlish glee. 'I could die of laughter at it, as they used to say at school,' Jane Austen remarked in one of her letters to Cassandra.[26]

After twenty months spent in the Abbey School she returned home for good in December 1786, just approaching her eleventh birthday. Her formal education was over. But the home to which she returned was one from which her brother Edward was now permanently absent.

As has been suggested, the transference of children from one home to another by formal adoption, as with Edward Austen Knight, or by a more informal arrangement, as with the fictional Fanny Price in *Mansfield Park*, was by no means uncommon. If the Knights, like Lord Mansfield and the Chutes, had wanted a girl rather than a boy, then Jane Austen would have been separated from her beloved Cassandra.

Jane Austen reworked the theme of adopted children several times in her novels and uses it to suggest her ideas about nature and nurture, good parents and bad parents, the importance of childhood in relation to the adult. 'Give me the child until he is seven and I will give you the man,' as the old Jesuit saying had it.

Jane Austen was close to her father, who supported her ambition to become a published writer. Her feelings towards her mother were far more complicated. There are few examples of effective parenting in the novels. This is partly a plot device: the heroine must make her own choices, judgements and mistakes before reaching maturity and finding an equal mate worthy of her. The exception to this rule of the flawed heroine is Jane Austen's most disliked (or least well-understood) heroine, Fanny Price. The fictional Fanny is almost the same age that the real Edward Knight was when he was first taken from his home. *Mansfield Park* is perhaps the first novel in history to depict the life of a little girl from within.[27]

Jane Austen enters intuitively into the feelings and consciousness of the child as she is uprooted from her family and transferred to Mansfield Park. Fanny's fear and anxiety, exacerbated by the vicious bullying of Mrs Norris, are brilliantly executed. Told that she must be a good grateful girl and given the treat of a gooseberry tart to comfort her, Fanny dissolves into tears. It is the careless neglect that affects her sensitive spirit: 'Nobody meant to be unkind, but nobody put themselves out of their way to secure her comfort.'[28]

One of the main themes of the novel is the importance of home. The word is repeated over 140 times in the course of the narrative. What does 'home' mean? Is it a place or is it a family? What happens when a home is left unprotected or badly governed? When Fanny returns home to Portsmouth she has an epiphany that shakes her to the core:

> Her eagerness, her impatience, her longing to be with them, were such as to bring a line or two of Cowper's Tirocinium for ever before her. 'With what intense desire she wants her home,' was continually on her tongue, as the truest description of a yearning which she could not suppose any school-boy's bosom to feel more keenly.
>
> When she had been coming to Portsmouth, she had loved to call it her home, had been fond of saying that she was going home; the word had been very dear to her; and so it still was, but it must be applied to Mansfield. *That* was now the home. Portsmouth was Portsmouth; Mansfield was home.[29]

The literary reference is crucial. William Cowper was Jane Austen's favourite poet. The poem to which she refers here, *Tirocinium*, was extremely well known. It bids a father not to send his son away to school, but to educate him at home so that the natural ties of affection are not damaged and so that the father's spiritual and moral guidance will be uppermost.

> Why hire a lodging in a house unknown
> For one whose tenderest thoughts all hover round your own?
> This second weaning, needless as it is,
> How does it lacerate both your heart and his!
> The indented stick, that loses day by day,
> Notch after notch, till all are smoothed away,
> Bears witness, long ere his dismission come,
> With what intense desire he wants his home.[30]

Indeed, *Mansfield Park* shares many of the concerns of *Tirocinium*. It is a profound exploration of the duty of parents to shape their children's moral and spiritual development. It includes a father who is emotionally distant, his children 'chill'd into respect'. It reflects on the importance of home, the nature of good education, the alienation of sons from their father, the importance of conscience: 'In early days the conscience has in most/A quickness, which in later life is lost.' At the centre of the book is a timid, shy displaced child with an unshakeable sense of conscience.

Fanny is a heroine who is deeply sensitive, and loves nature, poetry and biography, especially Shakespeare, Crabbe and Cowper. She is religious and her spirits are easily depressed. As well as quoting from *Tirocinium* she also loves Cowper's *The Task*, a poem inspired by his muse, Lady Austen (a distant relative of Jane's), an elegant and attractive widow who set him 'a task' to write a poem about a 'sofa'. This extraordinary poem in six books is the eighteenth century's great celebration of the retired and religious life. 'God made the country, and man made the Town' is among its most famous lines. Cowper undertakes a fierce assault on contemporary society, condemning the slave trade, French despotism, fashionable manners and lukewarm clergymen. 'England, with all thy faults, I love thee still –/My country!' writes Cowper, and the sentiments could have been Austen's own.

It was Henry Austen, Jane's brother, who revealed that Cowper was her favourite poet. But one could have guessed as much from her portrayal of Fanny Price and of Anne Elliot in *Persuasion*. As much admired by the Romantic poets Coleridge and Wordsworth as by Jane Austen, Cowper was a brilliant but deeply troubled man, a depressive who tried to kill himself at least three times and was for a time confined to a lunatic asylum before finding refuge from his despair in a profound Christian faith. He was a friend of slave trader turned Evangelical preacher John Newton, the author of 'Amazing Grace'. Cowper's poetry was pioneering because he wrote about everyday life and scenes of the English countryside. For Jane Austen, his work embodied love of the country as Dr Johnson's embodied the energetic life of the town.[31] He transformed English poetry rather in the way that Jane Austen herself would transform English fiction.

Though Jane Austen was to return to the theme of the adopted child in *Emma*, there she does not enter the mind of the child as she does in *Mansfield Park*. In that novel, Fanny's transference into the great house is a blessing and a final redemption, especially to Sir Thomas: 'Fanny was indeed the daughter that he wanted. His charitable kindness had been rearing a prime comfort for himself. His liberality had a rich repayment.'[32] The child of the impoverished branch of the family redeems the materially more prosperous but morally bankrupt household. By accepting Fanny, the Bertrams become more human.

Mansfield Park is not a retelling of the story of Jane Austen's wealthy relatives, the Knights of Godmersham Park. Her brother Edward Austen, who became Edward Knight, is not the 'original' of Fanny Price. But the theme of the bond between branches of a family with very different prospects came close to Austen's own experience. The liberality of the Knights eventually made it possible for her to become a novelist. Mrs Knight, her only patron, was described by her as 'gentle and kind and friendly'.[33] And, crucially, it was through the Knights that Edward was to give his mother and sisters a home. Had he not been adopted, he would not have grown up to inherit the great house at Chawton, from where he was able to give his poor relations the modest property near by in which Jane lived the last eight years of her life and wrote her novels.

at least three times and was for a time confined to a future asylum before finding refuge from his despair in a profound Christian faith. He was a friend of slave-trader turned Evangelical preacher, John Newton, the author of 'Amazing Grace.' Cowper's poetry was, in part, appealing because he wrote about everyday life and scenes of the English countryside, for Jane Austen, his work embodied love of the country; as Dr Johnson's embodied the essence of the town. It was in real places that Dr Johnson walked—rather in the way that Jane Austen based, would transform everyday reality.

Though Jane Austen is to return to the theme of the adopted child in emma, there she does not enter the mind of the child, as she does in Mansfield Park. In this novel, the adopted child in a great house is a blessing, and a triumph over her humble origins. Fanny was indeed the daughter the Austen novelist, and her daughters had been rearing a prime comfort to their parents in their old age requirement. The child of the impoverished Prices, she becomes the materially more prosperous Bertrams by adoption—preferring Fanny, the Bertrams become more...

Mansfield Park was, in some respects, Jane Austen's wealthy relatives, the Knight family, and her own brother Edward Austen who became Edward Knight, formerly Fanny Price. But the theme of the bond between branches in a family with very different prospects came close to Austen's own experience. The liberality of the Knights eventually made it possible for her to become a novelist. Mrs Knight, her only patron, was described by her as 'gentle and fond and friendly.' And crucially, it was through the Knights that Edward was to give his mother and sisters a home. Had he not been adopted, he would not have grown up to inherit the great house at Chawton, from where he was able to give his poor relations the modest property near by in which Jane lived the last eight years of her life and wrote her novels.

The East Indian Shawl

Shawls had been hand-woven in Kashmir since the eleventh century. The finest examples were made under Mughal patronage to be worn at court or presented as ostentatious gifts. They could take many months to complete, requiring the skills of spinners, dyers, pattern designers, craftsmen responsible for arranging the warp and weft, weavers and finishers. The best were made from the underbelly fleece of the wild central Asian goat, whereas pashmina, second-grade wool, came from domesticated goats. Many such shawls were brought back to Europe, where they became a popular fashion item in Jane Austen's lifetime. Western demand duly affected Kashmiri production: by the time the shawl illustrated here was made, the classic *boteh* design, derived from flowering plants, had become more formal and stylized. This particular 'moon shawl' is square, like most Kashmir shawls, and was intended to be worn over the shoulders.

In January 1772, Jane Austen's Aunt Phila was sent 'a piece of flowered shawl to make a warm winter morning gown' from her husband, who was living in Calcutta.[1] Seventy years later, Jane Austen's sister Cassandra mentioned in her last testament 'a large Indian shawl'. It had once belonged to the woman she had hoped would become her mother-in-law.[2] Jane Austen herself once gave a shawl to a Steventon neighbour. She observed her niece Cassy in a fine red shawl and a Bath acquaintance in a yellow one.[3] And in her house at Chawton today the visitor can still see a cream silk shawl that was a gift to her from Catherine Knight, her brother Edward's adoptive mother.

'Fanny,' says Lady Bertram in *Mansfield Park*, 'William must not forget my shawl, if he goes to the East Indies; and I shall give him a commission for any thing else that is worth having. I wish he may go to the East Indies, that I may have my shawl.' She hesitates for an instant, then ends with characteristic indulgence: 'I think I will have two shawls, Fanny.'[4]

When Jane Austen saw or wore or wrote about an Indian shawl, she entered a whole new realm of cross-cultural exchange, a world far from that of her own Hampshire village. Through her family connections, she became aware of that wider world and it entered subtly into her imagination, shaping her novels to a far greater extent than is often realized. Thanks in particular to a charismatic female cousin, there is a thread connecting Jane Austen to places we do not usually associate with her: not only the East Indies, but also the streets of revolutionary Paris.

The East India Company, with its many trading activities, was developing into a significant economic and political force within the global economy. Cottons and silks, indigo dyes and spices, not to mention diamonds and opium, were imported in vast quantities. As goods came west, so people went east. The Indies became the place to make your fortune when hope was lost at home.

A young woman, an orphan called Cecilia Wynne, leaves her home in England for Bengal. Her journey to the East Indies takes six months, the passage fraught with dangers and privations. She is going with one object in mind: to find a husband. Left penniless by her father, she is travelling at the behest of a rich relation who is eager to marry her off. The girl's younger sister, also destitute, has been offered a placement as a lady's companion in England.

When Cecilia arrives in the East Indies, her good looks ensure that she soon finds a rich husband. He is older than her, and very respectable: she is considered to be 'splendidly but unhappily married'. Back in England Cecilia is regarded by those who know her as a lucky girl. All except one friend, who harbours no such romantic illusions: 'Do you call it lucky, for a Girl of Genius and Feeling to be sent in quest of a Husband to Bengal, to be married there to a Man of whose Disposition she has no opportunity of judging till her Judgement is of no use to her, who may be a Tyrant, or a Fool or both for what she knows to the Contrary. Do you call *that* fortunate?' Another girl replies, cynically, 'She is not the first Girl who has gone to the East Indies for a Husband, and I declare it should be very good fun if I were as poor.'[5]

This story is fictional. It is called 'Catharine, or the Bower' and it was written by the young Jane Austen in 1792 when she was sixteen. But the facts of the story replicate almost exactly the fate of her own aunts: Philadelphia, elder sister of the Reverend George Austen, did indeed go to the East Indies for a husband, while Leonora, his younger sister, became a lady's companion at home in England. Even in her teens, the young Jane Austen was preoccupied with the hardships faced by women reduced to a state of absolute dependence on relations who often prove to be unkind and unfeeling. Her interest in the plight of impoverished women and the harsh realities of the Georgian marriage market never left her. She once advised her niece Fanny that 'Single Women have a dreadful propensity for being poor – which is one very strong argument in favour of Matrimony.'[6] The women sent out to the East Indies to find husbands because they had no dowry and little chance of finding an English match were but extreme examples of a widespread phenomenon.

So what was the story of these three children – Philadelphia, known to the family as Phila, George and Leonora – born in rapid succession in May 1730, May 1731 and January 1733? It is a tale of siblings separated, an uncaring stepmother and the prospect of penury or worse.

Perhaps one of the reasons why George Austen grew up to become such a loving, kind and attentive father, and to fill his house with children, was that his own childhood had been one of neglect and misery. His mother, Rebecca, died shortly after giving birth to Leonora. Their father, William Austen, a surgeon, remarried, but he too soon died. Little George was just six.

The stepmother was not interested in the three young children. William Austen's will had established his two brothers as trustees for the orphans. One of these uncles, Stephen, was a bookseller at St Paul's in London. He and his wife took in their nephew and two nieces. According to family tradition, the children were neglected, even mistreated.[7] But one can never be entirely sure how much to trust what one branch of a family says about another. The neglect cannot have been total, since little Leonora stayed in the household. Presumably she would have had the same kind of status as Fanny Price at Mansfield Park. Hardly anything is known of her later life, other than that she became a lady's companion. George, meanwhile, was sent to live with an aunt at Tonbridge in Kent. He went to the long-established school there and proved himself a clever boy, winning a scholarship to Oxford.

Philadelphia did not have such educational opportunities. When she was fifteen, she was apprenticed to a milliner in Covent Garden. She would have been set to work making shirts and shifts, aprons and neckerchiefs, caps and cloaks, hoods and hats, muffs and ruffles, trim for gowns. Apprentice milliners led tough, unhealthy lives with long hours and poor conditions. Many of them died young, but there was always a stream of young girls available to take their place. Some, especially those as attractive as Phila, were tempted or forced into another profession. The term 'Milliner of Covent Garden' was slang for a prostitute. In that part of London, the dividing line between different kinds of working girl was very thin.

Phila needed to get out. Having finished her apprenticeship and come of age, she inherited her small portion from her father's estate. In November 1751, she made a bold move, petitioning the Directors of the East India Company for leave to go to India aboard their ship, the *Bombay Castle*.

She set sail on 18 January 1752, together with ten other 'young beauties'. They all had the same ambition: to find a husband among the lonely white businessmen, soldiers and administrators who worked in the East Indies. In the colloquial language of the English in Bengal, women of this kind would become known as 'the fishing fleet'.

One of the other girls, Mary Elliott, had named the same two gentlemen as Phila in the role of 'sureties' to support her application, so it may be assumed that they were friends before they went aboard. Another, who would also become a good friend to Phila, was Margaret Maskelyne. Only sixteen, the orphaned and impoverished daughter of a minor civil servant, she was escaping a life of boredom with her maiden aunts in Wiltshire. The army had taken her wild brother Edmund to India and he reckoned he had lined up a match for her: a letter had arrived in England with the information that he 'had laid out a husband for Peggy if she chooses to take so long a voyage for one that I approve of extremely, but then she must make haste, as he is in such a marrying mood that I believe the first comer will carry him'.[8]

The beauties bound for Bengal finally arrived at Madras Harbour in early August. All eleven had survived the conditions aboard ship, described by Jane Austen as 'a punishment that needs no other to make it very severe'.[9]

Many people died in the passage. What must it have been like for these girls? Homesickness at leaving England coupled with the terrors of the voyage, seasickness, weeks upon weeks of cramped conditions, stink from the bilge, coldness on deck and heat below. Always the threat of shipwreck. If the girls were wealthy they could be wined and dined by the captain, but this came at a high price and many East India captains charged exorbitant sums and steep rates of interest if credit was required. The captains also acted as general suppliers of goods such as clothes, delicacies, even furniture, which they sold both to their passengers and to the inhabitants at their destination.

Their first sight of India was the long, low line of the Coromandel Coast. The contrast in journeying from a freezing English mid-winter to August in Madras (now Chennai) can readily be imagined: the heat and humidity, but also the glorious mountains and sea, the white buildings, the endless sky, the smell of Madras, with its mixture of hot dust, burnt dung and spices. From the deck, as the hot breeze hit them, they saw the battlements of Fort St George, with the steeple of St Mary's Church rising gracefully behind it. The church was a brilliant white, the surface covered with *chunam*, a cement that was made of burnt sea-shells. It glowed in the setting sun. To the right of the Fort was the native or 'Black Town', to the left was the old Portuguese settlement of Thome. Surrounding it all was golden sand and green palm-trees."

The girls were taken to the Sea Gate of the Fort in a flimsy *masula* boat. From there, they would be swept into a whirl of concerts, balls and picnics. Their quest for husbands was under way. Margaret Maskelyne was duly introduced to the man her brother had lined up for her. He was the Governor of Bengal, and within six months she had married him. He would go on to achieve fame under the name Lord Clive of India.

In 1745, the year when Phila began her apprenticeship in Covent Garden, a man called Tysoe Hancock, seven years her senior, set sail for the East Indies. Hancock held the post of Surgeon Extraordinary for the East India Company in Madras, but he was also involved in the shipment of diamonds and gold. And he was in search of a wife. He knew all about both the prospects and the perils faced by the 'fishing fleet beauties'. 'You know very well', he wrote in a letter, 'that no Girl, tho' but fourteen Years Old, can arrive in India without attracting the Notice of every Coxcomb in the Place, of whom there is very great Plenty at Calcutta, with very good Persons and no other Recommendation ... Debauchery under the polite name of Gallantry is the Reigning Vice of the Settlement.'[11]

Phila's wealthy uncle Francis, a well-to-do gentleman who made his money practising law and buying land at Sevenoaks in Kent, was Tysoe Hancock's lawyer and business agent. This connection brought them together. In February 1753, just over six months after her arrival in India, Jane Austen's aunt became Mrs Tysoe Hancock. At Fort St David, where she settled down to married life, she must have felt a million miles away from her days as a penniless seamstress for fine ladies. She was now the mistress of a large household of servants, including personal maids called Diana, Silima, Dido and Clarinda. She wore fine silks and muslins. The garden, shaded by rows of the evergreen tulip tree, was full of pineapples and pomegranates. The only thing she lacked was a baby. After six years of marriage the couple still remained childless.

In 1759 they moved to Fort William in Calcutta, at the request of Lord Clive. Here they became part of the elite British Bengal community, meeting and befriending Warren Hastings. Hastings had joined the East India Company in 1750 as a clerk, and by 1773 he would rise to become the first Governor-General of India. Hastings and Hancock entered into a business relationship, trading in salt, timber, carpets, rice and Bihar opium. Phila was reunited with her friend from the voyage out, Mary Elliott. She too had succeeded in making a quick match soon after arriving, but it had ended abruptly when her husband had the misfortune of being among the British soldiers who died when incarcerated in the Black Hole of Calcutta. With rather indecent haste, Mary married Warren Hastings just a few months later. In December 1757, she gave birth to a son called George. Then in 1758 she had a daughter called Elizabeth, who did not survive. The friends who had once been part of the fishing fleet did not have long together, for Mary Hastings died in July 1759, just weeks after Phila had moved to Calcutta.

Calcutta was grander and more luxurious than the Coast. Great mansions resembling Italian palazzi lined the river front. It was more like a European city than Madras, as its houses and public buildings were not all crammed into the confines of the Fort but were mingled on the streets of the town itself. Armenians mixed with Portuguese, providing the English with cooks and servants. Many of the English lived in large one-storey villas reached by outdoor stairs, boasting handsome verandas on which to sit in the cool of the evening. Walls were not papered but whitewashed and, the climate being too hot for carpets, the floors were covered in matting. The rooms were large, cool and airy, furnished with European imports. Many of the English had a 'garden-house' out of town, where they retired at the weekends, escaping the intense heat of the city. Siestas were necessary, the heat being so great that the ladies would retire wearing 'the slightest covering'. Only in the cool of the evening would everyone dress in their finery and go out into society. One of the most popular meeting places was Holwell's Gardens, where the British gathered together for supper parties and for their children to play. In early 1761 Philadelphia discovered that she was at last pregnant.

* * *

Phila's new life could hardly have been more different from that of her brother George, Jane Austen's future father. After Oxford, he was ordained deacon and became a master at his old school in Tonbridge. After his second ordination, as a full clergyman, in 1755 he resigned his schoolteaching post and returned to Oxford where he became assistant Chaplain at St John's College.

In 1762, George Austen met Cassandra Leigh. They married two years later and were accompanied on their honeymoon by a sickly seven-year-old

Jane Austen's aunt Phila

boy called George Hastings. The worlds of India and England were colliding again: the first child to come into the household of Jane Austen's father was the son of Warren Hastings.

George Hastings had been sent to England in 1761, at the time when Phila Hancock was pregnant. He was initially entrusted to the Leigh family of Adlestrop, who were old friends of Warren Hastings. In this sense, he came as part of the marriage package when George Austen proposed to Cassandra Leigh. George was rewarded with a salary from Hastings, and expenses incurred on behalf of the boy were reimbursed. After the honeymoon, the boy moved in with the newly married couple at the parsonage in Deane, Hampshire, where the Reverend George Austen had been granted a living. But the boy was in very poor health. He died of diphtheria in the autumn. According to family tradition, Cassandra Austen reacted as badly as if George had been her own child.

Meanwhile in Calcutta, sister Phila's seven barren years came to an end. On 22 December 1761, she finally gave birth to a daughter. This was Eliza Hancock, the little girl who would bring colour, danger and excitement into Jane Austen's world.

The Austen family still possesses an Indian rosewood writing desk that, it is said, was given as a present by Warren Hastings to Phila Hancock, in order to thank her for nursing his dying wife. The gossip among the British in Calcutta was that Phila had very quickly become much more than a nurse and a friend. It appears to have been an open secret in the community of the East India Company that Eliza was the illegitimate daughter of the great Warren Hastings. He was her acknowledged godfather, and Eliza was named after Hastings's daughter Elizabeth who had died in infancy. She in turn would name her only child, a son, after him: Hastings.

The gossip raged, fuelled by a jealous secretary of Clive's called Jenny Strachey. Lord Clive himself wrote to his wife, demanding that she dissociate herself from her fellow-traveller on the fishing fleet: 'In no circumstance whatever keep company with Mrs Hancock for it is beyond a doubt that she abandoned herself to Mr Hastings.'[12]

Warren Hastings remained profoundly loyal to Phila and her little girl, who quickly became known as Betsy. He settled a fortune of five thousand pounds on the child, later doubling the amount, giving her more than enough for a dowry to enable her to make a good marriage. The source of the money was a bond for forty thousand rupees made over to Hastings to be paid in China, which he then passed over to Eliza in English money. Sums of that kind coming from the India–China connection at this period always carry the smell of opium.

Hastings was famously generous and well known for his love of children, but his private letters to Phila are unusually affectionate and revealing: 'Kiss my dear Bessy for me, and assure her of my tenderest Affection. May the God of Goodness bless you both.'[13] Whether or not Hastings was Eliza's natural father, she always treated him like one. When she married her cousin Henry in 1797, she wrote at once to Hastings, seeking his approbation of the union. After Eliza's death, Henry visited Hastings. Reporting on the visit, Jane Austen wrote, somewhat mysteriously, that he had 'never *hinted* at Eliza in the smallest degree'.[14] She was clearly astonished that Hastings had said nothing about the last days of the child he had so adored. It may well be inferred that the relationship was so close, his pain so great, that he could not bear to speak of her.

In the summer of 1765, the Hancock family arrived back in England, accompanied by Warren Hastings and their maid Clarinda. It was reported that the first news he heard on his arrival was word from the Austens of the death of his son. He was deeply affected, his love for his god-daughter Eliza only intensified. In London, Hastings and the Hancocks rented houses close to one another. Eliza and her mother stayed on in England when Hancock returned to Bengal. He sent them wonderful supplies: spices for cooking, curry leaves, pickled mangoes and limes, chillies, balychong spice and cassoondy sauce. Perfumes, such as attar of roses from Patna, arrived too. Diamonds were sent worth thousands of pounds, and gold mohurs (coins). He also shipped over fine linen and silks for bed linen and for dresses for both mother and daughter. They received seersucker, sannow, doreas, muslin, dimity, Malda silks, chintz and flowered shawls. In return, Phila sent books, gin and newspapers. Hancock requested that his wife share her treasures with members of her family, including of course George Austen and his family, which by this time was growing rapidly. Little wonder that Jane Austen's juvenile writing contains references to consumer goods such as Indian muslins, not to mention curry sauces.[15]

Hancock wrote vivid letters to his wife, telling terrifying tales of servants killed by tigers in the Sunderbunds and reporting that her two maids, Diana and Silima, had become prostitutes. Phila shared this Indian news with Jane Austen's parents. She often visited Hampshire to help Mrs Austen in her confinements. She was definitely present at Cassandra's birth and probably at Jane's in 1775.

Warren Hastings met George Austen in London in July 1765. Austen was extremely impressed with Hastings, who had been a brilliant classicist at Westminster School and had always been disappointed that instead of proceeding to university he had been sent out to the East India Company as a young man. Hastings loved Latin poetry and had a taste for writing verse based on the Horatian model. George Austen urged his own children to emulate the great man's learning.

Eliza's parents wanted her to be educated in England or France. She was given the best London masters for drawing and dancing lessons, and for music. She played the guitar and the harpsichord. She was taught to ride, to play-act and to speak French. This was a typical education in female accomplishments with the express purpose of attracting a man of means. But Hancock also insisted that she had arithmetic and writing lessons: 'her other Accomplishments will be Ornaments to her, but these are absolutely necessary'.[16] He took advice on her education from Hastings, who urged 'an early practice in Economy', but also hinted that he would provide for Eliza: 'but if I live and meet with the success which I have the Right to hope for, she shall not be under the Necessity of marrying a Tradesman, or any Man for her Support'.[17] Hancock fretted about his daughter. He worried about her moral health, fearing that she might 'pick up the Levity or Follies of the French', and also about her physical health – when she got threadworms he noted that 'they cannot be watched with too much Caution, as they may be greatly detrimental to her Constitution'.[18]

After Hancock's death, alone in India in 1775, still trying and failing to make money, Eliza and her mother stayed in London another year. Then they began their travels in Europe, first going to Germany and Belgium, before reaching Paris in 1779. By 1780 Eliza had seen the French royal family at close quarters in Versailles, taken up the harp and sat for her ivory miniature. It was a present for her beloved uncle George Austen, dispatched to his rectory. She is wearing a pretty low-cut dress, adorned with blue ribbons, and her hair is heavily powdered, as was the fashion in Paris ('Heads in general look as if they had been dipped in a meal tub,' she wrote in a letter).[19]

Jane Austen was five when the miniature reached Steventon. A year later Eliza became engaged to a captain in Marie-Antoinette's regiment of dragoons, Jean-François Capot de Feuillide. Ten years older than Eliza, he was the son of a provincial lawyer – though he called himself the Comte de Feuillide, on somewhat dubious grounds. George Austen thoroughly disapproved of the match, fearing that the self-styled Count was a fortune-hunter and complaining that Eliza and her mother were giving up their friends, their country and even their religion.[20]

In December 1773, Hancock had drawn up letters of attorney enabling George Austen to act on his sister's behalf in the confidential handling of receipts from India. Invoices for assignments of diamonds were made out in George Austen's name. Hastings and Hancock were also involved in trading opium, among other commodities. It is startling to suppose that Jane Austen's education and the books in her father's library, which did so much to inspire her to become a writer, may well have been funded, at least indirectly, by the opium trade. So much for the notion of her family being wholly sequestered from the world in a cosy Hampshire village.

Hancock's death, back in Calcutta in 1775, was the occasion for Warren Hastings's doubling of his gift to his god-daughter Eliza. George Austen was one of the trustees named in the legal documents. It was just two months after Hancock's death that Jane Austen was born.

Cecilia Wynne in the early novella 'Catharine' is the only young woman in Austen's fiction to join the fishing fleet to seek marriage in India. But her family connections with Bengal periodically pop up in the mature novels. Lady Bertram's request for an East Indian shawl is one example. And in *Sense and Sensibility*, Marianne and Willoughby make fun of Brandon's experience there: "'he has told you that in the East Indies the climate is hot, and the mosquitoes are troublesome" ... "Perhaps," said Willoughby, "his observations may have extended to the existence of nabobs, gold mohrs and palanquins.'"[21] Jane Austen never based her stories directly on her own family's experiences, but in a life dominated by conversation, the exchange of family news, storytelling and letter-writing, it seems more than a little coincidental that the reason Brandon asks his regiment for a transfer to Bengal is his desire to escape from the heartbreak of losing his great love, who is called Eliza. She is forced to marry his brother, against her will, and later becomes a prostitute; her daughter, also called Eliza, is seduced by Willoughby when only sixteen, has his child and is abandoned. For Jane Austen, it would seem, the name of Eliza was inextricably connected with both the East Indies and sexual scandal.

* * *

Eliza

Eliza Hancock, now the Comtesse de Feuillide and bringing with her a baby boy, burst into the life of the Steventon parsonage just in time for the Christmas festivities of 1786. Slight of build and extremely elegant, she had high cheekbones, elfin features, large expressive eyes and masses of curly hair. Marriage had not tamed the vivacious Eliza. She had plenty of admirers at Steventon, male and female. Jane Austen, at the impressionable age of eleven, was simply enchanted by the cousin who brought tales of India and Europe to rural Hampshire.

For the young Jane Austen, Eliza Hancock was the living incarnation of her favourite character in one of her favourite novels: Charlotte Grandison in Samuel Richardson's *Sir Charles Grandison*. Reading Eliza's real letters is like reading Charlotte's fictional ones. Temperamentally, Eliza was unsuited to marriage, which she saw as giving up 'dear Liberty and yet dearer flirtation'. 'Flirtation's a charming thing,' she wrote: 'it makes the blood circulate!' Of her first husband, the Count, she remarked, 'it is too little to say he loves, since he literally adores me'. Of weddings she quipped, 'I was never but at one wedding in my life and that appeared a very stupid idea to me.'

Of herself she wrote, 'independence and the homage of half a dozen are preferable to subjection and the attachment of a single individual ... I am more and more convinced that She is not at all calculated for sober Matrimony.'[22]

Her liveliness mesmerized the Austens. She played piano for them every day, and arranged impromptu dances in the parlour. She told stories of Paris and of Marie Antoinette. She complained of French theatre that 'it is still the fashion to translate or rather murder, Shakespear'.[23] She gave Jane for her birthday a twelve-volume set of Arnaud de Berquin's stories *L'Ami des enfants.*

Jane and Cassandra, who had been at boarding school for the previous eighteen months, were now home for good. In Steventon rectory Eliza also encountered Henry Austen, no longer a child but a tall handsome man about to go up to Oxford. He soon made a point of visiting her when she went back to London, and arranging for her to visit him at college. At St John's in Oxford, Eliza 'longed to be a *Fellow* that I might walk [in the garden] every day'. 'Besides,' she added, 'I was delighted with the Black Gown and thought the Square Cap mighty becoming.'[24]

Eliza had confessed to Philadelphia ('Phylly') Walter, cousin to the Austens, that she was no longer in love with her husband. While he was in France she led, according to this cousin, a 'very dissipated life' in London.[25] To judge from Eliza's surviving letters, her life was full of socializing and adventure. She narrowly misses being robbed and attacked by highwaymen on Hounslow Heath. She takes her little boy Hastings to Hastings and other seaside resorts for the benefit of sea-bathing. She attends balls and the opera and moves back and forth between England and France.

Following the success of her visit to Steventon in 1786 she was keen to go down to Hampshire again, though her uncle had told her that he was able to entertain only at midsummer and Christmas. She made plans to return to Steventon for the following Christmas and she encouraged her cousins in their plans to put on private theatricals. As will be seen, Eliza led the way in choosing the plays and it is no surprise that those she chose featured spirited heroines who refuse to be cowed by men.

Both James and Henry Austen were 'fascinated' by the flirtatious Eliza, according to James's son, who wrote the first memoir of Jane. One of Jane Austen's comic stories written before the end of the 1780s was called 'Henry and Eliza'. Eliza is a beautiful little foundling girl discovered in a 'Haycock', rather as Austen's cousin was a beautiful little girl of uncertain origin called Eliza Hancock. The action turns on an elopement by the titular characters, who run off to France leaving only a curt note: 'Madam, we are married and gone.' With the real Eliza anything could happen and the young Jane Austen seems to have found it both exciting and amusing to imagine her eloping with Henry. Little did she know how the story of the real Eliza and Henry would end.

Eliza returned to Steventon in the summer of 1792, in much darker circumstances. She brought with her a fund of true tales as shocking as anything in the Gothic novels that young women were devouring at the time. Eliza, her mother and little Hastings had fled from France as trouble brewed in the months leading up to the storming of the Bastille in 1789. They were in London when news of the revolution broke. From then on, they were forced to stay in England.

By January 1791 Eliza's husband Jean-François, now no doubt regretting his title of 'Comte', had fled to Turin with the King's brother and other royalist émigrés. Eliza wrote from London to the Austen family at Steventon telling them the news and also giving bulletins of her mother's declining health. She comforted herself with gossip about her Steventon cousins, especially Jane and Cassandra: 'I hear they are perfect beauties and of course gain hearts by dozens.'[26]

After a long battle with breast cancer, Phila Hancock died in 1792. Eliza's husband managed, via a circuitous route, to join her in England to provide some comfort in her bereavement. They went to Bath for a period of recuperation and she became pregnant. The Count decided, however, to return to France for fear of having his land confiscated. As Eliza reported,

> M. de F proposed remaining here some time, but he soon received Accounts from France which informed him that having already exceeded his Leave of Absence, if he still continued in England he would be considered as one of the Emigrants, and consequently his whole property forfeited to the Nation. Such Advices were not to be neglected and M. de F was obliged to depart for Paris.[27]

Within days of his departure, Eliza's nerves, already frayed, were shattered when she was caught up in serious riots in London. On 4 June 1792, the King's birthday, a group of forty servants had been invited to a dance and dinner at a pub, the Pitts Head. There was no disturbance until the High Constable of Westminster along with his watchmen entered the pub, made trouble and arrested all the servants, taking them to the Watchhouse in Mount Street. The next morning a mob arrived at the Watchhouse and soldiers were called to read the Riot Act. Eliza's coach was attacked and her driver was injured, terrifying her out of her wits and causing her to miscarry the baby she had conceived on her husband's visit to England. She wrote a graphic account of the events:

The noise of the populace, the drawn swords and pointed bayonets of the guards, the fragments of bricks and mortar thrown on every side, one of which had nearly killed my Coachman, the firing at one end of the street which was already begun, altogether in short alarmed me so much, that I really have never been well since. The Confusion continued all that day and Night and the following Day, and for these eight and forty Hours, I have seen nothing but large parties of Soldiers parading up and down in this Street, to which Mount Street is very near, there being only Grosvenor Square between. My apprehensions have been that they would have set fire to the houses they were so bent on demolishing, and think if that was to be the case how soon in such a City as this a Fire very trifling in the beginning might be productive of the most serious Consequences.[28]

Parallels were instantly drawn with recent history in France. A caricature of the Mount Street riots, published two days later, showed a French manservant arguing with a violent watchman and saying 'Ah, Sacre Dieu! I did tink it vas all Dance in de land of Liberté!' On the back wall is a print of the Storming of the Bastille, with cannons and decapitated heads on pikes. The implication is clear: like Paris, London was in danger of being swept into revolution.[29]

Eliza immediately made plans to escape to Steventon. But as a result of her miscarriage and then a severe case of chickenpox, she didn't get there until August. So it was that she arrived at the Austen rectory with her head full of English riots and anxieties about her husband back in Paris. Weakened by miscarriage and illness, she cried when she saw the uncle whose features so resembled those of the beloved mother whom she had recently lost.

She noted how tall her cousin Jane had grown and assured Phylly Walter, who disliked Jane, that she 'was greatly improved in manners as in person'. Eliza also expressed her own sense of loyalty to the younger sister: 'My Heart gives the preference to Jane, whose kind partiality to me, indeed requires a return of the same nature.'[30]

She may have felt safe in rural Hampshire, sharing stories and books with her cousins, but news from France reached her in private letters from Jean-François and also via the English press: 'My private Letters confirm the Intelligence afforded by the public Prints,' she wrote to Phylly Walter, 'and assure me that nothing we read there is exaggerated.'[31] She was referring to the September Massacres, that wave of mob violence which began with the storming of the Tuileries Palace and culminated in the massacre of fourteen thousand people, including priests, political prisoners, women and children as young as eight. William Wordsworth would witness the aftermath as he passed through Paris soon afterwards. The unthinkable had happened: France abolished its monarchy and formally established the Republic.

The atrocities were reported in gruesome detail in the English press. The royal family were imprisoned and the London papers focused on the fate of the Queen's friend, the Princess de Lamballe. On 3 September she was killed by the mob, decapitated, her innards and her head carried away on pikes. The head was taken to a barber who dressed the hair with its striking blonde curls so as to render it instantly recognizable to Marie Antoinette when it bobbed up and down outside the window where she was incarcerated. Caricatures of decapitated heads being carried along the streets of Paris on pikes filled the windows of the London print shops.

Eliza must have been terrified for Jean-François as the English press reported that even those said to sound like an aristocrat or resemble one in the slightest way would be 'run through the body with a pike'. *The Times* reported that 'A ring, a watch chain, a handsome pair of buckles, a new coat, or a good pair of boots in a word, every thing which marked the appearance of a gentleman, and which the mob fancied, was sure to cost the owner his life. EQUALITY was the pistol, and PLUNDER the object.'[32]

Eliza was comforted by the calm and practical Austens. They fussed over her, soothed her worries and, most importantly, paid attention to her little son, Hastings – 'very fair', 'very fat' and 'very pretty', according to Mrs Austen.[33] Earlier, Eliza had worried that he had no teeth. And when he did begin teething, he started having convulsions. As he became a toddler and failed to start walking or talking properly it grew clear that something was wrong. Comparisons with little George Austen were inevitable. Cousin Phylly Walter wrote to her brother to tell him that Hastings had fits, was unable to walk or talk but made continuous 'great noise': 'many people says he has the appearance of a weak head; that his eyes are particular is very certain; our fears are of his being like poor George Austen'.[34] Later, she wrote, 'I'm afraid he is already quite an idiot.'[35]

For a long time, Eliza refused to believe that anything was wrong with her beloved 'son and Heir'. Her letters are full of references to him, as she took pleasure in his every tiny accomplishment: 'he doubles his prodigious fists and boxes quite in the English style'. There is something very touching in her attempt to convince herself that her boy was completely normal, despite his bad epilepsy, his strange noises and his struggle with speech and movement. She insisted on keeping him at home with her. There was no question of sending him away to join his similarly disabled Austen cousin at Monk Sherborne. Eliza devoted herself to teaching him his letters and to gabble in French and English. From all accounts, 'little Hastings' was a sweet-tempered child, who would offer people his 'half muncht apple or cakes'. When a doctor recommended sea-bathing, Eliza was happy to oblige and spent months at seaside resorts, insisting on their efficacious effect on his health. She 'breeched' him early (taking him out of 'petticoats' and into jacket and trousers) in order to ease his difficulties in walking. She fondly called him 'as great a pickle as any who ever deserved that appellation'. She would have never described him as an idiot, as cousin Phylly Walter was wont to do. His Austen cousins adored him and he often spent time in Steventon. He was, in Eliza's words, 'the Play Thing of the whole Family'.[36]

Eliza's adventurous and difficult life had a great impact on the vivid imagination of the teenage Jane Austen. This close familial connection to the reign of terror brought her much closer to the French Revolution than most of her English contemporaries. According to family tradition, Jane's dislike of the French never left her from this moment.

Eliza stayed at Steventon probably until the spring of 1793. On 1 February, the new French Republic declared war on Britain and Holland. The French Revolutionary and Napoleonic wars would continue for another twenty years. There is an uncorroborated, probably apocryphal, family tradition that Eliza went back to France and then escaped, heavily pregnant once again, in company with a maidservant (perhaps the Madame Bigeon who would become her housekeeper in later years). She was certainly back in London by March 1794. At one o'clock on a very wet Saturday, Warren Hastings called on her, by request, and she read out to him a paragraph in the émigré newspaper giving the very worst possible news: 'that on the 22nd February – Jean Capote Feuillide was condemned to death'.[37]

Jean was guillotined the day after he had been found guilty. Listed in the official record as 'Prisoner No. 396', he was bundled into a tumbrel and taken to the scaffold on the fifth day of the newly created month of *ventôse* in Year 2, according to the revolutionary calendar.[38] The revolutionary tribunal had found him guilty of two charges. First, for complicity with Nicolas Mangin, who was executed the same day, in conspiring against the unity and indivisibility of the Republic and the sovereignty of the French people. And secondly, for being 'the accomplice of the Marboeuf woman in trying to seduce, by means of a bribe, one of the secretaries of the Committee for Public Safety in an attempt to persuade this public official to steal or burn documents related to the said Marboeuf'.[39] The family had no doubt that these were trumped-up charges. From Eliza's point of view, her husband had nobly helped an elderly friend, the Marquise de Marbeouf, by trying to buy off her false accusers (she was executed a few weeks earlier for the crime of 'desiring the arrival of the Prussians and the Austrians',[40] enemies of the Republic). He had been betrayed and guillotined. There was a family tradition that he tried to save himself by claiming to be a valet impersonating his master, though no evidence of this fruitless plot came out in his trial.

There are no surviving letters of Jane Austen until 1796, so there is no way of knowing how the execution of prisoner 396 affected her, but her closeness to her cousin and little Hastings must have brought home the full horror of the guillotine. Eliza noted in her letters that the Austen children were rather special, each of them endowed with 'Uncommon abilities'. Jane, her clear favourite, returned Eliza's interest by dedicating stories to her, and by using her as a model for her clever coquettes. The notion that Jane Austen was somehow oblivious to the violent events of her time is belied by the fact that Eliza was with her and her family at the Steventon rectory in September 1792, one of the bloodiest and most dramatic months of that bloody and dramatic age, and that they remained in close contact at the time of the guillotining of Eliza's husband.

* * *

✄✄✄✄✄✄✄✄✄✄✄

To Madame la Comtesse
DE   FEVILLIDE
this Novel is inscribed
by her obliged Humble
Servant THE AUTHOR.

✄ ✄ ✄
✄ ✄
✄

For Eliza: Austen's affection for her cousin is apparent from her decision to dedicate the early novella 'Love and Freindship' to her

It was in the late summer of 1792, exactly at the time when Eliza arrived in Steventon with news from revolutionary France, that Jane Austen began the short novel, 'Catharine, or the Bower', which includes the story of Cecilia Wynne heading out on the fishing fleet to India. One of the other characters, Mr Stanley, 'never cares about anything but Politics',[41] while another, Mrs Percival, has fashionable disdain for the horrors of the modern world:

> After Supper, the Conversation turning on the State of Affairs in the political World, Mrs P, who was firmly of opinion that the whole race of Mankind were degenerating, said that for her part, Everything she beleived was going to rack and ruin, all order was destroyed over the face of the World ... Depravity never was so general before.[42]

Catherine,[43] the heroine, is a clever girl who is interested in politics and is shocked when her feather-brained friend, Camilla, professes, 'I know nothing of Politics, and cannot bear to hear them mentioned.'

Catherine finds succour in a garden bower that she has built. When Edward Stanley, recently returned from France, kisses Catherine's hand in the arbour, her aunt, Mrs Percival, is horrified: '*Profligate* as I *knew* you to be, I was not prepared for such a sight ... I plainly see that every thing is going to sixes and sevens and all order will soon be at an end throughout the Kingdom.' Catherine is dismayed by her aunt's rebuke: 'Not however Ma'am the sooner, I hope, from any conduct of mine ... for upon my honour I have done nothing this evening that can contribute to overthrow the establishment of the kingdom.' 'You are mistaken Child,' replies the older woman, 'the welfare of every Nation depends upon the virtue of it's individuals, and any one who offends in so gross a manner against decorum and propriety, is certainly hastening it's ruin.'[44]

This is one of Austen's most explicit references to the French Revolution. There is no mistaking what Mrs Percival means by the overthrow of the establishment of the kingdom. She sees no distinction between radical politics and dangerous sexual impropriety: in her view Edward Stanley has picked up both vices on his French travels. The stability of the state, she suggests, depends on proper behaviour between the sexes. She is horrified that Catherine has been neglecting the improving sermons and catechisms she has foisted upon her.[45] French influence, inappropriate reading and sexual licence mean only one thing: revolution. The fact that Jane Austen is clearly mocking Aunt Percival's political paranoia shows that she has no sympathy for mindless conservatism. But, at the same time, the presence of Eliza and her French news in the household at Steventon alerted the young Austen to the high stakes in the current 'State of Affairs in the political World'.

Later in the turbulent 1790s Jane Austen wrote the first draft of the novel that was eventually published after her death under the title *Northanger Abbey*. It includes a scene not dissimilar to Catherine's debate with Mrs Percival. The exchange takes place on Beechen Cliff, the hill above the city of Bath. Henry Tilney has been lecturing another Catherine, Miss Morland, on the picturesque, and then moves on to politics and the 'state of the nation':

Delighted with her progress, and fearful of wearying her with too much wisdom at once, Henry suffered the subject to decline, and by an easy transition from a piece of rocky fragment and the withered oak which he had placed near its summit, to oaks in general, to forests, the inclosure of them, waste lands, crown lands and government, he shortly found himself arrived at politics; and from politics, it was an easy step to silence.[46]

Strikingly, it is Catherine who puts an end to the silence: 'I have heard that something very shocking indeed, will soon come out in London.' Catherine is in fact talking about a new Gothic novel that is about to be published, but she is misunderstood by Henry's sister, Eleanor, to mean mob riots in London: 'Good Heaven! – Where could you hear of such a thing?'

'A particular friend of mine had an account of it in a letter from London yesterday' [replies Catherine]. 'It is to be uncommonly dreadful. I shall expect murder and every thing of the kind.'

'You speak with astonishing composure! But I hope your friend's accounts have been exaggerated; – and if such a design is known beforehand, proper measures will undoubtedly be taken by the government to prevent its coming to effect.'

'Government,' said Henry, endeavouring not to smile, 'neither desires nor dares to interfere in such matters. There must be murder; and government cares not how much.' ...

'Miss Morland, do not mind what he says; – but have the goodness to satisfy me as to this dreadful riot.'

'Riot! – what riot?'

The reference to reading about the London horrors in a letter from a friend echoes the real-life detail of Eliza writing to her family about the Mount Street riots. Henry's reproving speech to his sister blames female imagination for the misunderstanding:

'My dear Eleanor, the riot is only in your own brain ... You [Catherine] talked of expected horrors in London – and instead of instantly conceiving, as any rational creature would have done, that such words could relate only to a circulating library, she immediately pictured to herself a mob of three thousand men assembling in St George's Fields; the Bank attacked, the Tower threatened, the streets of London flowing with blood, a detachment of the 12th Light Dragoons, (the hopes of the nation,) called up from Northampton to quell the insurgents.'

Henry's graphic description recalls a series of violent insurgencies on the streets of London: the anti-Catholic Gordon Riots back in 1780, the Mount Street riots witnessed by Eliza, and also the Bread riots of 1795, when hungry mobs seized flour and bread, damaging mills and bakeries. The threat to the Tower and the image of the streets of London flowing with blood inevitably conjure up the Bastille and the September Massacres.

'Catharine, or the Bower' ends abruptly with Edward Stanley's return to France. The events that winter, culminating in the execution of Louis XVI and later Marie Antoinette, perhaps contributed to Jane's decision to leave it unfinished, though she continued making adjustments to the fragment until at least 1809. Many critics have complained that she ignored the historical events of her times. In 1913, the historian Frederick Harrison described her to his friend Thomas Hardy as 'a heartless little cynic … penning satirettes about her neighbours whilst the Dynasts were tearing the world to pieces, and consigning millions to their graves'.[47] This kind of accusation ignores the evidence of 'Catharine' and *Northanger Abbey*, where anxiety about revolution is clearly part of the narrative. And it neglects the fact that, because of her cousin Eliza, Jane Austen was brought exceptionally close to the events of revolutionary France. Why do Austen's novels not engage more frequently and directly with 'the Dynasts tearing the world to pieces and consigning millions to their graves'? Could it have been not so much because she knew and cared little about it all, but because she knew too much and cared all too deeply? Loving Eliza as she did, it would have been too painful to let her pen dwell on the guilt and misery of revolutionary Paris.

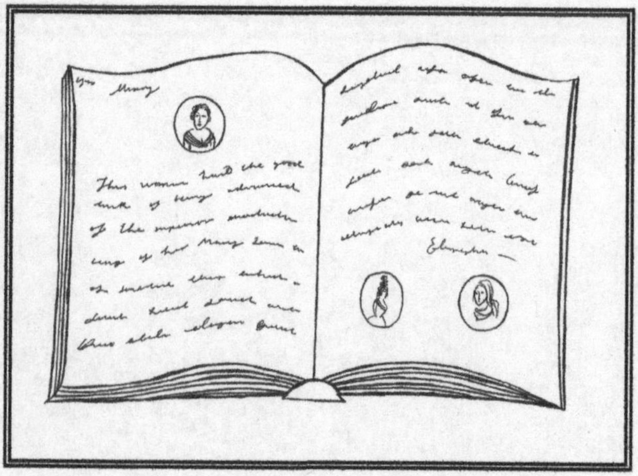

3

The Vellum Notebooks

There are three of them. Each is inscribed on the cover in careful handwriting, in imitation of a three-decker novel or a set of complete works: *Volume the First, Volume the Second, Volume the Third*. The first – a collection of little stories, plays, poems and satires – ends with the date 3 June 1793, but it is clear that some of the pieces were written much earlier, at the age of as little as eleven or twelve, and then transcribed in a fair hand when the author was in her eighteenth year. The notebook, purchased ready-made from a stationer, is bound in tanned sheepskin over marbled boards. It is now in the Bodleian Library in Oxford.

Volume the Second, illustrated here, is another miscellany, including two epistolary novelettes, a parodic 'History of England' and various 'Scraps', all probably composed when the author was in her mid-teens. It is another stationer's notebook, this time headed with the acknowledgement, in Latin, 'a gift from my father'. In small quarto format, it is bound in full parchment – vellum – pasted on to millboard. It is now in the British Library, London. So is *Volume the Third*, which is very similar in size and also covered in vellum, the front disfigured by a water-stained splodge. This final volume contains only two works: a fragmentary story called 'Evelyn' and the much longer, though still unfinished, 'Catharine, or the Bower'. The first page is signed and dated 'Jane Austen – May 6th 1792'. A pencil note on the inside of the board opposite, in her father's hand, sounds a note of paternal pride: 'Effusions of Fancy by a Very Young Lady consisting of Tales in a Style entirely new'.[1]

These are the earliest works of Jane Austen, copied in her best hand and preserved by her. Why did she write them out in this way? First and foremost, for the amusement of her family. Pasted to the inside front board of *Volume the First*, the most worn of the three, is a note penned by Cassandra after her sister's death: 'For my brother Charles. I think I recollect that a few of the trifles in this Vol. were written expressively for his amusement.' But Jane Austen also took the trouble of creating these books, which involved much labour with goose quill and inkwell, so as to present herself, at least in her own imagination, as a professional author. Though written by hand, the volumes have the accoutrements of proper published books: contents lists, dedications, chapter divisions. Even as a teenager, Jane Austen knew what she wanted from life: to be a writer.

Her literary career began in 1787, the year that she turned twelve. One could almost say that, like Mozart, she was a child prodigy. Throughout her teens she continued to write stories and plays, sketches and histories, burlesques and parodies. Their original manuscripts are lost, but the fair copies in the vellum notebooks amount to some ninety thousand words. This body of work has become known as her 'juvenilia'. Though the contents of the vellum notebooks are now well known to scholars, they are still often neglected by readers and even biographers. Yet these early works provide extraordinary insight into the vivid and often wild imagination of the real Jane Austen.

Virginia Woolf was the first to observe that Jane Austen's juvenile writings were 'meant to outlast the Christmas holidays'. That, at the tender age of fifteen, she was writing 'for everybody, for nobody, for our age, for her own'. Woolf's admiration for the sheer exhilaration and breathless energy of Austen's earliest comic sketches expresses itself in the adjectives 'astonishing' and 'unchildish'.[2] What do we make of a sentence such as this from Austen's first 'novel', which has an endearingly youthful spelling mistake in its title, 'Love and Freindship'? 'She was nothing more than a mere good-tempered, civil and obliging Young Woman; as such we could scarcely dislike her – she was only an Object of Contempt.'[3] Good girls the object of contempt? Not exactly the image of Austen that her family members sought to establish in the memoirs of her that they wrote after her death. 'The girl of fifteen is laughing, in her corner, at the world,' observed Woolf. 'Girls of fifteen are always laughing,' she adds – to which we might add: especially when like Austen and Woolf herself they are one of a pair of sisters in a household full of boys.

Very near the end of her life Jane Austen passed on a message to her niece that her one regret as a writer was that she wrote too much at an early age. She advised her niece to spend her time reading rather than taking up the pen too early.[4] So perhaps she would not be entirely pleased to know that her early teenage work is now widely read. But although the early stories were not intended for public consumption, she continued to enjoy and indeed to amend and edit her youthful writings well into her thirties.[5] Because she was writing for herself and her family, she allowed herself a lack of restraint unthinkable in the published novels. In this sense, the vellum notebooks give access to the authentic interior life of Jane Austen, free from the shackles of literary convention and the mask of respectability required by print. If the child is father to the man, as her contemporary William Wordsworth claimed, then the girl is mother to the woman. The not so secret life of Jane Austen aged eleven to seventeen is as a writer of wonderful exuberance and self-confidence. She also shows herself to be a young woman of firm opinions and strong passions.

A turning point was being allowed a room of her own. Shortly after Jane and Cassandra returned from boarding school for good in 1786 they were given the use of an upstairs drawing room, adjoining their bedroom. In her letters she referred to it as her Dressing Room. It had blue wallpaper and blue striped curtains and a chocolate-brown carpet. The room contained Jane's piano and her writing desk. There was a bookcase and a table for the sisters' workboxes.

Jane Austen was a supreme social satirist. Wit was valued highly in the Austen family. Most of the early stories are lampoons, burlesques or parodies. The point of such writing is that it copies or caricatures the style or spirit of serious works so as to excite laughter, often by ludicrous exaggeration. The great exemplar of the form in the eighteenth century was Henry Fielding, whose works Austen knew well. His *Tragedy of Tragedies, or the History of Tom Thumb the Great* was the classic burlesque of stage tragedy. The 'great' Tom Thumb is a heroic warrior who happens to be a midget. He is offered in marriage to the Princess Huncamunca, which makes Queen Dollalolla passionately jealous. Tom dies as a result of being swallowed by a cow, but his ghost returns. The ghost is put to death in turn and nearly all the rest of the cast kill each other in duels or take their own lives in grief. The young Jane Austen loved this sort of thing, and when she uses such names as Crankhumdunberry and Pammydiddle she is paying homage to Fielding.

Fielding's great rival Samuel Richardson had pioneered the heroine-centred courtship novel when he published the smash hit *Pamela, or Virtue Rewarded*. Pamela is a lowly maidservant who refuses the sexual advances of her master, Mr B, and tames him by her virtue and religious principles into making her an offer of marriage. Fielding loathed the hypocrisy of the idea that the reward for virtue should be so patently material: marriage to a wealthy man with a large house. He responded with his lampoon *Shamela*, in which the heroine, far from being an innocent and virtuous victim, is a scheming unscrupulous hussy who entraps her master into marriage. Reading *Shamela* is like reading the original novel through a distorted mirror. In the original novel, Pamela is distressed by her master's sexual advances, but in Fielding she is playing a long and sly game of sexual conquest:

He took me by the Hand, and I pretended to be shy: Laud, says I, Sir, I hope you don't intend to be rude; no, says he, my Dear, and then he kissed me, 'till he took away my Breath – and I pretended to be Angry, and to get away, and then he kissed me again, and breathed very short, and looked very silly; and by Ill-Luck Mrs Jervis came in, and had like to have spoiled Sport. – How troublesome is such Interruption![6]

Jane Austen loved to make her family laugh out loud when reading out her lampoons, but like Fielding she also approved of burlesque as a literary medium for exposing moral and social hypocrisy. And also like Fielding, she had a sharp eye for the absurdities and limitations of much of the fiction of her age.

The first story that she copied into her precious notebook was 'Frederic and Elfrida', a very funny parody of the sentimental novels of the day. For those who begin reading Jane Austen with *Pride and Prejudice* and come to the vellum notebooks only after the six mature novels, it is a disorienting experience to read 'Frederic and Elfrida: a novel'. Early in the story comes the news that a new family has taken a house near by. Frederic, Elfrida and her friend Charlotte go to pay their respects. The arrivals in the neighbourhood are Mrs Fitzroy and her two daughters. The conversation initially turns on the relative merits of Indian and English muslins. So far, so *Pride and Prejudice*. But one of the sisters is beautiful and foolish, the other ugly and clever. In this topsy-turvy world it is the ugly and hump-backed Rebecca who garners the compliments: 'Lovely and too charming Fair one, notwithstanding your forbidding Squint, your greasy tresses and your swelling Back, which are more frightfull than imagination can paint or pen describe, I cannot refrain from expressing my raptures, at the engaging Qualities of your Mind, which so amply atone for the Horror with which your first appearance must ever inspire the unwary visitor.'[7]

As in Fielding, the lampoon depends upon the pitch-perfect rendering of the stylistic clichés of the sentimental novel. In a serious novel of the day you would read such sentences as 'From this period, the families of Etherington and Cleves lived in the enjoyment of uninterrupted harmony and repose, till Eugenia ... had attained her fifteenth year.' In 'Frederic and Elfrida' Jane Austen writes 'From this period, the intimacy between the Families ... grew to such a pitch, that they did not scruple to kick one another out of the window on the slightest provocation.'[8]

'During this happy period of Harmony,' Austen continues, 'the eldest Miss Fitzroy ran off with the Coachman and the amiable Rebecca was asked in marriage by Captain Roger of Buckinghamshire.' The world of the vellum notebooks is so knowing and so uninhibited that one cannot be entirely confident that the young Austen was blissfully unaware of the Georgian slang meaning of the verb 'to roger'.[9] Mrs Fitzroy disapproves of the match 'on account of the tender years of the young couple': Rebecca is only thirty-six and Captain Roger sixty-three. Charlotte then becomes engaged to two men simultaneously. Realizing her breach of social decorum, she commits suicide by jumping into a stream, while Elfrida, who has a most delicate constitution, is reduced to 'a succession of fainting fits' in which 'she had scarcely patience enough to recover from one before she fell into another'.[10]

The second story, 'Jack and Alice: a novel', is dedicated by Austen to her younger brother Frank, 'Midshipman on board his Majesty's Ship the Perseverance'. Jane presumably sent a copy with a letter. We need to imagine Frank receiving it several months later, somewhere in the East Indies, and smiling at the deadpan humour of his clever sister. She has perfected the satirist's art of bathos or 'sinking', the abrupt transition from an elevated style to a ludicrous conclusion. An elegant evening party is described, until at the end of the chapter the whole party 'were carried home, Dead Drunk'.[11] And a character called Lady Williams waxes lyrical about her governess:

'Miss Dickins was an excellent Governess. She instructed me in the Paths of Virtue; under her tuition I daily became more amiable, and might perhaps by this time have nearly attained perfection, had not my worthy Preceptoress been torn from my arms e'er I had attained my seventeenth year. I never shall forget her last words. "My dear Kitty" she said "Good night t'ye." I never saw her afterwards' continued Lady Williams wiping her eyes, 'She eloped with the Butler the same night.'[12]

So many of Austen's greatest gifts are here in embryo: not only the comic timing and the revealing gestures (that sentimental teardrop), but also the sense of mischief and the sheer delight in human foibles – the incongruity of the 'worthy Preceptoress' in the 'Paths of Virtue' eloping with the butler. Already Austen has absolute control of her tone, and elsewhere in 'Jack and Alice' there are hints of the more deadly because more understated irony that is to come in the mature novels: 'Every wish of Caroline was centered in a titled Husband.'[13]

'Henry and Eliza: a novel' might be described as Fielding's *Tom Jones* meets Austen's *Emma* – in parody. Eliza, like Tom, is a foundling. She is taken into the household of the goodly Sir George and Lady Harcourt, who are first seen superintending the labours of their haymakers, rewarding the industrious with smiles of approbation and punishing the idle with a good cudgelling. They bring up Eliza in 'a Love of Virtue and a Hatred of Vice'. She grows up to be a delight to all who know her. Then the next sentence begins like an anticipation of *Emma* but ends with a twist: 'Beloved by Lady Harcourt, adored by Sir George and admired by all the World, she lived in a continued course of uninterrupted Happiness, till she had attained her eighteenth year, when happening one day to be detected in stealing a bank-note of 50£, she was turned out of doors by her inhuman Benefactors.'[14] From being a somebody, an Emma, she turns into a nobody, a Jane Fairfax, who has to seek a position 'in the capacity of Humble Companion'. She gains one in the household of a duchess, where Henry Cecil, the wealthy fiancé of the only daughter, falls in love with her. The Chaplain, who has also fallen in love with her, marries them privately (and illegally) and they run off to the continent.

A family of alcoholics and gamblers, a young woman whose leg is fractured by a steel mantrap set for poachers in the grounds of the gentleman she is pursuing, a child who bites off her mother's fingers, a jealous heroine who poisons her sisters, numerous elopements: the vellum notebooks do not contain the subject matter one might expect of a parson's daughter. But then Steventon rectory was not the typical parson's household. The family were all broad-minded and clearly loved black humour. Like Shakespeare, whose works they read aloud together, they knew that 'the web of our life is of a mingled yarn, good and ill together'.[15] Seeing the absurdity of the perpetual diet of virtue and piety in the orthodox literature in the family library, they relished the unshockable young Jane's array of loose women, drunkards, thieves and murderers.

'Lesley Castle', dedicated to Henry, begins with a married woman called Louisa leaving her child and her reputation behind her as she runs off with a certain Rakehelly Dishonor Esq. (a name straight out of Restoration comedy). But within a few pages the husband 'writes in a most chearfull Manner, says that the air of France has greatly recovered both his Health and his Spirits; that he has now entirely ceased to think of Louisa with any degree either of Pity or Affection, that he even feels himself obliged to her for her Elopement, as he thinks it very good fun to be single again'.[16] After Jane's death, Henry, by that time in holy orders, would write a brief memoir emphasizing his sister's piety. By then, he had long forgotten, or made a point of forgetting, the youthful story dedicated to him in which the consequence of a woman's adultery is a new life of 'very good fun' for the jilted husband.

'Very good fun' is indeed the watchword for the vellum notebooks. Brought up in a house full of boys, sharing jokes with the male lodgers and wanting to cheer up young Frank as he endured the rigorous conditions of a midshipman, she laid on the slapstick and revelled in the sheer joy of words. Every page of the vellum notebooks sparkles with Jane Austen's love of language. The story called 'A Collection of Letters', towards the end of *Volume the Second*, is a tour de force even in its dedication: 'To Miss Cooper – Cousin: Conscious of the Charming Character which in every Country, and every Clime in Christendom is Cried, Concerning you, With Caution and Care I Commend to your Charitable Criticism this Clever Collection

Two of Cassandra's watercolours in her sister's
'History of England': Henry V (left) perhaps
resembles Henry Austen and Edward IV (right)
cousin Edward Cooper

of Curious Comments, which have been Carefully Culled, Collected and
Classed by your Comical Cousin – The Author'.[17]

* * *

By the time she reached *Volume the Second*, she was writing fuller, more
sophisticated parodies. This time Oliver Goldsmith was the target of her
satire, and even Cassandra got in on the joke. Jane Austen's 'History of
England' with illustrations by Cassandra is a pro-Stuart, pro-Catholic skit
which makes fun of the standard school history books of the time. It mocks
the very textbook that her father used in his own schoolroom. She clearly
loved teasing her father. Oliver Goldsmith's popular four-volume *History
of England from the Earliest Times to the Death of George II* (1771) was itself
a heavily biased abridgement of David Hume's *History of England from the
Invasion of Julius Caesar to the Revolution in 1688* (six volumes, 1754–62).
Jane Austen had her own copy of Hume's work, which is greatly superior
to Goldsmith. Goldsmith later published a one-volume abridgement of his
History. Thus part of her joke was to abridge the already abridged history.

The Steventon copy of Goldsmith's *History*, inscribed with the name of her eldest brother James, contains marginal annotations in her hand. The volumes of Goldsmith are still in the family's possession and Jane Austen's annotations have recently been published in full for the first time.[18] Her first known scribbling had been a defacement of a book: her French textbook, from when she was eight, has her signature 'Jane Austen., 5th Decr. 1783' and then 'Mothers angry fathers gone out' and 'I wish I had done.'[19] Once she had a pen in her hand she couldn't stop herself from writing. Reading Goldsmith's biased opinions on English history, she displays the almost uncontainable urge to scribble that is the mark of the born writer.

The annotations on Goldsmith clearly reveal her own passionately royalist feelings. In Jane Austen's eyes, Oliver Cromwell was a 'Detestable Monster!'[20] Goldsmith informs us that he 'inherited a very small paternal fortune', to which Austen adds: 'And that was more than he deserved.' She praises Lady Fairfax ('Charming Woman!') for making loyalist remarks from the public gallery when the King was put on trial. The King's execution drew her most forceful denunciations. 'Such was the fortitude of the Stuarts when oppressed and accused!' she wrote of King Charles I. She finished and dated her parodic 'History of England' 26 November 1791, her hatred of the English revolution heightened by the French.[21]

In an account of the death of the Parliamentarian John Hampden, Goldsmith wrote of his character: 'affability in conversation, temper, art, eloquence in debate, and penetration in counsel'. Austen responded in the margin: 'what a pity that such virtues sh[oul]d be clouded by Republicanism'. Of other anti-royalists she wrote, 'Shame to such members' and 'Impudent Fellows'. She often substituted the word 'guilt' for 'innocence' in relation to anti-royalists. 'Fiddlededia', she writes – meaning nonsense or fiddledeedee.

Jane Austen adored the Stuarts. A touching speech attributed to Bonnie Prince Charlie is annotated 'Who but a Stuart could have so spoken?' Her loyalty was inspired by her Leigh ancestry. Of the Stuarts the young Jane Austen noted in her pencil marks: 'A family, who were always ill-used, BETRAYED or NEGLECTED, Whose virtues are seldom allowed, while their Errors are never forgotten'. These were strong opinions for a young girl. Her Jacobite sympathies meant that she shared Goldsmith's hostility to the Whigs, who dominated politics in the Georgian era. He claimed that 'the Whigs governed the Senate and the court ... bound the lower orders of people with severe laws, and kept them at a distance by vile distinctions; and then taught them to call this – Liberty', and she agreed: 'Yes, This is always the Liberty of Whigs and Republicans.' To his comment that 'all the severe and most restrictive laws were enacted by that party that are continually stunning mankind with a cry of freedom', she writes, 'My dear Dr G. – I have lived long enough in this World to know that it is always so.' She felt that the Whigs represented new money, selfishness and self-aggrandizement. Her sympathies were with the poor and oppressed. Beside an account of an impoverished couple who were forced to the last resort of cutting their child's throat and hanging themselves, she wrote, 'How much are the Poor to be pitied and the Rich to be blamed.' She shared with her father and all her family a paternalistic Christian Toryism.

In another of her Steventon books, Vicesimus Knox's anthology of *Elegant Extracts: or Useful and Entertaining Passages in Prose Selected for the Improvement of Scholars*, she disagreed with every slight on the character of her heroine, Mary Queen of Scots: 'No', 'No', 'A lie', 'Another lie', 'she was not attached to him'. Correspondingly, she vehemently opposed any praise for Queen Elizabeth I: 'a lie', 'a Lie – an entire lie from beginning to end'.[22]

Having defaced Goldsmith's *History* she eventually decided that she would write a sustained parody, showing up his inadequacies as a historian. She gave her work the title 'The History of England from the reign of Henry the 4th to the death of Charles the 1st. By a partial, prejudiced and ignorant Historian', dedicated it to Cassandra and added a *nota bene*: 'There will be very few dates in this History.' Austen parodies the tone and style of Goldsmith with unerring accuracy, pinpointing his incongruities and omissions.

Jane Austen made her dislike of Elizabeth I very clear, though she did cast some of the blame on to her male advisers: 'It was the peculiar Misfortune of this Woman to have bad Ministers – Since wicked as she herself was, she could not have committed such extensive Mischief, had not these vile and abandoned Men connived at, and encouraged her in her Crimes.' All her sympathies were with Mary Queen of Scots: 'firm in her Mind; Constant in her Religion; and prepared herself to meet the cruel fate to which she was doomed, with a magnanimity that could alone proceed from conscious Innocence'. Mary, she says, was friendless apart from the Duke of Norfolk and her only friends now 'are Mr Whitaker, Mrs Lefroy, Mrs Knight, and myself'. Whitaker was the author of a book called

Mary Queen of Scots Vindicated, just published in 1787. Mrs Knight was, of course, the wife of Thomas Knight, who had adopted young Edward Austen and who would play an important part in Jane's future literary career. Mrs Lefroy was a friend and mentor, who lived in a nearby parsonage.

Jane Austen also makes a series of knowing jokes about the homosexual preferences of King James I and his circle. The 'attentions' of his courtier Sir Henry Percy 'were entirely confined to Lord Mounteagle', while 'His Majesty was of that amiable disposition that inclines to Friendships and in such points was possessed of a keener penetration in Discovering Merit than many other people'. The nature of these 'Friendships' might be hinted at in the phrase 'keener penetration',[23] but it is made explicit in the charade that Austen then slips into her 'History': 'My first is what my second was to King James the 1st, and you tread on my whole.' The answer is of course, car-pet, an allusion to Sir Robert Carr, the most notorious of King James's homosexual lovers.[24] Those who believe that Jane Austen could never have made a joke about sodomy in the navy ('*Rears*, and *Vices*') may want to reconsider their opinion in the light of her King James joke, made as a teenager. And read aloud to family and friends. The Georgians, as is clear from the thriving trade in caricatures riddled with *double entendres*, were a far cry from the prudish Victorians.

Like all big families, the Austens had their own private language, their in-jokes. Many of the allusions are no doubt lost on us, but certain ones can be deduced. Jane was known to have red cheeks, so there are several jokes about young women who have too much red in their cheeks. Again, Jane drew on the names of family members in stories such as 'The Beautifull Cassandra' and 'Henry and Eliza'. It is hardly a coincidence that a story dedicated to Frank includes a pious young man who is torn between entering the Church and joining the navy, and thus becomes a chaplain on board a man of war. Another story describes a boy who, like Charles and Frank, is 'placed at the Royal Academy for Seamen at Portsmouth when about thirteen years old'. On graduating he is 'discharged on board one of the vessels of a small fleet destined for Newfoundland ... from whence he regularly sent home a large Newfoundland Dog every Month to his family'.[25] And one suspects some sort of family joke in a story dedicated to Austen's mother, in which Jane writes, 'I saw you thro' a telescope, and was so struck by your Charms that from that time to this I have not tasted human food.'[26]

The little 'History of England' in *Volume the Second* is a genuine family production: it is peppered with caricature illustrations of the kings and queens of England, drawn by Jane's sister Cassandra. They are jokily responsive to Jane's narrative. Cassandra's portrait of Queen Elizabeth presents her as shrewish and ugly with a long witch-like nose, while Mary Queen of Scots is full of face, pink-cheeked and beautiful with dark, curly hair. Edward IV, whom Jane notes is 'famous for his beauty', is drawn to look like a pig-farmer.

Comparison of the cartoons with surviving portraits has led to the recent suggestion that 'The History of England' may be even more of a family affair than previous biographers have realized.[27] Henry V, the exemplary soldier-king, bears an uncanny resemblance to Henry Austen, who was seriously considering a career in the army. James I looks somewhat like James Austen and Edward VI like Edward Austen. The ugly Edward IV, who appears to be wearing the garb of an Evangelical clergyman, is the spitting image of a cousin whom Jane heartily disliked – Edward Cooper, an Evangelical clergyman. Elizabeth I has Mrs Austen's hooked nose. If this hypothesis is correct, there can be only one candidate for resemblance to the heroine of the piece, Mary Queen of Scots. It would appear that Cassandra painted her in the likeness of her sister Jane. Mary Queen of Scots has red cheeks, a small mouth, large eyes and a strong nose, a small but perfectly formed miniature of the seventeen-year-old Jane. This could well be the biggest joke of all: that the young author might just be visible before our eyes.

* * *

'Run mad as often as you chuse; but do not faint –': so says Sophia, one of the (anti-) heroines of 'Love and Freindship'.[28]

Though Jane Austen was a great advocate of the novel as a literary form, she was well aware of its limitations. In order to break the mould with her writing, she had to establish what she disliked and what didn't work. Jane Austen loved the novels of Samuel Richardson and Fanny Burney, but she was not afraid to parody their conventions. Thus one of her characters, Sir Charles Adams, is based on Richardson's idealized hero Sir Charles Grandison. In a sly dig at Richardson, showing a finely tuned comic touch beyond her years, Austen has her egocentric hero remark: 'I expect nothing more in my wife than my wife will find in me – Perfection.'[29]

Cassandra's drawing of Mary Queen of Scots in
Jane Austen's 'History of England'

Anybody reading through the vellum notebooks will notice a seemingly
endless succession of heroines weeping and fainting. At the end of 'Edgar
and Emma', the heroine retires to her room and continues in tears for 'the
remainder of her Life'. In 'A beautiful description of the different effects of
Sensibility on different Minds', Melissa drapes herself in her bed – somewhat diaphanously wrapped in 'a book muslin bedgown, a chambray gauze
shift, and a french net nightcap' – so that the devoted Sir William can
minister to her in her distressed fit of extreme sensibility. A doctor asks
whether she is thinking of dying, to which the reply is that 'She has not
strength to think at all.' 'Nay then,' replies the witty doctor, 'she cannot
think to have Strength.'[30]

It is tricky for modern readers fully to understand the genius of the
vellum notebooks without placing them in the context of 'sentimentalism'
and the late eighteenth-century 'novel of sensibility'. Sentimentalism is a
slippery concept, not least because what was first an approbatory term
increasingly became pejorative. The cult of sensibility or sentimentalism
was acted out in a code of conduct which placed emphasis on the feelings

rather than on reason. A heightened sensitivity to emotional experience and an acute responsiveness to nature were perceived as the marks of the person of sensibility. Medical writers of the era connected sensibility to madness, over-taxed nerves and hysteria. In a sense, it was the eighteenth century's term for what we now call manic depression. In the literature of the time, suicide was sometimes seen as the ultimate manifestation of extreme sensibility.

Sensibility had its orgins in philosophy, but it became a literary movement, particularly in the newly emerging genre of the novel. Characters in sentimental novels are often fragile individuals, prone to sensibility, which manifests itself in tears, fainting fits and nervous excitability. Laurence Sterne's *Sentimental Journey*, Goldsmith's *The Vicar of Wakefield* and Henry Mackenzie's *The Man of Feeling* were exemplars of the genre which emphasized 'feeling' and aimed to elicit an emotional or sentimental response from the reader, usually by relating scenes of distress or tenderness. The most notorious of all sentimental novels was Goethe's *The Sorrows of Young Werther*, which depicted a highly sensitive hero who kills himself because of unrequited love. It was said that every teenager in the land identified with the hero and shed tears when reading the novel, some even going so far as to commit copycat suicide.

The flip-side of this popular sentimental craze was the contention that such extreme behaviour was mere narcissism and self-indulgent histrionics. Furthermore, anti-sentimental thinkers associated the emotional volatility of sensibility with the violence of the French Revolution. After all, Jean-Jacques Rousseau's *La Nouvelle Héloïse* was one of the bibles of sensibility and it was that same Rousseau whose *Social Contract* and theory of the 'general will' underpinned the ideology of the Jacobins. The young, passionately anti-revolutionary Jane Austen belonged firmly to the camp of anti-sensibility – though twenty years later her first published novel, *Sense and Sensibility*, would reveal a more nuanced and complex response to the phenomenon.

During the exact period when Jane Austen was preparing the vellum notebooks, her brothers were also engaged in a literary project that centred on the critique of sensibility. James Austen, sophisticated, creative and ambitious, went at the age of fourteen to his father's *alma mater*, St John's College, Oxford. He was already showing some talent as a poet. In 1786 he went on a Grand Tour on the continent, including a visit to cousin Eliza de

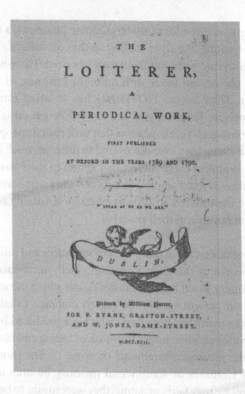

THE

LOITERER,

A

PERIODICAL WORK,

FIRST PUBLISHED

AT OXFORD IN THE YEARS 1789 AND 1790.

" SPEAK OF US AS WE ARE."

DUBLIN:

Printed by William Porter,

FOR P. BYRNE, GRAFTON-STREET,
AND W. JONES, DAME-STREET.

M.DCC.XCII.

Feuillide's estate in Guienne, France. After his return home he took holy orders and was ordained deacon in December 1787. While serving as a curate in Hampshire, but still spending most of his time in Oxford, he launched, with the assistance of his brother Henry, who was himself a St John's undergraduate by this time, a weekly literary periodical called the *Loiterer*. It was initially aimed at an Oxford student audience, but James eventually managed to get wider distribution for it, engaging a London publisher called Thomas Egerton and also advertising in the *Reading Mercury*, the local paper that served Steventon and the rest of East Hampshire. The periodical ran for a little over a year from 1789 to 1790. It eventually closed because, as James put it, the publisher's bills were too long and the readers' subscription list too short. James gave up on his ambition to be a published author, though he continued writing poetry for his own pleasure (when he wasn't riding to hounds) throughout his career in the Church.

The *Loiterer* contains a lot of undergraduate humour – a typical paper concerns 'tuft-hunting', the art of trailing on the coat-tails of an aristocratic student. The essays are witty, but frequently laboured. There is an epigrammatic turn of phrase, but never with quite the crispness of the brothers' younger sister. Thus James: 'NOTHING has so often interrupted the harmony of private families, and set the whole genealogical table of Relations in arms against each other, as that unfortunate propensity which the old and the young have ever discovered to differ as much as possible in their opinion on almost every subject that comes in their way.'[31]

But where there is exact alignment between the *Loiterer* and the vellum notebooks is in their shared attitude to excessive sensibility and its debilitating effects on novels and their readers:

What I here allude to, Sir, is, that excess of sentiment and susceptibility, which the works of the great Rousseau chiefly introduced, which every subsequent Novel has since foster'd, and which the voluptuous manners of the present age but too eagerly embrace. I shall not here enumerate the many baneful effects which are produced by it in the morals of mankind, when under the mask of feeling and liberality are concealed the grossest allurements of sense ... For though these Heroes and Heroines of sentimental memory be only imaginary characters, yet we may fairly presume, they were meant to be probable ones; and hence too we may conclude, that all who adopt their opinions will share their fate; that they will be tortured by the poignant delicacy of their own feelings, and fall the Martyrs to their own Susceptibility.[32]

Jane says the same in rather fewer words.

The tone is closer to hers in some of the essays written by brother Henry. For example this, on the rules for the education of a fine lady: 'As soon as she can understand what is said to her, let her know that she is to look forwards to matrimony, as the sole end of existence, and the sole means of happiness; and that the older, the richer and the foolisher her Husband is, the more enviable will be her situation.'[33]

But the wittiest and most stylish contribution in the entire run of the *Loiterer* appears in issue number nine. It is written in the voice of a female reader:

To the AUTHOR *of the* LOITERER ... You must know, Sir, I am a great reader, and not to mention some hundred volumes of Novels and Plays, have, in the last two summers, actually got through all the entertaining papers of our most celebrated periodical writers ... I assure you my heart beat with joy when I first heard of your publication, which I immediately sent for, and have taken in ever since.

I am sorry, however, to say it, but really, Sir, I think it the stupidest work of the kind I ever saw: not but that some of the papers are well written; but then your subjects are so badly chosen, that they never interest one. – Only conceive, in eight papers, not one sentimental story about love and honour, and all that ... Why, my dear Sir – what do you think we care about the way in which Oxford men spend their time and money – we, who have enough to do to spend our own. For my part, I never, but once, was at Oxford in my life, and I am sure I never wish to go there again ... Get a new set of correspondents, from among the young of both sexes, but particularly ours; and let us see some nice affecting stories, relating the misfortunes of two lovers, who died suddenly, just as they were going to church. Let the lover be killed in a duel, or lost at sea, or you may make him shoot himself, just as you please; and as for his mistress, she will of course go mad; or if you will, you may kill the lady, and let the lover run mad; only remember, whatever you do, that your hero and heroine must possess a great deal of feeling, and have very pretty names. If you think fit to comply with this my injunction, you may expect to hear from me again, and perhaps I may even give you a little assistance: – but, if not – may your work be condemned to the pastry-cook's shop, and may you always continue a bachelor, and be plagued with a maiden sister to keep house for you.

Your's, as you behave,

SOPHIA SENTIMENT.

A young female reader from outside Oxford, who is a passionate reader and has a wicked sense of humour, who takes her name from a character in a play in the library at Steventon (William Hayley's *The Mausoleum*), who loves to mock the novel of sensibility ('let the lover run mad'), and who ends the letter with a joke about being plagued with a sister ... There is a very strong probability that the letter from 'Sophia Sentiment' to the editor of the *Loiterer* is the first published work of Jane Austen.[34]

If Jane really was 'Sophia Sentiment', then, remarkably, her first appearance to an audience beyond the Oxford cognoscenti was at the hands of a Dublin 'pirate'. After the magazine folded, the remaining sheets were bound up and published in Oxford, but in 1792 an independent edition was printed in book form by P. Byrne and W. Jones of Dublin. Patrick Byrne was Ireland's leading Catholic publisher. He was later accused of involvement in a plot against King George III. He was arrested, accused of high treason and consigned to Newgate gaol, where he became ill. A petition for release was finally successful and he emigrated to Philadelphia, where he ran a successful printing business until his death in 1814, in the middle of the Anglo-American War.[35] He was an unlikely first publisher for Jane Austen.

The vellum notebooks exist in a dialogue with the essays in the *Loiterer*. There are many parallels of both phrasing and theme. At the beginning of Jane Austen's literary career, as in its maturity, there is a close relationship between her brothers and her path into print. 'Lesley Castle: an unfinished Novel in Letters' in *Volume the Second* is dedicated to Henry, with a joke imagining he has managed to get a very good book deal for her: 'Messrs Demand and Co – please to pay Jane Austen Spinster the sum of one hundred guineas on account of your Humbl. Servant. H. T. Austen'.[36] In later years, he would indeed act as her literary agent.

But the very best writing in the notebooks, the two works in which the modern reader can really see the seeds of the future novelist, were written for the all-important women in her family. One might have expected the dedications to have been the other way round: 'Catharine, or the Bower', with its East Indian connection and its political edge, is for Cassandra when it sounds more like Eliza de Feuillide's fare, whereas 'Love and Freindship' is for Eliza when it consists of comic versions of the kinds of letter that would later pass between Jane and Cassandra.

'Love and Freindship' is the young Austen's very best satire on the novel of sensibility. Emotional excess – the indulgence of luxuriance in feeling for its own sake – was the particular target of her satire. Many sentimental novels contained clichés such as lost orphans, swooning heroines, emotional reunions between lost children and parents, improbable chance meetings. 'Love and Freindship' mocks all these with a ruthless brilliance. Above all,

Austen shows how bad moral conduct, selfishness and hypocrisy can be disguised behind the façade of sensibility.

Her heroines Laura and Sophia lie, cheat and steal – all in the name of sensibility. It was, after all, a code of conduct that unashamedly placed the individual first. When Sophia is caught stealing money, or in her words 'majestically removing the 5th bank-note' from a drawer, she responds in the injured tones of a virtuous heroine: 'The dignity of Sophia was wounded; "Wretch (exclaimed she, hastily replacing the Bank-note in the draw) how darest thou accuse me of an Act, of which the bare idea makes me blush?"'[37] The heroines are overcome with excessive 'feeling'. When they witness an emotional reunion, they faint alternately on a sofa. At a moment of distress, one of them shrieks and faints on the ground, while the other screams and runs instantly mad.

'Love and Freindship' is in part a parody of Jane's cousin Cassandra Hawke's novel *Julia de Gramont* (1788), a book that contains many of the clichés that she satirized with such clear-eyed precision. Austen mirrors the plot-lines and sentimental language of *Julia*. She also borrows the name of the hero, Augustus, for her own unprincipled leading man.

Another of the clichés of the sentimental novel that Jane Austen parodies is the use of natural settings as a place of solace. In *Julia*, the heroine enters a shady grove which reminds her of the frequent visits that she made there with Augustus. 'Each seat, each shrub, recall[s] a dear idea to her mind.'[38] In 'Love and Freindship', Sophia and Laura enter a shaded grove, and turn to thoughts of their lovers:

'What a beautifull Sky! (said I) How charmingly is the azure varied by those delicate streaks of white!'

'Oh! my Laura (replied she, hastily withdrawing her Eyes from a momentary glance at the sky) do not thus distress me by calling my Attention to an object which so cruelly reminds me of my Augustus's blue Satin Waistcoat striped with white! In pity to your unhappy freind, avoid a subject so distressing.'[39]

After reading this sort of thing in 'Love and Freindship' it is hard to take the eighteenth-century sentimental novel altogether seriously.

Jane Austen loved burlesque and never altogether abandoned it. From her earliest full-length satire on the Gothic and sentimental novel,

Northanger Abbey, to her final uncompleted novel, *Sanditon*, she continued to use elements of it in her work. But her critique of sensibility is serious as well as playful. Shortly after the vellum notebooks were completed, Samuel Taylor Coleridge lectured in Bristol on the slave trade:

> True Benevolence is a rare Quality among us. Sensibility indeed we have to spare – what novel-reading Lady does not over flow with it to the great annoyance of her Friends and Family – Her own sorrows like the Princes of Hell in Milton's Pandemonium sit enthroned bulky and vast, while the miseries of our fellow creatures dwindle into pygmy forms, and are crowded, an unnumbered multitude, into some dark corner of the Heart where the eye of sensibility gleams faintly on them at long Intervals – a keen feeling of trifling misfortunes is selfish cowardice not virtue.[40]

As will be seen, Austen was a great admirer of Coleridge's friend, the leading abolitionist Thomas Clarkson. Coleridge's argument that 'sensibility' was fundamentally selfish and thus an impediment to that true 'Benevolence' which guides Christian behaviour – and which should make every true Christian an abolitionist – is one with which Jane Austen heartily concurred.

The Subscription List

This is a novel in five duodecimo volumes, dated 1796. The title page reads *Camilla: or, A Picture of Youth. By the Author of Evelina and Cecilia.* It was printed for two publishers, T. Payne at the Mews Gate, and Cadell and Davies in the Strand. A dedication to Queen Charlotte carries the name of F. d'Arblay, who some years earlier had been employed by Her Majesty as Second Keeper of the Robes. Madame d'Arblay was known to her friends as Fanny Burney, daughter of Dr Johnson's friend, the famous musical historian Charles Burney.

There was a huge sense of anticipation in the fashionable literary world for the third offering of one of the nation's favourite female authors. What increased the sense of excitement was Burney's shrewd decision to publish *Camilla* by subscription, with purchasers paying upfront in order to underwrite the production costs, guaranteeing that 'its sale becomes almost instantly as quick as general'.[1] The *Morning Chronicle* had made the first public announcement on 7 July 1795: 'PROPOSALS for printing by Subscription a NEW WORK, in Four Volumes, 12 mo. By the AUTHOR of EVELINA and CECILIA: To be delivered on or before the 1st day of July, 1796. The Subscriptions will be one Guinea; to be paid at the time of subscribing.'

Burney herself alphabetized her list of subscribers for the printed edition. She freely admitted that she also kept a sharp eye on protocol and title: the most elite subscribers were given due prominence. The list of

75

names, which followed the Dedication and Advertisement, ran to thirty-eight pages. Royalty, aristocracy, politicians and writers were there – a thousand subscribers in all. Edmund Burke signed up for five sets and the widow of the renowned actor David Garrick for two. Warren Hastings promised to 'attack the East Indies' on the novelist's behalf. Mrs Hannah More, Miss Edgeworth and Mrs Radcliffe of Babington, leading novelists of the day, all put down their names, as did the naturalist Sir Joseph Banks, the celebrated Duchess of Devonshire, the actress Sarah Siddons, the landscape gardener Humphry Repton, various members of the Leigh family of Adlestrop and, sandwiched between 'George Aust, Esq.' and 'Mrs Ayton', a certain 'Miss J. Austen, Steventon'. She was in her twentieth year; the guinea was paid by her father, a sign of his commitment to her literary interests. This was Jane Austen's first appearance in print. Indeed, since her novels would be published anonymously, it was one of only two occasions on which her name appeared publicly in her lifetime. The other was in a subscription list to a volume of sermons.

Jane Austen's copy of *Camilla* was bought in boards, uncut, and was later half-bound, probably by Cassandra, who inherited the volumes after her sister's death. Though Jane cherished her novels, she was not averse to defacing them for the sake of a good joke. As a fledgling writer, she just couldn't resist scribbling, even in places where it was rather inappropriate. On the back of the novel there is an inscription, its final word obscured by the half-binding: 'Since this work went to the Press a Circumstance of some importance to the happiness of Camilla has taken place, namely that Dr Marchmont has at last [?died].'[2]

Jane Austen's joke here refers to the meddling Dr Marchmont, who is the chief obstacle to the union of the lovers. For five long volumes, he manages to keep Camilla and Edgar from marrying, despite the fact that they adore, and are suitable for, one another. Austen knows perfectly well that the story is fictional, but the characters have been made to seem so real that she cannot resist imagining their continuing life after the end of the book. In its tiny way, her intervention on the endpapers of *Camilla* is a licence to those many lovers of Jane Austen's novels who have taken it upon themselves to imagine how the marriage of Elizabeth and Darcy might unfold.

Austen was forced to sell many of her belongings when she moved to lodgings in Bath, but this was one novel that she was never going to sell. It stayed in the family and was eventually given to the Bodleian Library in

Oxford. Austen's father, who held an account at John Burdon's bookshop in College Street, Winchester, owned a library of several hundred books, but that resource dried up when the family left their home and much of the library was sold. When Jane visited Kent there was always her wealthy brother Edward's well-stocked library, which included many novels. And when she eventually joined the publishing house of John Murray, Murray himself loaned her books.

Most of the dozens of novels that Austen read were borrowed from libraries. Commercial subscription libraries began when booksellers rented out copies of new titles in the mid-eighteenth century. By 1790, about six hundred rental and lending libraries were in business, with a clientele of some fifty thousand.[3] To the consternation of moral commentators, there was a veritable epidemic of female novel reading.

When she lived in Bath and Southampton Jane Austen depended on public circulating or subscription libraries. Most of the novels in libraries were unbound and tattered from heavy use. There may be a hint of this neglect in Mr Collins's horrified backward start when he is offered a book to read aloud in *Pride and Prejudice*: 'every thing announced it to be from a circulating library'.[4] In *Sanditon*, Austen's final unfinished novel, Sir Edward Denham is at pains to emphasize that the new seaside resort boasts a smart and upmarket 'subscription' library. Mr Parker pays a visit, not to take out a book but to inspect the all-important subscription list. He wants to see if there are enough fashionable people in town: 'The List of Subscribers was but commonplace. The Lady Denham, Miss Brereton, Mr. and Mrs. P. – Sir Edward Denham and Miss Denham ... were followed by nothing better than – Mrs. Mathews – Miss Mathews, Miss E. Mathews, Miss H. Mathews.'[5]

Some libraries charged an entrance fee, others charged a rate for borrowing books. Reading was becoming a social activity. Libraries were places where you met friends and exchanged gossip. Some were attached to a milliner's shop or a draper's, as is the one in *Sanditon*, where the heroine picks up a copy of *Camilla* and also buys trinkets: Charlotte pays for her goods 'as she had not Camilla's youth, and had no intention of having her distress'.[6] This refers to a famous scene in Burney's novel, concerning the winning of a gold locket, which is set in a library. Lydia Bennet in *Pride and Prejudice* meets officers at the library and sees 'such beautiful ornaments as made her quite wild'.[7]

The family memoir insists that Jane Austen's clerical brother James formed and directed her taste in reading.[8] But she required no such teacher. Her taste was wide-ranging and eclectic. She was left free to roam library shelves at her leisure, both public and private. She read novels and discussed them mainly with her female friends, most notably her mentor Anne Lefroy, but she also read sermons, essays, travel literature, biography and poetry.

Novels were a relatively new genre of literature and they came with a poor reputation: 'the mere trash of the circulating library', as Sheridan wrote in his smash hit stage-play *The Rivals*. The comic paradigm of the giddy novel reader was his Lydia Languish, a misguided reader of fiction: 'the girl's mad! – her brain's turned by reading' is the cry of Sir Anthony Absolute. Lydia tears out pages from Fordyce's *Sermons* to use as curling paper for her hair. Jane Austen's own Lydia in *Pride and Prejudice* also greatly dislikes Fordyce's sermons. Sheridan's play helped to perpetuate the idea that novels were an inferior form of writing. The idea that the wrong kind of books were dangerous to young females recurs throughout the eighteenth century, with commentators tut-tutting about 'Romances, Chocolate, Novels and the like Inflamers'.[9] Literary parody associated with the harmful effects of novel-reading on the naive mind is frequently found in late eighteenth-century essays and magazines and indeed in novels such as Charlotte Lennox's *The Female Quixote*.

Jane Austen did not conform to the view that circulating libraries were the repositories of pap. In 1798 she commented on the opening of a subscription library in Basingstoke, which she intended to join: 'As an inducement to subscribe Mrs Martin tells us that her Collection is not to consist only of Novels, but of every kind of Literature etc etc – She might have spared this pretension to *our* family, who are great Novel-readers and not ashamed of being so.'[10]

When the family moved to Chawton, Austen joined a reading group and borrowed books from the Alton Book Society. Every member paid an annual subscription of a guinea. There were fines for the late return of books. By 1811, the club had well over two hundred works, kept in a special bookcase at the house of Mr Pinnock in Alton. A large proportion were of a serious non-fiction kind – on politics, travel, biography, history and theology. But novels were also available. In 1813, Jane read *Rosanne*, a deeply Christian novel, by Laetitia M. Hawkins. 'We have got "Rosanne" in our

Society, and find it much as you describe it; very good and clever, but tedious. Mrs Hawkins' great excellence is on serious subjects. There are some very delightful conversations and reflections on religion: but on lighter topics I think she falls into many absurdities.'[11] Falling into absurdities and lack of realism were Jane Austen's chief criticism of particular kinds of novels, whether the excessively didactic, such as those of Mrs More, or the excessively romantic, such as those of Mrs Radcliffe. She preferred novels that were 'natural' and 'true to life' – those that, in the words given ironically to a foolish character in *Sanditon*, consist of 'vapid tissues of ordinary Occurrences from which no useful Deductions can be drawn'.[12]

Since the form was held in such low esteem, Fanny Burney herself was wary of using the word 'novel', even though she had undertaken a sterling defence of the form in the preface to her first book, *Evelina*. *Cecilia* was sub-titled 'memoirs of an heiress' and *Camilla* 'a picture of youth'. In the Advertisement, Burney described *Camilla* as 'this little Work' and even in 1814, by which time one would have expected her to have full confidence in the form, she wrote of the novel as a 'species of writing never mentioned, even by its supporter, but with a look that fears contempt'.[13] Austen borrowed the phrase 'this little work' for her Advertisement to *Northanger Abbey*, but within the book itself she is effectively telling her sister-authors that the time has come to stop apologizing and to stand up in defence of both the form and the word – 'Oh! It is only a novel!'

Historically speaking, the flighty novel reader was as likely to be male as female. Certainly Jane Austen took this view from the beginning of her writing career to the end. In her early work 'Love and Freindship' it is Edward the hero who is directly accused of gleaning absurd notions from reading fiction, and in *Sanditon* Sir Edmund Denham is enthralled by sensational novels and determined to be a 'dangerous man, quite in the line of the Lovelaces' (his allusion is to the charismatic rapist in Richardson's *Clarissa*). Henry Tilney in *Northanger Abbey* claims to have read 'hundreds and hundreds of novels' and teasingly defends his rights as a male reader: 'for they read nearly as many as women', he tells Catherine Morland.[14]

Though *Northanger Abbey* is a parody of the fashionable Gothic novel, it is also the occasion for Austen's most impassioned defence of the form: 'there seems almost a general wish of decrying the capacity and undervaluing the labour of the novelist, and of slighting the performances which have only genius, wit, and taste to recommend them'.[15] In *Northanger Abbey*, literary taste is a guide to character; thus John Thorpe, the thuggish, boorish, booby squire, enjoys the Gothic lubricity of M. G. Lewis's *The Monk* and the 'fun' of Mrs Radcliffe, but dislikes the kind of novels that Austen is intent on defending – such as those of Fanny Burney:

> 'I was thinking of that other stupid book, written by that woman they make such a fuss about, she who married the French emigrant.'
> 'I suppose you mean Camilla?'
> 'Yes, that's the book; such unnatural stuff! – An old man playing at see-saw! I took up the first volume once, and looked it over, but I soon found it would not do; indeed I guessed what sort of stuff it must be before I saw it: as soon as I heard she had married an emigrant, I was sure I should never be able to get through it.'
> 'I have never read it.'
> 'You had no loss, I assure you; it is the horridest nonsense you can imagine; there is nothing in the world in it but an old man's playing at see-saw and learning Latin; upon my soul there is not.'[16]

The 'justness' of this critique is 'unfortunately lost' on Catherine because at that moment they arrive at Mrs Thorpe's lodgings, where John proves himself as 'dutiful and affectionate' a son as he is 'the discerning and unprejudiced reader of Camilla': he gives his mother a hearty shake of the hand and tells her that her 'quiz of a hat' makes her look like an old witch.

Henry Austen claimed that his sister's favourite novelists were the two giants of eighteenth-century English fiction, Samuel Richardson and Henry Fielding. Richardson's *Clarissa* and *Sir Charles Grandison* were of enormous importance to her, and it is clear that she had an intimate knowledge of Fielding's *Tom Jones*, which was often considered unsuitable for young ladies. But in her own magnificent defence of the novel in *Northanger Abbey* the exemplars are not the works of Richardson and Fielding:

> 'I am no novel-reader – I seldom look into novels – Do not imagine that *I* often read novels – It is really very well for a novel.' – Such is the common cant. – 'And what are you reading, Miss –?' 'Oh! it is only a novel!' replies the young lady; while she lays down her book with affected indifference, or momentary shame. – 'It is only Cecilia, or Camilla, or Belinda'; or, in short, only some work in which the greatest

powers of the mind are displayed, in which the most thorough knowledge of human nature, the happiest delineation of its varieties, the liveliest effusions of wit and humour are conveyed to the world in the best chosen language.[17]

This passage makes clear that the novels she admired above all others were Fanny Burney's *Cecilia* and *Camilla* and Maria Edgeworth's *Belinda*.

Richardson had pioneered the heroine-centred novel of manners in *Pamela*, *Sir Charles Grandison* and *Clarissa*, but, much as Jane Austen admired him, his heroines are idealized 'pictures of perfection' of the kind that she avoided in her own works. She much preferred his 'anti-heroines' such as the spirited sister of Sir Charles, Lady G. Fanny Burney was pioneering in her quest to draw 'characters from nature', as her preface to *Evelina* (1778) suggested. Burney was also pioneering in her decision to bring her second novel, *Cecilia* (1782), to its close with a 'realistic' ending: 'the Hero and Heroine are neither plunged into the depths of misery, nor exalted to *unhuman happiness*, – is not such a middle state more natural? more according to real life, and less resembling every other Book of Fiction?'[18]

The final chapter of *Cecilia* includes a phrase that inspired Jane Austen: '"The whole of this unfortunate business," said Dr Lyster, "has been the result of PRIDE and PREJUDICE ... Remember: if to PRIDE AND PREJUDICE you owe your miseries, so wonderfully is good and evil balanced, that to PRIDE AND PREJUDICE you will also owe their termination."'[19] *Pride and Prejudice* is indeed a homage to *Cecilia*. Burney's heroine, Cecilia Beverley, is beautiful, clever, spirited and rich, but her wealth comes at a price. The condition of her inheritance is that whoever wins her hand must relinquish their surname and take hers. The hero is Mortimer Delville, a nobly born man whose family pride is uppermost. He loves Cecilia but, like Darcy with Elizabeth, says it will 'degrade' him to marry her because of her lack of nobility. He will never agree to become Mr Beverley. His mother, Mrs Delville, is a magisterial older woman, who first opposes, then sanctions, the marriage. Lady Catherine de Bourgh is a version of this kind of powerful and proud older woman who opposes the young usurper.

Burney wrote that her intention in *Cecilia* was to depict characters who were neither wholly good nor wholly evil, but true to life: 'I meant in Mrs Delville to draw a great, but not a perfect character; I meant, on the contrary, to blend upon paper, as I have frequently seen blended in life, noble and rare qualities with striking and incurable defects.' Of the Delvilles, she wrote, 'I merely meant to show how differently pride, like every other quality, operates upon different minds.'[20] The latter sentence could be a description of *Pride and Prejudice*.

In many ways, *Cecilia* is a deeply shocking and unsettling novel. It shows that as a young girl Jane Austen was free to read emotionally and morally challenging material. With its large cast of characters, it is a prototype of the great Victorian novels of George Eliot, Dickens and Thackeray. One of Cecilia's guardians, Mr Harrel, a gambling addict, who has blackmailed her, shoots himself at the Vauxhall Pleasure Gardens while she is there. A back-story is the seduction of an innocent young girl who is then forced into prostitution. Cecilia, abandoned by her husband, descends into poverty and madness. Her nervous breakdown at the end of the book is graphically rendered. The hero and heroine are finally united but at great personal cost to Cecilia's mental health and physical beauty.

Burney had, ever since the success of *Evelina*, wanted to create an ugly, poor but clever heroine. She called it her 'ugly scheme'. Her original intention was for Cecilia to be this new kind of plain heroine (called Eugenia), but she was persuaded to abandon her idea. Burney would not give up on Eugenia, however, and she appears in her third novel, *Camilla*, as the pock-marked crippled sister of the heroine. Eugenia contracts smallpox and is badly disfigured and then falls off a see-saw, injuring her spine in the process. It is ugly, clever, kind Eugenia who is the real heroine of the novel.

Strikingly, Jane Austen's heroines are rarely described as beautiful and accomplished. Even Emma Woodhouse is 'handsome' rather than 'beautiful'. Physical descriptions of her heroines are rare. Austen shows instead how they grow into loveliness or possess a particular fine feature, such as sparkling eyes. Jane Bennet is the beauty of the family but the heroine is feisty Elizabeth, who ridicules the common tendency of over-idealizing the female species. Burney was the first novelist to create heroines who were plain or even downright ugly. Without her, it would not have been possible for Jane Austen to reject the convention that a heroine must be beautiful.

Jane Austen would have felt particular pleasure and pride when she received her five-volume set of *Camilla* in 1796. Not only was there the anticipation of a read as good and as lengthy as *Cecilia*. There was the added frisson of seeing her own name in the list of subscribers, as well as a

Prologue: Captain Harville's View

1. The Family Profile

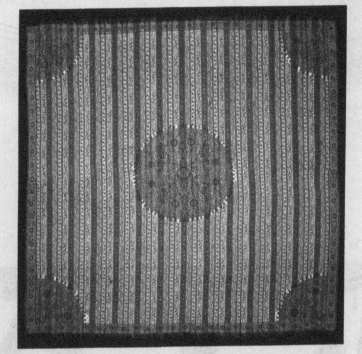

2. The East Indian Shawl

3. The Vellum Notebooks

4. The Subscription List

Fanny Burney

personal connection: her godfather Samuel Cooke was a close friend of Burney.[21] The Reverend Samuel Cooke was married to Mrs Austen's first cousin, who shared the name Cassandra Leigh. She was the daughter of Theophilus Leigh, Master of Balliol College, Oxford. The Cookes lived in a village in Surrey called Great Bookham. Opposite them in a little house called The Hermitage lived Fanny Burney, now married, as John Thorpe in *Northanger Abbey* puts it, 'to an emigrant', General Alexandre d'Arblay. Burney had first met her future husband at Juniper House, a former coaching inn nestled in a valley at the foot of Box Hill, that had become home to a group of émigrés who had fled from revolutionary Paris.

Fanny was a frequent visitor to the Cookes. She didn't really like their teenage daughter, Mary, whom she found 'stiff and cold', but she was very fond of Cassandra Cooke, who was herself a novelist. It may have been Cassandra who asked Jane to be a subscriber to *Camilla*. Burney lived close to the Cookes from 1793 to 1797, whereupon she moved near by to build Camilla Cottage. Samuel Cooke baptized Burney's only and beloved son, who was named Alexandre after his father. Jane Austen later joked about marrying him, so it is clear that she and her sister gossiped about the d'Arblay family life.

The Cookes particularly admired *Mansfield Park*, and Samuel wrote to Jane Austen to tell her so, observing that he would not like Madame d'Arblay's new novel (*The Wanderer*, published the same year) so well. We know that Jane Austen visited her godfather in Surrey. The topography of the fictional Highbury in *Emma* bears some resemblance to that of Great Bookham, and there can be no doubt that Jane Austen knew Box Hill. She would have discussed novels when she spent time with Cassandra Cooke. The publication of Cassandra's novel *Battleridge* in 1799 might have helped to persuade Jane Austen that she too could be a published author. She may well have read the novel in manuscript.

Jane wrote to her sister Cassandra in October 1798, 'Your letter was chaperoned here by one from Mrs Cooke, in which she says that *Battleridge* is not to come out before January; and she is so little satisfied with Cawthorn's dilatoriness that she never means to employ him again.'[22] Cawthorn, of Cawthorn and Hutt in Cockspur Street, London, was Mrs Cooke's publisher. Here, Jane Austen shows her interest in her cousin's publishing problems. Cassandra Cooke's openness in discussing such matters suggests that the Austens were supportive of her attempts to be a published novelist. Later, as we will see, Jane experienced similar frustrations with her first publisher.

Jane and her Leigh cousins had loyal Cavalier ancestors during the Civil War. In 1642, Sir Thomas Leigh had entertained King Charles I at Stoneleigh for three days when the gates of Coventry were shut against him. The Leighs were heavily fined by Cromwell's government but held on to their lands and their royalist sympathies.

Cooke's preface to *Battleridge: An Historical Tale* claims that the novel was based on a true story set in the interregnum. The chief character is the historical figure Doctor Scott, who was a favourite of Charles I but manages to earn the admiration of Oliver Cromwell (who appears as a character in volume one). *Battleridge* actually tells two different tales, both allegedly based on 'facts'. The main story concerns the abduction and imprisonment of a young girl whose family fortunes are restored by the recovery of a lost deed which has been locked into the false bottom of a cedar chest. It has typically Gothic features: madness, old castles, lost documents, cruel fathers and sons, beautiful but crazed maidens, wise divines. In her preface, Cooke acknowledges the novels of Goldsmith, Richardson and Burney as exemplars for not representing their heroines as 'angels', and Mrs Radcliffe as the

'Queen of the tremendous'. Cooke also writes that she was advised by friends to enlarge her book by adding a second 'Scottish story founded on fact'. *Battleridge* is the type of Gothic novel parodied in *Northanger Abbey*. Austen certainly seems to make teasing use of it at various points. For example, Catherine Morland's tomboyish taste for baseball and cricket is a playful echo of a male character's complaint on the second page of *Battleridge*: 'No more cricket, no more base-ball, they are sending me to Geneva.' The novel's pro-Stuart sympathies would, nevertheless, have appealed to Jane Austen, as they would to Mary Leigh, Cassandra Cooke's sister, who wrote a history depicting the Leigh family's connections with and support for the Stuarts.[23]

Jane Austen also had another cousin novelist on the Leigh side of the family. She was Cassandra Hawke, who wrote the well-reviewed sentimental novel *Julia de Gramont* (1788)[24] and boasted of it, much to the irritation of Fanny Burney, who described it as 'love, love, love, unmixed and unadulterated with any more worldly materials'.[25] Cassandra Hawke's sister Elizabeth described her as being 'never without a pen in her hand; she can't help writing for her life'.[26]

Fanny Burney met these sisters, Elizabeth and Cassandra, at a party in 1782 and wrote a lengthy, satirical account in her journals. Burney was half amused and half irritated by Elizabeth, Jane Austen's rattle of a cousin, who insisted on introducing her to Cassandra Hawke as a 'sister authoress'. The account reads like a scene in a play, with the young Burney seated beside the two 'Ladyships'. Elizabeth talks non-stop of writing, of the 'hundreds of novels' she has read, of plays and authoresses. Did Burney know any of the authoresses? Was not *Evelina* 'the most elegant novel' ever written? 'Such a style … there's a vast deal of invention in it! And you've got so much humour, too! Now my sister has no humour – hers is all sentiment.' Was Burney, she enquired, 'writing another novel'? 'No, ma'am.' 'Oh, I daresay you are. I daresay you are writing one at this very minute!'

Burney, with typical sharp powers of observation, noted that, in contrast to her loud-mouthed sister, the pretty Cassandra was 'extremely languishing, delicate, and pathetic; apparently accustomed to be reckoned the genius of her family, and well contented to be looked upon as a creature dropped from the clouds'.[27] Little did the Leighs know that the real genius of the family would be a humble Hampshire cousin.

* * *

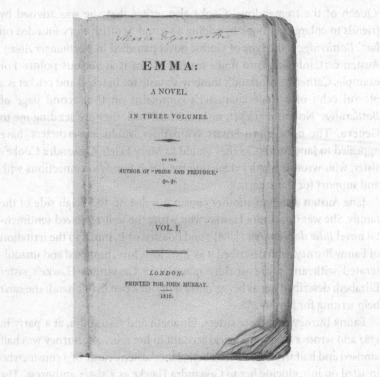

EMMA:

A NOVEL.

IN THREE VOLUMES.

BY THE
AUTHOR OF "PRIDE AND PREJUDICE."
&c. &c.

VOL. I.

LONDON:
PRINTED FOR JOHN MURRAY.
1816.

Presentation copy sent by Jane Austen to
Maria Edgeworth

Jane Austen greatly admired the novelist Maria Edgeworth. When *Emma* was published, Austen asked John Murray to send a presentation copy to Edgeworth in Ireland. Maria knew Jane Austen's aunt and uncle Mr and Mrs James Leigh-Perrot,[28] but it is not clear that she made the connection, saying, 'The authoress of Pride and Prejudice has been so good as to send me a new novel just published, Emma.'[29] Edgeworth was not impressed with the novel, judging by the comments she made to her half-brother: 'There was no story to it, except that Miss Emma found that the man whom she designed for Harriet's lover was an admirer of her own – and he was affronted at being refused by Emma … and smooth, thin water-gruel is according to Emma's father's opinion a very good thing and it is very difficult to make a cook understand what you mean by smooth thin water gruel.'[30]

Edgeworth was a prolific writer of novels, essays and children's fiction. Several of her novels, including the highly successful *Castle Rackrent* (1800), were set in Ireland, where she was brought up. Her novels of London society were *Belinda* (1801), *Leonora* (1806), *Tales of Fashionable Life* (1809–12) and *Patronage* (1814). Walter Scott claimed that he turned from poetry to fiction as a result of her influence.

Belinda, the novel that Jane Austen singled out for special praise through its mention in *Northanger Abbey*, was a controversial book. It depicted an opium-addicted (anti-)heroine and featured an inter-racial marriage between a farm-girl called Lucy and a Jamaican servant called Juba. By the third edition, Edgeworth removed this plot-line. Belinda herself comes close to marrying a rich West Indian Creole. The novel also depicts a character called Harriet Freke, who is closely based on the feminist Mary Wollstonecraft. Harriet dresses like a man, is sexually aroused by Belinda and repelled by men. 'I am a champion for the Rights of Woman,' she tells the astonished hero, Clarence Hervey.[31]

The novelists that Jane Austen mentions in her own novels and surviving letters are probably only a fraction of the dozens whose works she knew. Her reading is very difficult to piece together because of her reliance on lending libraries. There was no doubt that she had strong opinions. She was unimpressed with the popular novel by Sydney Owenson (Lady Morgan), *The Wild Irish Girl.* In January 1809, as the Austens were preparing to move to Chawton, Jane wrote to Cassandra, 'We have got *Ida of Athens* by Miss Owenson; which must be very clever, because it was written as the Authoress says, in three months. – We have only read the Preface yet; but her Irish Girl does not make me expect much. – If the warmth of her Language could affect the Body, it might be worth reading in this weather.'[32]

One author she disliked vehemently was Jane West. She was a conservative and didactic writer, not at all in Jane Austen's style. She firmly believed that a woman's place was in the home, declaring 'My needle always claims the pre-eminence of my pen.'[33] In September 1814, Jane Austen wrote to her niece Anna that she was 'quite determined … not to be pleased with Mrs West's Alicia de Lacy, should I ever meet with it, which I hope I may not. – I think I *can* be stout against any thing written by Mrs West. – I have made up my mind to like no Novels really, but Miss Edgeworth's, Yours and my own.'[34] The fact that she so despised the reactionary Jane West is a sure sign that Austen herself was no reactionary.

THE REAL JANE AUSTEN

Her taste was for the rebels against literary convention: Burney with her plain or disabled heroines and her uncertain endings, Edgeworth with her feminists and her inter-racial marriages. Jane Austen's novels were essentially heroine-centred novels of courtship, not conduct books disguised as novels in the manner of Jane West. They are coming-of-age novels in which guardians and parental figures are often flawed. The heroine is not taught a lesson: she learns from her own mistakes.

In a letter written from Bath in 1805, Jane Austen reflected on the fact that she was moving in very different company from that of an earlier visit: 'What a different set are we now moving in! But seven years I suppose are enough to change every pore of one's skin, and every feeling of one's mind.'[35] The self and the emotions evolve. We change, we grow through experience: that is what makes us human, and it is the process that the novel can track in more detail and with more nuance than any other creative endeavour. Catherine Morland, the Dashwood sisters, Elizabeth Bennet, Emma Woodhouse, Fanny Price, Anne Elliot: none of them is the same at the end of the story as she was at the beginning. It was Fanny Burney and Maria Edgeworth who led Jane Austen to see that the novel could be a medium for showing how seven years, or seventeen, were enough to change every pore of one's skin and every feeling of one's mind.

It has become fashionable in our own time to be dismissive of 'Janeites' who speak of Elizabeth Bennet, Mr Darcy and the rest as if they were real people, so it may come as a surprise to find that the supremely self-aware ironist Jane Austen considered, if playfully, her fictional creations as flesh and blood figures. In conversation with her family – as in her scribbled comment on the back of her copy of *Camilla* – she gave afterlives to the characters in her novels. She suggested that Jane Fairfax dies young in childbed, that Kitty Bennet marries a young clergyman and that the large sum of money Mrs Norris gives to William Price is One Pound. According to the family memoir, she thought of fictional characters as people she knew: 'Every circumstance narrated in Sir Charles Grandison, all that was ever said and done in the cedar parlour, was familiar to her; and the wedding days of Lady L. and Lady G. were as remembered as if they had been living friends.'[36]

She loved Burney's comic creations, such as the voluble leader of the fashionable world the 'inimitable Miss Larolles'[37] in *Cecilia* and the endearing but foolish Hugh Tyrold in *Camilla*.[38] She shared that love with her dear sister. Allusions to Fanny Burney are a kind of affectionate code in her letters to Cassandra: 'Take care of your precious self, do not work too hard, remember that Aunt Cassandras are quite as scarce as Miss Beverleys.'[39] And again, 'Give my love to Mary Harrison, and tell her I wish whenever she is attached to a young Man, some *respectable* Dr Marchmont may keep them apart for five Volumes.'[40]

By a strange coincidence, 1814 saw not only the publication of Jane Austen's third novel, *Mansfield Park*, but also highly anticipated novels by her favourites Burney and Edgeworth – *The Wanderer* and *Patronage*. Walter Scott also published his first novel that year and Jane Austen joked to her niece Anna that he should have stuck to writing poetry: 'Walter Scott has no business to write novels, especially good ones. – It is not fair. – He has Fame and Profit enough as a Poet, and should not be taking the bread out of other people's mouths. – I do not like him, and do not mean to like Waverley if I can help it – but fear I must.'[41] The fame of Scott did indeed eclipse that of Burney and Edgeworth, but they are the writers to read if one wants to get a sense of the models that inspired Jane Austen to become a novelist.

5

The Sisters

Two young ladies are dressed in white muslin.[1] Their gowns are high-waisted, classical and flowing in the Regency style. Their hair is piled on top of the head and secured with beautiful headbands. One is wearing a pink shawl draped around her waist, the other a blue shawl. They resemble Grecian statues, but their pink cheeks and bright eyes show their vitality. One is holding an unfolded letter, from a suitor, or from a friend or relative. They are standing in the grounds of a stately home, sharing a confidence, perhaps related to the contents of the letter. They look as if they belong in a Jane Austen novel. They could be Marianne and Elinor Dashwood, Jane and Elizabeth Bennet, Julia and Maria Bertram, Emma and Isabella Woodhouse, Anne and Mary Elliot.

The young woman on the left is actually Charlotte Trevanion. A label attached to the portrait says that she 'married 1803'. On the right is Georgiana Trevanion, 'unmarried'. They are sisters-in-law. Charlotte, née Hosier, was born in 1783. She married John Purcell Bettesworth Trevanion, a major in the Dragoons, who was later described as 'a gentleman who, to the pretensions of birth and lineage, to brilliant talents, the finest taste, and the most polished manners, united ardent and enlightened attachment to the cause of civil and religious liberty'.[2] Charlotte did what was expected of young women of her class: she bore him children. Five of them, over seven years. In 1810 she suffered the fate of so many of her peers: she died in childbirth. In St Michael, Caerhays, the church near the family seat in

Cornwall, there is a stone monument to her with weeping putti and a crocketed gable over a tomb chest with an elegiac inscription.

One of Charlotte's sons, Henry Trevanion, married Georgiana Augusta Leigh, daughter of Lieutenant-Colonel George Leigh and his cousin Augusta, Lord Byron's half-sister. Now it gets complicated: Augusta was the daughter of Lady Amelia Darcy and Captain 'Mad Jack' Byron, whose father Admiral 'Fairweather' Jack Byron had married into the Trevanion family. Colonel Leigh's father, General Charles Leigh, had married Mad Jack Byron's sister. As shorthand, one might say that almost everybody in the story was the cousin of everybody else. The tentacles of the Leigh family spread so widely that the marriage between General Leigh and Byron's aunt means that Jane Austen and Lord Byron may have been distant cousins.[3]

But Henry Trevanion was unfaithful. He was passionately drawn to his wife's younger sister Medora, who was almost certainly the child of an incestuous union between Byron and Augusta. Medora became pregnant and her father locked her up in an establishment in Maida Vale where upper-class girls went to have their illegitimate offspring. Henry arranged her escape and they eloped to Normandy, where their child was stillborn. They then removed themselves to a remote and decrepit chateau in rural France, where they passed for brother and sister. Medora became a Catholic and declared her intention of entering a convent. However, she got pregnant again. The Abbess was tolerant and found her lodgings, where a daughter was born in 1834, christened Marie-Violette Trevanion – she was said to bear an uncanny resemblance to her probable grandfather Lord Byron. After a series of miscarriages, Henry Trevanion and Medora Leigh finally parted. In her autobiography, Medora wrote of Henry that he gave himself up to religion and shooting. The impoverished Medora travelled with her daughter (who eventually became a nun), married a Frenchman and died in 1849.

'I have read *The Corsair*, mended my petticoat, and have nothing else to do,' Jane Austen would write to Cassandra on 5 March 1814.[4] Byron's *Corsair* was the bestselling poem of the age – its first edition sold ten thousand copies on the day of publication. Its popularity owed not a little to the growing scandals around his name. Stories of his incestuous union with Augusta Leigh were beginning to circulate in society. In *The Corsair*, the hero's beloved is called Medora.

The tangled story that flows from the sprightly figure of Charlotte Trevanion reminds us that it was common among the gentry in Jane Austen's time for people to marry their cousins. And that it was not uncommon for a man to marry one sister and yet desire another. That brothers and sisters could have very intense, even incestuous, relationships. That an early death in childbirth was a very strong possibility for any young woman who married. And that letters are a key conduit of sisterly intimacy and affection.

Around the time that she turned twenty-one, Cassandra Austen became engaged to a young clergyman who was due to take a living in faraway Shropshire. Mrs Austen, preparing herself for the eventual removal of her two daughters, who were now entering the marriage market, rather despaired of the younger one's prospects. To one of her daughters-in-law, she confided that 'I look forwards to you as a real comfort to me in my old age, when Cassandra is gone into Shropshire, and Jane – the Lord knows where.'[5]

Visits to Southampton, Gloucestershire and Kent had exposed the girls to a selection of eligible young men, but Cassandra's engagement was not to a mysterious stranger met at a ball or a fashionable watering hole. It was to a young man who had been like a brother to her. Tom Fowle was one of the boarders, educated in the schoolroom at the family home. We know very little about him except that he was liked enormously by the Austen family and was an active participant in amateur dramatics at Steventon. Tom Fowle, who gained his MA from Oxford in 1794, was destined for the Church. But a home and an income were dependent on the living in Shropshire, so the lovers had to wait for their wedding day.

In the meantime, in January of 1796, Cassandra went to stay with Tom's family at their parsonage near Newbury. Jane and Cassandra had undergone some temporary separations when one or other of them had been on family visits, but this was the harbinger of something new and unwelcome: a life apart, in which letter-writing would become the prime means of sustaining the sisterly relationship. Jane Austen's first surviving letter dates from precisely this moment. The surviving letters to Cassandra are the most intimate record we have of Jane's inner life. The first of them was written on Cassandra's twenty-third birthday – almost certainly the first birthday the sisters were apart – and it begins with the words 'In the first place I hope you will live twenty-three years longer.'[6] This is playful, but it barely conceals the thought that Cassandra might not live another twenty-three years: marriage meant childbirth which often meant death.

In the letters that Jane wrote to Cassandra at this time, she gives the impression of trying out several voices: gossipy, jokey, affectionate, mock-pompous ('I am very much flattered by your commendation of my last Letter, for I write only for Fame, and without any view to pecuniary Emolument').[7] She makes light of the gap that is opening up between them, but in her heart she is thinking of the great distance between Steventon and Shropshire. When she came to write her novels, she was always acutely aware that distance from a sister was one of the penalties of marriage: in her most 'perfect' novel, *Pride and Prejudice*, Jane and Elizabeth 'in addition to every other source of happiness' are separated only by 'thirty miles'.[8]

Jane Austen liked women. She had several cherished female friends and was devoted to those she esteemed. She deeply valued the loyalty and companionship of those friends whom she could regard almost as sisters. She was particularly fond of the Bigg sisters, Catherine and Alethea, and the Lloyd sisters, Martha and Mary.

Relationships between female friends were extremely close-knit and it was common for such bonds to be strengthened by marriage to brothers, as was the case with the Austens and the Lloyds. Mary Lloyd married James Austen, and Martha, when she was sixty-two, married Frank Austen. Furthermore, the Lloyds were cousins to Cassandra's betrothed, Tom Fowle. Mary and Martha's sister Eliza married her cousin, Fulwar Fowle, who was another of Mr Austen's Steventon pupils. The proposed marriage between Cassandra and Tom would have made her a cousin by marriage to the Lloyds as well as their sister-in-law. The relationships are almost as involuted as those of the Trevanions, the Byrons and the Leighs: the Lloyds and the Fowles were descended from the Cravens, who were themselves related to the Leighs of Stoneleigh, so Tom Fowle was also a distant cousin of Cassandra by descent.[9]

Cath Bigg was Jane's choice of partner at balls where men were in short supply. She described her as 'nice and composed-looking', which was something of a tease since Cath and Alethea, like the fictional Catherine Morland, had a propensity for misusing the word 'nice': 'The Biggs would call her a nice woman,' Austen once joked. Henry Tilney's taking Catherine to task – 'and this is a nice day, and we are taking a very nice walk, and you two are very nice young ladies' – may well have been a private joke between Jane

Austen and the Biggs.[10] As will be seen, a time would come when Jane herself almost became a sister-in-law to the Biggs. She didn't, but she remained on the best of terms with Catherine and Alethea.

The Lloyd sisters had lost a small brother to smallpox, and though the girls survived the epidemic both Martha and Mary were severely scarred. Martha was among the most beloved of Jane Austen's friends. She was gentle, sweet-tempered and deeply Christian. She was probably for some time a lady's companion to a Mrs Dundas, an invalid at Barton Court in Kintbury. She was also an excellent cook. After her mother's death, she lived with the Austens as a family member. Martha was ten years older than Jane Austen, who was always drawn to older women as friends. 'With what true simpathy our feelings are shared by Martha, you need not be told; – she is the friend and Sister under every circumstance,' she wrote to Cassandra.[11]

But it was always her blood sister to whom she remained closest. So the period following the announcement of the engagement was a time of great uncertainty. Some sentences of the letter sent by Jane to Cassandra at the home of her future in-laws are unusually stiff, even distant, in tone: 'I am very glad to find from Mary that Mr and Mrs Fowle are pleased with you. I hope you will continue to give satisfaction.'[12]

The Shropshire living still had not come through, so Tom Fowle accepted a temporary post as chaplain to his patron, Lord Craven, in the West Indies. In April 1797, Cassandra heard the tragic news that her fiancé had died of yellow fever in San Domingo. It was a blow to the whole family, and Jane immediately wrote to cousin Eliza to inform her of the news. Eliza in turn reported the mood at Steventon: 'I have just received a letter from Steventon where they are all in great Affliction ... for the death of Mr. Fowle ... Jane says that her Sister behaves with a degree of resolution and Propriety which no common mind could evince in so trying a situation.'[13] It is tantalizing that we have only Eliza's report of this key Jane Austen letter, not the thing itself.

Tom was buried at sea, so there was no grave, nowhere to go to mourn him. All Cassandra had left of him was a small legacy in his will. Lord Craven later said that he would never have taken him to the West Indies if he had known that he was engaged to be married. Cold comfort indeed.

Cassandra's conduct in bereavement might have been impeccable, but she all too quickly adopted widow's weeds and abandoned all further thoughts of matrimony. She resigned herself to spinsterhood and didn't change her mind.

Jane Austen was a very private person. In her letters to Cassandra she allowed herself a freedom of expression and thought denied to many others of her family and friends. They were, according to their niece Caroline Austen, 'open and confidential'. In the Georgian era, letters were like newspapers, passed around and read aloud to members of the family and friends, but we can see from Jane Austen's comments that some parts of them were intended to remain private. She was careful to share only selected parts of Cassandra's letters: 'I read all the scraps I could of your letter' (to Sackree the maid), and, again, 'I read the chief of your letter' (to Edward).[14]

Jane Austen's letters to Cassandra catch her in the act of private conversation, which is one reason why her voice sounds so modern and familiar. It's true that most of the letters pass on news and exchange information, sometimes trivial or seemingly incomprehensible, but that inimitable voice can't be supressed. 'We left Guildford at 20 minutes before 12 – (I hope somebody cares for these minutiae),'[15] she says to Cassandra. She greatly looked forward to receiving her letters and feigned jealousy at the thought of her sister writing to other siblings: 'I shall not take the trouble of announcing to you any more of Mary's children, if, instead of thanking me for the intelligence, you always sit down and write to James. I am sure nobody can desire your letters so much as I do, and I don't think anybody deserves them so well.'[16]

Despite the fact that neither of them married, in later years the sisters were separated for long periods of time, and in Jane's letters her disappointment at their separation always shines through. She admired and adored her elder sister, as Caroline Austen noted: 'the habit of looking up to her begun in childhood, seemed always to continue ... she would frequently say to me ... Aunt Cassandra could teach everything much better than *she* could – Aunt Cass *knew* more ... she did always *really* think of her sister, as the superior to herself.'[17] The finest comic writer of the age actually described her sister Cassandra as 'the finest comic writer of the present age'.[18]

Jane Austen's profound capacity for female friendship is not always obvious from her letters. Her deliciously irreverent and unguarded remarks have upon occasion aroused some readers' contempt, such as when she makes tasteless jokes about miscarriage, death or adultery. She could be sharp and acerbic with silly females of her acquaintance, especially those who doted (stupidly) on their children or their husbands.

It is well known that she made a tasteless joke about miscarriage: 'Mrs Hall of Sherbourn was brought to bed yesterday of a dead child, some weeks before she expected, oweing to a fright. – I suppose she happened unawares to look at her husband.'[19] 'Only think', she wrote, 'of Mrs Holder being dead! Poor woman, she has done the only thing in the world she could possibly do, to make one cease to abuse her.'[20] She could also be rude to respected family members: 'my Aunt may do what she likes with her frigates'.[21]

But all of these wickedly funny remarks were made to her sister in private correspondence with the express purpose of making Cassandra laugh. The infamous remark about miscarriage has been quoted many times as proof of her callousness, but, as Christopher Ricks notes in a brilliant essay on Jane Austen and children, when this quotation is read aloud to an audience of women it usually provokes great guffaws of laughter.[22] It tends to be male critics who find her joke distasteful; women are made of sterner stuff. Often Jane Austen's bad-taste jokes are made at the expense of men: 'Mr Waller is dead, I see; – I cannot grieve about it, nor, perhaps, can his Widow very much.'[23] Nevertheless, the jokes about death do come close to the bone. 'I am sorry for the Beaches' loss of their little girl,' she wrote to Cassandra, 'especially as it is the one so much like me.'[24]

Apart from the obvious point that the Georgians had a different way of dealing with death, such comments are key to understanding the particular workings of Jane and Cassandra's relationship. Jane's letters show how she liked to play the role of the naughty little sister, confessing to Cassandra that she has a hangover, that she has overspent her allowance on trivialities, or that she has behaved indecorously: 'imagine everything most profligate in the way of flirting', she writes. And 'If I am wild Beast, I cannot help it.'[25]

Many of her letters show her entertaining her sister with rude remarks, often about other pairs of sisters. She could be critical and catty, especially when it came to physical attractiveness. In one account of a ball she describes 'the two Miss Coxes' as 'vulgar, broad featured', the Miss Maitlands with 'large dark eyes, and a good deal of nose', the Debary sisters reeking of 'bad breath', the Miss Atkinsons, 'fat girls with short noses', and Mrs Blount with her 'broad face, diamond bandeau, white shoes, pink husband, and fat neck'.[26] As for Lady Fagg and her daughters: 'I never saw so plain a family, five sisters so very plain!'[27]

She makes the women she is describing seem like figures in a caricature by the great satirical artist Gillray. The more outrageous the comment, the more she made her sister laugh. Anna Austen confirms this picture in her memoir when she claimed that she and Jane made Cassandra laugh so much that she would 'beg us to leave off', saying 'How *can* you both be so foolish?'[28]

The more absurd the wordplay the better: 'I shall keep my ten pounds too, to wrap myself up in next winter.' 'I took the liberty a few days ago of asking your black velvet bonnet to lend me its cawl,' 'We shall have pease soon – I mean to have them with a couple of Ducks from Wood Barn and Maria Middleton.' Two tables 'covered with green baize send their best love'. 'I will not say that your Mulberry trees are dead, but I am afraid they are not alive.'[29] It is only really in her letters to Cassandra, not the few surviving ones to her brothers, that the 'naughty little sister' voice comes through.

The unique bond with Cassandra can be highlighted by considering Jane Austen's relationships with her sisters-in-law. Her relationship with brother James's second wife, her old friend Mary Lloyd, soured over the years. Jane intimates that Mary was jealous of the family's closeness, resenting her husband for spending so much time with them.[30] By 1813, the gloves were off: 'How can Mrs J. Austen be so provokingly ill-judging? – I should have expected better from her professed if not real regard for my Mother.'[31] Jane wrote to Cassandra, who had been on a shopping commission for Mary: 'I hope the half of that sum will not greatly exceed what you had intended to offer upon the altar of sister-in-law affection.' That last is a tart phrase. It shows that Jane could say anything to Cassandra in complete confidence, and that they shared the belief that a sister-in-law could never be quite the same as a real sister.

Mary was careful with money, a trait that Jane despised. In one of her last letters before her death she described her sister Mary as 'in the main *not* a liberal-minded Woman' and told a close friend that her character would not mend: 'expect it not my dear Anne; too late, too late in the day'.[32] It has been suggested that she gave Mrs Norris some of Mary's unpleasant traits,[33] but there is perhaps more of a resemblance to the tight-fisted Mrs John Dashwood in *Sense and Sensibility*. Sisters-in-law fare badly in this novel. The disinheritance with which it begins is one of the most unsisterly acts in all of the novels:

Mrs. John Dashwood did not at all approve of what her husband intended to do for his sisters. To take three thousand pounds from the fortune of their dear little boy, would be impoverishing him to the most dreadful degree. She begged him to think again on the subject. How could he answer it to himself to rob his child, and his only child too, of so large a sum? And what possible claim could the Miss Dashwoods, who were related to him only by half blood, which she considered as no relationship at all, have on his generosity to so large an amount. It was very well known that no affection was ever supposed to exist between the children of any man by different marriages; and why was he to ruin himself, and their poor little Harry, by giving away all his money to his half sisters?[34]

Another of Jane's sisters-in-law, the wealthy and beautiful Elizabeth Bridges who married her lucky brother Edward, appears to have disliked her. Jane was jealous of Elizabeth's claim on Cassandra, as Elizabeth took every opportunity to invite the older girl for extended visits first at Rowling House and then later at Godmersham. Elizabeth was usually pregnant or recovering from a pregnancy, and even Jane admitted that she did the 'Business of Mothering' very well. But she could not love Elizabeth as a sister. One of the nieces observed that although Elizabeth's children enjoyed their clever aunt as 'a playfellow, and as a teller of stories', they were 'not really fond of her'. Anna remarked that their mother was not fond of Jane and 'preferred the elder sister'.[35] When Jane Austen says of the Bridges of Goodnestone, 'a little talent went a long way', she meant that although they were fashionable and entertained lavishly, they were not intellectual. Nevertheless Jane enjoyed the luxury of Kent. 'I shall eat Ice and drink French wine, and be above Vulgar Economy,' she said during a visit when Elizabeth was once more pregnant, and 'unusually active for her situation and size'.[36] Jane was shocked but not unduly distressed when she later heard the news that Elizabeth had died giving birth to her eleventh child, a boy called Brook. 'We need not enter into a Panegyric on the Departed,' she remarked drily.[37] Her concern was for the children and her own dear brother Edward.

Another sister-in-law who died in childbed was Fanny Palmer. Jane liked this delicate-featured pretty young blonde, who was just seventeen when she married brother Charles in Bermuda. She drew on her sister-in-law's experience as a naval wife when she created the character of Mrs Croft in

Persuasion. Charles was devoted to his wife, whom he called 'Fan'. The couple had three small daughters who lived with them aboard the *Namur*. Twelve of Fanny's letters survive from this time and they paint a compelling picture of the life of a young sailor's wife bringing up her children in cramped and confined conditions. Her letters describe her making 'tidy little Spencers' (short jackets) for the small girls, taking them to feed the pigeons, reading in the ship's library and going to the ship's theatre, which she loved.[38]

In *Persuasion*, there is a long discussion about the suitability of women living on board ship. Captain Wentworth's old-fashioned belief that a ship is no place for a woman is given short shrift by his sister: 'Oh, Frederick! – But I cannot believe it of you. – All idle refinement! – Women may be as comfortable on board, as in the best house in England. I believe I have lived as much on board as most women, and I know nothing superior to the accommodation of a man of war.' For good measure, Mrs Croft adds, 'I hate to hear you talking so, like a fine gentleman, and as if women were all fine ladies, instead of rational creatures. We none of us expect to be in smooth water all our days.'[39]

Fanny Palmer fitted well into the category of wives who have had their happiest times aboard ship. When she stayed on shore with Charles's patron, Sir Tom Williams (who had once been married to Charles's cousin Jane Cooper), she was anxious to get back on board. 'Tho I received every kindness and attention from them both,' she told her sister, 'I cannot help feeling a great desire *to be at home*, however uncomfortable that home may be – but I must submit and pretend to like it. I believe Capt. Austen rather wishes to stay than otherwise.'[40]

Charles returned home after an absence of years to show off his new wife and new family. He was a devoted family man, which sometimes irked Jane: 'I think I have just done a good deed – extracted Charles from his wife and children upstairs and made him get ready to go out shooting.'[41] Nevertheless, she liked Fanny and was always pleased when they visited, noting in one letter that they had arrived to stay at Chawton after a very rough sea passage: 'here they are safe and well, just like their own nice selves, Fanny looking as neat and white this morn as possible, and dear Charles all affectionate, placid, quiet, cheerful good humour'.[42]

Charles and Fanny were in a dilemma as their eldest daughter had been suffering badly from seasickness. Cassandra Austen had offered to babysit her for the winter, but the devoted couple could not bear to leave her. By 1814, Fanny was expecting a fourth baby. Jane heard that she was 'safe in bed with a Girl – It happened on Board, a fortnight before it was expected' (the use of the word 'safe' is a reminder of the danger of childbirth), but tragically Fanny died and the baby followed two weeks later.

Cassandra relayed the news to her old aunt Elizabeth Leigh, who recorded in her diary: 'The Austin family have a great loss in the attach'd and beloved wife of Captn. C: Austin; who died (by a mistake) on board a Ship from whence she ought sooner to have been removed.'[43] Charles had no choice but to send his three bereaved little girls to be looked after by their Palmer grandparents and their aunt Harriet in Bloomsbury. His diary recorded his deep sense of loss: he 'dreamed of my ever lamented dearest Fanny'.[44] Another dream brought back the memory of playing with his dear little daughter Harriet in her bed, as he had often done 'in happier days'.[45] Still grieving, and still away at sea over a year later, he comforted himself by reading *Emma*, which 'arrived in time to a moment': 'I am delighted with her, more so than even with my favourite Pride and Prejudice.'[46] He reread

Cassandra Austen

it three times on a long voyage home. Charles later found comfort by marrying his wife's sister Harriet.

* * *

The highest praise from Jane Austen was when she described her niece Fanny Knight as 'almost another sister' – the 'almost' is important. No one could be as important as Cassandra. The family agreed that in the aftermath of Tom Fowle's death the sisters, always close, drew even closer. 'They seemed to lead a life to themselves, within the general family life, which was shared only by each other,' wrote a perceptive great-niece. 'I will not say their true but their full feelings and opinions were known only to themselves. They alone fully understood what each had suffered and felt and thought.'[47]

From the start of her career, Jane Austen wrote about sisters. 'I would refuse him at once if I were certain that neither of my Sisters would accept him,' says one of 'The Three Sisters' in *Volume the First*. 'I am now going to murder my sister,' announces the narrator of 'A Letter from a Young Lady' among the 'Scraps' in *Volume the Second*.[48] It is highly significant that it was during Cassandra's engagement to Tom Fowle that Jane Austen began drafting what became her first two published novels. Both were about pairs of sisters. One of them certainly and the other quite possibly took the form of letters: 'Elinor and Marianne', probably begun in 1795, was an epistolary novel in the manner of Richardson's *Clarissa* and *Sir Charles Grandison* and Burney's *Evelina*. 'First Impressions', probably begun the following year, may also have been epistolary.

Cassandra played her own part in encouraging Jane in her ambition to become a published author. She was Jane's first reader and she knew 'First Impressions' well. Anna Austen, who lived at the parsonage at Dean, near Steventon, recalled her aunt reading from the manuscript of 'First Impressions' while she was in the room and, as a very small child, not expected to listen: 'Listen however I did, with so much interest, and with so much talk afterwards about "Jane and Elizabeth" that it was resolved for prudence's sake, to read no more of the story in my hearing.'[49] In 1799, Jane wrote to Cassandra, 'I do not wonder at your wanting to read *first impressions* again, so seldom as you have gone through it, and that so long ago.'[50] The idea of her only having 'seldom' read it is clearly a joke: she followed her sister's progress every inch of the way.

Jane Austen was one of the first novelists to write about pairs of sisters. In *Sense and Sensibility* and *Pride and Prejudice*, we are given pairs of sisters whose relationship to one another matters as much as their interest in a romantic match (there was a long tradition in both drama and fiction of contrasting a lively lady with a rational female figure, but they were often friends rather than sisters). Readers have accordingly been tempted to draw parallels between the sisters in the novels and Cassandra and Jane Austen. Invariably it is the younger sisters, such as Elizabeth Bennet and Marianne Dashwood, who are portrayed saying shocking things to their elder sisters, provoking both their outrage and their laughter. This seems very like Jane in her letters to Cassandra.

So it is that the wiser, calmer, exquisitely well-mannered and more cautious elder sisters have been compared to Cassandra. Is not Elinor Dashwood fond of drawing, as Cassandra was? Does not the younger and more tempestuous Marianne Dashwood in *Sense and Sensibility* share her love of music and novels with her creator, the younger sister Jane? And in *Pride and Prejudice* could it be a deliberately witty touch to have given the name *Jane* Bennet to an elder sister resembling Cassandra when Jane herself had a worldview closer to that of the younger sibling? Elizabeth Bennet's view of the world is far more jaded, and she is not unlike her father in making jokes to cover her natural cynicism: 'There are few people whom I really love, and still fewer of whom I think well. The more I see of the world, the more am I dissatisfied with it; and every day confirms my belief of the inconsistency of all human characters, and of the little dependence that can be placed on the appearance of either merit or sense.'[51] That is very much the sort of thing Jane Austen might have said herself in one of her letters.

The Victorian family record comments on the difference between the two sisters: 'They were not exactly alike. Cassandra's was the colder and calmer disposition; she was always prudent and well judging, but with less outward demonstration of feeling and less sunniness of temper than Jane possessed.'[52] 'Prudent and well judging' Cassandra might have been, but it is erroneous to believe that she was somehow less passionate than her sister. Her decision to remain a spinster after the death of her fiancé was deeply romantic.

In *Sense and Sensibility*, Austen depicts three pairs of sisters, the Dashwoods, the Steeles and the Jenningses. Her portrayal of all three pairs reflects upon her theme of reason versus passion. One of the ideas that she was interested in was how people in the same situation act in very different ways. Thus, Marianne and Elinor are both depicted suffering from a broken heart. Elinor shows fortitude and selflessness in her silent suffering, while Marianne freely indulges in her grief.

One of the questions that the novel asks is whether it is possible to have a second attachment. Marianne's belief is that you can only love once, but she is forced to reassess her views, when she does fall in love for the second time:

> Marianne Dashwood was born to an extraordinary fate. She was born to discover the falsehood of her own opinions, and to counteract, by her conduct, her most favourite maxims. She was born to overcome an affection formed so late in life as at seventeen, and with no sentiment superior to strong esteem and lively friendship, voluntarily to give her hand to another! – and *that* other, a man who had suffered no less than herself under the event of a former attachment, whom, two years before, she had considered too old to be married, – and who still sought the constitutional safeguard of a flannel waistcoat![53]

Jane Austen, contrary to what people might expect, was firmly not of the belief that there is only one person in the world whom you can love. She said as much to her niece Fanny Knight when she was advising her on matters of the heart, telling her that her only mistake was to believe that first love is real love. 'Oh! dear Fanny, Your mistake has been one that thousands of women fall into. He was the *first* young Man who attached himself to you. That was the charm, and most powerful it is.' As she then goes on to say, 'it is no creed of mine, as you must be well aware, that such sort of disappointments [in love] kill anybody'.[54]

Yet in *Sense and Sensibility* disappointment in love very nearly does kill someone. Marianne Dashwood, beautiful, passionate, trusting, has her heart broken in the most callous way. There is no other such raw depiction of grief in any of the novels. Marianne almost dies as a result. But her self-discovery includes the realization that she has harmed herself and her beloved sister:

Had I died, – it would have been self-destruction. I did not know my danger till the danger was removed; but with such feelings as these reflections gave me, I wonder at my recovery, – wonder that the very eagerness of my desire to live, to have time for atonement to my God, and to you all, did not kill me at once. Had I died, – in what peculiar misery should I have left you, my nurse, my friend, my sister! – You, who had seen all the fretful selfishness of my latter days; who had known all the murmurings of my heart! – How should I have lived in *your* remembrance![55]

Despite Cassandra's 'Elinor-like fortitude', when it came to her feelings about love and the impossibility of finding a second attachment, she is closer to the 'sensibility' of Marianne than to the 'sense' of Elinor.

The scant evidence that can be drawn regarding Cassandra Austen suggests her deeply romantic nature. Her refusal to entertain another man after Tom Fowle shows that she could never replace him. Jane Austen wrote in *Persuasion*: 'How eloquent could Anne Elliot have been, – how eloquent, at least, were her wishes on the side of early warm attachment, and a cheerful confidence in futurity, against that over-anxious caution which seems to insult exertion and distrust Providence! – She had been forced into prudence in her youth, she learned romance as she grew older – the natural sequel of an unnatural beginning.'[56] After her sister's death, Cassandra wrote beside this in her own copy of the novel: 'Dear dear Jane! This deserves to be written in letters of gold.'[57] To judge from this, Cassandra, not Jane, was the romantic.

A few years after Jane's death, Cassandra Austen risked censure from the family by supporting a romantic attachment between her nephew Edward Knight and his sister Fanny's stepdaughter. Fanny Knight had made an excellent match to Sir Edward Knatchbull, who was a widower with six children. (Their London residence was a fine townhouse in Great George Street, where Lord Byron's body lay on the night before his funeral that brought the streets of London to a standstill.) In 1826 Edward Knight, Fanny's brother, eloped to Gretna Green in the middle of the night with her stepdaughter, Mary Knatchbull. Thus Fanny was sister-in-law and stepmother to the same woman. Edward Knight, Jane Austen's brother who had been adopted and had inherited a fortune, had always been the lucky one. But now he was distraught: the shocking elopement, he wrote, had 'thrown us all into a sad state of agitation and distress'.[58] The Knights and the Knatchbulls were horrified by the match, considering it to be an incestuous union, but Cassandra supported the young lovers. She kindly offered to 'receive the fugitives' at Chawton.[59]

It can hardly be a coincidence that Jane Austen returned to 'Elinor and Marianne', the original version of *Sense and Sensibility*, soon after Cassandra's loss of her great and only love. Was the revised version, eventually published in 1811, both a love letter from Jane to Cassandra – a way of sharing the pain of her broken heart – and a gentle rebuke, a way of suggesting that it was possible to find true love again, that falling in love is something that can happen more than once?

Anna Austen wrote movingly of the sisters' strong bond in her memoir, and paints a memorable picture of them walking in the muddy roads of Steventon in pattens (outdoor shoes), wearing identical bonnets, 'precisely alike in colour, shape and material', and being referred to by their father as 'the girls', though they were in fact women.[60] Jane, with more precision, jokingly gave herself and Cassandra the moniker 'the formidables'. Anna wrote that, 'Their affection for each other was extreme; it passed the common love of sisters; and it had been so from childhood.'[61] But the true indicator of the strength of their attachment is in Cassandra's own words, written after her sister's death, when she had indeed been to Jane 'my nurse, my friend, my sister': 'I *have* lost a treasure, such a Sister, such a friend as never can have been surpassed, – She was the sun of my life, the gilder of every pleasure, the soother of every sorrow, I had not a thought concealed from her, and it is as if I had lost a part of myself.'[62]

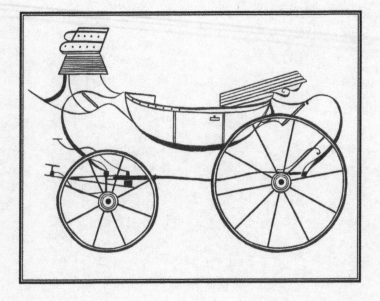

6

The Barouche

The barouche, illustrated here in one of a series of engravings of carriages published by Rudolph Ackermann in 1816, was a very upmarket set of wheels, pretty much the equivalent of a modern convertible. Four-wheeled and shallow, its seats were arranged *vis-à-vis*, so that the passengers on the front seat faced those on the back. It had a soft collapsible half-hood that folded like a bellows over the back seat. There was a high outside box seat in front for the driver. The entire carriage was suspended on C-springs. It was drawn by a pair of high-quality horses and was used principally for leisure driving in the summer. This particular model is a 'high-perch sociable', very fashionable and rather dangerous. Maria Edgeworth's father spoke with horror of the reckless height to which perches had ascended by 1817. 'Carriages', he wrote, 'have arisen to a preposterous elevation. That private phaetons and barouches should be mounted out of the town dust, and above the country hedges, is a dangerous luxury.'[1]

'Mr Clifford lived at Bath; and having never seen London, set off one Monday morning determined to feast his eyes with a sight of that great Metropolis.' So writes the young Jane Austen in a story in *Volume the First* called 'The Memoirs of Mr Clifford'. She continues, 'He travelled in his Coach and Four, for he was a very rich young Man and kept a great many Carriages of which I do not recollect half. I can only remember that he had a Coach, a Chariot, a Chaise, a Landeau, a Landeaulet, a Phaeton, a Gig, a Whiskey, an Italian Chair, a Buggy, a Curricle and a wheelbarrow.'[2] The passage is notable not only for coming to a climax with a bump, and for being one of the first moments when Austen experiments with the intervention of a first-person authorial voice, but also because it reveals her knowledge of the many varieties of road transport vehicles available in the late Georgian era.

In the popular imagination, Jane Austen spent nearly all her life sitting in a parsonage, working on her embroidery, gossiping about the neighbours and writing novels confined to 'three or four families in a country village'. But two of her novels are set predominantly in the fashionable city of Bath, where she lived for several years herself. Another is set in a newly peopled seaside resort, the kind of place where she loved to spend her summer holidays. Throughout the body of her fiction there are frequent trips to London – whether by Mr Clifford feasting his eyes on the great metropolis, Frank Churchill allegedly going up to town for a haircut, or Darcy visiting Elizabeth's city relatives in order to sort out the indelicate problem of Lydia. And even in the 'country' novels, there are frequent expeditions by road to tourist sites near and far (Blaize Castle, Box Hill, the Derbyshire Peak District).

It should not therefore come as a surprise that Austen herself was a very well-travelled woman. In thinking about the forces that shaped her imagination, we should add to her family and her books her experience of the road and of different places. By the time she was ten, she had lived in Reading, Oxford and Southampton. When she was twelve she visited Sevenoaks in Kent, travelling back via London. In later years, we can track her to a house in Goodnestone, also in Kent, but much further east, indeed at the extreme east of southern England. She went into the heart of England, to Adlestrop in Gloucestershire and Stoneleigh in Warwickshire. In 1806 she travelled across the River Trent, the traditional dividing line between north and south: she stayed for over a month in Staffordshire, some 150 miles north of her old family home. According to her nieces, she even went as far as the coast of mid-Wales, 250 miles and in both landscape and custom a world away from the southern shires. She was quite familiar with town and city life, moving with ease from the naval hub of Portsmouth to the spa of Bath to the seaside resorts of the west country to what her contemporary William Cobbett called the 'great wen' of London itself. She was often away from home for months at a time.

At the age of sixteen her travels began in earnest. It was then that her brother Edward wed and began his married life at his elegant brick house called Rowling in the village of Goodnestone in a remote location between Canterbury and Sandwich in Kent. She frequently visited him there and later at his home in Godmersham, halfway between Canterbury and Ashford. Accompanied by a male sibling, she would make London her overnight stop-off on the journey from Hampshire to Kent, usually taking in a theatre visit in the capital. In 1798, 1802, 1803, 1805, 1808, 1809 and 1813, Jane Austen spent lengthy periods at Godmersham, as well as two summer vacations at nearby Rowling. Her letters often give details of travel arrangements. In 1813 she writes of travelling to London with her nieces by coach. The journey took twelve hours: 'the first three stages for 1s – 6d … all 4 within, which was a little crowd'.[3]

Travel was time-consuming, costly and uncomfortable. Ninety per cent of the population never set foot more than a few miles from their own community. But Jane Austen, with her large and widely scattered family, was a good and experienced traveller. The introduction of the turnpike system led to greatly improved roads. Unlike her mother, she did not suffer from travel sickness. She positively enjoyed being away from home. She did not go abroad, because throughout her adult life England was at war with France and there were severe restrictions on continental travel. But she participated in the boom in domestic tourism. Like others of her class, she started taking holidays – usually by the seaside, once close to the mountains of the Peak District.

Jane used her brother's carriages but she also travelled by stage-coach, the equivalent of modern public transport. Journeys were undertaken in 'stages' of ten to fifteen miles after which the horses would be changed, the length of each day's journey being determined by the hours of daylight. This was the cheapest way to travel long-distance. Different rates were charged for seats inside or outside the coach – the expression 'to drop off', to fall asleep, once had a very literal meaning. At the time of Jane Austen's birth there were four hundred registered stage-coaches on the road. They could carry up to eighteen passengers at up to eight miles per hour. It was also possible to travel, either inside or out, in a mail coach, where mailbags would be piled on the roof and luggage was carried in receptacles called boots. The Royal Mail stage-coach, introduced in 1784, hastened the improvement of the road system in the British Isles. As well as facilitating the art of letter-writing, which was so central to Jane Austen's life and the fiction of her time, it was one of the fastest ways to travel.

Coaching inns provided accommodation and refreshment to travellers, as well as stabling and smithies for the horses. But of course the best way to travel, if you could afford it, was in your own carriage. Richer people wanting to avoid public transport could hire their own post-chaise, a small carriage usually pulled by one or two horses. These were small, light and fast. They were driven by a postilion or 'post-boy'. Hired post-chaises were often travelling chariots that had been discarded by gentlemen – they were like a fleet of used cars serving as long-distance taxis. They could be hired for about a shilling a mile.

Genteel women were usually accompanied on the stage-coach. Jane Austen was no exception and her travel plans were nearly always scheduled around a male escort in the shape of her father or one of her brothers. She wanted to ride to London in a stage-coach in 1796, but her brother Frank would not allow it.[4] By contrast, travel in a private post-chaise could be undertaken with a female friend, as suggested by a hilarious letter from Jane to Cassandra following a visit to Martha Lloyd in Ibthorpe: 'Martha has promised to return with me, and our plan is to [have] a nice black frost for walking to Whitchurch, and there throw ourselves into a postchaise, one upon the other, our heads hanging out one door, and our feet at the opposite.'[5] Lady Catherine in *Pride and Prejudice* is horrified at the idea of two young women 'riding post' by themselves.[6]

The Reverend George Austen bought a carriage in 1797 and had the family crest painted on the panels. But he was forced to mothball it or 'lay it down' the following year as the result of the introduction of a new tax.[7] Jane's difficulties arose in returning from her visits to houses such as Rowling. She complained that waiting for Henry to bring her home was the equivalent of 'waiting for Dead-men's shoes'. Her visit in this instance was prolonged: 'I am sorry for it, but what can I do?' Her letters from Rowling and London in this period of her life hint at her frustration: 'My father will be so good as to fetch home his prodigal Daughter from Town, I hope, unless he wishes me to walk the Hospitals, Enter at the Temple, or mount Guard at St James.'[8]

In *Mansfield Park*, Fanny Price is left in the similar predicament of having to wait in Portsmouth until she is fetched by Edmund. Little wonder that Anne Elliot in *Persuasion* truly feels her independence only when she becomes the proud owner of her own 'very pretty landaulette'.[9] A vehicle of one's own was a sign that one had arrived in society. In *Pride and Prejudice* Elizabeth's aunt Mrs Gardiner imagines driving around the park at Pemberley with Mrs Darcy: 'A low phaeton, with a nice little pair of ponies, would be the very thing.'[10] A phaeton was a sporty open carriage, low-slung and fast. Jane joked about the dangers of the road, fantasizing that she might be abducted like a heroine in a sentimental novel if some friends failed to meet her at Greenwich: 'for if the Pearsons were not at home, I should inevitably fall a Sacrifice to the arts of some fat Woman who would make me drunk with Small Beer'.[11]

In the vellum notebooks, Austen loved making jokes about road accidents. In 'Love and Freindship' her two unscrupulous heroines are sitting on a turnpike road when they have the good fortune to witness the 'lucky overturning of a Gentleman's Phaeton': 'Two Gentlemen most elegantly attired but weltering in their blood was what first struck our Eyes – we approached – they were Edward and Augustus –. Yes dearest Marianne they were our Husbands.'[12] She could not know when writing this that she would lose two of the people closest to her in road accidents. Austen's final unfinished novel, *Sanditon*, begins dramatically with a stage-coach being overturned.

There were other dangers involved in travel, chief among them the dreaded footpad or highwayman. Jane Austen's aunt and cousin crossed dangerous Bagshot Heath, renowned as a haunt for highwaymen, alone in a post-chaise. Austen's mother sent an account of the 'courage' of her plucky sister Hancock:

> She set out in a Post Chaise with only her little Bessy [Eliza] … in the middle of Bagshot Heath the Postilion discover'd She had dropped the Trunk from off the Chaise. She immediately sent him back with the Horses to find it, intending to sit in the Chaise till he return'd, but was soon out of patience and began to be pretty much frightened, so began her Walk to the Golden Farmer about two miles off, where she arrived half dead with fatigue, it being in the middle of a very hot day.[13]

In *Northanger Abbey*, Catherine is left 'breathless and speechless' with shock upon learning that she is to be turned out of the house to return home in a carriage on an eleven-hour journey unaccompanied even by a servant: 'A heroine in a hack post-chaise, is such a blow upon sentiment, as no attempt at grandeur or pathos can withstand.'[14] The General's private carriage carries her only as far as Salisbury, and from that point she endures the indignities and dangers of a hack post-chaise: 'after the first stage she had been indebted to the post-masters for the names of the places ... so great had been the ignorance of her route'. In other words, she has to take responsibility for getting herself home by public transport and she is utterly reliant upon the post-masters to tell her where to travel at each 'stage' of the journey home. Catherine's parents express indignation at her 'long and lonely' journey, forcing them to conclude that 'General Tilney had acted neither honourably nor feelingly – neither as a gentleman nor as a parent.'[15] They also worry that she might have left some of her belongings in the pockets of the post-chaise.

Among the other anxieties associated with carriage rides was the possibility of inappropriate words or behaviour in the unusual situation of men and women being pressed tightly together in an enclosed space. One might, for example, find oneself courted by an inebriated clergyman on the way home from a party. Mr Elton follows Emma Woodhouse into a carriage and to her dismay she is forced into a 'tete-a-tete drive':

[Emma] was immediately preparing to speak with exquisite calmness and gravity of the weather and the night; but scarcely had she begun, scarcely had they passed the sweep-gate and joined the other carriage, than she found her subject cut up – her hand seized – her attention demanded, and Mr. Elton actually making violent love to her: availing himself of the precious opportunity, declaring sentiments which must be already well known, hoping – fearing – adoring – ready to die if she refused him.

The abduction of young heroines in a carriage is a cliché that Austen exploits here to great effect, as this becomes a scene of comic misunderstanding. Emma is horrified by Elton's conduct as she mistakenly believes he loves Harriet, while he believes that Emma has given him romantic encouragement:

If there had not been so much anger, there would have been desperate awkwardness; but their straightforward emotions left no room for the little zigzags of embarrassment. Without knowing when the carriage turned into Vicarage-Lane, or when it stopped, they found themselves, all at once, at the door of his house; and he was out before another syllable passed.[16]

It is typically brilliant of Jane Austen to apply to the encounter in the carriage the word 'zigzags', so suggestive of the vehicle's motion as it bumps its way along the country road.

Carriages used for abduction and ultimately rape feature in many of the sentimental novels that Austen loved, particularly those of Richardson, who has two of his heroines abducted by coach. There's a good joke in *Northanger Abbey* to the effect that Catherine would not be the victim of abduction by Frederick Tilney: '*He* cannot be the instigator of the three villains in horsemen's great coats, by whom she will hereafter be forced into a travelling-chaise and four, which will then drive off with incredible speed.'[17]

A privately owned vehicle, the ultimate example of conspicuous consumption, is often a guide to status, and sometimes to character, in the novels. Jane Austen's most wicked villain is John Willoughby. He drives the Regency equivalent of a sports car, a curricle. It was a fast, two-wheeled open carriage for two people. Jane's brother Henry bought one when he became a banker and started moving in a fast set in London – he took Jane for a drive in it in 1813.

Marianne Dashwood in *Sense and Sensibility* exposes herself to gossip when she rides out unchaperoned in Willoughby's curricle. Gentlemen who drove their own carriages were often considered to be both glamorous and dangerous. Foolish John Thorpe in *Northanger Abbey* can't quite aspire to a curricle but he owns a 'well-hung' gig: 'What do you think of my gig, Miss Morland? a neat one, is not it? Well hung; town built; I have not had it a month ... Curricle-hung you see; seat, trunk, sword-case, splashing boards, lamps, silver moulding, all you see complete; the iron-work as good as new.'[18] In the same novel, Henry Tilney drives Catherine around Bath in his curricle, which she finds a rather erotic experience, and a great contrast to being in the gig of the buffoon Thorpe:

A very short trial convinced her that a curricle was the prettiest equipage in the world … But the merit of the curricle did not all belong to the horses; – Henry drove so well, – so quietly – without making any disturbance, without parading to her, or swearing at them; so different from the only gentleman-coachman whom it was in her power to compare him with! … To be driven by him, next to being dancing with him, was certainly the greatest happiness in the world.[19]

* * *

Chawton Cottage stood hard against the road itself, opposite the inn and close by the village pond. From its windows Jane Austen could see all of human life. She wrote to her nephew Edward, with her uncanny insight into the mind of a child: 'We saw a countless number of Postchaises full of Boys pass by yesterday morn – full of future Heroes, Legislators, Fools, and Villains.'[20] Each day a number of coaches passed through nearby Alton – three up and three down each day between London and Southampton and London and Gosport. Two were called the *Age*, two the *Times* and two the *Red Rover*. There were also two night coaches, one of which carried the mail.[21] It made Alton a busy town.

Austen was also alive to the joys and travails of travel. In one of her letters she gave her brother Frank details of a large family exodus in various modes of transport:

My Br[other, Edward], Fanny, Lizzy, Marianne and I composed this division of the Family, and filled his Carriage, inside and out. – Two post-chaises under the escort of George conveyed eight more across the Country, the Chair brought two, two others came on horseback and the rest by Coach – and so by one means or another we are all removed. – It puts me in mind of the account of St Paul's Shipwreck, where all are said by different means to reach the Shore in safety.[22]

On another occasion she went alone on Yalden's stage-coach. It was unusual for a genteel lady to be unescorted. Mr Yalden, who was based in Alton, ran a business in which he drove to London one day and back the next. It seems surprising that she travelled alone to London in a public stage-coach, but she clearly relished the experience:

I had a very good Journey, not crouded, two of the three taken up at Bentley being Children, the others of a reasonable size; and they were all very quiet and civil. – We were late in London, from being a great Load and from changing Coaches at Farnham, it was nearly 4 I believe when we reached Sloane St; Henry himself met me, and as soon as my Trunk and Basket could be routed out from all the other Trunks and Baskets in the World, we were on our way to Hans Place in the Luxury of a nice large cool dirty Hackney Coach. There were 4 in the Kitchen part of Yalden – and I was told 15 at top, among them Percy Benn; we met in the same room at Egham, but poor Percy was not in his usual Spirits ... We took up a young Gibson at Holybourne; and in short everybody either *did* come up by Yalden yesterday, or wanted to come up. It put me in mind of my own Coach between Edinburgh and Sterling.[23]

Her reference here is to a scene in her early novella 'Love and Freindship', which is set inside a busy public stage-coach. The heroine is left alone after the untimely deaths of her nearest friends and relations, whereupon she boards the coach from Stirling to Edinburgh. She takes her place in the dark, where she is disturbed by snoring:

'What an illiterate villain must that Man be! (thought I to myself) What a total Want of delicate refinement must he have, who can thus shock our senses by such a brutal Noise! He must I am certain be capable of every bad Action! There is no crime too black for such a Character!' Thus reasoned I within myself, and doubtless such were the reflections of my fellow travellers.[24]

To the heroine's surprise she finds herself among friends and relations both inside the coach and out:

> Great as was my astonishment, it was yet increased, when on looking out of Windows, I beheld the Husband of Philippa, with Philippa by his side, on the Coach-box and when on looking behind I beheld, Philander and Gustavus in the Basket. 'Oh! Heavens, (exclaimed I) is it possible that I should so unexpectedly be surrounded by my nearest Relations and Connections?' These words rouzed the rest of the Party, and every eye was directed to the corner in which I sat. 'Oh! my Isabel (continued I throwing myself, across Lady Dorothea into her arms) receive once more to your Bosom the unfortunate Laura.'[25]

The absurdity increases as Laura relates her 'history', and is told by Augusta that she is taking a tour to Scotland after having read Gilpin's *Tour to the Highlands*. Rather than travel in a relatively comfortable and private post-chaise, Augusta and her father take the public stage-coach to support their friends who have spent their fortune and taken up a coaching business:

> She told me that having a considerable taste for the Beauties of Nature, her curiosity to behold the delightful scenes it exhibited in that part of the World had been so much raised by Gilpin's Tour to the Highlands, that she had prevailed on her Father to undertake a Tour to Scotland ...
> 'It has only been to throw a little money into their Pockets (continued Augusta) that my Father has always travelled in their Coach to veiw the beauties of the Country since our arrival in Scotland – for it would certainly have been much more agreable to us, to visit the Highlands in a Postchaise than merely to travel from Edinburgh to Sterling and from Sterling to Edinburgh every other Day in a crowded and uncomfortable Stage.'[26]

Gilpin's book cited here is *Observations, relative chiefly to Picturesque Beauty Made in the Year 1776 in Several Parts of Great Britain, particularly in Scotland.*

The Reverend William Gilpin, Rector of Boldre in Hampshire, was a pioneering travel writer whose books encouraged an interest in natural beauty. He was one of the originators of the 'picturesque' movement, defining the picturesque, of course, as 'that kind of beauty which is agreeable in a picture'. He granted that nature was good at producing textures and colours, but argued that it was rarely capable of creating the perfect composition. Some extra help was required from the artist, perhaps in the form of a carefully placed tree. A ruined abbey or castle would add 'consequence'. In one much quoted passage, Gilpin suggested that 'a mallet judiciously used' might render the insufficiently ruinous gable of Tintern Abbey more picturesque.[27] Playwrights and novelists couldn't resist satirizing Gilpin: 'It has just cost me a hundred and fifty pounds to put my ruins in thorough repair,' says a vulgar merchant in Garrick and Colman's comedy – a favourite of Austen's – *The Clandestine Marriage*.[28]

There was a symbiotic relationship between the improvement of roads, the increased availability of carriages and the fashion for picturesque tourism. Jane Austen was a great satirist of Gilpin, much as she admired him. In 'A History of England' she wrote of Henry VIII, 'nothing can be said in his vindication, but that his abolishing of Religious Houses and leaving them to the ruinous depredations of time has been of infinite use to the landscape of England in general, which probably was a principal motive for his doing it': the point was that Gilpin considered nothing to be more picturesque than a ruined abbey.[29] In *Pride and Prejudice*, Elizabeth Bennet notably refuses to join Mr Darcy and the Bingley sisters in a stroll. She justifies her absence with the teasing observation, 'You are charmingly group'd ... The picturesque would be spoilt by admitting a fourth.'[30]

In all sorts of respects, then, Jane Austen's own knowledge and experience of travel gave her opportunities for pointed comment in the novels. 'My dear Edmund,' says the ghastly Mrs Norris in *Mansfield Park*, 'taking out *two* carriages when *one* will do, would be trouble for nothing; and between ourselves, coachman is not very fond of the roads between this and Sotherton; he always complains bitterly of the narrow lanes scratching his carriage, and you know one should not like to have dear Sir Thomas when he comes home find all the varnish scratched off.'[31]

There is nothing like a trip out in a carriage for stoking jealousy between rivals. The Bertram sisters quarrel over who gets to sit next to Henry Crawford when – very ostentatiously – he takes the reins of the barouche:

Wednesday was fine, and soon after breakfast the barouche arrived, Mr. Crawford driving his sisters; and as everybody was ready, there was nothing to be done but for Mrs. Grant to alight and the others to take their places. The place of all places, the envied seat, the post of honour, was unappropriated. To whose happy lot was it to fall? While each of the Miss Bertrams were meditating how best, and with the most appearance of obliging the others, to secure it, the matter was settled by Mrs. Grant's saying, as she stepped from the carriage, 'As there are five of you, it will be better that one should sit with Henry, and as you were saying lately that you wished you could drive, Julia, I think this will be a good opportunity for you to take a lesson.'

Happy Julia! Unhappy Maria! The former was on the barouche-box in a moment, the latter took her seat within, in gloom and mortification; and the carriage drove off.[32]

A lesson in driving, a lesson in the art of flirtation: they are much the same thing. Only a writer who loved the whole business of travel could have written an exchange such as this.

Even during her last illness Jane Austen continued to travel. In May 1816, she went to the spa town of Cheltenham in search of a cure. And eventually she took her final sixteen-mile journey to Winchester to place herself under the care of a highly renowned doctor, Giles King Lyford. James Austen lent Jane and Cassandra his family carriage. They were accompanied by Henry and her nephew Edward, who both rode beside them on horseback. Jane was distressed at the sight of the men riding on horseback in the pouring rain. It makes for a poignant picture: the sick woman enduring yet another uncomfortable journey in what must have been great physical pain and suffering, her devoted relations getting soaked as they followed.

Brother Charles, whose own seven-year-old daughter was very ill, had not been alerted to the severity of Jane's illness. Once he had been informed, he executed his travel plans swiftly: 'Received a letter from Henry acquainting me with Dear Jane's illness took a place in the mail for Winchester ... Arrived at Winchester at 5 in the morning found my Sister very ill ... Rode to Chawton on Henry's Horse … returned to Winchester on top of the Coach … Jane a little better. Saw her twice and in the evening for the last time in this world … Left Winchester at 1/2 past nine by the Telegraph Coach.'[33]

But in surveying the travels of Jane Austen we should not leave her on her last sad journey. One of her happiest letters describes her feelings of independence and liberty in London at the time when her literary career was reaching its peak. She rejoices in the experience of being driven unaccompanied around 'that great Metropolis' in her brother's barouche landau, with the top down: 'I had great amusement among the Pictures; and the Driving about, the Carriage been open, was very pleasant. – I liked my solitary elegance very much, and was ready to laugh all the time, at my being where I was. – I could not but feel that I had naturally small right to be parading about London in a Barouche.'[34]

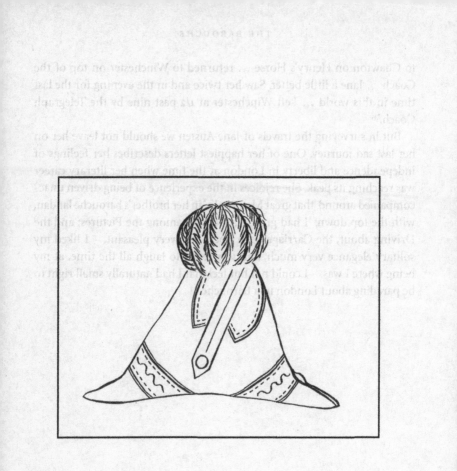

The Cocked Hat

This cocked hat belonged to Captain John Meadows of the Oxfordshire Militia – Henry Austen's regiment. In the 1790s, in both Britain and France, a black-coloured bicorne hat was adopted as the uniform of the officer class. The front and rear halves were turned up and pinned together. The shorter front brim was called the cock – hence 'cocked hat' – and the longer rear brim was known as the fan. A cockade, typically white, was worn at the front.[1]

'I really believe', says Henry Crawford in *Mansfield Park*, 'I could be fool enough at this moment to undertake any character that ever was written, from Shylock or Richard III down to the singing hero of a farce in his scarlet coat and cocked hat.'[2] For the fictional rake Henry Crawford, a scarlet coat and cocked hat are the costume of a hero in a farce. For the real-life Henry Austen, the brother to whom Jane grew closest, it was the uniform of a soldier. One can readily imagine Henry Austen proudly showing his Oxfordshire cocked hat to his sisters Jane and Cassandra.

Most of Jane Austen's adult life was lived against the backdrop of war. 'The profession, either navy or army, is its own justification. It has everything in its favour: heroism, danger, bustle, fashion. Soldiers and sailors are always acceptable in society. Nobody can wonder that men are soldiers and sailors.'[3] Just as Frank's and Charles's careers were instrumental in shaping the naval background to *Mansfield Park* and *Persuasion*, so Henry's military associations had a subtle impact on his sister's literary career.

Henry Austen did not enlist with the regulars. The regular army was typically used for service in the colonies. One recalls Colonel Brandon in *Sense and Sensibility*, serving in the East Indies. Henry, like many men from the gentry, joined the militia. They were essentially the reserves, the Home Guard, the equivalent of the modern Territorial Army in Britain or the National Guard in the United States. They frequently incurred a poor reputation for dancing and drinking in the towns where they were quartered. Wickham in *Pride and Prejudice* has joined his corps expressly for 'the prospect of constant society, and good society'.[4]

Jane Austen danced with redcoats from the South Devons at the Basingstoke Balls. They were often stationed in towns during the winter, moving to coastal camps for the summer months. She also knew the Surrey Regiment, of which her fictional Captain Weston from *Emma* was a member. Redcoats were attacked by Mary Wollstonecraft in *A Vindication of the Rights of Woman* (1792), where she warned about the dangerous attraction of military men for young women: 'nothing can be so prejudicial to the morals of the inhabitants of country towns as the occasional residence of a set of idle superficial young men, whose only occupation is gallantry'.[5]

Much as they were criticized, the militia performed a vital role in protecting the home front from foreign invasion. Austen's militia novel *Pride and Prejudice* drew on Henry Austen's experiences with the Oxfordshire Militia, such as his posting with them to Brighton. Elizabeth Bennet's younger sister envisages the soldiers setting up camp in that famous resort:

In Lydia's imagination, a visit to Brighton comprised every possibility of earthly happiness. She saw, with the creative eye of fancy, the streets of that gay bathing place covered with officers. She saw herself the object of attention, to tens and to scores of them at present unknown. She saw all the glories of the camp; its tents stretched forth in beauteous uniformity of lines, crowded with the young and the gay, and dazzling with scarlet; and to complete the view, she saw herself seated beneath a tent, tenderly flirting with at least six officers at once.[6]

Wickham, we are told 'wanted only regimentals to make him completely charming'.[7] He tells Elizabeth Bennet that 'a military life is not what I was intended for … The church ought to have been my profession.' Jane Austen may have been drawing on her brother Henry's experiences here, as he, too, was destined for the Church until the outbreak of war in 1793.

Henry Austen has acquired a reputation as a rather brilliant but unstable, mercurial character. His change of career from soldier to banker to clergyman and his various failed money-making schemes have all added to this somewhat unfair picture of his hopelessness. His niece, Anna Lefroy, summed him up succinctly: 'Brilliant in conversation, and like his Father, blessed with a hopefulness of temper, which, in adapting itself to all circumstances, even the most adverse, seemed to create a perpetual sunshine of the mind. The Race is not however always to the swiftest … and though so highly gifted by Nature, my Uncle was not prosperous in life.'[8]

The phrase 'perpetual sunshine of the mind', even in adverse circumstances, encapsulates Henry Austen's particular charm. 'Oh! what a Henry,' his sister Jane wrote about him upon hearing that he had gained entrance to a grand society ball in 1814 to celebrate the victory over the French.[9] There is something amused but exasperated in her exclamation. The family view seems to have been that brilliant, amusing Henry had not fulfilled his potential. As well as being tall and handsome, he was cultivated and literary, as his contributions to the *Loiterer* show. He later became in effect Jane Austen's literary agent. Henry's eldest brother, James, inherited Steventon and brother Edward was adopted into a wealthy family, but Henry had to make his own way in life. In 1816 he wrote to the Bishop of Winchester and explained why he had abandoned the Church in his early years: 'Soon after taking my degree … I not being old enough for ordination, and the political circumstances of the times 1793 calling on everyone not otherwise employd to offer his services in the general defence of the country, I accepted a Commission in the Oxfordshire Militia.'[10] Although Henry had no land, being the son of a respectable clergyman he was taken on as a 'Gentleman to be Lieutenant'.

He was first posted to Southampton. The Oxfordshire's task was to escort a thousand French prisoners of war to Stapleton Prison near Bristol. Late that summer of 1793, the Oxfords were assigned to Brighton. We don't know Jane Austen's whereabouts in that year, so there is no way of knowing whether she visited him in the resort she uses as the scene for Lydia's elopement with Wickham.

Then in 1795 Henry was appointed acting Regimental Paymaster. Up to £15,000 could pass through his hands in a year. Henry's promotion was great testament to his trustworthiness and competence. The winter of 1794–5 was long and cold. The Oxfords were in barracks at East Blatchingford, near Brighton. The conditions there were appalling, as the buildings were unfinished and many necessities such as cooking houses and hospital facilities were lacking. Henry asked for and was granted two months' leave to continue his studies at Oxford. In his absence, a serious riot took place among the men of his militia. It made headline news and caused great damage to the reputation of his regiment. In time of war, mutiny in the ranks was the worst fear of the government.

The crop failures of the previous year, due to bad weather and poor harvests, led to food shortages and high prices. That year the Prime Minister William Pitt the Younger even put a tax on hair powder, which was made from wheat and considered to be wasteful in wartime. A number of food riots occurred, where mobs seized flour or bread, sometimes damaging or destroying mills or bakeries. Anxiety about the revolution in France meant that the authorities were more concerned than usual, and were ready to take a tough line. Increasingly, magistrates would call upon the militia or even the regular army to help restore order.

Things came to a head in April 1795. Henry was sent a message at Oxford, instructing his immediate return to his regiment. He pleaded illness. A note appeared against his name on the muster call: 'Austen, sick at Oxford'.[11] On Friday 17 April four hundred men left their barracks in Blatchingford and marched 'in a disorderly manner' to nearby Seaford and Newhaven. All the flour and other food that could be found was seized by the insurgents and sold at reduced prices to the poor. The riots lasted for two days. Ale was freely distributed and officers tried unsuccessfully to regain order.

Finally, a battery of the Royal Horse Artillery was set up on the hills overlooking the town. They fired shots to warn the rioters of their presence. A detachment of the Lancashire Regiment of Fencible Dragoons then rode into town and captured the mutineers.

The authorities considered disbanding the regiment, but it was finally decided to disarm them and make an example of the ringleaders. Ten thousand soldiers (including Royal Artillery, five militia and three fencible regiments, as well as the 12th Light Dragoons) were marched to Goldstone Bottom, Hove, to witness the executions – and help keep the peace, since the Sussex people were highly sympathetic to the prisoners in the light of their distribution of bread to the poor. On 13 June, the punishments were carried out. Of the six to be flogged, two were pardoned, one remanded into custody and the other three received 300 lashes each. One man was transported to Australia. Edward Cooke, a former blanket weaver, and Chipping Norton's Sam Parish were condemned to death. The day before the execution, Cooke wrote to his brother: 'I am going to die for what the regiment done. I am not afraid to meet death for I have done harm to no person and that is a great comfort to me.'[12]

Though he had been absent when the riot took place, Henry Austen was among the thousands of soldiers who watched as the men were executed by firing squad. Cooke and Parish were first made to witness the floggings. Then they were forced to kneel on their own coffins and were shot by ten comrades, who had been selected from among the other mutineers. The audience of soldiers marched around the bodies. The High Sheriff of Sussex noted down an eyewitness account of the 'poor fellows': 'I am just returned from the ground where two soldiers were shot this morning, about quarter past eight. One of them knelt down upon one coffin and one upon the other, and they both instantly fell dead. Though left there, lest there be any remains of life, a firelock was left close to the head of each immediately after.'[13]

The news was widely reported and Jane Austen would have been well aware of the incident. As with the Mount Street riots, witnessed by Eliza de Feuillide, the press drew comparisons with the revolution in France, as echoed in *Northanger Abbey* in Henry Tilney's 'streets of London flowing with blood' speech.

That summer, Henry Austen was back with the Oxfords at Sheerness Camp. They underwent an intense period of drill and training, aimed at restoring discipline and credibility: 'no care shall now be wanting to restore the good Order and Discipline of the Regiment, trusting that before long it will retrieve its lost Character, and recover from the Disgrace under which, by late Misconduct, it now deservedly lays'.[14]

In Nottingham in the same year, 1795, there were bread riots that were put down by the 12th Dragoons. In *Northanger Abbey*, the rake Frederick Tilney is one of the raffish Prince of Wales's Regiment, the 12th Dragoons

– 'the hope of the nation' as Austen drily remarks, 'called up from Northampton to quell the insurgents'.[15] There was indeed a cavalry barracks built at Northampton. It is a mark of Jane Austen's realism that in writing about Frederick Tilney's army career she is highly specific about military leaves of absence. Frederick is on leave in March, but this was the month during which all army leaves expired, so in a letter dated early April Isabella duly writes that Frederick 'went away to his regiment two days ago'.[16]

Jane Austen wrote her first version of *Pride and Prejudice* ('First Impressions') in 1797, exactly at the time when her brother was firmly ensconced in military life. Her detailed knowledge of the army may well have been derived from his experiences. The presence of the militia, which enlivens the dreary countryside and the romantic lives of the young women, is brilliantly captured. The details of the soldiers dancing and flirting at the balls, the young private who is flogged, the cross-dressing antics of the young Bennet girls' favourite redcoat, Denny, the decampment to Brighton in the summer months: all would have elicited a smile of pleasurable familiarity from Henry when he read the book. At the end of the novel, the unscrupulous rake Wickham plans to quit the militia to go into the regulars: 'He has the promise of an ensigncy in General —'s regiment, now quartered in the North.'[17] It cost somewhere in the region of £500 to buy such a commission and Mrs Gardiner informs Elizabeth that Mr Darcy has paid for it.

Henry Austen planned to leave the militia and enter the regulars. He first planned to purchase the Adjutancy of the Oxfordshire Regiment, a senior administrative role. But, lacking the necessary financial backing, he entertained hopes of joining the regulars. He told Jane of his plans, and she duly informed Cassandra:

Henry is still hankering after the Regulars, and as his prospect of purchasing the adjutancy of the Oxfordshire is now over, he has got a scheme in his head about getting a lieutenancy and adjutancy in the 86th, a new-raised regiment, which he fancies will be ordered to the Cape of Good Hope. I heartily hope that he will, as usual, be disappointed in this scheme.[18]

Again, there is that tone of exasperation. This is another of Henry's failed 'schemes' and Jane is heartily grateful that he is not to be shipped off to the heat and disease of the colonies.

Soldier, banker, clergyman: Henry Austen

One of the reasons why he may have been attracted to the regulars was to get over his heartache. Henry had renewed his love interest in cousin Eliza, who rejected his proposal of marriage around 1795. A year later, with his usual capacity to overcome adversity, he was engaged to a Miss Mary Pearson. But he carried on visiting Eliza whenever he was in London and by October the engagement to Mary was off. Following a couple of important promotions, Eliza was writing letters to Phylly Walter full of news of Henry. Having previously thought that his brother James might make the better match, her favour seemed to be turning towards Henry. His abandonment of the Church and the potential for promotion in the army played a part – after all, her first marriage had proved her love of a soldier. Eliza was delighted at his prospects: 'Captn. Austen has just spent a few days in Town; I suppose you know that our Cousin Henry is now Captain, Pay Master, and Adjutant ... I believe he has now given up all thoughts of the Church, and he is right for he certainly is not so fit for a Parson as a Soldier.'[19] The foreshadowing of Mary Crawford and Edmund Bertram in

Mansfield Park is hardly coincidental. The beautiful coquette begs the younger son to quit ordination for the army: 'I am just as much surprised now as I was at first that you should intend to take orders. You really are fit for something better. Come, do change your mind.'[20]

By 1797, Eliza and Henry had grown closer and she finally agreed to marry him. She wrote to her godfather, Warren Hastings, to tell him the good news: 'the excellence of his Heart, Temper and Understanding, together with his steady attachment to me, his Affection for my little Boy … have at last induced me to an acquiescence which I have withheld for more than two years'.[21] Jane's little fantasy in *Volume the First* of the union of 'Henry and Eliza' had turned to reality.

To Jane Austen's delight, Eliza retained her coquettish manner. Though she professed to have 'left off trade' (her expression for flirtation), she adored male attention and still loved to shock prudish Phylly: 'if I was married to my third husband instead of my husband I should still be in love with him … alas he is married as well as myself'.[22]

She firmly believed that the marriage to Henry was a success because he bowed to her strong will, 'to say nothing of the pleasure of having my own way in every thing, for Henry well knows that I have not been accustomed to controul and should probably behave rather awkwardly under it, and therefore like a wise Man he has no will but mine, which to be sure some people would call spoiling me, but [I] know it is the best way of managing me'.[23] She called Henry by his name: 'I have an aversion to the name *Husband* and never make use of it.'[24]

Henry Austen resigned his commission in 1801. It was time to spend more time with his new wife. But he retained his strong connections with the military. Within a month of his resignation, he reappeared in the pay list of the Oxfordshire Regiment of the Militia, in a new role: 'Agent: H. T. Austen and Co.'[25] Together with Henry Maunde, another ex-officer, he had set himself up as a banker. Their first lucrative account was the handling of the regiment's payroll. They also made a secret agreement with a certain Charles James 'to profit from speculation in army commission brokerage and in the agency of half pay'.[26] James had held captaincies in two different militias. He was at this time working on a *Military Dictionary*, which was completed the following year and would go through many editions. It was published by Thomas Egerton, 'Bookseller to the Ordnance, Military Library, near Whitehall'.[27]

PRIDE

AND

PREJUDICE:

A NOVEL.

IN THREE VOLUMES.

BY THE

AUTHOR OF " SENSE AND SENSIBILITY."

VOL. I.

London:

PRINTED FOR T. EGERTON,
MILITARY LIBRARY, WHITEHALL.
1813.

The most enduring publication of
Egerton's Military Library

This was the surprising connection that got Jane Austen into print for the first time. Few modern readers are aware that *Sense and Sensibility* and its successor *Pride and Prejudice*, among the most beloved works of romantic fiction in the English language, originally bore title pages announcing the publisher as 'T. Egerton, Military Library, Whitehall'.

* * *

Henry and Eliza moved to a new house in the fashionable London location of Upper Berkeley Street. They invested in over three thousand pounds' worth of '5% Stock' – the equivalent of about two hundred thousand pounds ($300,000) in today's terms. The six-monthly dividends provided them with a stable income. The banking business, meanwhile, was highly speculative. Promissory notes were written at will and large sums were advanced to people with very questionable credit records, including £6,000 to the notorious spendthrift Lord Moira. He never repaid the bank loan. Given the volatility of the credit market, the agency for army payroll provided some much needed stability – though it also meant that when the war came to an end and a huge part of the army was discharged or put on to half-pay, the handling fees plummeted. This would be a major cause of the collapse of the bank. In March 1816, Henry would be declared bankrupt.

Eliza was a remarkable person and a good mother. When her son Hastings died in 1801, the last link to Jean-François,[28] she refused platitudes from her cousin Phylly that his death must have been a 'desirable relief'. 'So awful a dissolution of a near and tender tie must ever be a severe shock,' she replied.[29] Jane was deeply moved at the loss. She continued to adore her 'outlandish cousin', who was now also her sister.

She visited the Henry Austens in London where they lived 'quite in style' with a French chef. As will be seen, they fostered her love of the theatre. After her own father's death, Jane took it upon herself to send Eliza a mourning brooch. She also retained special fondness for Eliza's housekeeper, a French émigrée called Madame Bigeon.

On one memorable occasion, when she was on the brink of becoming a professional author, Jane stayed with Henry and Eliza. In her long struggle to get published, it was Henry's connections with Thomas Egerton's Military Library that provided her breakthrough. Some pressure from the banker was enough to persuade Egerton, more used to publishing such volumes as *The Royal Military Chronicle* and James's *Military Dictionary*, to take on *Sense and Sensibility*.[30]

Jane was in town to correct proofs for Egerton when she wrote to Cassandra with details of a fabulous party that Eliza had thrown for eighty people. In preparation Jane and Eliza had walked into London to buy chimney lights. Jane was excited by the musical entertainment: '5 professionals, 3 of them Glee-singers … One of the Hirelings, is a Capital on the Harp, from which I expect great pleasure.'[31] She later described the cut flowers and the elegance of the company: 'I was quite surrounded by acquaintance, especially Gentlemen.'[32]

On another occasion, she accompanied sister-in-law Eliza on a visit to the Comte d'Antraigues and his wife, an opera singer. Jane liked them apart from their habit of 'taking quantities of snuff'. She reported that 'Monsieur the old Count, is a very fine looking man, with quiet manners, good enough for an Englishman.'[33] A year later, the Count and his wife were stabbed to death in a brutal murder by an Italian servant, who then committed suicide. There were rumours that this murder had a political motive.

It must have been gratifying that Eliza saw her clever cousin in print, having done so much to encourage her as a child. But by the spring of 1812, just as *Sense and Sensibility* received its first reviews, Eliza was ill, probably with breast cancer. She endured a long and painful illness, and Jane was asked to come up from Hampshire to be with her in her last days. She died in April 1813, two months after the publication of *Pride and Prejudice*. Jane stayed with Henry that September, sleeping in Eliza's bed.

Eliza was a muse for Jane Austen and it has often been suggested that, as well as dedicating the youthful story 'Love and Freindship' to her, Jane used details of her vivacious cousin for two of her fictional characters: the fascinating widow Lady Susan, and Mary Crawford in *Mansfield Park*, the novel that she was working on in the last year of Eliza's life. Jane Austen was adept at drawing *femmes fatales* such as these. Both characters are spirited, irreverent, charming and amoral. They resist marriage as an infringement of their liberty. Like the real Eliza, the fictional Mary plays the harp, is elegant and fashionable, adores London, laces her vocabulary with French phrases, is witty, loves amateur dramatics and enchants every man she meets. It is unlikely that Jane Austen could have drawn an anti-heroine so beguiling as Mary Crawford without her cousin Eliza.

And then there is their disdain for clergymen. After her death Henry entered the Church, something that would have been most unlikely while Eliza was alive. This third and final career began in December 1816, when he took orders at Winchester or Salisbury. Jane lived long enough to hear him preach at the village church in Chawton. She had always considered him an eloquent speaker. Jane's favourite brother and the member of the family who had had the most influence in furthering her literary ambitions was in constant attendance throughout the final two months of her illness in 1817. Henry, Cassandra and the mysterious housekeeper Madame Bigeon were the only names mentioned in Jane Austen's will. But of all the surprising connections in her life, few are greater than that which led, by a crooked path, from Henry's donning of the cocked hat of the Oxfordshires to the publication of *Pride and Prejudice* in Egerton's Military Library.

Steventon Parſonage near Overton, Hants

To be SOLD by AUCTION,
By Mr STROUD.

On the premiſes, on Tueſday the 5th of May, 1805,
and two following days, at eleven o'clock.

The neat HOUSHOLD FURNITURE, well made
Chariot (with box to take off) and Harneſs, Volumes
of Books Stump of Hay, Fowling Pieces, three Norman
Cows and Calves, one Horſe, and other Effects.

8

The Theatrical Scenes

The auction for the sale of the contents of Steventon parsonage took place on the premises, conducted by Mr Stroud of Newbury. Advertisements had appeared in the local papers. The one illustrated here is from the *Reading Mercury*, the newspaper read by the Austen family. The sale was scheduled to last for three days, commencing at eleven o'clock each morning, from Tuesday 5 May 1801. The Reverend George Austen had announced that he was going to retire and that the family would be moving to rented premises in the city of Bath. Jane Austen, now aged twenty-five, would have to say goodbye to the family home. Apart from her time at boarding school and those visits to relations, she had lived in the parsonage at Steventon since the day when she was born.

For all its prosaic dreariness, the sale advertisement is a curiously moving testament to all that she was losing. Her father's nearly new carriage is there, the greater part of his library, all the household goods and even the livestock from his smallholding: 'The neat HOUSEHOLD FURNITURE, well made Chariot (with box to take off) and Harness, 200 volumes of Books, Stump of Hay, Fowling Pieces, three Norman Cows and Calves, one Horse, and other Effects.' The loss of the books would have been a particular blow to Jane. And among the 'four-post and field bed-steads, with dimity, moreen and other furnitures, fine feather beds and bedding, mattresses, pier and dressing glasses' would have been her own bed and the mirror in front of which she dressed. The table at which the family dined was there, the mahogany sideboard and the Wedgwood crockery, the card table at which they played. Also Jane's pianoforte in its 'handsome case (by Ganer)', her music, the huge six-doored bookcase from her father's library, and finally, presumably from the barn, '13 ironbound casks, an end of hops, set of theatrical scenes etc. etc.'.

A set of theatrical scenes. Years before, young James Austen had composed a 'Prologue to the Tragedy of Matilda, acted at Steventon Hants. Spoken by Edward Austen':

When Thespis first professed the mimic art,
Rude were his Actors, and his stage a cart;
No scene gay painted, to the eye displayed
The waving honours of the sylvan glade.[1]

The scenes in the barn, what would now be called flats, perhaps 'gay painted', are a reminder of the family theatricals of Jane Austen's youth. James, who was to take over the parish and the rectory, had clearly put such childish things away. His days as stage manager, director, writer and actor were over now that he was ordained as a clergyman.[2]

The 'set of theatrical scenes' suggests the attention to detail and the high ambition of the Steventon theatricals. Jane Austen's first-hand knowledge of the art of amateur dramatics enabled her to create her vivid and compelling account of private theatricals in *Mansfield Park*. 'A love of the theatre is so general,' she writes in that novel.[3] Jane Austen loved Shakespeare, and spoke of him as running through our veins, 'a part of an Englishman's constitution' with whom we are 'intimate by instinct'.[4] She was a supporter of the public theatres, in London and also in the provinces, at Bath and Southampton. Her taste was eclectic; she enjoyed farces, musical comedy and pantomimes considered to be 'low' drama, as much as she enjoyed Shakespeare and the leading contemporary comic dramatists such as George Colman and David Garrick.[5]

From an early age, Jane Austen showed her awareness of what the newspapers called 'the Theatrical Ton' – the fashion for private theatricals – that obsessed genteel British society in the late Georgian era. In a short story dating from 1792, she has one of her characters demand a purpose-built theatre as part of her marriage settlement.[6] Here, she is satirizing the extreme end of the craze, whereby members of the gentrified classes and the aristocracy built their own scaled-down imitations of the London play-houses. The most famous was that erected in the 1770s at Wargrave in Berkshire by the spendthrift Earl of Barrymore, at a reputed cost of £60,000. It seated seven hundred people.

In *Mansfield Park* the public interest in aristocratic private theatricals is regarded ironically: 'To be so near happiness, so near fame, so near the long paragraph in praise of the private theatricals at Ecclesford, the seat of the Right Hon. Lord Ravenshaw, in Cornwall, which would of course have immortalized the whole party for a least a twelvemonth.'[7] Jane Austen carefully distinguishes between the fashionable elite theatricals of the aristocracy, which were mercilessly lampooned by the press, and the more modest efforts of the gentry. Despite Tom Bertram's best efforts to professionalize his theatre, the young people at Mansfield Park fall back on the measure of converting a large room of the family home for the production of *Lovers' Vows*. This is one of Jane Austen's private family jokes, as this is exactly what the Austens did when they first began to put on plays at Steventon.

Jane Austen was only seven when the first play was performed in the dining room of the rectory at Steventon. Later on, the Austens used the family barn, which is no doubt why the theatrical scenes were still there at the time of the 1801 sale. The theatricals at Steventon were not solely a family affair. The Cooper cousins and some local friends, the Digweeds, helped to make up numbers, while George Austen's pupils joined in. Tom Fowle, who was to become engaged to Cassandra, was part of the Steventon theatricals and spoke the epilogue to *Matilda*. It helped that George Austen always encouraged his pupils in the art and practice of good reading aloud.

James and Henry Austen, the clever boys of the family, were the ringleaders. James, who fancied himself as a writer and poet, wrote his own prologues and epilogues. They survive, so we know several of the plays that were performed at Steventon. After the tragedy of *Matilda*, Sheridan's hilarious comedy *The Rivals* was performed 'by some young Ladies and Gentlemen at Steventon' in July 1784. By the time that the Austens had converted the barn into a theatre they were performing *The Wonder: A Woman Keeps a Secret*, by Susanna Centlivre, one of the finest dramatists of the early eighteenth century, and *The Chances*, an adaptation by the great David Garrick of a comedy that ultimately went back to Shakespeare's collaborator John Fletcher. Jane Austen's cousin Phylly Walter wrote: 'My uncle's barn is fitting up quite like a theatre, and all the young folks are to take their part.'[8] Eliza de Feuillide egged on her cousins. She also tried to persuade shy Phylly to take part in the Steventon theatricals: 'You know we have long projected acting this Christmas at Hampshire ... on finding there were two unengaged parts I immediately thought of you.' She told Phylly that she need not worry about costumes: 'Do not let your dress neither disturb you, as I think I can manage it so that the Green Room should provide you with what is necessary for acting.'[9] She sounds just like Mary Crawford twisting the arm of the shy Fanny Price into participating in *Lovers' Vows*.

Mrs Austen was very keen on the young people taking part in the acting scheme, and was irritated when Phylly reported back that she was reluctant about 'appearing in public'. Eliza wrote to tell Phylly to 'bring yourself to act, for my Aunt Austen declares "she has not room for any *idle young people*"'. Eliza was convinced that it was interfering Aunt Walter who prevented her daughter from joining in the theatricals: 'The insuperable objection to my proposal is, some scruples of your Mother's about your acting – If this is the case I can only say it is [a] Pity so groundless a prejudice should be harboured in so enlightened [and so] enlarged a mind.'[10]

The theatricals seemed to be a Christmas event. During 1787–9 the Steventon company performed a wide variety of comedies: *The Wonder*, *Bon Ton*, *The Chances*, *The Tragedy of Tom Thumb*, *The Sultan* and *High Life below Stairs*. Eliza took on the female leading roles and flirted outrageously with her cousins, James and Henry. James, home from his foreign travels, wrote a prologue and epilogue for *The Wonder*. Eliza played the spirited heroine, Donna Violante, who risks her own marriage and reputation by choosing to protect her friend Donna Isabella from an arranged marriage to a man she despises. The play engages in the battle-of-the-sexes debate that Eliza and the Austens particularly enjoyed. Women are 'inslaved' to 'tyrant men'.[11] Whether they be fathers, husbands or brothers, men 'usurp authority and expect a blind obedience from us, so that maids, wives, or widows, we are little better than slaves'.[12] The play's most striking feature is a saucy proposal of marriage from Isabella, though made on her behalf by Violante in disguise, to a man she barely knows: an anticipation of *Lovers' Vows*, with its daring proposal from a vivacious young woman. In the New Year, *The Wonder* was followed up by Garrick's *The Chances*, a racy comedy depicting jealous lovers, secret marriages and confused identities. It is likely that Eliza played the role of the low-born 'second Constantia', a favourite of the great comic actress Dora Jordan. The flirtation, the battle-of-the-sexes banter and the intimacy between cousins are later recreated in the Mansfield theatricals: all observed by the rather envious outsider, Fanny Price.

We know from the vellum notebooks that young Jane was writing short playlets, which may well have been performed as afterpieces to the main plays. The part of the diminutive hero Tom Thumb in Fielding's outrageous burlesque was often played by a child, whose high-pitched voice added to the comic incongruity of the valiant hero – it is tempting to think that either she or little Charles took on the role.

Jane Austen's intimate knowledge of the drama is evident in her habit of repeating key phrases from plays, often those considered for performance at Steventon. Twenty years after Hannah Cowley's popular *Which is the Man?* was considered and then rejected for performance, Jane was still quoting one of its catchphrases, 'tell him what you will'. She also loved to quote from Cowley's other hit comedy, *The Belle's Stratagem*: 'Mr Doricourt has travelled; he knows best.'[13]

The Steventon theatricals took place between 1782 and 1790, coinciding with the period in which Jane Austen's earliest literary works were written. It is sometimes assumed that she turned against amateur theatricals when she grew older. But this is not the case. When she was well into her thirties, she 'drew the character of Mrs Candour in Sheridan's *School for Scandal*'. She 'assumed the part with great spirit'.[14] This was the recollection of Sir William Heathcote of Hursley Park, Hampshire, after he was invited to a Twelfth Night party. Mrs Candour is a witty gossip-monger who professes she can never speak ill of a friend, and then spreads idle gossip with enormous relish. This party was either at Manydown, home of the Austens' friends the Bigg-Withers, or in the big house at Chawton.

There was an intimate relationship between the comic novel and the comic theatre. Henry in his biographical notice remarked on his sister's 'gifts of the comic muse'. She was from an age when reading novels and plays aloud was an essential part of social recreation and entertainment. One of her nieces remembered her aunt reading a comic part from Fanny Burney's *Evelina* and said 'it was almost like being at a play'. The Edward Austens held an annual celebration at the climax of the Christmas season, with masquerades, dressing up and private theatricals. In contrast to his brother James, who sold off the theatrical scenes and gave up his love of theatre, Edward and his large family loved to act. His eldest daughter, Fanny, recorded a Twelfth Night party in 1806, in what was then the family home at Godmersham in Kent. There was a masquerade in which Fanny and her brother Edward were the Shepherd King and Queen, her mother was a Savoyarde, Miss Sharp a witch, Henry Austen a Jew and another uncle cross-dressed as a Jewess. There were parts for all of the children, except baby Louisa. Little Charles was a cupid, with a 'little pair of wings and a bow and arrow'. They paraded into the library which was lit up with 'a throne and a grove of Orange trees'.[15]

Jane Austen was there for a party the previous summer when there was dressing up and acting. Fanny recorded in her diary a game of school in which her aunts, grandma and governess, Anne Sharp, dressed up and acted:

Wednesday 26 June We had a whole holiday. Aunts and Grandmama played at school with us. Aunt C was Mrs Teachum the Governess, Aunt Jane, Miss Popham the teacher, Aunt Harriet, Sally the Housemaid, Miss Sharpe the Dancing Master, the Apothecary and the Searjeant, Grandmama Betty Jones the pie woman, and Mama the bathing woman. They dressed in Character and we had a most delightful day – After dessert we acted a play called Virtue Rewarded.[16]

Anne Sharp, Fanny Knight's real governess, was clearly fond of taking on the cross-dressed roles. It was at this time that she met and forged a close friendship with Jane Austen, who no doubt relished playing the role of a teacher. That Godmersham summer Jane Austen also participated in performances of The Spoilt Child and Innocence Rewarded. Bickerstaff's The Spoilt Child was a great favourite on the London stage, popularized by Dora Jordan who played the cross-dressed role of the child, Little Pickle.

It was during this visit to Kent that Jane Austen was reading Thomas Gisborne's dour Enquiry into the Duties of the Female Sex. Gisborne was a close friend and Staffordshire neighbour of her Evangelical cousin Edward Cooper. No doubt she would have been amused to discover his assertion that play-acting was injurious to the female sex through encouraging vanity and destroying diffidence, 'by the unrestrained familiarity with persons of the other sex which inevitably results from being joined with them in the drama'.[17] He particularly recommended that children should not be allowed

The lobby of the Theatre Royal, Drury Lane
(where in *Sense and Sensibility* Sir John Middleton
tells Willoughby that Marianne is dying)

to act in plays. Jane had been determined not to read Gisborne, but professed herself rather coolly, maybe ironically, to Cassandra as 'pleased with it'.[18] But she did not share his views on the dangers of play-acting. It may well have been at this time that she helped Anna Austen with the writing of a five-act burlesque play, *Sir Charles Grandison or the Happy Man*. Much as she loved Richardson's novel about a virtuous man, she could not resist the challenge of abridging its seven long volumes into a very short play and parodying its morality and sentimentality.

Jane Austen was as avid a theatregoer as she was a participant in amateur dramatics. She loved nothing more than to take her nephews and nieces to see a show. The first surviving documented reference to her theatregoing sees her visiting Astley's theatre in Lambeth in August 1796: 'we are to be at Astley's to night, which I am glad of'.[19] Astley's was one of London's so-called 'illegitimate' theatres – it did not hold a Royal Patent to perform serious drama, which was the unique preserve of the Theatres Royal at Drury Lane and Covent Garden, together with the Haymarket for the short summer season. Astley's accordingly provided a wide variety of entertainment from pantomime, acrobatics and sword-fighting to musicals. Jane Austen had no snobbery about this kind of popular theatre.

It is revealing that she chose Astley's as the location for a major turning point in *Emma*. It is there that Harriet Smith accidentally meets Robert Martin and they rekindle their relationship. Astley's was known for its socially diverse audience: the genteel John Knightleys take their children there, alongside the farmer Robert Martin. It was friendly and unpretentious. Precisely because of its status as a minor, illegitimate theatre, it was a place where a yeoman farmer and a girl who is without rank (carrying the 'stain of illegitimacy', as we are reminded in the same chapter) could mingle freely with the gentry. The setting of the scene is Austen's way of ridiculing her heroine's snobbery towards the kind-hearted Robert Martin.

In her journals, Fanny Knight complained that she found Drury Lane too immense and preferred 'the dear enchanting Haymarket'.[20] Haymarket or the 'Little Theatre' was the only theatre licensed to open in the summer months. In *Pride and Prejudice* Austen shows her scrupulous sense of realism when Lydia, who is in London for the summer season, remarks, 'To be sure London was rather thin, but however the Little Theatre was open.'[21] By contrast, when Elizabeth Bennet and her aunt Mrs Gardiner have a long and important conversation in London, it is in one of the boxes of the patented theatres, though we are not told whether it is Covent Garden or Drury Lane. Equally, Willoughby in *Sense and Sensibility* discovers the news of Marianne Dashwood's serious collapse when he bumps into John Middleton in the lobby of Drury Lane. Fanny Burney had staged a vivid suicide at Drury Lane in *Cecilia*. Jane Austen refrains from melodrama of this kind, but still uses the theatre as a place where key encounters and important conversations take place. In *Northanger Abbey* it is in the Theatre Royal Bath that John Thorpe falsely informs General Tilney that Catherine is an heiress, and the same location is the background for a reconciliation between Catherine and Henry Tilney.

In 1808, Jane Austen visited Henry and Eliza Austen at 16 Michael Place in the London suburb of Brompton. The famous actress and singer Jane Pope lived next door to them at number 17. Pope had been the original Mrs Candour in *The School for Scandal*, that role which Jane Austen took on in an amateur production the following year. On the other side, at 15 Michael Place was Elizabeth Billington, a celebrated soprano singer. The comedian John Liston lived just along the road at number 21. Jane stayed until July, enjoying the rounds of dinner-parties, theatre trips and concerts arranged by Henry and Eliza.

Henry owned his own box at one of the illegitimate theatres, the Pantheon in Oxford Street.[22] The Pantheon was a fine building, often used for masquerades and concerts. Henry's passion for the theatre endured throughout his life. Whenever Jane (or Cassandra) was in town, he was to be found arranging seats at the various London theatres. Had the majority of Jane Austen's letters not been destroyed after her death in 1817, we would have had a much more detailed sense of the passion that she shared with the brother who was closest to her. But there is enough evidence in the surviving letters to suggest that she was utterly familiar with contemporary actors and with the range and repertoire of the theatres.

In April 1811, when she was in London, staying with Henry and Eliza again – they had now moved to Sloane Street, though his bank was in Henrietta Street – she expressed a desire to see Shakespeare's *King John* at Covent Garden. She was unwell so she sacrificed a trip to the Lyceum Theatre in the hope of saving her strength for something special:

> To night I might have been at the Play, Henry had kindly planned our going together to the Lyceum, but I have a cold which I should not like to make worse before Saturday ... Our first object to day was Henrietta St to consult with Henry, in consequence of a very unlucky change of the Play for this very night – Hamlet instead of King John – and we are to go on Monday to Macbeth, instead, but it is a disappointment to us both.[23]

Her preference for *King John* over *Hamlet* may seem curious by modern standards, but it can be explained by one of the intrinsic features of Georgian theatres: the orientation of the play towards the star actor in the lead role. Her disappointment is accounted for in the next letter to Cassandra: 'I have no chance of seeing Mrs Siddons. – She *did* act on Monday, but as Henry was told by the Boxkeeper that he did not think she would, the places, and all thoughts of it, were given up. I should particularly have liked seeing her in Constance, and could swear at her with little effort for disappointing me.'[24] It was not so much *King John* she wanted to see as the great Sarah Siddons in one of her most celebrated roles as Queen Constance, the quintessential portrait of a tragic mother.

Austen's phrase 'I should particularly have liked seeing her in Constance' suggests that she had seen her before in some other role: perhaps as Lady

Macbeth, which she performed several times that 1811 season. That she had seen Siddons perform is also suggested in a comment she made about her Knight nieces: 'That puss Cassy, did not shew more pleasure in seeing me than her Sisters, but I expected no better, – she does not shine in the tender feelings. She will never be a Miss O'neal; – more in the Mrs Siddons line.'[25] This comment also shows how fully aware she was of debates in the theatre world. Miss Eliza O'Neill was London's new acting sensation, heralded as the only tragedienne worthy to take over the mantle of Siddons as the queen of the stage neared her retirement.[26]

It was rumoured that some audience members fainted under the spell of the divine Eliza, who was slim and beautiful, which could not by this time be said of Siddons. Jane Austen was keen to see the new star and in late 1814 she was granted her wish. She went with Henry, Edward and his daughters to see O'Neill in the tragedy of *Isabella*. She joked to her niece Anna that she took along two pocket handkerchiefs. This was a reference to O'Neill's reputation as an actress of extreme sensibility: 'I do not think that she was quite equal to my expectation. I fancy I want something more than can be. Acting seldom satisfies me. I took two Pocket handkerchiefs, but had very little occasion for either. She is an elegant creature, and hugs Mr Younge delightfully.'[27] The latter phrase suggests an intimate shorthand between Jane and her niece: O'Neill was known to the cognoscenti as a 'hugging actress', so the comment suggests real awareness of the gossip of the theatre world.

The Mr Young who had the privilege of Miss O'Neill's hugs on this occasion was the great rival of Edmund Kean, the star of tragedy who burst on to the London theatre scene in that very year of 1814. Jane had written, with great excitement, to tell Cassandra that they had been successful in getting tickets for *Richard III*: 'Prepare for a Play the very first evening, I rather think Covent Garden, to see Young in Richard.'[28] The management at the Garden were bringing forward Young in order to try to win audiences back from Drury Lane, which was packed out night after night as a result of Kean's electrifying debut performance as Shylock in *The Merchant of Venice* and his follow-up as the charismatically villainous Richard. The news of Kean's conquest of the stage had quickly reached Jane Austen, and in early March 1814, while she was staying with Henry during the negotiations for the publication of *Mansfield Park*, she made plans to see the latest acting sensation: 'Places are secured at Drury Lane for Saturday, but so great is the rage for seeing Keen that only a third and fourth row could be got. As it is in a front box however, I hope we shall do pretty well. – Shylock – A good play for Fanny.' They duly saw Kean on 5 March, but Jane complained to Cassandra that there was too little of him for her taste: 'We were quite satisfied with Kean. I cannot imagine better acting, but the part was too short.' Later she wrote, 'I shall like to see Kean again excessively, and to see him with You too; – it appeared to me as if there were no fault in him anywhere; and in his scene with Tubal there was exquisite acting.'[29] She had high standards for what she called 'real hardened acting' and Kean fulfilled her expectations, unlike Eliza O'Neill.

Though she relished a big performance in tragedy, comedy was her true love. She had very particular tastes. 'Downton and Matthews were the good actors,' she remarked after seeing Isaac Bickerstaff's Molière adaptation The Hypocrite.[30] Charles Mathews was a comic genius, most famous for a 'monodramatic entertainment' called At Home – that is to say, the first one-man show, in which he played all the parts.

Each new actor who appeared on the London stage was sized up with careful scrutiny. When Daniel Terry took over the role of Lord Ogleby in The Clandestine Marriage, Jane Austen was not quite convinced: 'the new Mr Terry was Ld Ogelby, and Henry thinks he may do; but there was no acting more than moderate'.[31] Strikingly, she was more wrapped up in the character of Don Juan in a pantomime version based on Thomas Shadwell's The Libertine: 'I must say I have seen nobody on the stage who has been a more interesting Character than that compound of Cruelty and Lust.'[32] Here is another unusual glimpse of Jane Austen in the equivalent of an 'off-Broadway' theatre, relishing the performance of Cruelty and Lust.

She was fortunate enough to see the superb comic actress Dora Jordan, star of Covent Garden and mistress to the Duke of Clarence, playing the part of Nell in The Devil to Pay, one of her most famous roles. Nell is a timid cobbler's wife who is magically transformed into an aristocratic society mistress who makes a better wife to her husband, Sir John, and a kinder mistress to her servants than the irascible Lady Loverule. Because of her success in this role, Dora was known as 'Nell of Clarence'. Jane was 'highly amused' – strong praise from a woman with her standards. Back in 1801 she had commiserated with her sister when Cassandra was compelled to abandon a trip to Covent Garden to see the celebrated comic actress: 'You speak with such noble resignation of Mrs Jordan and the Opera House that it would be an insult to suppose consolation required.'[33]

Her judgements on actors were always acute and sharply observed: 'the parts were ill-filled and the Play heavy', she said of a production of *The Merchant of Venice*; Catherine Stephens was 'a pleasing person' but with 'no skill in acting'; a comedy featuring 'Mathews, Liston and Emery' provided 'of course some amusement'. Of Elizabeth Edwin, star of Drury Lane, and leading actress in the Earl of Barrymore's private theatricals at Wargrave, she was coolly dismissive: 'Mrs Edwin was the Heroine – and her performance is just what it used to be.'[34]

Probably her favourite actor of all was Robert Elliston, star of the Theatre Royal Bath. He was known as 'the fortnightly actor', as he was loaned to the London theatres, where he played once a fortnight. Despite lucrative offers from Covent Garden and Drury Lane, he refused to leave Bath because of his wife's business. She ran her own dance and deportment Academy in the city and he would not leave her. Eventually in 1804, he was lured to London, while his wife Elizabeth remained in Bath. In 1807, Jane Austen shared with Cassandra some Bath gossip gleaned from her aunt Leigh-Perrot: 'Elliston, she tells us has just succeeded to a considerable fortune on the death of an Uncle. I would not have it enough to take him from the Stage; she should quit her business and live with him in London.'[35] The remark demonstrates her loyalty to Elliston, in both his professional and his private lives. She clearly disapproved of Elizabeth's controversial decision to continue her own career without her husband. Elliston played the part of Frederick in *Lovers' Vows* several times during his tenure at the Theatre Royal Bath when Jane Austen was in residence.[36]

Austen was fortunate to live in Bath when the Theatre Royal was at the 'zenith of its glory'.[37] The appearance of London stars, coupled with the allure of Elliston, ensured its reputation as a theatre of the highest standing. Elliston was unusual in being a player of both comic and tragic roles. Jane Austen followed his career and saw him on stage in London, but complained of the falling standards of his acting following his move to the 'great Metropolis'. She saw him perform in an oriental 'melodramatic spectacle' called *Illusion; or the Trances of Nourjahad*, but she was disappointed with her old favourite: 'Elliston was Nourjahad, but it is a solemn sort of part, not at all calculated for his powers. There was nothing of the *best Elliston* about him. I might not have known him, but for his voice.'[38] She clearly preferred him in comedy, a view shared by most critics. Jane Austen may or may not have known that he was by now a hardened drunk and addicted to gambling (Kean would follow the same road to ruin), but her comments about his changed physical appearance suggest his sad decline.

Jane Austen especially loved plays where social roles were turned topsy-turvy. For example, *The Devil to Pay* exemplifies the comic theatre's obsession with social mobility and its endless play on rank and manners. Goldsmith's *She Stoops to Conquer* was probably her age's finest comedy of class divide and social stratification: the Georgians revelled in comedies that depicted scenes in which a person crossed the boundary from 'low' life to 'high' or vice versa.

Jane Austen was particularly attuned to the discrepancies between rank and manners within the tightly circumscribed social structure of her world. That understanding was profoundly shaped and informed by her interest in the drama. Dramatic confrontations such as that between Elizabeth Bennet and Lady Catherine de Bourgh could have come straight out of comedies such as *The Devil to Pay*. Lady Catherine is a Lady Loverule. Highly charged battle-of-the-sexes scenes between Elizabeth and Darcy are reminiscent of those in the comic tradition that reaches back through Congreve and the Restoration dramatists to the banter of Beatrice and Benedick in *Much Ado about Nothing*, as some of Jane Austen's earliest critics perceived. Austen's superb art of dramatic dialogue in *Pride and Prejudice* owes much to the influence of both contemporary and Shakespearean comedy; that is one reason why the novel adapts so well to stage and screen.

* * *

Astonishingly, for many years critics and readers of Jane Austen believed that she disapproved of the theatre and the drama. The reason for this was that they mistook Fanny Price's distrust of private theatricals for her own. The truth is much more complex: for the theatre-loving Austen, the debacle of the private theatricals in *Mansfield Park* is not so much an occasion to moralize as an opportunity to give her fictional characters licence to reveal their secret sexual desires through acting.

The theatrical episode is erotically highly charged. The character who voyeuristically observes and guides our response is Fanny Price. She perceives that the young people are using play-acting to engage in 'dangerous intimacies'. The plot of *Lovers' Vows* parallels the main plot in the novel: the prohibited love between a dull but respectable clergyman and a

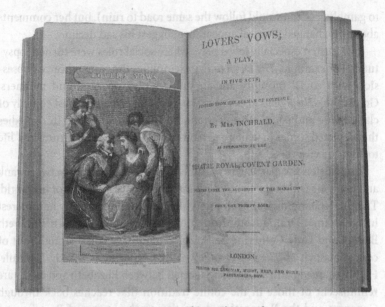

LOVERS' VOWS;

A PLAY,

IN FIVE ACTS;

ADAPTED FROM THE GERMAN OF KOTZEBUE

By Mrs. INCHBALD,

AS PERFORMED AT THE

THEATRE ROYAL, COVENT GARDEN,

PRINTED UNDER THE AUTHORITY OF THE MANAGERS

FROM THE PROMPT BOOK;

LONDON:

PRINTED FOR LONGMAN, HURST, REES, AND ORME,
PATERNOSTER-ROW.

On opening their copies of *Lovers' Vows*, the young
people of Mansfield Park would have immediately
seen the prospect of staging moments of high
sentiment (with body contact)

beautiful coquette (Edmund plays the clergyman Anhalt and Mary
Crawford the coquette Amelia). Another plot-line involves a fallen woman
(Agatha, played by Maria Bertram) and a dangerously attractive soldier
(Frederick, played of course by Henry Crawford). Like her stage counter-
part, Maria eventually becomes a social outcast through sexual
misconduct.

As Fanny is all too aware, the play rehearsals give the lovers freedom to
express their real feelings. Scenes with Maria Bertram and Henry Crawford
license, and indeed demand, flirtation and physical contact. The stage
directions reveal the extent of the physical contact between the young man
and woman: '*Rising and embracing him, leans her head against his breast, he
embraces her, Agatha presses him to her breast, Frederick takes her hand and
places it to his heart.*'[39] Fanny of course is observing the action closely and
even Mary Crawford quips, 'those indefatigable rehearsers, Agatha and
Frederick, should excel at their parts, for they are so often embracing. If

they are not perfect, I shall be surprised.'⁴⁰ Their conduct, by Georgian standards, would be risqué enough in the absence of chaperones, but the fact that Maria Bertram is engaged (to a rich fool whom she despises) makes her behaviour particularly unpleasant. Mr Rushworth is hurt and made jealous by his betrothed's flirtation. Lovers in Jane Austen's novels very rarely make physical contact, so when they do it is always sexually charged. When Julia makes her melodramatic announcement that the play must be stopped immediately as her father has returned, she alone notices that Henry retains Maria's hand throughout the crisis.

It is not merely the erotic charge of the physical contact that resonates but also the racy lines spoken by the actors. Mary Crawford, the sexiest of Jane Austen's *femmes fatales*, asks brazenly, 'What gentleman among you, am I to have the pleasure of making love to?' Edmund is unable to resist taking his part as her lover. 'None but a woman can teach the science of herself' is one of Amelia/Mary's lines, spoken to the abashed clergyman Edmund/Anhalt. Poor bemused Edmund, wholly out of his depth in the face of Mary's overpowering sexuality, is torn, we are told, 'between his theatrical and his real part'.⁴¹

Mary's fondest memory of Edmund involves recalling him in a position of sexual submission to a vivacious and sexually confident woman:

'The scene we were rehearsing was so very remarkable! The subject of it so very – very – what shall I say? He was to be describing and recommending matrimony to me. I think I see him now, trying to be as demure and composed as Anhalt ought … If I had the power of recalling any one week of my existence, it should be that week, that acting week … I never knew such exquisite happiness in any other. His sturdy spirit to bend as it did! Oh! It was sweet beyond expression.'⁴²

Whereas the Gothic novels of the age are full of 'demure' heroines cowed in submission beneath the gaze or hand of villains reminiscent of Richardson's rapist Lovelace, here it is the woman who feels the 'exquisite happiness' of bending a man's 'sturdy spirit' to her will.

For the Crawfords, sexual conquest is the motivating force in a romantic relationship. Henry later decides with callous detachment to 'make a hole in Miss Price's heart' simply because he can, or thinks that he can. When to his surprise she rejects him and he responds by falling in love with her, Mary entreats Fanny to bask in the conquest she has made over a man who has been desired by so many women: 'the glory of fixing one who has been shot at by so many'.[43]

Henry is regarded by the others as an accomplished actor, with 'more confidence than Edmund, more judgement than Tom, more talent and taste than Mr. Yates'.[44] His acting style is 'natural' in stark contrast to that of Tom Bertram's theatre-mad friend, the 'ranting' melodramatic Mr Yates. It is Mr Yates and Tom Bertram, the heir to Mansfield Park, who are responsible for bringing the theatricals to the young people. As with the real Steventon theatricals, everything is undertaken with the greatest professionalism, despite Tom's claims that all they require is a 'green curtain, and a little carpenter's work'. There is to be a green room, costumes and make-up. An expensive scene painter is hired from London. Lighting is arranged. Tom gives out invitations 'to every family who came in his way'.[45] His own preference for the choice of play is *The Heir at Law* by George Colman, which would have given him the chance to abnegate his real role as heir to a great estate and take on instead the part of a comic Irishman.

Tom is one of the most intriguing characters in Austen's fictional world: he loves theatre and dressing up, he is very close to the dandyish Yates, he is not very good at understanding women and the social customs of courtship, and he never marries, with the result, we may assume, that a future son of Edmund and Fanny may well inherit Mansfield. Jane Austen was well aware of several high-profile homosexual scandals, including one involving the writer William Beckford, to whom she seems to have been distantly related. The association between theatre and homosexuality had a very long history. If there is a homosexual character in Austen's novels, it is surely Tom Bertram.

What with Tom's behaviour, the impertinence of Mr Yates, the illicit love-play of Maria and Henry, and the general disruption to the household – especially to Sir Thomas's study – it is hardly surprising that the master explodes with anger on his return to Mansfield Park. As the Austen family's theatrical scenes were disposed of in the Steventon auction, so the Mansfield theatricals are halted, all copies of *Lovers' Vows* are burned, and 'The scene painter was gone, having spoilt only the floor of one room, ruined all the coachman's sponges and made five of the under-servants idle and dissatisfied.'[46]

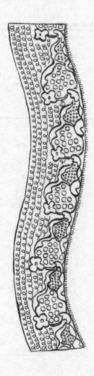

THE REAL JANE AUSTEN

9

The Card of Lace

Early one September morning in 1813, while staying with her brother
Henry in London, the 'Metropolis of England', Jane Austen bought some
'very nice plaiting Lace'. It would have been kept by the draper on a card.
The required length would have been rolled out and snipped off.
Domestically produced bobbin lace, typically from the English midlands,
used patterns copied from Flemish Mechlin lace worked with a simple
twist-net ground or from strong French Valenciennes lace, which consisted
of four threads braided together with eight threads at the crosses, as illustrated on the card shown here, which still retains its nineteenth-century
manufacturer's label.[1]

There are some characters in Jane Austen's novels who live to shop. Kitty
and Lydia, the youngest Bennet sisters in Pride and Prejudice, are 'tempted
three or four times a week' into the nearby town of Meryton 'to pay their
duty to their aunt and to a milliner's shop just over the way'.[2] For Isabella
Thorpe in Northanger Abbey, the shops are among the principal delights of
Bath: 'Do you know, I saw the prettiest hat you can imagine, in a shop
window in Milsom-street just now – very like yours, only with coquelicot
ribbons instead of green; I quite longed for it.'[3] Her new best friend
Catherine Morland, ever the ingénue, catches the shopping bug: 'Towards
the end of the morning, however, Catherine, having occasion for some
indispensable yard of ribbon which must be bought without a moment's
delay, walked out into the town.'[4]

Men, more often than not those of dubious character, can also be shopping addicts: the first we see of Robert Ferrars in *Sense and Sensibility* is a man causing a long delay in Gray's, a real shop in London, 'examining and debating for a quarter of an hour over every toothpick-case in the shop'.[5] Caring too much about consumer goods is a bad mark, as is made clear in the wonderful closing paragraph of *Emma*:

> The wedding was very much like other weddings, where the parties have no taste for finery or parade; and Mrs. Elton, from the particulars detailed by her husband, thought it all extremely shabby, and very inferior to her own. – 'Very little white satin, very few lace veils; a most pitiful business! – Selina would stare when she heard of it.' – But, in spite of these deficiencies, the wishes, the hopes, the confidence, the predictions of the small band of true friends who witnessed the ceremony, were fully answered in the perfect happiness of the union.[6]

(It is neat that Mr Elton does get to marry Emma after all, though not in the sense he desired, and it is pointed that Mrs Elton has to rely on him for a fashion report – she is not among the 'small band of true friends' who are present.)

Notwithstanding the clear implication here, that 'finery and parade' are not the route to happiness, Jane Austen herself very much enjoyed shopping. Her best opportunities came when she stayed with Henry in London. On the day in September 1813 when she bought that 'very nice plaiting Lace' she went to Wilding and Kent, a busy drapery store in New Bond Street, before breakfast so as to avoid the queues and get 'immediate attention'. The lace cost three shillings and fourpence, a not insignificant sum, the equivalent of about £10 or $15 today. She returned to Henry's premises in Henrietta Street to fortify herself and they had scarcely finished eating when the carriage was at the door. From eleven till a quarter past three, together with Henry, his children and niece Fanny, they were 'hard at it'. They took in Newton's in Leicester Square (Irish linen for Fanny), Remmington's (silk stockings for twelve shillings and cotton at four and threepence, 'great bargains'), Crook and Besford's for an over-priced white silk handkerchief (six shillings – she wished she'd remembered to get a cheaper one on the pre-breakfast trip), Wedgwood's for a dinner service ('I beleive the pattern is a small Lozenge in purple, between Lines of narrow

Gold') and Birchall's music shop. They even managed to fit in a dental appointment for the children – the painful part of the day.[7]

There was nowhere else on the planet that could match London for its shops. Robert Southey, appointed Poet Laureate that year (Walter Scott had refused the post), wrote of the 'opulence and splendor of the shops: drapers, stationers, confectioners, pastry-cooks, seal-cutters, silver-smiths, book-sellers, print-sellers, hosiers, fruiterers, china-sellers, – one close to another, without intermission, a shop to every house, street after street, and mile after mile'.[8] In the interiors, the displays were the envy of the world. Before the war, a visitor from the continent, Sophie von la Roche, had noted the superiority of the art of English shopkeeping to the French:

> Every article is made more attractive to the eye than in Paris or in any other town … We especially noticed a cunning device for showing women's materials. Whether they are silks, chintzes or muslins, they hang down in folds behind the fine high windows so that the effect of this or that material, as it would be in the ordinary folds of a woman's dress, can be studied. Amongst the muslins all colours are on view, and so one can judge how the frock would look in company with its fellows.[9]

'Beware my Laura', a young girl is warned in 'Love and Freindship', 'Beware of the insipid Vanities and idle Dissipations of the Metropolis of England; Beware of the unmeaning Luxuries of Bath and of the Stinking fish of Southampton.'[10] Jane Austen was no mere country mouse: she spent much of her life in the city. Five years of her life were spent in Bath and she was a frequent visitor to London, especially in the years when she became a published author.

The royal spa of Bath was second only to London for its shopping potential. In *Northanger Abbey*, the journey from a country village to the bustle of Bath is the heroine's rite of passage into the world. The novel seems to have been begun soon after Jane's first recorded visit to the city in 1797. That November, the *Bath Chronicle*, which was scrupulous in recording the comings and goings of the gentry, noted the arrival of 'Mrs and 2 Miss Asten'.[11] Her arrival was thus heralded by a spelling mistake. Jane, Cassandra and their mother stayed with her maternal uncle and aunt, the Leigh-Perrots, at the fashionable address of Paragon Buildings.

Aunt Leigh-Perrot

Mrs Austen, as was often the case, was unwell, so she would have been glad of the opportunity to 'take the waters'. Mr Leigh-Perrot was her wealthy brother who lived in a grand house called Scarlets, but who came to Bath frequently, also to take the waters, in his case to alleviate his gout. The couple were childless and made James Austen their heir. Jane disliked her aunt, who had a reputation for being bossy, critical and stingy, but she appears to have been fond of her uncle, who gave her presents of books from his own library.

They stayed until just before Christmas, giving Jane ample time to get to know the city and conceive her first 'Bath' novel. She returned there in May 1799, this time to accompany her brother Edward. Suffering from 'a nervous complaint' and gout, he was under doctor's orders to try the waters. Edward and his wife Elizabeth collected Jane from Steventon and they made the journey to Bath, stopping off at Devizes on the way, where they dined on asparagus, lobster and cheesecake.

Their lodgings were at the elegant 13 Queen Square. Their landlady, 'a fat woman in mourning', showed them their quarters, 'two very nice-sized rooms, with dirty quilts and everything comfortable', while a little black kitten ran around the stairs. They arrived in pouring rain, so they were unable to view the pavements due to the sea of umbrellas. But Jane was in high spirits, spotting a friend, Dr Hall, from the carriage, 'in such very deep mourning that either his mother, his wife, or himself must be dead'.[12]

It would seem that she planned to work on another novel during this visit. Judging by a joking comment she made to Cassandra, she had taken the manuscript of 'First Impressions' with her. She pretended that the reason she kept it with her was that if left at Steventon it would have been stolen by her friend Martha Lloyd: 'I would not let Martha read First Impressions again upon any account, and am very glad that I did not leave it in your power. – She is very cunning, but I see through her design; – she means to publish it from Memory, and one more perusal must enable her to do it.'[13] The idea that Jane Austen did not want her family and friends to know of her novel-writing is belied by the information here that she had shared the draft of the book that became *Pride and Prejudice* not only with Cassandra but also with Martha.

But it is probable that she was also still thinking about and planning the Bath novel, originally to be called 'Susan' and eventually *Northanger Abbey*. Edward's wealth and connections gave her access to assemblies, shopping, dances, pleasure gardens and theatre-visits, all of which would be transformed into fiction. Bath seems to have energized her: 'I do not know what is the matter with me today, but I cannot write quietly; I am always wandering away into some exclamation or other.'[14]

Edward, in contrast, was in poor spirits, depressed and tired. Jane hoped that shopping for tea, coffee, sugar and cheese would cheer him up. He planned to take the water, try bathing and then even to try 'electricity'. Bath had been famous for new-fangled electroanalgesia, ever since the celebrated sexologist Dr James Graham began offering electrical treatments for a spectrum of conditions ranging from modish nervous disorders and infertility to fevers, rheumatism and the gout.

Graham had begun his career in Bath. His offer of 'Effluvia, Vapours and Applications ætherial, magnetic or electric' attracted celebrity patients. Among the first was the redoubtable bluestocking historian Catherine Macaulay, who was so stimulated by Graham's apparatus that she married his twenty-one-year-old brother, who was less than half her age. This propelled Dr Graham to national fame. He moved to London and in prime premises in Pall Mall set up his electromagnetic musical 'Grand State Celestial Bed', an exotic form of infertility treatment. The Celestial Bed had a tilting inner frame that allegedly put couples in the best position to conceive. Their movements set off music from organ pipes which breathed out 'celestial sounds' whose intensity increased with the ardour of the bed's occupants. Stimulating fragrances were released into 'the temple of Hymen', the canopy that encircled the electrical bed. A pair of live doves fluttered above. Though Dr Graham died in 1794, electrical treatment continued to be popular in spa towns such as Bath and Bristol.

Jane was dubious about the efficacy of electricity for Edward's jaded nerves, but a little retail therapy seemed to improve his spirits. He bought a handsome matched pair of black coach horses for sixty guineas. She was clearly delighted to be in Bath with its shopping and cultural opportunities. Bath was the queen of the spa towns. Christopher Anstey's *New Bath Guide*, published that very year of 1799, extolled its virtues and set out the rules for polite company:

> In the morning the rendezvous is at the Pump-Room; – from that time till noon in walking on the Parades, or in the different quarters of the town, visiting the shops, etc; – thence to the Pump-Room again, and after a fresh strole, to dinner; and from dinner to the Theatre (which is celebrated for an excellent company of comedians) or the Rooms, where dancing, or the card-table, concludes the evening.[15]

The family took advantage of the amusements on offer. At the theatre they enjoyed a performance of the comedy *The Birth-Day*, by August von Kotzebue, author of the German original of *Lovers' Vows*. And they especially enjoyed Sydney Gardens, supposed to be the best pleasure gardens outside London.

Filled with exotic plants and trees entwined with variegated lamps, it boasted spectacular water cascades, well-rolled gravel paths for promenading and enjoying the views, a stone pavilion with seating for taking refreshments and looking out over to the well-lit orchestra below, and there were even swings for the ladies. For lovers there were intimate covered boxes or grottoes. Famously, one of the most private grottoes had been a courting spot for the dramatist Richard Sheridan and the exquisitely beautiful singer and actress Elizabeth Linley (they eloped to France, below the age of legal marriage, when she was seventeen and he was not quite twenty-one). There was also a charming maze or labyrinth, half a mile long, which could take up to six hours to traverse, at a cost of an extra three pence per person. On gala nights, in the summer, there were spectacular fireworks, illuminations and showings of transparencies.

'There was a very long list of Arrivals here, in the Newspaper yesterday, so that we need not immediately dread absolute Solitude,' Jane Austen reported one day in May 1799, 'and there is a public breakfast in Sydney Gardens every morning, so that we shall not be wholly starved.' She then told Cassandra of plans to attend a gala night: 'There is to be a grand gala on tuesday evening in Sydney Gardens; – a Concert, with Illuminations and fireworks.'[16] Jane was disappointed when it rained, but they returned to another gala evening two weeks later: 'We did not go till nine, and then were in very good time for the Fire-works, which were really beautiful, and surpassing my expectation; – the illuminations too were very pretty.'[17]

Shopping was superb ('one can step out of doors and get a thing in five minutes'), and she had commissions from family and friends back in Hampshire: stockings for her little niece Anna, shoes for Martha Lloyd, fabric for Cassandra. She told the girls that for modish headwear 'Flowers are very much worn, and Fruit is still more the thing ... I cannot help thinking that it is more natural to have flowers grow out of the head than fruit. – What do you think on the subject?'[18] Cassandra requested a sprig of flowers and Mary a black muslin veil. Jane shopped around for lace to edge a new cloak that she was having made up and drew a picture of its delicate pattern in her letter home: 'I am very glad You liked my Lace, and so are You and so is Martha. – and we are all glad together.'[19] Lace was soon to take on a less happy aspect for the Austen family.

* * *

Jane Austen was not the type of young woman who was prone to hysterics or fainting fits. In the vellum notebooks she satirizes giddy heroines who 'faint alternately on the sofa'. Yet, according to family tradition, she was greatly distressed – even to the point of fainting – when in early December 1800 she returned from a stay with her friend Martha Lloyd to be told by her mother that the family had made a decision in her absence: they would be leaving Steventon for Bath. According to family legend Jane

'Here follows the pattern of its lace': holograph
letter from Jane to Cassandra, Bath 1799

Austen was greeted by her mother's shock announcement: 'Well, girls, it is all settled, we have decided to leave Steventon in such a week and go to Bath.'[20]

Anna Lefroy thought that the move was because of Mrs Austen's health. Brother Frank believed that his father 'felt too incapacitated from age and increasing infirmities to discharge his parochial duties in a manner satisfactory to himself'.[21] George Austen would turn seventy in the spring and the children were all grown up. It was time to hand the parsonage over to James. And Bath might provide some better marriage prospects for the two unmarried daughters of advancing age. Jane's twenty-fifth birthday came a couple of weeks after the unwelcome news.

But since she had so clearly enjoyed her visits to Bath, why was she so taken aback at the news that the family were to relocate there? Of course it was partly shock at the thought of leaving the home where she had been brought up. But there was something else: Bath had been the location of a major scandal involving the very aunt who had hosted her in Paragon Buildings, a scandal that had come to a head in a nationally reported court case of March 1800.

Just two months after Jane Austen had returned home following the happy visit to Bath with brother Edward, her aunt Leigh-Perrot was arrested and imprisoned for shoplifting. It was alleged that she had stolen a card of expensive white lace from a millinery shop in Bath Street, just round the corner from Westgate Buildings. The very grand and wealthy Mrs Leigh-Perrot was committed to Ilchester Gaol, remanded in custody pending the Taunton Assizes.

When the news reached the Austen family in Steventon, Mrs Austen immediately offered to send her daughters to keep her company. It is extraordinary to think of Jane and Cassandra Austen going voluntarily to gaol. But Mrs Leigh-Perrot would not hear of allowing 'those Elegant young Women [to] be ... Inmates in a Prison'.[22] Her husband, despite his ill-health, insisted on accompanying her. Thanks to their wealth, they were able to secure accommodation in the gaol-keeper's own house, so conditions were not so bad as they might have been – though they must have felt a very long way from the elegance and spaciousness of Scarlets.

There is, unsurprisingly, no mention of the scandal in the Victorian family memoir of Jane Austen, and none of her letters from this period survive. But the trial was published in a pamphlet and Mrs Leigh-Perrot's letters to a cousin give an account of the horrors she endured.[23] Scadding the gaoler and his wife had five small noisy children, and their house was dirty and cramped. Mr Leigh-Perrot, for whom 'cleanliness has ever been his greatest delight', was forced to endure a room full of chimney smoke and dirt, and greasy toast laid on his knees by the children who didn't use plates and spilt their father's small beer over him. Mrs Scadding's method of dishwashing was to lick the fried onions from her knife before using it. The details of the dirty children and rooms are similar to the Portsmouth scenes in *Mansfield Park*. Mrs Leigh-Perrot reported that her worst misery was seeing her husband enduring 'Vulgarity, Dirt, Noise from Morning to Night'. The Leigh-Perrots lived with this from August to the following March.

In light of the evidence, it seems likely that she was guilty. Mrs Leigh-Perrot had shopped for a card of lace to edge a new cloak from a haberdasher's called Smiths in Bath Street. She bought a card of black lace and left the shop to meet her husband. The couple walked past the shop some time later and were apprehended by a shop assistant who accused Mrs Leigh-Perrot of stealing a card of white thread lace, worth twenty shillings (one pound – the equivalent of about £68 or $100 today). Mrs Leigh-Perrot opened her parcel and the card of white lace was retrieved and taken back to the shop. The couple thought no more of it until days later she was arrested for Grand Larceny.

The issue at stake was the cost of the lace. Because it was worth twenty shillings the theft was a serious offence punishable by death by hanging or at the very least by transportation. Because of Mrs Leigh-Perrot's standing in the local community the latter was more likely, so the devoted Leigh-Perrot began to put his affairs in order so that he could accompany his wife to Australia if the worst were to happen. Gossips said that he was dominated by her and his letters to her do indeed suggest that she had much the stronger personality.

As the trial approached the family rose to Mrs Leigh-Perrot's support. James Austen had broken a leg in a riding accident so was unable to rush to her side, but once again Mrs Austen offered to send Cassandra and Jane. Mrs Leigh-Perrot once again refused: 'nor could I accept the Offer of my Nieces – to have two Young Creatures gazed at in a public Court would cut one to the very heart'.[24]

Her supporters were convinced that she had been framed by unscrupulous blackmailers, but there were many others convinced that she was guilty. Damningly, her own counsel, Joseph Jekyll, thought that she was guilty. A family member who was in the know wrote privately, 'Jekyll considered Mrs. L. P. was a kleptomaniac and that she did steal the material and probably meant to.' Years later another story circulated: that Mrs Leigh-Perrot had been caught stealing plants from a garden centre.

The plausibility of her guilt is underlined by the fact that her four defence lawyers did not bring a blackmail charge against the shopkeeper, who had immediately consulted local magistrates. Instead they argued that the assistant had mistakenly put the white lace into the package. And one wonders why Mr Leigh-Perrot made plans for deportation if he thought his wife innocent.

Her own lawyer called her a 'smoocher', someone who could and did steal small things. Kleptomania was first defined in the eighteenth century as a psychological condition that involves 'recurrent, strong, sudden urges to steal items that one does not need and that can have little value, or that one can afford to purchase'.[25] Kleptomaniacs are usually females who, as modern psychology now puts it, experience tension before the theft and then a release of tension following the act. One wonders whether Mrs Norris is merely being greedy or exhibiting symptoms of the condition when, after the debacle of *Lovers' Vows*, she 'contrived to remove one article from [Sir Thomas's] sight that might have distressed him. The curtain over which she had presided with such talent and such success, went off with her to her cottage, where she happened to be particularly in want of green baize.'[26]

After a full day's hearing at the Taunton Assizes in March 1800, Mrs Leigh-Perrot was – rather against the balance of the evidence – unanimously acquitted by the jury. The couple returned to Bath and a warm reception from all their friends. But mud sticks and, as a prominent figure in the city, Mrs Leigh-Perrot was frequently lampooned. Shortly after the acquittal she received an anonymous letter suggesting that a print had been found and would be published: it was a caricature of a parrot holding a card of lace in his bill. Furthermore, the two-shilling pamphlet reporting the trial in all its gory detail was readily available at all good booksellers, the editor proclaiming that 'the general curiosity which has been excited' by the 'various and contradictory accounts in the public prints' made the venture worth while.

The trial allegedly cost Mr Leigh-Perrot two thousand pounds, money that James Austen (the Leigh-Perrots' heir) may well have felt was misused. Nevertheless, family relations remained good. The scandal was not sufficient to make the Austens think twice about the move to Bath, even if it did play some part in their daughter's reaction to their impulsive departure. Jane herself wrote of her aunt Leigh-Perrot's delight at the news of their impending arrival: 'she thinks with the greatest pleasure of our being settled in Bath'.[27]

Despite the 'great distress' that Jane felt on being uprooted from her family home in Steventon without consultation of any kind, her letters suggest that her mood soon changed. There is a sense of excitement at the prospect of city life: 'I get more and more reconciled to the idea of our removal,' she wrote to Cassandra. 'We have lived long enough in this Neighbourhood, the Basingstoke Balls are certainly on the decline, there is something interesting in the bustle of going away, and the prospect of spending future summers by the Sea or in Wales is very delightful. – For a time we shall now possess many of the advantages which I have often thought of with Envy in the wives of Sailors or Soldiers.'[28]

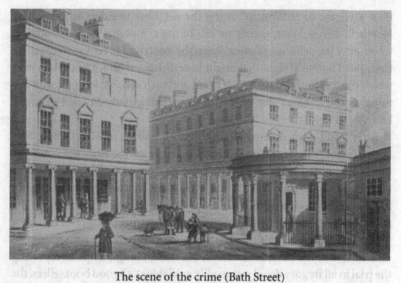

The scene of the crime (Bath Street)
and the report of the case

THE

TRIAL

OF

JANE LEIGH PERROT,

WIFE OF

JAMES LEIGH PERROT, Esq;

CHARGED WITH

STEALING a CARD of LACE,

IN THE SHOP OF

ELIZABETH GREGORY,

HABERDASHER and MILLINER, at BATH,

BEFORE

Sir SOULDEN LAWRENCE, Knight,

ONE OF THE JUSTICES OF HIS MAJESTY'S COURT OF
KING'S BENCH.

AT TAUNTON ASSIZES,

On Saturday the 29th Day of March, 1800.

TAKEN IN COURT BY

JOHN PINCHARD, Attorney,

OF TAUNTON.

TAUNTON:

Printed by and for THOMAS NORRIS, White-lion-court;
And Sold by CARPENTER and Co. 14, Old Bond-street ; E. NEWBERY,
St. Paul's-Churchyard ; HURST and Co. Paternoster-Row, London ;
MEYLER, Bath ; SHEPPARD, Bristol ; COLLINS, Salisbury ;
NORRIS, and POOLE, Taunton ; and all other Booksellers,

The family discussed various locations with all the enthusiasm of first-time city house-hunters: Mrs Austen liked the sound of Queen Square, but her husband preferred Laura Place and Jane thought it would be fun to be near Sydney Gardens so that 'we might go into the Labyrinth every day'.[29] Other matters to be settled were the servant question. Jane joked that 'We plan having a steady Cook, and a young giddy Housemaid, with a sedate, middle aged Man, who is to undertake the double office of Husband to the former and sweetheart to the latter. – No Children of course to be allowed on either side.'[30]

But there were also matters to be settled at Steventon, not least the auction of the furniture. In a letter written on the day of the move Jane mentions the loss of her pianoforte and her own library – a sorry detail given how much her books and her music meant to her. She made no attempt to disguise her chagrin towards her brother James and his wife, whom she suspected had encouraged the retirement plan in her absence and who offered to buy many of the rectory chattels at far below what she considered a fair price: 'The whole World is in a conspiracy to enrich one part of our family at the expense of another.'[31]

Jane Austen and her mother left Steventon to spend a few days house-hunting before Cassandra and her father arrived. The houses they saw first were damp and unsuitable, but they eventually took a lease of three and a quarter years on 4 Sydney Place, facing Sydney Gardens, where Jane had expressed a preference for living. The plans for the next few years were winters in Bath and summers at the seaside.

It was a happy time for Jane Austen's parents. Anna Austen, James's daughter by his first wife, vividly recollected their contented retirement in Bath and how they 'seemed to enjoy the cheerfulness of their Town life, and especially perhaps the rest which their advancing years entitled them to … I have always thought that this was the short Holyday of their married life.'[32]

There are only five surviving letters from the five years that Jane Austen lived in Bath. This has led to much misunderstanding and speculation. Some biographers have suggested that this period was a dead time for her writing. One much read account suggests that she was 'disabled as a writer', falling into silence, if not depression.[33] But she had her portable writing desk and nothing was going to stop her from writing. She began a new novel, *The Watsons*, and she finalized and sold her first Bath novel, 'Susan'.

It was actually advertised as forthcoming in the spring of 1803. She must have believed that she was on her way to being what she wanted to be – an author. With her in Bath were the manuscripts of no fewer than three completed novels, 'Elinor and Marianne' (probably rewritten as *Sense and Sensibility* by this time), 'First Impressions' and *Lady Susan*, all no doubt frequently tinkered with and thought and spoken about.[34]

Many twentieth-century readings of Jane Austen were fixated on the assumption that she was immovably attached to village life and deeply suspicious of urban pleasures – the theatre foremost among these. But she herself parodied such a clichéd view when she wrote from London: 'Here I am once more in this Scene of Dissipation and vice, and I begin already to find my Morals corrupted.'[35] There is every reason to believe that she enjoyed urban life. In *Northanger Abbey*, Catherine Morland declares her enthusiasm for Bath, observing that 'there is much more sameness in a country life than in a Bath life. One day in the country is exactly like another.'[36] It was just such boredom that Jane Austen was ready to escape.

She was quick to explore the circulating libraries. There were over ten of them in Bath by the end of the eighteenth century. In the year that she moved, the *Bath Journal* advertised the opening of a new public library. Its purpose was to benefit both residents and visitors, with a collection of books not commonly met with in the circulating libraries: books of reference, foreign journals, history and mathematics and astronomical tables and so forth. Also in 1801 there was news of a new coffeehouse serving breakfasts, dinners and suppers, on the same plan as in London.

Of all the leisure facilities that developed in Bath in this period, the two most popular were the public assemblies and the walks. Walking and dancing could be regarded as a form of exercise, but more importantly these pastimes provided for socializing and personal display. Jane Austen loved both activities. In the few extant Bath letters, she lists the long walks she has taken, one lasting for two hours – a trip to Beacon Hill and across the fields to Charlcombe. She also enjoyed promenading the Royal Crescent, and walking by Crescent Fields and Lansdown Hill. Walks to Weston, Lyncombe and Widcombe were other favourites. The squares and circuses were in effect open-air rooms, where people promenaded, flirted and gossiped.

In Bath, assemblies were divided into the regular assemblies, and ones associated with special occasions, for example the Queen's birthday ball. The Lower Rooms, according to Anstey's *New Bath Guide*, had a fabulous ballroom ninety feet in length and thirty-six feet in breadth with a stucco ceiling and fine views of the river, valley and adjacent hills. Paintings adorned the walls – most prominent was a portrait of Beau Nash – and the rooms were elegantly furnished with chandeliers and girandoles. There were two tea rooms, an apartment devoted to the games of chess and backgammon and a sixty-foot-long card room. The balls, according to the *Guide*,

> Begin at six o'clock and end at eleven … About nine o'clock the gentlemen treat their partners with tea, and when that is over the company pursue their diversions till the moment comes for closing the ball. Then the Master of the Ceremonies, entering the ballroom, orders the music to cease, and the ladies thereupon resting themselves till they grow cool, their partners complete the ceremonies of the evening by handing them to the chairs in which they are to be conveyed to their respective lodgings.[37]

It is at a ball in the Lower Rooms that Henry Tilney is first introduced to Catherine Morland in *Northanger Abbey*: when he is 'treating his partner to tea' he laughingly accuses her of keeping a journal in which he fears he should make but a poor figure. '"Shall I tell you," he asks, "what you ought to say? … I danced with a very agreeable young man, introduced by Mr King; had a great deal of conversation with him – seems a most extraordinary genius."'[38] Mr King was the real-life Master of the Ceremonies at the Lower Rooms, from 1785 to 1805, when he became Master of the Ceremonies for the Upper Rooms, another example of Austen making her novels realistic by introducing details from reality.

The ballroom was also used during the daytime as a promenade, as its windows commanded extensive views of the Avon. It was the fashion for the company to invite each other to breakfast at the Lower Rooms after taking their early baths or first glass of spa water.

The New Assembly Rooms, which had opened in September 1771, were located at the east end of the Circus. They were built by subscription under the direction of John Wood. The ballroom was 105 feet long and 42 feet wide, furnished with Gainsborough portraits and boasting five spectacular chandeliers from its ornate panelled ceiling. At the end of the room were gilt-framed looking glasses. On the way to the concert or tea room one would cross the octagon room, with its elegant domed roof and frieze, opening out to the ballroom, the tea room and the card room. The open-plan architecture was deliberate: the rooms were built in a roughly circular fashion to encourage the free flow of guests. It is in the octagon room that Catherine Morland and Isabella Thorpe arrange to meet their brothers for a rendezvous, and this room is also the setting for the scene in the much later Bath novel, *Persuasion*, between Anne Elliot and Captain Wentworth when Anne allows herself to hope that he still loves her.

The Bath assemblies were organized on a subscription basis. Balls and concerts were held at least twice weekly. According to the *New Bath Guide* there were two dress balls every week, at the New Rooms on Monday and on Friday at the Lower Rooms. Then there were two fancy balls every week, at the Lower Rooms on Tuesday and at the New Rooms on Thursday, subscription half a guinea. Concerts were held on Wednesdays. The Monday dress ball was devoted to country dances only, and at the fancy ball on Tuesdays and Thursdays two cotillions were danced, one before and one after tea. The fancy ball was not a fancy dress or masquerade ball but an occasion when the stringent rules regarding evening dress were relaxed. The ladies wore shorter skirts for the cotillion, with their over-dresses pinned up, as in *Northanger Abbey* when Isabella and Catherine pin up each other's train for the dance.

As well as the twice-weekly assemblies and the mid-week Wednesday concert, the theatre held performances on Tuesdays, Thursdays and Saturdays. In *Northanger Abbey*, the regulated uniformity of the Bath social circuit is parodied in a dialogue between Catherine and Henry in the Lower Rooms:

'Were you never here before, Madam?'
'Never, sir.'
'Indeed! Have you yet honoured the Upper Rooms?'
'Yes, sir, I was there last Monday.'
'Have you been to the theatre?'
'Yes, sir, I was at the play on Tuesday.'
'To the concert?'
'Yes, sir, on Wednesday.'
'And are you altogether pleased with Bath?'
'Yes – I like it very well.'
'Now I must give one smirk, and then we may be rational again.'[39]

When Jane Austen arrived at Bath in May 1801 she attended the penultimate ball of the season. She was surprised that the Assembly Rooms were so quiet, with merely four couples dancing before tea:

> I dressed myself as well as I could, and had all my finery much admired at home. By nine o'clock my Uncle, Aunt and I entered the rooms and linked Miss Winstone on to us. – Before tea, it was rather a dull affair; but then the beforetea did not last long, for there was only one dance, danced by four couple. – Think of four couple, surrounded by about an hundred people, dancing in the upper rooms at Bath! – After tea we *cheered up*; the breaking up of private parties sent some scores more to the Ball, and tho' it was shockingly and inhumanly thin for this place, there were people enough I suppose to have made five or six very pretty Basingstoke assemblies.[40]

Nevertheless she enjoyed staring at a distant cousin, the notorious Mary-Cassandra Twiselton: 'I am proud to say that I have had a very good eye at an Adulteress'; she was 'not so pretty as expected', being indeed somewhat bald and highly rouged.[41] Mary-Cassandra had recently been divorced by her husband, always a high-profile affair at the time, since it involved an action in the House of Lords. A maid had testified that Mary-Cassandra had bragged about the sexual prowess of her lover in comparison with that of her husband.

Jane Austen's Twiselton cousins certainly had a chequered history: Mary-Cassandra's elder brother had eloped to Scotland after forming an unsuitable liaison during some amateur theatricals. The marriage was a disaster and he eventually divorced his wife and became a clergyman. Austen mentioned him in a letter of 1813.

Austen continued her account of that first ball after her arrival in Bath with an enthusiastic description of her own new white dress. Jane seemed to prefer larger parties: 'I detest tiny parties – they force one into constant exertion.'[42] Catherine Morland is less favourably inclined towards large gatherings. When she attends her first assembly, she is shocked to find Mr Allen heading off for the card room, leaving the ladies to negotiate their way through the throng of young men by the door. So crowded is the room that she can only glimpse the high feathers of the ladies.

Austen's first Bath novel depicts a city of amusement, sociability and pleasure, though it can of course also be painful and humiliating if the social codes are misunderstood. Catherine's innocent breaches of propriety do cause her distress, as do broken engagements and the absence of a dancing partner at a ball. Like the teenager that she is, Catherine oscillates between extreme happiness and despair; one minute her 'spirits danced within her, as she danced in her chair all the way home', the next she experiences the 'heart-rending tidings' that the Tilneys have called on her only to discover that she has gone out driving with John Thorpe.[43] That night she cries herself to sleep. Austen's ironic third-person narration maintains the necessary distance from her heroine, but she is never callous about how seemingly trivial things matter to the feelings of a young girl. She is much harsher towards characters who, in her phrase, tell lies to increase their importance, or manipulate others for their own ends, regardless of everything but their own gratification. Catherine's entrance into society is an education in growing up, as it was for her literary predecessor, Fanny Burney's *Evelina*.

Jane Austen was well aware of Bath's reputation as a marriage market. In *Emma* Mrs Elton tells Emma, 'And as to its recommendations to you, I fancy I need not take much pains to dwell on them. The advantages of Bath to the young are pretty well understood.'[44] In *Northanger Abbey*, the spa town fulfils its reputation as a place devoted to the pursuit of social and sexual liaison. Isabella hooks Frederick Tilney by playing him off against Catherine's brother. Henry Tilney's affection for Catherine 'originated in nothing better than gratitude, or, in other words, that a persuasion of her partiality for him had been the only cause of giving her a serious thought'. For Catherine Bath is a city of pleasure, where she finds a husband in the first man she dances with: 'Here are a variety of amusements, a variety of things to be seen and done all day long, which I can know nothing of there ... I really believe I shall always be talking of Bath ... I *do* like it so very much ... Oh! who can ever be tired of Bath?'[45]

If 'Susan', as it then was, had been published in 1803, the first words of the published Jane Austen[46] would have established her from the very start as someone different from the run-of-the-mill lady novelists whose sentimental romances and melodramatic Gothic tales filled the shelves of the circulating libraries: 'No one who had ever seen Susan Morland in her infancy, would have supposed her born to be a heroine.' Susan was later renamed Catherine because of the publication in 1809 of a novel by another anonymous lady with the title *Susan*. Catherine Morland is a plain child, with a 'thin awkward figure, a sallow skin without colour, dark, lank hair, and strong features'.[47] But it is her very ordinariness that is the point. Jane Austen makes her readers interested in a very unremarkable girl who grows up in the course of the novel.

Catherine learns the folly of expecting 'real-life' to be the same as events in novels. Her imagination leads her to think that General Tilney has murdered his wife and she is rebuked by the hero in a very striking passage: 'consider the dreadful nature of the suspicions you have entertained. What have you been judging from? Remember the country and the age in which we live. Remember that we are English, that we are Christians. Consult your own understanding, your own sense of the probable, your own observation of what is passing around you.'[48]

But Catherine is right and Henry is wrong. Catherine's distrust of the General is justified when he turns her out of the house, forcing her to endure that long coach journey of seventy miles alone. Austen's novel reveals a paradoxical doubleness beloved of the author: the novel-reading heroine, contrary to expectation, does learn about life from reading books: 'Catherine, at any rate, heard enough to feel, that in suspecting General Tilney of either murdering or shutting up his wife, she had scarcely sinned against his character, or magnified his cruelty.'[49]

Ultimately, Jane Austen had mixed feelings about Bath – as most of us do about the cities in which we live. But it inspired two remarkable novels. She took advantage of all that this vibrant environment could offer and it was here that she thought she would see the first of her books in print. But it would also be the place where she suffered her greatest loss.

The Form of an Entry of a Marriage.

A.B. of _____ and C.D of _____
were married in this Church by {Banns / Licenfe*} this
Day of _____ in the Year One Thousand Seven
Hundred and _____ by me
                    J.J. Rector }
                        Vicar }
                        Curate }
This Marriage was folemnized between us A.B.C.B. late C.D
in the Prefence of E.F.G.H.

10

The Marriage Banns

St Nicholas's, Steventon, the thirteenth-century church where Jane worshipped until the family left for Bath, stands almost unchanged from the time when the Austen family made their way by foot to Sunday services. The path ascended the steep hill behind the parsonage. It was flanked by hedgerows, giving shelter to primroses in the spring and anemones in May and June. The church was set apart, flanked by sycamore trees. An ancient yew hung over the north-west corner. The main change to the modest stone-built grey church between Austen's time and ours was the addition of a needle spire in the middle of the nineteenth century.

In the church, there are now memorial tablets to James Austen, Jane's eldest brother, who took over the parish from her father, to his two wives and to some of his relations. Their graves are in the churchyard. Austen herself is commemorated on the north wall of the nave with a bronze plaque which simply states her dates and the fact that she worshipped at the church. There is also a reproduction of one of her prayers on the wall. Many of the graves and memorials have connections to the Austen family, such as those of their close friends the Digweed family who lived in the Steventon Manor House.

One day in the late eighteenth century the young Jane Austen made her way to St Nicholas's, to search out the parish register over which her father presided. At the front of the volume, which dated back to 1755 and was not filled until 1812, there were specimen entries to show clergymen how to complete marriage records. Jane Austen, whose name appears in the birth register for December 1775, filled out one of the forms. Already a fiction writer of sorts, she decided to get married – several times over. She picked up a pen and scribbled in names for the calling of the banns, the entry of the marriage itself and the witnessing:

The Banns of Marriage between *Henry Frederic Howard Fitzwilliam* of *London* and *Jane Austen* of *Steventon*.
The Form of an Entry of a Marriage. *Edmund Arthur William Mortimer* of *Liverpool* and *Jane Austen* of *Steventon*.
The Marriage was witnessed between us. *Jack Smith, Jane Smith*, late *Austen*, in the presence of *Jack Smith, Jane Smith*.[1]

Jane Austen's facetious defacing of her father's parish register suggests her easy relationship with him. The last entry is particularly amusing as the couple, Jack Smith and Jane Smith née Jane Austen, are witnesses to their own nuptials. One can only imagine how different the history of English fiction would have been if the young Jane Austen's fleeting fantasy about love and marriage had been fulfilled.

One certainty of a marriage would have been separation from her beloved sister. Jane was thought not to be as pretty as Cassandra, but she did not lack suitors. It would appear that she did not take the idea of marriage very seriously, but when Cassandra got engaged to Tom Fowle, Jane must have had some hesitation at the thought of being left alone with her parents. She loved them, but she adored Cassandra. The prospect of living without her was daunting. So perhaps it is not coincidental that Jane's most active period of flirtation occurred in the years when Cassandra was engaged and waiting to be married. The oft-quoted remark from author and neighbour Mary Mitford that Jane was 'the prettiest, silliest, most affected, husband-hunting butterfly' relates to this sensitive time in her life, when she was forced to confront her own future.[2]

At Christmas 1795, Jane began her own flirtations, most notably with a blond, handsome Irishman called Tom Lefroy. Her letters reveal that 'other Admirers' such as a wealthy Mr Heartley were also showing interest. And there was another ex-pupil of Steventon, John Warren: people thought that he was in love with Jane, though she refused to believe this. John Lyford, son of a local surgeon and male midwife, tried to dance with her but she managed to get away: 'I was forced to fight hard.' Charles Powlett, who according to Mrs Lefroy had deformed hands, tried to kiss her at a ball. He later became Chaplain to the Prince Regent. More alluringly, there was Edward Taylor, a year younger than her and whom she described as having 'beautiful dark eyes'.[3]

Her brief flirtation with Tom Lefroy has been well documented and, mistakenly, presented as the great love of her life, cruelly cut short by the machinations of Mrs Lefroy, Jane's mentor and Tom's aunt. Jane's account of the affair is recorded in her letters to Cassandra, who was staying with her future in-laws in Berkshire. Her sister's absence underlined the fact that she was in the market for a suitor.

Jane's tone is one of studied nonchalance, writing to tell her sister of her 'profligate' conduct at this very time. She had attended the Manydown Ball given by their friends the Bigg family. She refers to the fact that Cassandra has sent her a 'scolding letter' about her behaviour, but she playfully and provocatively expresses her indifference: 'I am almost afraid to tell you how my Irish friend and I behaved. Imagine to yourself everything most profligate and shocking in the way of dancing and sitting down together.'[4]

She does however go on to reassure her sister that there is nothing serious in this romance: Tom Lefroy was due to leave the country. She enjoyed his attentions – in her own words he was 'gentleman-like, good-looking, pleasant' – and she was flattered that he was teased about his crush on her: 'he is so excessively laughed at about me at Ashe, that he is ashamed to come to Steventon, and ran away when we called on Mrs Lefroy a few days ago'.[5] A man who ran away at her approach would never do for her, one suspects.

Later she joked, 'I rather expect to receive an offer from my friend in the course of the evening. I shall refuse him, however, unless he promises to give away his white Coat.'[6] The white coat was a literary joke, a reference to Fielding's roguish hero Tom Jones, who, famously, wore a white morning coat. It seems clear that this real-life Tom was as keen on Jane as his admired Tom Jones was on the lovely Sophia Western in Fielding's novel. Jane clearly liked him well enough. They discussed novels, danced and flirted. Her friend John Warren, also a Steventon boy, drew a likeness of Tom Lefroy to give to her. She fell a little in love. But she was ripe to fall in love.

Later in life Tom Lefroy, who became Chief Justice of Ireland, admitted that he had indeed been in love with the novelist Jane Austen, though it was a 'boy's love'.[7] According to family tradition, Mrs Lefroy was furious with him for leading Jane on, and banned him from her rectory. Thus Mrs Lefroy has been seen as the obstacle separating the young lovers, a proto-type Lady Russell in *Persuasion*, whose interference causes such misery. In fact, Mrs Lefroy acted honourably. She felt Tom had acted badly towards her protégée as Jane might have fallen in love with him and had her heart broken when he left the country.

Tom was not in a financial position to offer marriage; as one of the Austen nieces later said firmly, 'there was *no* engagement'.[8] There were very strict though often tacit rules about courtship in the eighteenth century. Men who deliberately flirted with dowryless girls such as Jane Austen, with no intention of following through, could quickly find themselves very unpopular. Austen's novels consistently address the complex rules of court-ship conduct. In *Pride and Prejudice*, Jane Bennet convinces herself that she has misread the signals with Mr Bingley: 'It is very often nothing but our own vanity that deceives us. Women fancy admiration means more than it does.' But Lizzy retorts, 'And men take care that they should.'[9]

But what did Jane really think? She told Cassandra, 'I mean to confine myself to Mr Tom Lefroy, for whom I don't care sixpence.' Then later she joked: 'At length the Day is come on which I am to flirt my last with Tom Lefroy, and when you receive this it will be over – My tears flow as I write, at the melancholy idea.'[10] It seems clear from this comment that she was ambivalent about him, that his crush on her was stronger than her feelings for him and that she never took him entirely seriously but was flattered by his interest. The couple barely had time to get to know one another. The flowing tears as she writes, misread by some biographers as signs of Jane's broken heart, are in reality little more than the author of the vellum note-books projecting herself into the role of the heroine of a novel of sensibility.

Nevertheless, she liked him and three years later she was keen to hear news of him: 'I was too proud to make any enquiries; but on my father's afterwards asking where he was, I learnt that he was gone back to London in his way to Ireland, where he is called to the Bar and means to practise.'[11] Once again, George Austen comes across as a sensitive and thoughtful father, asking the question that he knew his daughter wanted to hear but was too proud to ask. Perhaps the fact that Tom lived in Ireland would have been enough to soften the blow to her pride. Going off to Shropshire was one thing, going to Ireland quite another; it would be the destiny of her Knight nieces, Louisa and Cassandra, to be forced to leave their beloved Kent for Ireland when they were married. Thankfully, Jane was spared such separation.

She probably assumed that once Cassandra was married she would soon marry herself. But the death of Tom Fowle changed everything: it put an end not only to Cassy's but also to Jane Austen's matrimonial plans. In the years ahead Jane was to encounter several men who came close to proposing or indeed did propose marriage. Each time she shied away. There is strong evidence of an attachment between Jane and Edward Brook Bridges, brother of Elizabeth who married Edward Austen. She probably met him in 1794 when she first visited East Kent as the guest of her brother Edward. Two years later she opened a ball with Brook and he showed her great attention, playfully calling her 't'other Miss Austen'.[12] Whenever they met he singled her out for attention: 'it is impossible to do justice to the hospitality of his attentions towards me', she told Cassy, 'he made a point of ordering toasted cheese for supper entirely on my account'.[13] It seems that he proposed to Jane some time after he was ordained an Anglican priest, but was rejected. The proposal must have been before 1808 as she referred to his 'unaltered manners' to her when she saw him in June of that year.[14] She made a more explicit reference to his proposal in October 1808 when she wrote this to Cassandra: 'I wish you may be able to accept Lady Bridges's invitation, tho' *I* could not her son Edward's.'[15]

A year later when she discovered news of his engagement to someone else, she showed surprise but wished him well: 'Your news of Edw: Bridges was *quite* news ... I wish him happy with all my heart, and hope his choice may turn out according to his own expectations, and beyond those of his family.'[16] His marriage was unhappy and Jane did not approve of his choice of wife: 'she is a poor Honey – the sort of woman who gives me the idea of being determined never to be well – and who likes her spasms and nervousness and the consequence they give her, better than anything else'.[17] Later she remarked of Edward: 'Poor Wretch! He is quite the Dregs of the Family as to Luck.'[18]

She took an interest, clearly, in the wives of her ex-beaux. Upon meeting the wife of Charles Powlett, who had tried to kiss her at the ball in 1796, she described her as being 'everything that the Neighbour could wish her, silly and cross as well as extravagant'.[19]

One little-known romance, if Jane Austen's aunt Leigh-Perrot is to be believed, was between Jane and Harry Digweed. The Digweeds were a very close family, and Steventon Manor, where they lived, adjoined the grounds of Steventon rectory. Jane referred to him as 'my dear Harry'. Mrs Leigh-Perrot claimed that one of the reasons for the family's move to Bath was to separate 'Jane and a Digweed man'.[20] Another of her supposed beaux was Charles Fowle, brother to Cassandra's betrothed. When Jane found she couldn't afford the stockings she wanted, he insisted on buying them for her, a rather intimate commission. Charles was more likely to have been a brother figure, another of the surrogate siblings that had boarded at the rectory, but whether or not he was one of her suitors, his behaviour shows how capable she was of inspiring affection in the men around her.

Another abortive romance was engineered by Mrs Lefroy in 1797. Perhaps distressed by her part in the Tom Lefroy debacle, she began matchmaking in earnest. She found Jane a man she clearly thought more suitable than her nephew and invited to Ashe parsonage a young man with good prospects, fellow of a Cambridge college, the Reverend Samuel Blackall. Mrs Lefroy had talked to him at length about her friend Jane, though Jane was surprised that Blackall was prepared to fall in love 'knowing nothing of me'. After he had met Jane, he told Mrs Lefroy that he was interested in her as a suitable wife but had to wait some years before becoming financially secure. Jane wrote to Cassandra to relay the odd situation and her feelings towards him. She reported that Mrs Lefroy had shown her a letter which she had received from Blackall in which he had written, 'I am very sorry to hear of Mrs Austen's illness. It would give me particular pleasure to have an opportunity of improving my acquaintance with that family – with the hope of creating to myself a nearer interest. But at present I cannot indulge any expectation of it.'[21]

Jane might, reading between the lines, have suspected that Blackall was trying to placate Mrs Lefroy, who had pushed for the match. It is clear that Blackall had written previously to Mrs Lefroy to express his admiration for Jane, but was perhaps now pulling back. She went on to tell Cassandra:

This is rational enough; there is less love and more sense in it than sometimes appeared before, and I am very well satisfied. It will all go

5. The Sisters

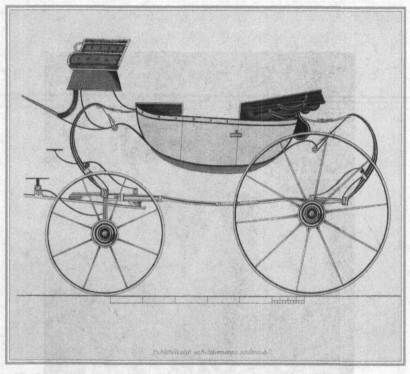

Published 1816 at R. Ackermanns 101 Strand.

6. The Barouche

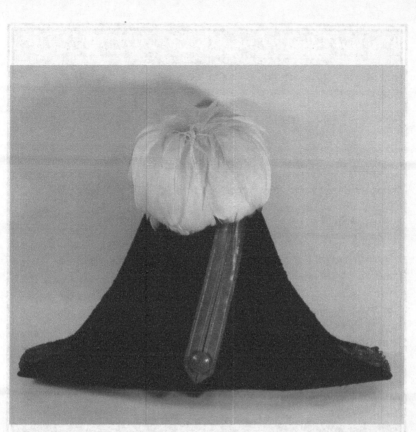

7. The Cocked Hat

Steventon Parsonage, near Overton, Hants.

TO be SOLD by AUCTION,
By Mr. STROUD,

On the premises, on Tuesday the 5th of May, 1801, and two following days, at eleven o'clock,

The neat HOUSHOLD FURNITURE, well made Chariot (with box to take off) and Harness, 200 Volumes of Books, Stump of Hay, Fowling Pieces, three Norman Cows and Calves, one Horse, and other Effects.

The furniture comprises four-post and field bed-steads, with dimity, moreen and other furnitures, fine feather beds and bedding, mattresses, pier and dressing glasses, floor and bedside carpets, handsome mahogany sideboard, modern set of circular dining tables on pillar and claws, Pembroke and card ditto, bureaus, chests of drawers and chairs, a piano forte in a handsome case (by Ganer), a large collection of music by the most celebrated composers, an 18-inch terrestial globe (by Adams), and microscope, mahogany library table with drawers; bookcase with six doors, eight feet by eight feet; a smaller ditto, tea china, a table set of Wedgwood ware, eight-day clock, side of bacon; kitchen, dairy and brewing utensils, 13 iron-bound casks, an end of hops, set of theatrical scenes, &c. &c.

The cows, nag horse, carriage and hay will be sold on the first day.

To be viewed on Monday the fourth.

Catalogues may be had at the Excise Offices, Basing-stoke and Winchester; Dean Gate; Inns at Overton; White Hart, Whitchurch; Angel, Reading; Hare and Hounds, Beenham; Hind's Head, Aldermaston; Anchor, Kingsclere; place of sale, and of the Auctioneer, Newbury.

8. The Theatrical Scenes

on exceedingly well, and decline away in a very reasonable manner ... our indifference will soon be mutual, unless his regard, which appeared to spring from knowing nothing of me at first, is best supported by never seeing me.[22]

The tone in this letter suggests that Austen was irked by the behaviour of her adored Mrs Lefroy, complaining that she 'made no remarks on the letter, nor did she indeed say anything about him as relative to me. Perhaps she thinks she has said too much already.' Jane Austen was not a woman to be pushed into marriage by anyone.

Nevertheless, she kept up an interest in Blackall and when he finally married she noted the fact to her brother Francis, who was clearly aware of the situation: 'I wonder whether you happened to see Mr Blackall's marriage in the papers last January. We did.' She went on to say, 'He was a piece of Perfection, noisy Perfection himself which I always recollect with regard.' Regard, that is, not regret: after all, as she said in another letter, 'pictures of perfection as you know make me sick and wicked'.[23] She also – as was her wont with ex-suitors – expressed a wish to know more about his wife, whose father had owned a plantation in Antigua: 'I should very much like to know what sort of woman she is ... I would wish Miss Lewis to be of a silent turn and rather ignorant, but naturally intelligent and wishing to learn; – fond of cold veal pies, green tea in the afternoon, and a green window blind at night.'[24]

According to family tradition it was a 'seaside romance' that was the most important of Jane Austen's romantic life. This occurred when she was living in Bath, and the family escaped the city in the summer. The various accounts of the romance are riven with discrepancies and inconsistencies. Some of them confuse the man with Samuel Blackall. The best account is from her niece Caroline, who relates that the family were holidaying in Devonshire when Jane Austen met and fell in love with a charming young man: 'I never heard Aunt Cass. speak of anyone else with such admiration – she had no doubt that a mutual attachment was in progress between him and her sister. They parted – but he made it plain that he would seek them out again – and shortly afterwards he died!'[25] Cousin Eliza wrote in 1801 that the Austens had just holidayed in Devonshire, so it was likely to have been on this visit.

One version of the story says that the mysterious gentleman was 'a young clergyman visiting his brother, who was one of the doctors of the town'. He and Jane allegedly fell in love with each other, and when the Austens left the resort, probably Sidmouth, 'he asked to be allowed to join them again further on in their tour, and the permission was given'. By this account, the family were encouraging a potential match. But instead of his arriving as expected, they received a letter announcing his death. In the more reliable version, the timescale is not quite so compressed: the mysterious gentleman asks where the family will be holidaying next year, perhaps implying that he will make a point of going there himself, but they hear of his death soon afterwards. All the accounts agree that he was someone special. Long after Jane's death, Cassandra was telling family members that his 'charm of person, mind and manners' had made him 'worthy to possess and likely to win her sister's love'.[26]

Harris Bigg-Wither (His father, Lovelace
Bigg, added the 'Wither' when he inherited
property in 1789)

Just a year after the supposed seaside romance, Jane Austen came the closest to marriage she would ever come. She accepted a proposal from a family friend, only to rescind her acceptance the following morning. This was a most unlikely pairing, and it shows Jane Austen appearing to behave in a most uncharacteristic way. Was her disposition after all more highly strung and fragile than we would assume from the cool and ironic voice of the novels and the letters?

The story is told in the family record from the perspective of Mary Austen, brother James's wife. She recorded the dates in her journal and then passed on the story in later years to her daughter Caroline. Jane and Cassandra had been staying with James and Mary back at the old family parsonage in Steventon late in the year of 1802. They took the opportunity to visit all their old friends, including Alethea and Catherine Bigg at Manydown Park, the lovely manor house where Jane had once danced and flirted with Tom Lefroy. The house, just two miles from Steventon, was set in fifteen hundred acres, and had a wing dating back to Tudor times, although the interior was beautifully modernized with an elegant staircase leading up to a spectacular first-floor drawing room.

Cassandra and Jane had intended to stay at Manydown for three weeks, but after only one week Mary Austen was surprised to see the arrival of the Biggs' carriage containing the four young women in a state of distress. They parted in the hall with tears and affectionate farewells. Without a word of explanation to Mary, Jane and Cassandra requested that James should take them home straight away to Bath. Mary tried to discourage them, pleading his weekend rectorial duties, but Jane was not to be detained and insisted on their immediate removal.

Eventually Mary and James were given an explanation. They were told that Catherine and Alethea's brother Harris had proposed to Jane and she had accepted him. However, on the following morning she had changed her mind and withdrawn her consent. According to Caroline, who had discussed the episode with her mother, Harris was 'very plain in person – awkward, and even uncouth in manner'. To judge from a surviving portrait sketch, though, his appearance was not so very unpresentable. He was tall, just down from Worcester College, Oxford, and six years younger than Jane, who was a couple of weeks short of her twenty-seventh birthday, an age at which prospects of any decent marriage would rapidly start receding. He did have a speech impediment, but he was kind, sensible and respectable. And, of course, he stood to inherit a considerable fortune. His elder brother had died as a teenager, so he stood to inherit Manydown. As Caroline reported, 'a great many would have taken him *without* love'.[27]

Why did she initially accept him? One explanation is that she was at a vulnerable moment, unhappy to be living in Bath, longing for a return to the locality of her childhood, and possibly recovering from news of the death of her seaside lover. The seeming evidence of a lost letter suggests that she herself described her decision as 'a momentary fit of self-delusion'.[28] Caroline believed that her aunt's acceptance was based on the advantages of the match and her long friendship with the family, but that on overnight reflection she thought that it would prove a miserable marriage: 'the place and the fortune which would certainly be *his*, could not alter the *man*'. In Caroline's interpretation of events, it was the 'worldly advantages' that momentarily appealed: 'My Aunts had very small fortunes and on their Father's death they and their Mother would be, they were aware, but poorly off – I believe most women so circumstanced would have taken Mr. W. and trusted to love after marriage'.[29]

But Jane Austen was not 'most young women'. She simply wasn't in love with Harris and – whether as an agony aunt or a novelist – she was never someone to advise matrimony for financial gain without love, whatever the temptations of security and status. When advising her niece Fanny on marriage she counselled that 'Anything is to be preferred or endured rather than marrying without Affection' and that 'nothing can be compared to the misery of being bound *without* Love'.[30]

We can only assume that during the long night when she changed her mind she took her own advice. She knew she was not in love with this man, whom she always thought of as her friend's little brother. He was not very clever: he failed to complete his studies at Worcester College. And he had health problems – a couple of years before, Austen had written in passing, 'Harris seems still in a poor way, from his bad habit of body; his hand bled again a little the other day, and Dr Littlehales has been with him lately'.[31] The year before that, she reported that he had been seized one morning at Winchester with 'a return of his former alarming complaint'; he recovered quickly from the 'attack', but 'in such a disorder his danger, I suppose, must always be great'.[32] This all sounds alarmingly reminiscent of the seizures of poor little George Austen. The prospect of a marriage that lacked scintillating conversation and that might descend into mere care for an invalid was not, on reflection, so very inviting after all. Having impulsively agreed, Jane Austen had the courage to come down in the morning and make a graceful withdrawal of her acceptance.

For Bigg-Wither, the consequence was more a degree of humiliation than a broken heart. He was only just twenty-one and he duly married less than two years later. He found a well-to-do girl from the Isle of Wight who bore him ten children before he died of apoplexy aged just over fifty.

Her decision to reject Harris greatly upset her sister-in-law Mary, who thought it was a good match for Jane. The telling detail in the story is not Harris's distress but that of the two pairs of sisters, crying in the hall. Jane and Cassandra were greatly attached to the Bigg sisters, and she must have felt that she had let them down. We can only imagine the scenes of jubilation when Jane accepted the proposal that night of 2 December only to have to face Harris, Catherine and Alethea in the morning with her retraction. It is to the credit of one and all that the family remained friends.

Other interested suitors were to be treated as little more than a joke. There was Mr Papillon, rector of Chawton ('I *will* marry Mr Papillon, whatever may be his reluctance or my own'), Henry's lawyer friend William Seymour who (Mr Elton-like) 'almost' proposed to her on a long coach ride, and the Prince Regent's librarian Stanier Clarke who was smitten by her. When she was at Stoneleigh in 1806, she was greatly admired by a Member of Parliament from Wigan, a distant relation of the Leigh family, but she gave him little encouragement. As one modern Janeite blogger has written, 'is there no end to the list of men who fancied Jane Austen'?[33]

There is something admirable about her decision to reject Harris Bigg-Wither. If her niece was correct in saying that she was tempted by his wealth, before coming to her senses, it is easy to see why, as a dowryless woman, she had her moment of madness. In *Pride and Prejudice*, she invites us to consider the ethics of marrying a repulsive man for security. Plain but clever Charlotte Lucas marries Mr Collins, one of Jane Austen's most sexually repellent characters, for social and economic reasons. Charlotte views marriage as a job: 'Without thinking highly either of men or of matrimony, marriage had always been her object; it was the only honourable provision for well-educated young women of small fortune, and however uncertain of giving happiness, must be their pleasantest preservative from want.'[34]

Though Charlotte is presented sympathetically – marriage is a contract and each side knows what they're getting from the transaction – Lizzy

Bennet ultimately rejects Charlotte's mercenary motives for marrying a man she does not and cannot love. Mary Wollstonecraft famously described marriage 'for support' as tantamount to 'legal prostitution'.[35] The sub-text to Lizzy's rejection of Mr Collins's proposal is her sexual antipathy towards him. Perhaps her creator was also repelled by the thought of having sex with the oafish, awkward, stammering Harris.

This brings us to sex and childbirth. No one knows what went through Jane Austen's mind in the long night when she thought about what the reality of marriage to Harris would mean, and then changed her mind, but she must have weighed up the costs and going to bed with him would surely have been one of them.

Jane Austen was certainly not prudish about sex. Illicit sex, either in adultery or sex before marriage, is explored in several of the novels. Poor Eliza Williams in *Sense and Sensibility* is seduced and left pregnant by the cad Willoughby: that he comes close to harming Marianne in the same way is made clear. Maria Bertram cuckolds her husband with the rake Henry Crawford. Sir Edward Denham in *Sanditon* plans to rape Clara Brereton in the manner of Richardson's Lovelace.

But she does not only present us with women as victims of predatory men. Jane Austen also wrote about woman's sexual pleasure. In the character of Lydia Bennet she presents us with a lusty teenage girl who enjoys sex before marriage with Wickham with very little concern for the consequences. They live together in lodgings in London. When Lizzy tells Darcy that Lydia is 'lost for ever', she is making it clear that he will never marry her: 'She has no money, no connections, nothing that can tempt him to ...'[36] Lydia's 'infamy' (a strong word for Jane Austen) is emphasized, and Wickham's 'violation of decency, honour and interest'. The long discussion between Elizabeth and Mrs Gardiner about Lydia's sexual transgression is remarkably open: 'But can you think that Lydia is so lost to everything but love of him, as to consent to live with him on any other terms than marriage?' asks Mrs Gardiner. Elizabeth, fully aware of her sister's 'animal spirits', knows that she is very capable of living in sin with him. She has not been seduced or forced by Wickham. She enters into her relationship with her eyes wide open. Lydia herself is indifferent to her disgrace: 'she would not hear of leaving Wickham. She was sure they should be married some time or the other, and it did not much signify when.'[37]

In *Mansfield Park*, Maria Bertram's adultery with Henry Crawford is foreshadowed in a scene at Sotherton where she leaves behind her betrothed, Mr Rushworth, to climb around an iron gate with Henry Crawford to enter the wilderness beyond. Fanny Price urges her cousin to consider her actions: 'You will hurt yourself, Miss Bertram ... you will certainly hurt yourself against those spikes – you will tear your gown – you will be in danger of slipping into the ha-ha.'[38]

The image of the torn dress as a symbol of sexual disgrace is also used in *Pride and Prejudice*. Lydia sends a request to her maid that she should 'mend a great slit in my worked muslin gown'.[39] We do not have to be Freudians to recognize a shocking image of her sexual transgression. Lydia's 'slit' can't be mended, except by a forced marriage, which is exactly what happens, though no one is fooled by the 'patched-up business'.[40] Jane Austen allows Lydia to be free from repentance or shame. Indeed, the moral torchlight is shone upon the odious Mr Collins when he tells Mr Bennet to 'throw off your unworthy child from your affection for ever, and leave her to repay the fruits of her own heinous offence'.[41] Lydia is fortunate not to share the fate of Eliza Williams in *Sense and Sensibility*, who is abandoned by Willoughby when she falls pregnant with his child.

Sex leads to pregnancy and in Georgian England that often led to death. Jane Austen seems to have had a phobia of childbirth, which is hardly surprising given the number of women she knew who died in childbed, including two of her sisters-in-law. There are many glimpses in her letters of her fears and anxieties around what she called 'the business of mothering'. In the same letter in which she wrote about her suitors Tom Lefroy and Samuel Blackall her thoughts turned to her sister-in-law Mary Austen, who was shortly expecting to give birth, 'she was glad to get rid of her child, of whom she is heartily tired'. Jane noted that 'Mrs Coulthard and Anne, late of Manydown, are both dead, and both died in childbed. We have not regaled Mary with this news.' She added drily but revealingly, 'Mary does not manage matters in such a way as to make me want to lay in myself.'[42]

A niece remembered that Jane Austen was thankful to have been spared the ordeal of childbirth and that she often expressed her relief in her letters. One of the great friends that she made in London was Frances Tilson, who was the wife of one of Henry Austen's banking colleagues: 'poor Woman! how can she honestly be breeding again?'[43] Frances Tilson was about to give birth to her eighth child – she eventually had eleven. Again, when Jane

THE REAL JANE AUSTEN

heard the news that her niece Anna was pregnant for the third time, she was dismayed: 'Poor Animal, she will be worn out before she is thirty. – I am very sorry for her.'[44] To another acquaintance, who seemed to be permanently tired and pregnant, she advised 'the simple regimen of separate rooms'. Another friend, Mrs Benn, 'has a 13th': 'I am quite tired of so many children.'[45]

She warned Fanny Knight of the perils of an early marriage, seeing the example of Anna, and not wanting Fanny to wear herself out by having children too young. A letter from aunt to niece counselling against over-hasty progress from love to marriage is wisely phrased:

Do not be in a hurry; depend upon it, the right Man will come at last; you will in the course of the next two or three years, meet with somebody more generally unexceptionable than anyone you have yet known, who will love you as warmly as ever *He* [John Plumptre, with whom Fanny was in love] did, and who will so completely attach you, that you will feel you never really loved before. – And then, by not beginning the business of Mothering quite so early in life, you will be young in Constitution, spirits, figure, and countenance, while Mrs Wm. Hammond is growing old by confinements and nursing.[46]

Few of Jane Austen's suitors had made a lasting impression on her. As she herself noted, she had high standards. It is gratifying to have in her own words her description of the ideal husband: 'There *are* such beings in the World perhaps, one in a Thousand ... where Grace and Spirit are united to Worth, where the Manners are equal to the Heart and Understanding.' But she was realist enough to know 'such a person may not come in your way'.[47]

The details of the seaside romance that were revealed many years after her death tell us far more about Cassandra than they do about Jane. The story came to light in the first place only because Cassandra was struck by another young man (a Mr Henry Eldridge of the Engineers) who reminded her of Jane's seaside lover: a good-looking, clever man who died young. This was Cassandra projecting her own tragedy on to her sister. Maybe it was her own story of loving and losing Tom Fowle and her own romantic nature, her belief in the irreplaceable 'one great love', that deep down she was really remembering. For the nieces who had known Jane Austen well, the seaside romance left no lasting legacy: she 'never *had* any attachment that overclouded her happiness, for long. *This* had not gone far enough, to leave misery behind.'[48]

People sometimes wonder how Jane Austen could write so compellingly about love when she never married or had a grand passion of her own. We are fortunate to have a letter to her niece, Fanny Knight, in which she has been solicited for, and gives, advice on what Fanny Burney had once called 'the minute and complex intricacies of the human heart'.[49] It gives exceptional insight into her own view of such matters: 'I read yours through the very evening I received it, getting away by myself. I could not bear to leave off when I had once begun. I was full of curiosity and concern,' she begins. She finds Fanny's dilemma of the utmost interest: 'I really am impatient myself to be writing something on so very interesting a subject, though I have no hope of writing anything to the purpose … I could lament in one sentence and laugh in the next.'

Then, turning agony aunt, she tells Fanny that it is her own belief that no one dies from disappointment in love. This is the down-to-earth wisdom of Shakespeare's Rosalind in *As You Like It* ('men have died from time to time but not for love'), as opposed to the romantic fantasy of the novel of sensibility (the suicide of Goethe's Young Werther on the loss of his beloved Charlotte). 'Wisdom is better than Wit,' writes Austen. She tells it to Fanny as she sees it: 'from the time of our being in London together, I thought you really very much in love. – But you certainly are not at all there is no concealing it. – What strange creatures we are! – It seems as if your being secure of him … had made you indifferent.'

But her advice is firm: 'And now, my dear Fanny, having written so much on one side of the question, I shall turn round and entreat you not to commit yourself farther, and not to think of accepting him unless you really do like him. Anything is to be preferred or endured rather than marrying without Affection; and if his deficiences of Manner etc etc strike you more than all his good qualities, if you continue to think strongly of them, give him up at once.' But Jane Austen can't suppress her wit, even for the sake of all this wisdom. She betrays herself by a revealing comment, which was excised from the first edition of letters. Fanny had confided in her aunt the rather shocking detail that she had sneaked off to take a peep in her suitor's bedroom: 'Your trying to excite your own feelings by a visit to his room amused me excessively. The dirty shaving rag was exquisite! Such a circumstance ought to be in print. Much too good to be lost.'[50]

A dirty shaving rag in a man's private bedroom: once again, it is an object, a small thing, that takes us to the heart of Jane Austen's vision of the world. In this case, the thing that embodies marriage is mundane and rather unpleasant.

One of her last letters written to Fanny Knight is a response to yet another dilemma in love. A letter dating just a few months short of her death reveals her delight in her niece, but there is also a sadness that this lovely voice will be suppressed by the state of marriage:

> You are inimitable, irresistable. You are the delight of my Life. Such Letters, such entertaining Letters, as you have lately sent! – Such a description of your queer little heart! – Such a lovely display of what Imagination does. – You are worth your weight in Gold, or even in the new Silver Coinage. – I cannot express to you what I have felt in reading your history of yourself – how full of Pity and Concern and Admiration and Amusement I have been. You are the Paragon of all that is Silly and Sensible, common-place and eccentric, Sad and Lively, Provoking and Interesting. – Who can keep pace with the fluctuations of your Fancy, the Capprizios of your Taste, the Contradictions of your Feelings? – You are so odd! – and all the time, so perfectly natural – so peculiar in yourself, and yet so like everybody else! – It is very, very gratifying to me to know you so intimately. You can hardly think what a pleasure it is to me, to have such thorough pictures of your Heart. – Oh! What a loss it will be, when you are married. You are too agreable in your single state, too agreable as a Neice.[51]

The thought of Fanny married was almost more than she could bear: 'I shall hate you when your delicious play of Mind is all settled down into conjugal and maternal affections.' She truly believed that marriage could stifle women's voices. This was the fate to which she would not submit herself in her own life. The delicious play of her own mind would never be settled into conjugal and maternal affections.

Jane Austen writes brilliantly about courtship and love, but always in a way that is leavened with a healthy dose of realism. Hers are not novels in which the heroine falls in love at first sight with a handsome stranger who becomes an ideal husband. The handsome stranger – Willoughby,

Wickham, Henry Crawford, Frank Churchill – turns out to be a bad bet. More often than not, the true love is a fraternal figure, such as Edmund Bertram, George Knightley or Edward Ferrars. When Fanny Price marries the cousin with whom she has been brought up and who has always treated her as a little sister, there is a whiff of brother–sister incest, a motif that is surprisingly common in the literature of the age.[52] The closest Austen comes to the romantic cliché of the romantic stranger is the relationship between Elizabeth and Darcy, and yet they begin by disliking one another. Love often comes slowly, surprisingly.

In her novels, Austen boldly abstains from reporting the grand speeches of 'romantic' lovers. At the point where the hero and heroine are finally united, she leaves much to the imagination of the reader. Mr Knightley resolutely says, 'I cannot make speeches … If I loved you less, I might be able to talk about it more.' Emma's internalized emotions are beautifully expressed but never spoken: 'What did she say? – Just what she ought, of course. A lady always does.'[53] Edmund Bertram's love for Fanny takes time: 'I only intreat everybody to believe that exactly at the time when it was quite natural that it should be so, and not a week earlier, Edmund did cease to care about Miss Crawford, and became as anxious to marry Fanny, as Fanny herself could desire.'[54]

The closest she comes to depicting extreme passion is Captain Wentworth's emotional declaration to Anne Elliot: 'You pierce my soul. I am half agony, half hope. Tell me that I am not too late, that such precious feelings are gone forever. I offer myself to you again with a heart even more your own, than when you almost broke it eight years and a half ago.'[55] In the first draft of the novel, his declaration of love is much more mildly phrased (merely 'Anne, my own dear Anne!') and the bulk of the scene is given in reported speech. The unsaid is more important than the said: Wentworth plays awkwardly with the back of a chair in the course of 'a silent, but a very powerful Dialogue'.[56] Jane Austen then revised her closing chapter so that the speech was made more passionate – but it is given via a letter. There is always a feeling of being at one remove, of authorial detachment. It is the distance that confers the intensity.

'I have no doubt that Aunt Jane was beloved of several in the course of her life and was herself very capable of loving', wrote her niece Caroline. Contrariwise, 'Aunt Jane never *had* any attachment that overclouded her happiness for long', wrote her nephew James Edward. But perhaps the voice of the novels is more to be trusted than the words of the family memoirs: 'It is always incomprehensible to a man that a woman should ever refuse an offer of marriage,' says Emma Woodhouse. 'A man always imagines a woman to be ready for anybody who asks her.'[57] For Jane Austen herself it was perfectly comprehensible to refuse Harris Bigg-Wither. She was not ready for anybody who asked her.

She did not want her own voice to be stifled by marriage. She was, I believe, happy to remain single: apart from the Bigg-Wither episode, the closest she ever got to marriage was her fictionalizing in her father's parish register. Perhaps she genuinely preferred the appellation that her father gave her in one of the vellum notebooks: 'Miss Jane Austen, Spinster'.[58] Once Cassandra had made the decision to remain a spinster, Jane saw that she did not have to be separated from the sister she adored. They could be together, for ever.

As for children, her books were the only offspring she desired. Catherine Hubback, a niece, wrote: 'she always said her books were her children, and supplied her sufficient interest for happiness; and some of her letters, triumphing over the married women of her acquaintance, and rejoicing in her own freedom from care were most amusing'.[59] The words 'rejoicing in her own freedom from care' are very revealing. Austen simply did not envy the women of her acquaintance who were married and exhausted by husband and children. She gave birth to her novels. They were her 'sucking child' or 'my own darling child'. 'My dear Anna,' she wrote in 1816 following the birth of her niece's daughter, 'As I wish very much to see *your* Jemima, I am sure you will like to see *my* Emma.'[60]

11

The Ivory Miniature

On 29 May 1780, the accomplished society artist Richard Crosse meticulously recorded in his ledger that he had 'received of Mrs Lefroy eight pounds eight shillings' for her ivory miniature.[1] It is a little bit, two inches high, of ivory worked with a fine brush in watercolour. It shows a most elegant woman, her hair powdered and tied. There is intelligence in her eyes and kindness in her half smile.

The miniature portrait was a very particular genre, highly popular in Jane Austen's day: it was almost always drawn from life, with the intention of creating as accurate a representation of the subject as possible. Typically, such pieces would be executed as keepsakes, intended to hold the image of a beloved person in the memory during their absence. The portrait would be given to a close friend or a lover or a family member – perhaps sent to a brother away at sea. The modern equivalent would be the photograph placed on the mantelpiece. And indeed it was with the advent of photography in the mid-Victorian era that the genre went into decline.

When a person died, their miniature could be turned into a piece of mourning jewellery, as is the case here, where the date of Mrs Lefroy's death is engraved on the tiny gilded frame.

Anne Lefroy, sometimes known, because of her sophistication, as Madam Lefroy (though Jane always referred to her as Mrs Lefroy) was one of the Austens' closest neighbours. The Reverend George Lefroy and his wife moved to Ashe rectory, just down the road from Steventon, in 1783.

They expanded the cultural horizons of the area. George Lefroy transformed the undistinguished rectory into a suitable residence for a Georgian gentleman and made it a place where he could entertain. His parents had lived abroad and the home was furnished with lovely artefacts from Italy. He was described as 'an excellent man, of courtly manners, who knew the world and mixed in it'.[2] His wife was a great beauty and a cultured woman, with 'an exquisite taste for poetry'. Allegedly, she 'could almost recite the chief English poets by heart, especially Milton, Pope, Collins, Gray, and the poetical passages of Shakespeare'.[3] The Lefroys had a carriage, which Anne would often lend out to families without one, such as the Austens.

Anne's brother, the author and genealogist Egerton Brydges, was devoted to her, describing her as 'one of the most amiable and eloquent women I ever knew. She was a great reader, and her rapidity of apprehension was like lightning.'[4] He attributed his own love of poetry to her influence. She wrote and was indeed a published poet. Three of her poems appeared in *The Poetical Register and Repository of Fugitive Poetry* and a larger collection was published posthumously.[5] She was also an accomplished amateur painter, particularly of flowers and insects. She was 'fond of society and was the life of every party into which she entered'. All in all, she was 'universally beloved and admired'.[6]

The Lefroys loved the theatre and had a wide circle of friends, who were introduced to the Austens. Mrs Lefroy was not, however, an amateur actress herself. She was a great friend of the Duchess of Bolton, but refused to take part in her amateur production of *Jane Shore* at Hackwood Park, just nine miles from Ashe. She declined by verse: 'Can I a wife, a mother, tread the Stage,/Burn with false fire and glow with mimic Rage?'[7]

Firm in her Christian faith, Anne Lefroy was devoted to her charity work and opened a school for the poor children of the surrounding neighbourhood, where she taught them to read. Remarkably, she also personally vaccinated the people of her husband's parish against smallpox. She wrote to her son, telling him all about her admiration of Dr Edward Jenner's work with the cowpox vaccine and told him that she had inoculated 'upwards of 800 poor with my own hands'.[8] As a young mother living in Basingstoke, she had experienced a severe outbreak of smallpox which greatly affected her, and accounted for her interest in Jenner and his inoculations. Of her seven children, three died, two of them in infancy in Jane Austen's lifetime.

She was famous for driving a donkey cart around the area, as Jane was later to do. Many of her visits to the poor were made on this.

A friend who knew her in the early days of her marriage wrote that George and Anne were 'so pleasant': 'Anne was one of the happiest beings I ever saw. She laughed almost the whole time, but it did not seem a mockery of joy but genuine mirth.'[9] The same could have been said of Jane Austen. Born in 1749, Mrs Lefroy was many years older than Jane but they formed a close and loving friendship, beginning from the time when the Lefroys invited the bright young Austen girl to play with their daughter. Anne was in many ways a more congenial mother figure to Jane than the rather less accomplished and certainly less attractive Mrs Austen (who lost her teeth at an early age, making her look older than she was). Jane's literary aspirations were encouraged and she was given free rein in the library at the Ashe parsonage. Mrs Lefroy influenced Austen's taste and judgements, just as she shaped her own brother's bent for poetry.[10]

There are few direct references to Mrs Lefroy in Jane Austen's surviving letters, the great majority of which are to Cassandra, who was not so close to her and who may even have been jealous of the close friendship between her younger sister and the older woman. Such references as there are include such mundane information as the fact that Mrs Lefroy admired Jane's new velvet cap at a ball. Nevertheless, her involvement in the aborted romances with nephew Tom Lefroy and the Reverend Samuel Blackall suggests her centrality to Austen's early life.

Even after she moved away from Steventon, Jane continued to visit her mentor in the rectory at Ashe. In September 1801, Mrs Lefroy told her son that Jane and her sister had spent the day with her at the rectory, adding, rather wistfully, 'they mean to return to Bath and after that I suppose it will be long before they again visit Steventon'.[11] They were reunited in 1803 for a longer visit, during which she described a charming picture of Jane and Cassandra helping with her school: 'I am now writing surrounded by my school and with the [Miss Austens] in the room.'[12] This may have been the last happy time that they spent together.

Mrs Lefroy had continued her life of good works. During the bad winter of February 1800, she set up a straw manufactory to give the women and children of the district a chance to earn a little money. Straw was in demand for making hats. As well as performing charitable acts such as this, she encouraged her children to look to the wider world. One of her sons,

Christopher Edward Lefroy, grew up to be a poet and an author of tales set in foreign parts. He eventually oversaw the suppression of the slave trade in Surinam.

Mrs Lefroy worried greatly about a French invasion. She told her son of how James Austen was helping to raise a Corps of Volunteers in the summer of 1803. She fantasized about defending her country herself: 'In case of actual invasion ... I think I could handle Cartridges if not fire a musket myself upon such an occasion.'[13] One can see why she was a woman whom Jane Austen revered.

One winter's day in 1804 Anne Lefroy set off on horseback with a servant to do some shopping. Meeting James Austen in the village, she remarked on the stupidity and laziness of her horse. It bolted on the way home and the Lefroy servant couldn't catch it. In trying to get off, Anne fell and hit her head on the road. She died twelve hours later. She was only fifty-five. It was 16 December, Jane Austen's twenty-ninth birthday. Anne Lefroy was deeply mourned in the neighbourhood and by all who knew her. According to an obituary in the *Gentleman's Magazine*, 'It would be almost impossible to find an individual, in a private station, whose death will be more generally and deeply felt ... In intellect, in heart, in temper, in manners, in strict and elevated principles, in pure and untainted conduct, she has left no second behind her.'[14]

A poem by Jane Austen reveals the depth of her devotion. Here Anne is described as 'the best of women':

> Angelic woman! past my power to praise
> In language meet thy talents, temper, and mind,
> Thy solid worth, thy captivating grace,
> Thou friend and ornament of human kind.[15]

This is the orthodox poetic language of the age, but no less sincere for that. There is a clear impression of Mrs Lefroy's good sense, her creativity, her sweetness of manner and evenness of temper, her beauty and her Christian spirit, her 'grace of tongue' which meant that she 'never misapplied' language – praise indeed from the young author.

Jane Austen never got over the shock of Anne's sudden demise. Every birthday brought her pain because it was a reminder of the day she had lost her 'Beloved Friend':

The day returns again, my natal day;
What mix'd emotions in my mind arise!
Beloved Friend; four years have passed away
Since thou wert snatched for ever from our eyes.[16]

There is something especially poignant in Jane Austen's acknowledgement that it was Mrs Lefroy's interest in her as a young girl that initiated the love they felt for each other: 'Her partial favour from my earliest years/ Consummates all.' She had lost a friend who was almost a second mother, a mentor who had nurtured both her talent and her character in her formative years.

A second, even worse blow fell just a few weeks later. Mrs Austen had always been the one in poor health, but then the Reverend George Austen began suffering from a persistent feverish complaint. He was taken ill one Saturday morning early in 1805. He seemed to be a little better by the evening, and the next day he got up and walked around the house.

But his 'fever' got worse towards the end of the day, and he died the following morning. Jane cut off a lock of her beloved father's hair and kept it in a wrap of paper. The loss was especially painful because it came so soon after Mrs Lefroy's fatal accident. This was the darkest period of Jane Austen's life.

The funeral took place in St Swithin's, the parish church of genteel Bath, the following Saturday. George Austen was buried in the crypt and a simple ledger stone was carved for his grave: 'Under this stone rests the remains of the Revd. GEORGE AUSTEN Rector of Steventon and Deane in Hampshire who departed this life the 21st January 1805 Aged 73 years'. James and Henry were in attendance, but the naval brothers were not able to make it (widows and daughters did not usually attend funerals).

Jane Austen wrote to her brother Frank on the day of their father's death, comforting herself with the thought that it was not a prolonged illness and that 'his worth and constant preparation for another World' must have assured his salvation.[17] He had done his duty, as the ledger stone said, as a rector; he would now be rewarded in heaven. His daughter wrote again the following day: 'We have lost an Excellent Father ... To have seen him languishing long, struggling for Hours, would have been dreadful! – and thank God! we were all spared from it. Except the restlessness and confusion of high Fever, he did not suffer.' 'His tenderness as a Father', she added, 'who can do justice to?'[18] A week later she sent Frank some small tokens of remembrance: a miniature compass and sundial in a black shagreen case, together with a pair of scissors.

* * *

Jane Austen's own religious faith saw her through this worst of times, as it did through all her life. The following words are not in the voice that we are familiar with from the novels, but they were written in Jane Austen's hand: 'Teach us to understand the sinfulness of our own hearts, and bring to our knowledge every fault of temper and evil habit which we have indulged in to the discomfort of our fellow creatures and the danger of our own souls.' And again,

> Heartily do we pray for the safety of all that travel by Land or by Sea, for the comfort and protection of the Orphan and Widow and that thy pity may be shewn upon all Captives and Prisoners. Above all

Jane Austen's beloved father

other blessings Oh! God, for ourselves, and our fellow-creatures, we implore Thee to quicken our sense of thy Mercy in the redemption of the World, of the Value of that Holy Religion in which we have been brought up, that we may not, by our own neglect, throw away the salvation thou has given us, nor be Christians only in name.

Cassandra Austen, at her death in 1845, left her niece, Cassandra Esten ('Cassy') Austen, the eldest daughter of their brother Charles, two sheets of paper containing the prayers from which these quotations are taken.[19] The inscription 'Prayers Composed by my ever dear Sister Jane' appears on the outside of the folded sheets.

These prayers were probably written for the purpose of family devotion. It does seem likely that the Austen family observed evening prayers at home. A letter written to Cassandra on a Sunday night in 1808 refers to evening devotions (which would include prayers): 'In the evening we had the Psalms and Lessons, and a sermon at home.'[20] In *Mansfield Park* Fanny Price says of morning and evening prayers at Sotherton, 'A whole family assembling regularly for the purpose of prayer, is fine.'[21]

Jane Austen was a devout Christian. Her surviving letters barely touch on her faith precisely because it was deeply personal and not to be treated lightly or with frivolity. To Cassandra she did not need to write about the faith that they shared. Among those few letters to others that do survive, several, notably those written following a death, and above all the two to Frank in the immediate aftermath of her father's parting, are testimony to her profound and sincere faith.

Her faith is also apparent from her admiration for a painting that she saw when she was in London in 1814 correcting proofs and changing her publisher. She went to an art exhibition in Pall Mall and was especially impressed by Benjamin West's vast canvas *Christ Rejected*, as she reported to Martha Lloyd:

I have seen West's famous Painting, and prefer it to anything of the kind I ever saw before. I do not know that it *is* reckoned superior to his 'Healing in the Temple', but it has gratified *me* much more, and indeed is the first representation of our Saviour which ever at all contented me. 'His Rejection by the Elders', is the subject. – I want to have You and Cassandra see it.[22]

Her words 'our Saviour' are particularly striking.

With her enlightened upbringing and knowledge of human nature, she was never shocked by adultery, yet when she read in the local newspaper that a married neighbour, Mrs Powlett, had eloped, she was saddened and surprised – not by the adultery but more because the previous Sunday Mrs Powlett had 'staid the Sacrament' (stayed behind after Morning Prayer in order to receive Holy Communion) at church alongside Jane and Cassandra.[23]

Henry Austen described his sister as 'thoroughly religious and devout; fearful of giving offence to God, and incapable of feeling it towards any fellow creature'. It must be remembered that by the time he wrote this he was a clergyman with Evangelical leanings and a very enthusiastic one at that. Certainly the comments in Jane Austen's letters would suggest that she was quite capable of giving offence to people. Henry was right to emphasize her deep and sincere faith, but it was of great importance to her that it remained private and sacred, not to be openly discussed.

Henry attested that her opinions 'accorded strictly with those of our Established Church'.[24] By this he meant the conservative Anglican Church. She was the daughter of a High Church Tory rector at a time when there was a great deal of laxity in the Church. Many clergymen were pluralists, which meant that they held several livings at the same time – her father was rector of both Steventon and Deane. As a child she showed a deliberately provocative, if playful, fondness for Roman Catholicism. Writing about King James I she wrote, 'As I am myself partial to the roman catholic religion, it is with infinite regret that I am obliged to blame the Behaviour of any Member of it … in this reign the roman Catholics of England did not behave like Gentlemen to the protestants.'[25] But of course the real allegiance she is showing here is not to the Church of Rome but to the Stuart line.

During her lifetime, the Evangelical movement burgeoned, sweeping some of her own family into its wake, much to her dismay. Evangelicals had no time for ritual and placed emphasis on the individual, the sinner, who repents, is saved and 'converted' by the Holy Spirit. Biblical authority was paramount, as well as the need for actively sharing the Gospel and expressing one's faith. They viewed the Holy Spirit as above 'reason', decrying the 'deist' theologians of the eighteenth century, intellectual descendants of John Locke, for 'the fashion in introducing a pompous display of *reasoning* into religion'.[26] As a woman whose faith was so personal and quiet, Jane Austen found the zeal of the Evangelicals repugnant. It was their overbearing 'enthusiasm' that she found especially unseemly.

Her own cousin Edward Cooper, of whom she was once fond, became a fervent Evangelical. 'We do not much like Mr. Cooper's new Sermons,' she wrote late in her life, 'they are fuller of Regeneration and Conversion than ever – with the addition of his zeal in the cause of the Bible Society.'[27] (The British and Foreign Bible Society, founded in 1804 by the Evangelicals, distributed free copies of the Bible to the poor and the heathen.) Jane Austen had been reading cousin Cooper's latest book, *Two Sermons Preached in the Old and the New Churches at Wolverhampton, preparatory to the Establishment of a Bible-Institution*, published in 1816. The 'zeal' to which she refers is apparent throughout: 'Bear in mind that it is not enough to live under the light, you must also walk in the light. It is not enough that the light is *around* you, it must be also *in* you.'[28]

She was also familiar with Cooper's most popular work, his *Sermons* of 1809, which went into many editions. Here he writes of the sinner, the promise of the Gospel, the Holy Spirit and the need for Conversion. She was keen to hear Cassandra's view of this drearily written tirade, adding that Edward's son had also become a 'Pompous Sermon-writer'.[29] She could not abide Cooper's zeal, his pomposity, his lack of humour and his childlike belief that some were saved and others not. Following the death of her sister-in-law Elizabeth Knight, she hoped that Edward would not send one of his letters of 'cruel comfort' (that is to say a sermon on the world as a vale of tears and the delights of the afterlife).[30]

One particularly influential group of Evangelicals, based in south London, were known as the 'Clapham sect' or 'The Saints'. As committed to social reform as they were to the Gospel, they included figures such as the anti-slavery campaigner William Wilberforce, the theologian and preacher Thomas Gisborne and the schoolmistress, philanthropist and bestselling novelist Hannah More. All of them were friends of Jane Austen's Evangelical cousin Edward Cooper. She was determined to dislike them. When Cassandra recommended More's 'sermon novel' *Coelebs in Search of a Wife* in 1809, she made her feelings quite clear: 'You have by no means raised my curiosity after Caleb; – My disinclination for it before was affected, but now it is real; I do not like the Evangelicals. Of course I shall be delighted when I read it, like other people, but till I do, I dislike it.'[31] She refused to call the novel by its ridiculous name *Coelebs* – Cassandra thought that Jane had referred to it as 'Caleb' because she had misread her handwriting, but Jane replied that 'Caleb' had an 'honest, unpretending sound' whereas *Coelebs* was 'pedantry and affectation'.[32]

Nevertheless, when advising her niece Fanny on courtship matters in 1814 – Fanny was worried that her suitor might be attracted to Evangelicalism – she jumped to their defence: 'I am by no means convinced that we ought not all to be Evangelicals, and am at least persuaded that they who are so from Reason and Feeling, must be happiest and safest.'

But this remark must be seen in context. It comes from the extraordinarily beautiful and complex letter of courtship advice discussed earlier, in which Austen begins by trying to show Fanny that she can't be in love with the man in question, but then the more she writes the warmer her feelings become towards him. It is a letter that, like a great work of art, considers not just 'one side of the question' but both; a letter that reveals Austen's suppleness of thought and openness of opinion – 'I am feeling differently every moment, and shall not be able to suggest a single thing that can assist your Mind. – I could lament in one sentence and laugh in the next, but as to Opinion or Counsel I am sure none will [be] extracted worth having from this Letter.'[33] This is a superb reminder that we should be very hesitant about 'extracting' Jane Austen's 'Opinion or Counsel' – about Evangelical faith or anything else – from her novels and letters. It was precisely the imposition of 'Opinion or Counsel' on the reader that she disliked about the didacticism of writers such as More and Gisborne (she may have softened in her prejudice against Gisborne because on reading him she discovered that he was slightly less rigid and opinionated than she had imagined he would be from his titles and reputation). For Jane Austen, it was not the business of writers to tell people what to do. It was their business to track the endlessly fascinating process of how human beings find themselves 'feeling differently every moment'.

What she is also saying to Fanny is that one should not generalize about classes of people. Not all Evangelicals are the same. If someone comes to an Evangelical position from both 'Reason and Feeling' (both sense and sensibility), all well and good. Especially good, she no doubt thought, if that faith led to good works among the poor and support for the abolition of the slave trade. Fanny's response to her aunt's letter is lost, but she obviously took it seriously because Austen wrote back to say 'I cannot suppose

Fanny Knight, to whom Austen wrote about her
'ideas of the Christian Religion'

we differ in our ideas of the Christian Religion. You have given an excellent description of it. We only affix a different meaning to the Word *Evangelical*.'[34]

If Austen was such a devoted Christian, how was that reflected in her novels? In one of the first extended accounts of her literary career, Richard Whately, later Archbishop of Dublin, writing in the *Quarterly Review* in 1821, perceived that while she was a Christian writer, she was not, like her contemporaries Maria Edgeworth and Hannah More, morally didactic. She did not write 'dramatic sermons' rather than novels. Her primary aim was to please, so she did not allow her morality and religion to obtrude:

> Miss Austin has the merit (in our judgment most essential) of being evidently a Christian writer: a merit which is much enhanced, both on the score of good taste, and of practical utility, by her religion not being at all obtrusive ... The subject is rather alluded to, and that

ANE AUSTEN

incidentally, than studiously brought forward and dwelt upon. The
moral lessons ... spring incidentally from the circumstances of the
story; they are not forced upon the reader.[35]

Whately's review would no doubt have pleased her. Moral didacticism she
abhorred. Her dislike for Hannah More, whose books really were drama-
tized sermons, was evident. Her joke about inserting one or two of her
brother Henry's sermons in a novel, to be discussed in a later chapter, shows
that a sermonizer was not the sort of novelist she wanted to be. She was a
quintessential Anglican: spiritually sincere but undemonstrative, with a
quiet religion characterized, in Whately's fine phrase, by 'practical utility'.
And it is the practical utility of Christianity that interests her in the novels.

Importantly, not one of the clergymen in her novels shows any affinity
with the Evangelical movement. In her unfinished novel *The Watsons*, Mr
Howard is praised for speaking his sermon, 'without any Theatrical grimace
or violence'. He preaches 'with great propriety and in a very impressive
manner ... much better calculated to inspire Devotion'.[36] Measured and
reasoned discourse is what she approves of – not the fire and brimstone of
the histrionic Evangelicals. Had *The Watsons* been finished, this worthy
clergyman would have married the heroine.

But her fictional clergymen are by no means all paragons of virtue.
Henry Tilney is a charming picture of a young clergyman who still loves
secular pleasures such as dancing, reading novels and theatre-visits – all
pursuits frowned upon by 'The Saints'. Austen had observed enough clergymen in her lifetime to know that many of them were far from being saintly.
Dr Grant in *Mansfield Park* is a glutton and Mr Collins in *Pride and
Prejudice* a toady. Mr Elton in *Emma* is odious. In the 'Opinions of Emma'
that she gathered from family and friends, she noted down the views of a
Mrs Wroughton: 'Thought the Authoress wrong, in such times as these, to
draw such Clergymen as Mr Collins and Mr Elton'.[37]

Her knowledge of the clergy was precise. Her father was a clergyman,
and two of her brothers became clergymen. The heroes of *Sense and
Sensibility*, *Northanger Abbey* and *Mansfield Park*, Edward Ferrars, Henry
Tilney and Edmund Bertram, are clergymen. When she tells us that Edward
Ferrars has reached the age of twenty-four, she expects her readers to know
that this is highly significant. Under the Clergy Ordination Act of 1804, a
man had to be twenty-four before he could be ordained to the Anglican

priesthood or hold a living in the Church of England. Now that he is twenty-four Edward is able to take the incumbency of Delaford. It is a small but important point.

One of the sermon writers she admired was Bishop Thomas Sherlock: 'I am very fond of Sherlock's Sermons, prefer them to almost any.'[38] Turning to Sherlock after Cooper, it feels a relief to read his cool, balanced, classically Anglican prose. In one characteristic passage he reflected upon Psalm 19 verse 12: 'Who can understand his errors? Cleanse thou me from secret faults.' Sherlock explains that the deadliest faults are those secret ones that result from self-ignorance, habit or simply a failure to reflect upon the consequences for others of one's own actions. These were very much the concerns of Austen in her novels.

One of the books Jane Austen owned was *A Companion to the Altar: shewing the nature and necessity of a sacramental preparation in order to our worthy receiving the Holy Communion, to which are added Prayers and Meditations* (1793). Her great-niece Florence Austen claimed that 'this book of devotions [was] always used by Jane Austen'.[39] The book is inscribed with her signature and the date 1794.[40] It may have been presented to her at the time of her own confirmation. In order to be prepared for the blessed sacrament, a devout communicant was expected to embrace six particulars, the first being *self-examination*: 'we must search our hearts, and examine our consciences'. This seems a sentiment close to Jane Austen's own heart.

Many of her heroines endure a journey of self-discovery. Elizabeth Bennet is forced to admit, 'I have courted prepossession and ignorance, and driven reason away ... Till this moment, I never knew myself.'[41] Emma Woodhouse undergoes a similar moment of self-revelation. However it is Marianne Dashwood, one of Austen's most interesting heroines, the only one shown in the grip of an all-consuming erotic passion, who is forced to admit her sins against a higher being: 'I wonder at my recovery, – wonder that the very eagerness of my desire to live, to have time for atonement to my God, and to you all, did not kill me at once ... Whenever I looked toward the past, I saw some duty neglected, or some failing indulged.'[42]

Austen's most pious heroine is Fanny Price, described by Henry Crawford as 'well-principled and religious'. Fanny appeals to the demands of conscience: 'We have all a better guide in ourselves, if we would attend to it, than any other person can be.' Her purity of mind provides a strong contrast to that of Mary Crawford: 'still shewn a mind led astray and bewildered, and without any suspicion of being so; darkened, yet fancying itself light'.[43] The morally aberrant characters in *Mansfield Park* have a distinctly jaundiced view of established religion: Maria Bertram expresses her approval that Sotherton Court is placed far from the church and Mary Crawford expresses her approbation for the closure of the family chapel there: 'every generation has its improvements'.[44]

Fanny Price, along with Marianne Dashwood and Anne Elliot, has a deep love of nature: 'Here's harmony! ... Here's repose! ... When I look out on such a night as this, I feel as if there could be neither wickedness nor sorrow in the world; and there certainly would be less of both if the sublimity of Nature were more attended to, and people were carried more out of themselves by contemplating such a scene.'[45] One of the strongest threads in the tapestry of eighteenth-century Anglicanism was deism or 'natural religion', the belief that the harmony of the universe bore witness to a Creator. In 1802, William Paley in *Natural Theology or Evidences of the Existence and Attributes of the Deity Collected from the Appearances of Nature* used the analogy of the watch and the watchmaker to prove the existence of God. Fanny's train of thought from 'the sublimity of Nature' to religious and moral precepts comes from within this tradition.[46]

Mansfield Park is Austen's most moral and religious novel. Her clerical cousin George Cooke, whom she admired as an 'impressive preacher of earnest awakening sermons', considered it 'the most sensible Novel he had ever read', and was particularly delighted by 'the Manner in which the Clergy are treated'.[47] The Cookes no doubt approved of Edmund Bertram, for whom the priesthood is not simply a career but a religious vocation. 'Do you think the church itself never chosen then?' he asks Mary Crawford. She replies, '*Never* is a black word. But yes, in the *never* of conversation which means *not very often*, I do think it.' For her, ordination for religion's sake without a living is 'madness indeed, absolute madness'.[48]

When Mary Crawford tells him that a 'clergyman is nothing' Edmund responds: 'I cannot call that situation nothing, which has the charge of all that is of the first importance to mankind, individually or collectively considered, temporally and eternally – which has the guardianship of religion and morals, and consequently of the manners which result from their influence. No one here can call the *office* nothing.'[49] And when he finally extricates himself from Mary, she fires a wounding parting shot, accusing him of Evangelical tendencies: 'At this rate, you will soon reform every body at Mansfield and Thornton Lacey; and when I hear of you next, it may be as a celebrated preacher in some great society of Methodists, or as a missionary in foreign parts.'[50]

It is sometimes said that Jane Austen described *Mansfield Park* as being *about* 'Ordination'; that view is based on a misreading of one of her letters, but there is no doubt that Edmund's vocation is at the centre of the novel. In January 1813, she wrote a lovely letter to Cassandra, describing the arrival of the first edition of *Pride and Prejudice* and speaking of her love of the character of Elizabeth Bennet. She tells of how she had cut the length of the second volume to sharpen up the narrative: 'I have lopt and cropt so successfully however that I imagine it must be rather shorter than S. and S. altogether.' Then she says, 'Now I will try to write of something else; – it shall be a complete change of subject.' In other words, the *letter* will now change subject. She then writes: 'Ordination. I am glad to find your enquiries have ended so well.' That is to say, she has previously asked Cassandra, who was staying with James, the cleric of the family, to confirm some technical details about the process of ordination. So the joke is that it is not a 'complete change of subject': she is moving from the final revisions of her previous novels to the preliminary research for her next one. Ever the writer, she is still talking about the writing process. Concerned as ever with her realism, she wants to get the details right with regard to Edmund's ordination. She also wants to get her topography right, so she then asks Cassandra 'if you could discover whether Northamptonshire is a County of Hedgerows'. In short, then, 'Ordination' is not the 'subject' of *Mansfield Park*, but it plays a crucial – and accurately rendered – part within the novel.[51]

At the close of the novel, Sir Thomas blames his daughters' misconduct on a lack of 'principle' but also on their having merely paid lip-service to religion: 'they had been instructed theoretically in their religion, but never required to bring it into daily practice'.[52] It is a lesson that Sir Thomas had also had to learn. What mattered to Austen was the way in which religion shaped the 'daily practice' of living a good life.

Jane Austen gave full rein to her sincere religious faith in *Mansfield Park*, but, just as more modern readers have been puzzled by the seriousness of Fanny Price and the morality of the novel, some of her family and friends were uncomfortable with her more serious voice. Jane copied out their opinions, keen to know what they truly thought of her novels: one opinion was 'Edmund objected to, as cold and formal', while another reader 'could not bear Fanny'. 'Of its good sense and moral Tendency there can be no doubt,' said a third, 'but as you beg me to be perfectly honest, I must confess I prefer P and P.'[53]

The majority of her intimates shared this belief that *Pride and Prejudice* was greatly superior. Gentle timid Fanny Price is no Lizzy Bennet, yet she surprises everyone in the novel by her quiet strength. She refuses to be bullied by Sir Thomas into marrying a man she doesn't love, and she alone sees the moral corruption that lies behind the charm of the Crawfords. Edmund, she perceives,

'is blinded, and nothing will open his eyes; nothing can, after having had truths before him so long in vain. – He will marry her, and be poor and miserable. God grant that her influence do not make him cease to be respectable!' – She looked over the letter again. '"So very fond of me!" 'tis nonsense all. She loves nobody but herself and her brother. "Her friends leading her astray for years!" She is quite as likely to have led *them* astray. They have all, perhaps, been corrupting one another.'[54]

'God grant ...': Austen uses the word 'God' as an exclamation only in the most serious of moments. Marianne at her most vulnerable shows her despair when she is coldly 'cut' by Willoughby: 'Good God! Willoughby what is the meaning of this?' Darcy is compelled to exclaim at seeing Elizabeth's distress at Lydia's elopement: 'Good God! What is the matter!' Captain Wentworth after Louisa's fall from the Cobb exclaims in the bitterest agony: 'Oh God! her father and mother.'[55] Fanny's ardent words at this key moment are about the closest Austen ever comes to speaking, sermon-like, of being 'led astray'.

She fervently believed however in the importance of fortitude and 'exertion', a word she often repeated at stressful times. In *Persuasion*, Captain Benwick's excessive grief for his betrothed is presented as self-indulgent and Anne urges him to take solace from works of prose and memoirs of real-life characters who have suffered 'religious endurances'.[56] Austen's own long illness in 1816 and 1817 forced her into great spiritual exertion and endurance of her own. She had time to think and reflect and prepare herself for death.

That she knew she was dying is suggested by an account left by Caroline Austen. She remembered that Jane and Cassandra made a fruitless journey to Cheltenham to find a cure. Their return journey to Chawton took a detour to Kintbury to visit the Fowles: 'Mary Jane Fowle, told me afterwards, that Aunt Jane went over the old places, and recalled old recollections associated with them, in a very particular manner – looked at them, my cousin thought, as if she never expected to see them again.'[57]

In her final illness Jane Austen told her friend Anne Sharp of her gratitude to God for having her family around her: 'I have so many alleviations and comforts to bless the Almighty for! … if I live to be an old Woman I must expect to wish I had died now, blessed in the tenderness of such a Family, and before I had survived either them or their affection.'[58] Henry related in his biographical notice of how on her deathbed she took the sacrament while she was still mentally aware. And Cassandra described her beloved sister's last moments in a detailed letter to Fanny Knight:

She felt herself to be dying about half an hour before she became tranquil and apparently unconscious. During that half hour was her struggle, poor Soul! she said she could not tell us what she sufferd, tho she complaind of little fixed pain. When I asked her if there was any thing she wanted, her answer was she wanted nothing but death and some of her words were 'God grant me patience, Pray for me, Oh Pray for me.'[59]

She died in the rented house to which she had moved in College Street, Winchester, during the small hours of a warm summer night, Friday 18 July 1817.

The following week she was laid to rest in Winchester Cathedral. The ledger stone over her grave narrates that she endured her illness with 'the patience and the hopes of a Christian'. It praises her 'charity, devotion, faith and purity', 'The benevolence of her heart, the sweetness of her temperament, the extraordinary endowments of her mind'. The latter phrase is a tacit recognition of her greatness as a novelist (since the novels had been published anonymously, it would have been inappropriate to say more of them than this). But the primary emphasis is on her Christian virtues. That was as it should have been: for all her wit and irreverence, Jane Austen was devoutly and profoundly Christian, as both a woman and a writer.

Fittingly enough, her final literary work was a poem, written two days before her death, on the feast day of St Swithin, the saint in whose church in Bath lay the bones of her beloved father. Winchester races were held that day. Tradition had it that if it rained on St Swithin's, it would rain for forty days more. Jane Austen, on her sickbed, woke up on St Swithin's Day, 15 July 1817, to 'hard rain in the morning'[60] and wrote the poem, playfully adopting the voice of the Saint:

> These races and revels and dissolute measures
> With which you're debasing a neighboring Plain
> Let them stand – You shall meet with your curse in your pleasures
> Set off for your course, I'll pursue with my rain.[61]

Talking about the weather was as English as anything could be – with the possible exception of being a faithful but unostentatious middle-of-the-road Anglican.

The Daughter of Mansfield

The large oil painting, attributed to Zoffany, hung in Kenwood House, the Hampstead seat of Lord Mansfield. It depicts two beautiful young girls. The blonde in the foreground is sitting down and is dressed in a pink silk and lace dress. She has flowers in her hair and a double strand of pearls around her neck and is holding a book. She is reaching out to the girl behind her, taking her hand and pulling her into the frame. She hardly needs to do so as the eye is drawn irresistibly to this other girl, with the high cheekbones and enigmatic smile. She rests a forefinger quizzically on her cheek and gazes confidently out at the artist.

She is dressed in sumptuous white satin and wears a string of large pearls around her neck, droplet pear and diamond ear-rings and a bejewelled turban with a feather perching jauntily at the back. She carries an armful of fruit and is wearing an exquisite blue and gold shawl which floats in the breeze as she walks. She is in motion, bursting with vitality and energy, while the girl in pink sits still.

The girls are Lady Elizabeth Murray and Dido Belle. They are the adopted daughters of Lord Mansfield on the terrace overlooking the grounds of Kenwood House with a spectacular view of St Paul's Cathedral in the distance. Kenwood House had been redesigned by Robert Adam in the 1760s, and later in the century its grounds were laid out with a lake and parklands by Humphry Repton.

The girls are cousins. Lady Elizabeth Murray lost her mother as a child and was brought to live with her uncle and aunt, the childless Mansfields, who made her their heir. Dido Belle was the illegitimate daughter of Mansfield's nephew Captain John Lindsay and an enslaved black woman called Maria Belle. The girls were companions and equals, as the portrait confirms. Mansfield doted on Dido. She was described by visitors as a much loved family member, though an American loyalist called Thomas Hutchinson who was living in London was scathing about her valued position in the family. He called her 'pert' and was shocked by her status in the family:

A Black came in after dinner and sat with the ladies and after coffee, walked with the company in the gardens, one of the young ladies having her arm within the other. Lord M … calls her Dido, which I suppose is all the name she has. He knows he has been reproached for showing fondness for her – I dare not say criminal [that is, sexual].[1]

Jane Austen might have well have visited Kenwood House to view the portraits and the grounds. Genteel members of the public were often shown round at times when the owner was absent, as at many great houses (including the imaginary Pemberley in *Pride and Prejudice*). Fanny Burney recorded a visit to Kenwood in her diary in June 1792. Whether or not Jane Austen saw this extraordinary painting, she did have a connection with one of the women in the portrait: Lady Elizabeth Murray was a friend and neighbour of her wealthy brother Edward.

Lady Elizabeth grew up to marry George Finch-Hatton of Eastwell Park near Godmersham. On a visit to Edward in 1805, Jane went to dinner at Eastwell Park and was seated next to Mr Finch-Hatton. She was very disappointed with the woman who had been brought up with Dido: 'I have discovered that Ly Elizabeth: for a woman of her age and situation, has astonishingly little to say for herself.' She was equally unimpressed with her daughter, Miss Hatton, but liked her small boys: 'George is a fine boy, and well-behaved, but Daniel cheifly delighted me; the good humour of his countenance is quite bewitching.'[2] She met the Finch-Hattons on many occasions when she was staying at Godmersham, but always found Elizabeth quiet and dull. Nevertheless, to have known and been on friendly terms with Lord Mansfield's heir and adopted daughter was of great interest to Jane Austen, since Mansfield was one of the heroes of the age.

Dido was the most celebrated mixed-race woman in England. When Lord Mansfield died in 1793, he left her a legacy and an annuity, while officially confirming her freedom. She married an Englishman later that year and had three sons. They lived in Hanover Square until her death in 1804. The Austens had many acquaintances among plantation families, so Jane may have had direct acquaintance with other mixed-race girls, but Dido is the one whose life she certainly knew about. In her unfinished last novel, *Sanditon*, there is a 'half Mulatto' heiress called Miss Lambe. A wealthy girl of seventeen, in delicate health, she has been brought to England from the West Indies to finish her education. 'Chilly and tender' in the English weather, she 'had a maid of her own, was to have the best room in the lodgings, and was always of the first consequence in every plan of Mrs. G.'[3] – rather, we might say, as Dido was always of the first consequence in every plan of the real-life Lord M.

For Jane Austen and her contemporaries, the name of Mansfield was synonymous with the great civil rights question of the age: the campaign against slavery. The first stepping-stone towards the abolition of the slave trade was laid in 1772 when Mansfield, Lord Chief Justice, made a monumental ruling in the James Somersett case. Somersett, an enslaved African who had been brought to England by his American owner, escaped, having endured brutal beatings. He was caught and readied to be sent to Jamaica, to be sold on as a plantation labourer. But following an intervention from three people claiming to be his godparents when he was baptized a Christian in England, he was brought before Mansfield under the Habeas Corpus Act. Asked to decide whether Somersett's imprisonment was legal, Lord Mansfield heard both sides of the argument and then reserved his judgment for five weeks. He eventually ruled that forcibly sending Somersett abroad because 'he absented himself from his service or for any other cause' was illegal: 'No authority can be found for it in the laws of this country and therefore ... James Somersett must be discharged.' Within his judgment was a general principle: 'The state of slavery is of such a nature, that it is incapable of now being introduced by Courts of Justice upon mere reasoning or inferences from any principles, natural or political.'[4]

The case was widely reported, and was generally interpreted to mean that all enslaved people in England must be 'discharged'. Though Mansfield himself drew back from this conclusion, his judgment gave great momentum to the abolitionists. A phrase used in the trial, 'that England was too pure an air for a slave to breathe in', became a campaign slogan, echoed by William Cowper in the famous abolitionist sequence in *The Task*, Jane Austen's favourite poem:

> I had much rather be myself the slave
> And wear the bonds, than fasten them on him.
> We have no slaves at home – then why abroad?
> And they themselves, once ferried o'er the wave
> That parts us, are emancipate and loosed.
> Slaves cannot breathe in England; if their lungs
> Receive our air, that moment they are free,
> They touch our country and their shackles fall.[5]

Mansfield would long be associated with freedom for slaves, not only because of the Somersett case, but also as a result of the infamous *Zong* case of 1781. The *Zong* was a Liverpool slaving vessel from which nearly 150 sick men, women and children were thrown overboard and drowned so that the owners could claim compensation for lost 'cargo'. The court found for the owners, but in an appeal before the King's Bench Mansfield ruled that humans could not be insured. He called for a retrial. He also ruled that there could be no compensation for the owners. At that point, they abandoned their case (though neither they nor the ship's captain were ever brought to trial for murder). Again, this was a Mansfield ruling that gave great impetus to the abolitionist cause.

A young girl is brought to a large country house to be raised with wealthy relations. Just as the story of Edward Austen's adoption by the Knights must have been in the background of Jane Austen's mind as she prepared to send a third novel to her publisher Egerton, so the famous story of Dido Belle is a shadow flickering in the background of the tale of Fanny Price. It is hard to believe it a coincidence that the Austen novel most connected with the slave trade was given the title *Mansfield Park*.

Mansfield Park, the great English country house, has often been seen by critics as a symbol of England itself. The interlopers, who create havoc, are London strangers, Mary and Henry Crawford, who threaten the ways and values of the country. But the Crawfords are merely the agents of change: the real corruption rests at the door of the flawed custodians of the house, Sir Thomas and Lady Bertram and Mrs Norris. Furthermore, Mansfield

George Cruikshank, caricature of 'Midshipman
William B. on the Middle Watch' (with escaped
slave on the loose)

Park is not an ancient English home, redolent of the paternalistic English
gentry, as Pemberley in *Pride and Prejudice* and Kellynch Hall in *Persuasion*
are. It is a new build, erected on the fruits of the slave trade.

The shadow story of *Mansfield Park* is slavery, to which the Austens were
fiercely opposed, despite their own family interest in plantations. Following
a campaign that lasted for over twenty years, the slave trade – that is to say
the carriage of slaves on British vessels – was abolished in 1807, though it
continued to flourish illicitly. Emancipation of slaves within the Empire did
not happen until 1833. Opinions on the slave trade in Jane Austen's time
were part of everyday conversation, as Austen suggests in *Emma*, where the
subject is treated in a brutally casual way by the odious Mrs Elton: "'Oh!
my dear, human flesh! You quite shock me; if you mean a fling at the slave-
trade, I assure you Mr. Suckling was always rather a friend to the abolition.'"[6] The phrase 'rather a friend' is revealingly defensive: Maple Grove,
Mr Suckling's ostentatious seat near the slave port of Bristol, would
undoubtedly have been another house contaminated by the trade in human
flesh.[7]

Both Jane Austen's naval brothers were involved in the interception of slave vessels. Frank was certainly pro-abolition: 'slavery however it may be modified is still slavery, and it is much to be regretted that any trace of it should be found to exist in countries dependent on England or colonized by her subjects'.[8] It was the job of the Royal Navy to enforce the abolition, though captains were permitted to act only against vessels of British ownership with slaves actually on board. But this did not stop them pursuing ships sailing under other flags: 'Chaced a ship which proved to be a Portuguese bound for Rio Janeiro,' Frank once noted in his log. 'She had on board 714 slaves of both sexes, and all ages.'[9]

Three of Jane Austen's favourite writers were staunchly anti-slavery: William Cowper, Dr Johnson and Thomas Clarkson. The latter's *History of the Rise, Progress and Accomplishment of the Abolition of the African Slave-Trade* (1808) was the bible of the anti-slavery movement. In writing of another polemicist, Charles Pasley, author of *An Essay on the Military Policy and Institutions of the British Empire*, Austen observed, 'I am as much in love with the Author as ever I was with Clarkson.'[10] The *History of the Abolition* is a brilliantly written, pacy, emotionally charged account of the author's own conversion to the abolitionist cause. It is easy to see why Jane Austen fell in love with Thomas Clarkson.

His interest was sparked at Cambridge when he wrote and won a prize for an essay on slavery. After reading the essay aloud at his college he returned to London determined to abandon his calling as a clergyman and dedicate his life to the cause: 'I sat down disconsolate on the turf by the roadside and held my horse. Here a thought came into my mind, that if the contents of the essay were true, it was time some person should see these calamities to their end.'[11] Clarkson raised money to fund his calling to write his history and went to Liverpool and Bristol to interview and amass information from both slavers and freed slaves. He spared no detail in his description of the conditions aboard the vessels and the atrocities committed, including the notorious *Zong* case. He gave speeches in which he used visual aids to great effect, such as shackles and irons, including the horrific 'speculum oris': slaves aboard ship so often refused to eat that a device was invented to pry their jaws open so that the sailors could force-feed them.

He also amassed a collection of African goods of astounding beauty and workmanship: carved figures, different types of wood, items made of ivory, leather, gold and cotton, swords and daggers fashioned from iron, four different kinds of pepper, even a tooth-whitening paste. His point was that trade should be in goods, not people. To help his cause, snuff boxes were made with the emblem of a freed slave, and ladies wore brooches so that 'fashion, which usually confines itself to worthless things, was seen for once in the honourable office of promoting the cause of justice, humanity, and freedom'.[12]

Clarkson quoted Cowper as a friend to the cause, printing his 'The Negro's Complaint' in the *History* and exclaiming how its popularity spread throughout England, and became a popular song in every right-thinking person's drawing room. And of course he made much of Mansfield's famous judgment in Somersett's case.

The root of Clarkson's passion for the cause of abolition was his deep Christianity. He also argued that the slave trade was highly destructive and dangerous to the Royal Navy – in time of war, there should be no distractions from the defence of the realm. Christianity and the navy: these things were also most dear to Jane Austen's heart.

Austen was intimately connected with the slave trade and plantation owners. In her own family, there were the Hampson and the Walter cousins on her father's side, and the Leigh-Perrots on her mother's (as well as being a kleptomaniac, Mrs Leigh-Perrot was heir to an estate in Barbados). What is more, the first wife of her brother James was the daughter of the Governor of Grenada.

Her closest connection to a plantation family was through her father's family. Jane's father had a half-brother by his mother Rebecca Hampson, who had previously been married to a William Walter. After the latter's death she married William Austen (Jane's grandfather), who inherited a stepson, William Hampson Walter, who became close to his step-siblings (George, Philadelphia and Leonora Austen). As was common in this age of premature deaths, the extended family resulting from the second marriage rubbed along very well together. William Hampson Walter lived in relative comfort and had a large family of six children.

The Hampson family had a plantation in Jamaica, and two of William's sons were sent there. It was their sister Philadelphia Walter (named after their aunt) who preserved Eliza de Feuillide's letters, which we have seen to provide a great source of information about the Austens. This was the girl who refused to partake in the Steventon theatricals, much to the chagrin of Mrs Austen. In one of her few surviving letters, Mrs Austen wrote to Phila

Walter, whom she considered her 'third niece', complaining that 'You might as well have been in Jamaica keeping your Brother's House, for anything that we see or are likely to see of you.'[13]

In 1773 Mrs Austen wrote to Susannah Walter to say that she was sorry to hear about Sir George Hampson's accident and that she hoped he would still be able to take Susannah's son George back to Jamaica with him the following spring. Sir George, the sixth Baronet of Taplow, was Rebecca Hampson's nephew. He married Mary Pinnock of Jamaica and was succeeded by his son, Sir Thomas Hampson. In other words, Jane Austen had a cousin twice removed who was called Sir Thomas and who owned a plantation in Jamaica.

Another intriguing connection was the Nibbs family, who were very close to the Austens. James Nibbs was taught by George Austen at Oxford and sent his son, George, godson to George Austen, to be tutored at Steventon. James owned a plantation in Antigua. In 1760 George Austen was made a trustee of Nibbs's Antiguan property called Haddon's or Week's plantation, containing 294 acres with slaves and stock. George Austen was one of the parties to the marriage settlement of James Nibbs and his cousin Barbara. This meant that if Nibbs had died early, George Austen would have been responsible for the plantation and its slaves. George Nibbs grew into a wild and troublesome boy and his father eventually took him to Antigua to separate him from undesirable company, a plot-line Austen used in *Mansfield Park* when Sir Thomas removes his son, Tom, from bad connections.

In 1801, Jane Austen, in talking about her house move to Bath, mentions a picture of Mr Nibbs hanging on the walls at Steventon. It's very possible that George Nibbs had a map of Antigua in Steventon. Such maps gave the names of the plantation owners. It may not be a coincidence that many of Austen's characters' names – including Willoughby, Wickham, Lucas and Williams – are the same as those of West Indian plantation owners.[14]

Another Steventon/Antigua connection came via the tenants of Ashe Park, who came to the area in 1771. Mrs Austen gave a warm welcome to these 'two very young single gentlemen'.[15] They were William and James Holder, who had made their fortune in the West Indies. James Holder took to handing on his newspaper to his neighbours at Steventon.

Yet another Hampshire connection was William Beckford. His father, Alderman Beckford, was the richest plantation owner – he held over twenty thousand acres – in the West Indies. He was known as the 'uncrowned king of Jamaica'. His son William inherited, when he was just ten, a fortune of a million pounds in cash (£150 million or $225 million today), together with estates and plantations worth millions more. He was a Gothic novelist, travel writer, art collector, builder of the extraordinary Fonthill Abbey and an infamous bisexual. His daughter's shocking elopement was mentioned by Jane Austen, who called her 'our cousin Margaret' and noted that she had been disinherited by her father.

There were other connections with the Caribbean. Jane's youngest brother Charles, 'our own particular little brother', got married in Bermuda to Fanny Palmer, the youngest daughter of the island's former Attorney-General. When she died, he married her elder sister, Harriet. 'We do not call Bermuda or Bahama, you know, the West Indies,' says Mrs Croft in *Persuasion*, casually revealing Austen's intimate knowledge of the distinction between the various Caribbean islands.[16]

Given all these associations, it is hardly surprising that Jane Austen's novels reveal her interest in plantations and the slave trade in the years following the 1807 Act. In *Emma*, it is made clear that Augusta Hawkins (later Mrs Elton) is the daughter of a Bristol slave trader. Bristol was second only to Liverpool as a slaving port and dealt primarily in slave-produced commodities such as sugar. Jane Austen gives a clear hint about the trade of Mrs Elton's father: 'Miss Hawkins was the youngest of the two daughters of a Bristol – merchant, of course, he must be called.'[17] The dash of hesitation indicates that 'merchant' is a euphemism for 'slaver'. Moreover, the name Hawkins had obvious resonance, since the Elizabethan mariner John Hawkins was the father of the English slave trade.

It is, however, in *Mansfield Park* that Jane Austen shows her support for the abolition of slaves and her disapproval of plantation owners. The background to the plot of the novel is Antigua and the problems that Sir Thomas is having with his 'poor returns'. Why are his estates in trouble? Antigua's main crop was sugar, the production of which was labour intensive, dependent upon a large slave force. The American War of Independence greatly disrupted the sugar trade, so much so that in the first quarter of the nineteenth century sugar exports fell by a third.[18] Furthermore Antigua, as one of the oldest colonies, was suffering from soil exhaustion as well as competition from other sugar islands.[19] There was also periodic unrest among the slaves.

We learn quickly that a large part of Sir Thomas's income is 'unsettled', exacerbated by Tom's gaming habit. The money problems have cost Edmund a valuable church living. From the opening pages, we hear of Sir Thomas's 'West Indian property' in Mrs Price's desperate wish that her son William might be of use to Sir Thomas. As with Jane Austen's cousins George and William Hampson, it was common practice for impoverished young relatives to be sent out to assist in the running of plantations. Though William Price becomes a midshipman, like the Austen boys, the possibility is raised here of an alternative narrative in which he would have been constantly sending Fanny letters from the West Indies.

We are also introduced in the opening paragraph of *Mansfield Park* to Mr and Mrs Norris. Mrs Norris is Jane Austen's most unremitting portrait of meanness and corrupted power. Fanny, initially timid and weak, is an easy target for her bullying instincts, and we cringe at her heartlessness. Fanny's early life is made a misery by this unpleasant adult, who treats her like a slave. But it is Mrs Norris' power in the Bertram household that causes the real damage. It is one of the supreme ironies of the novel that Sir Thomas goes to Antigua to sort out the problems in his plantation, only for his house in England to be thrown into chaos and subversion by his absence. During that absence, with Lady Bertram comatose on her sofa like some Chinese opium addict, the house is left under the dangerous guardianship of Mrs Norris. Eventually, Sir Thomas comes to see the error of his ways. Like Shakespeare's Prospero, he acknowledges that Mrs Norris is his Caliban, a monster that he has created: 'His opinion of her had been sinking from the day of his return from Antigua ... He had felt her as an hourly evil, which was so much the worse, as there seemed to be no chance of its ceasing but with life; she seemed a part of himself, that must be borne for ever.'[20]

If the name of Mansfield was synonymous with the cause of abolition, then that of Norris was its opposite. Any reader familiar with Clarkson's *History of the Abolition* would have known the infamous Robert Norris. He was a slave trader in West Africa turned 'merchant', who was a key figure in Clarkson's account. When Clarkson went on his first research trip to Liverpool, Norris was charming and helpful, claimed that he deplored the slave trade, abhorring the cruelty with which its victims were treated. But Norris was a hypocrite. He provided Clarkson with valuable testimony, promised to serve the cause of abolition and then betrayed him.

When it came to a parliamentary inquiry, instead of testifying in support of the abolitionists he argued against them, brazenly proposing that the slave trade had positive effects in Africa, as the poor were more humanely treated as slaves abroad than they were in their barbaric homeland. 'There was a great accession of happiness to Africa since the introduction of the Trade,' Norris insisted. In Clarkson's opinion, Norris's testimony greatly damaged the abolitionists' case. Clarkson exacted his revenge on Norris when they later met face to face in the chamber and Norris was discredited for his duplicity: 'Norris seemed to have no ordinary sense of his own degradation; for he never afterwards held up his head, or looked the abolitionists in the face, or acted with energy as a delegate, as on former occasions'.[21] We will never know how self-conscious Jane Austen was in her choice of names, but there can be little doubt that the vile Norris lodged himself in her mind when she read Clarkson and emerged as the perfect name for the villain of *Mansfield Park*.

To make clear the connection between the great house and Sir Thomas's ill-gotten gains in Antigua, Fanny describes Mansfield Park's grounds as 'plantations' – a not so subtle reminder of where the money for the house and grounds came from. And it is Fanny alone who is brave enough to ask the intimidating Sir Thomas about the slave trade:

'Did not you hear me ask him about the slave trade last night?'
'I did – and was in hopes the question would be followed up by others. It would have pleased your uncle to be inquired of farther.'
'And I longed to do it – but there was such a dead silence!'[22]

Fanny Price – a reader, a thinker, a close observer of the world – is no coward or weakling. She speaks truth to power and asks of England the question that dared not speak its name elsewhere in the novel: 'we have no slaves at home – then why abroad?' She, not the adulterous Maria or the flighty Julia Bertram, is the true daughter of Mansfield.

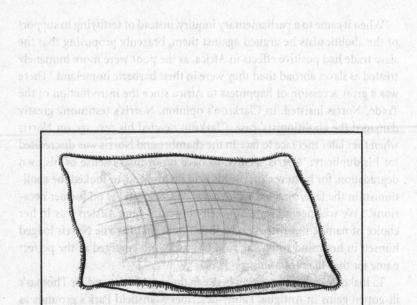

13

The Crimson Velvet Cushions

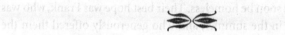

Jane Austen visited many fine houses. And the inheritance of great houses is at the heart of her novels. But only the grandest families could boast a private chapel. Of all the houses Austen visited, only one had this feature. In the chapel at Stoneleigh Abbey in Warwickshire, it is still possible to see today a row of 'crimson velvet cushions on the ledge of the family gallery'. The phrase is from *Mansfield Park*, where they are observed – along with a profusion of mahogany – by Fanny Price upon first entering the private chapel at Sotherton Court.[1] The little detail of the cushions conveys her disappointment that the room does not seem more like a proper church. It was an observation from the author's own experience. At Stoneleigh, as so often, Jane Austen's sharp eye took in seemingly inconsequential minutiae and turned them to unexpected use. But what was she doing there in Warwickshire?

Following the death of the Reverend George Austen in January 1805, his widow and her daughters remained in the city till the summer, when they stayed with Edward Knight at Godmersham in Kent. There Jane is to be glimpsed going to the occasional ball in Canterbury or playing at shuttlecock and battledore with her little nephew William. Cassandra also had several invitations to Goodnestone Park, the family home of Edward's wife, Elizabeth Bridges. In September they maintained their habit of taking a late summer and autumn trip to the seaside, but this time it was Hastings and Worthing instead of Dorset or Devon. They remained in the bracing sea air of Worthing until at least the end of November. It is not known where Jane Austen spent her first Christmas without her father. In January 1806, they were at Steventon, where there were so many memories. The girls stayed for a while with the Bigg-Withers at Manydown – facing an uncertain future, Jane might have wondered about her decision to reject Harris four years before.

Mrs Austen returned to Bath, but retrenchment was necessary. They had given up the spacious premises in which they had lodged when George Austen was alive. She found temporary accommodation in Trim Street, where Cassandra and Jane joined her in March. But within a few weeks someone offered to take the whole house, and they could afford only part of it, so they would soon be homeless. Their best hope was Frank, who was due to be married in the summer, and who generously offered them the chance to live with him and his new wife Mary in Southampton. While he was away for the wedding and honeymoon, they lived an itinerant life – first Clifton, just outside Bristol, then Adlestrop rectory in Gloucestershire, the home of Mrs Austen's cousin the Reverend Thomas Leigh. They could not have helped noticing that, since their last visit, the Leighs had greatly improved the estate (Thomas's nephew, James Henry Leigh, lived in the big house). The celebrated landscape gardener Humphry Repton had been engaged, at five guineas a day, to enclose the village green, plant out the cottages, move the entrance to the rectory, open up the back of the house, divert a stream through the garden and create a picturesque view of the lake, visible from both rectory and big house.[2] This all provided Jane Austen with raw material to put to good use with Mr Rushworth's improvements at Sotherton in *Mansfield Park*.

They left Adlestrop on 5 August in company with Thomas Leigh and his lawyer, Joseph Hill. Their destination was Stoneleigh. Their mission was to press a claim on a much greater estate. On 2 July 1806, the very day when, with what Jane recalled as 'happy feelings of escape', the Austen women left the city of Bath, the Honourable Miss Mary Leigh, mistress of Stoneleigh Abbey, had died. She was eccentric, diminutive and without an obvious heir. Thomas Leigh reckoned that the prize might just be his.

In 1786 the last Lord Leigh of Stoneleigh had died unmarried. Edward Leigh, fifth Baron Leigh, was, like Jane Austen's mother, a descendant of Sir Thomas Leigh, an Elizabethan lord mayor of London. Edward was a clever young man and a scholar of Oriel College, Oxford, a keen collector of art, furniture, scientific equipment, musical instruments and books. He made

'Mrs and Miss Austens will be of the party': letter
from Thomas Leigh to Joseph Hill

substantial improvements to Stoneleigh and before settling to marriage planned to embark on a Grand Tour in 1767. Prior to this, he seemed perfectly normal and sane, but payments made in 1767 to a leading doctor specializing in mental illness, John Monro, who practised at Bedlam Hospital, and to Francis Willis, who later treated the King, suggested that he was in the first stages of serious mental illness.[3] By 1774 he was declared insane. A prayer written by his sister speaks of 'frightful imaginations' and self-harming.

He left his estate to his sister Mary, to whom he was extremely close. She was also described as 'half-mad'. Thereafter, his Lordship specified, Stoneleigh should go 'to the first and nearest of my kindred, being male and of my name and blood that shall be living at the time of the determination of the several estates'.[4] So an heir had to be sought among the various branches of the Leighs. The Reverend Thomas Leigh and his nephew James Henry were well in the frame. Thomas Leigh's lawyer advised him to take immediate possession – hence the hasty trip with the Austen women. But there was also the possibility that he might resign his claim to the estate in return for a substantial pay-off and annuity. In that case, there was a possibility that Mrs Austen's brother, Leigh-Perrot, would inherit. This was of interest to the Austen family because their son James was Leigh-Perrot's heir. Perhaps the day would come when he might inherit Stoneleigh and find quarters for them in one of its many wings.

Stoneleigh Abbey looks as one might imagine the fictional Pemberley. A first glance at its palatial exterior and it could be mistaken for Chatsworth.[5] It is sometimes said that Pemberley was based on Chatsworth, since it is in Derbyshire. Austen *may* have seen Chatsworth when she went north to visit Edward Cooper, but Stoneleigh is a likelier model: it was the biggest house she ever stayed in.

Sitting in 690 acres of parkland overlooking the River Avon, deep in Warwickshire, the Abbey was founded in 1154, when Henry II granted lands to a small community of Cistercian monks. Following the dissolution of the monasteries the Abbey passed into the hands of Thomas Leigh. This was where, as Mrs Austen's family never ceased to remember, Sir Thomas Leigh, grandson of the second Thomas, entertained Charles I when the gates of Coventry were shut against him. As a reward, Charles gave Leigh a barony. For four hundred years, then, Stoneleigh Abbey had been the country seat of Jane Austen's elevated relatives, the Leighs. Edward Leigh, the third Lord Leigh, built the imposing baroque façade, the West Wing. The west range is in ashlar stone, fifteen bays long, three and a half storeys high.

The group arrived on 5 August and stayed for nine days. Joseph Hill, the lawyer who travelled with them, was agent and executor for Mary Leigh as well as friend and lawyer to the Reverend Thomas. He was the right man to be with at the time. He was also a great friend of Jane Austen's favoured poet, William Cowper. Hill was made Secretary of Lunatics in 1778, good preparation for service to mad Mary. During most of his life Cowper, who suffered from depression bordering on madness, was financially dependent on Hill. In his honour Cowper wrote an 'Epistle to Joseph Hill', which was published along with Jane Austen's beloved *The Task*, describing him as 'honest man, close-buttoned to the chin,/Broad-cloth without, and a warm heart within'.[6] Joseph, clearly sensitive to mental illness, assisted the Leighs, both Edward and Mary. He was a remarkable man and one yearns for a fragment of the table talk he shared with Jane Austen at Stoneleigh. She may have heard tales of the last days of poor Cowper, who had died in deep depression in 1800.

Mrs Austen immediately wrote to Mary Lloyd, giving a vivid description of the house and grounds. She captures its vastness – forty-five windows in the main range, twenty-six bedrooms in the new part alone, ample grounds ideal for walking:

And here we all found ourselves on Tuesday … Eating Fish, venison and all manner of good things, at a late hour, in a Noble large Parlour hung round with family Pictures – every thing is very Grand and very fine and very Large – The House is larger than I could have supposed – we can *now* find our way about it.

She expected to find 'everything about the place very fine and all that', but she had not anticipated its being 'so beautiful' in the modern way – she had imagined 'long Avenues, dark rookeries and dismal Yew Trees'. But there were 'no such melancholy things'. Instead she found that 'The Avon runs near the house amidst Green Meadows bounded by large and beautiful Woods, full of delightful Walks.'[7] She continued with a description of the interior:

I will now give you some idea of the inside of this vast house, first premising that there are 45 windows in front, (which is quite strait, with a flat Roof) 15 in a row – you go up a considerable flight of steps (some of the offices are under the house), into a large Hall, on the right hand, the dining parlour, within that the Breakfast room, where we generally sit, and reason good, tis the only room (except the Chapel), which looks towards the River, – on the left hand the Hall is the best drawing room, within that a smaller one, these rooms are rather gloomy, Brown wainscot and dark Crimson furniture, so we never use them except to walk thro' to the old picture Gallery; Behind the smaller drawing Room is the State Bed chamber with a high, dark crimson Velvet Bed, an *alarming* apartment just fit for an Heroine, the old Gallery opens into it – behind the Hall and Parlour a passage all across the house containing 3 staircases and two back Parlours – there are 26 Bed Chambers in the new part of the house, and a great many (some very good ones) in the Old. There is also another gallery, fitted up with modern prints on a buff paper, and a large billiard-room. Every part of the house and offices is kept so clean, that were you to cut your finger I do not think you could find a cobweb to wrap it up in. I need not have written this long letter, for I have a presentiment that if these good people live until next year you will see it all with your own eyes.[8]

Mrs Austen clearly had something of a Gothic imagination, what with her expectation of dismal yews and her image of that '*alarming* apartment just fit for an Heroine'.

The Abbey is entered through the hall or saloon, a spectacular room decorated with rococo plasterwork depicting the myth of Hercules. The rooms to the left of the saloon, which Mrs Austen thought dark and gloomy, are north-facing which makes them feel cold. The women preferred the rooms to the right which are filled with light and warmth.

Mrs Austen was herself an excellent 'huswife' and she greatly enjoyed inspecting the kitchen garden, bursting with ripe fruit in the summer sunshine:

I do not fail to spend some time every day in the Kitchen Garden where the quantities of small fruit exceed anything you can form an idea of ... The ponds supply excellent fish the Park excellent Venison; there is also plenty of Pigeons, Rabbits, and all sort of Poultry, a delightful Dairy where is made Butter food Warwickshire Cheese and

Cream ditto. One man servant is called the Baker, He does nothing but Brew and Bake. The quantity of Casks in the Strong Beer Cellar is beyond imagination.

After morning prayer in the family chapel, they had breakfast of 'Chocolate, Coffee and tea, Plumb Cake, Pound Cake, Hot Rolls, Cold Rolls, bread and butter, and *dry toast* for me'.

Despite her preference for 'dry toast', Mrs Austen loved her food, as did Elizabeth Twiselton, the Dowager Lady Saye and Sele, who was known to be an epicure. She was also there at Stoneleigh, as her daughter Julia was married to James Henry Leigh of Adlestrop, another strong claimant to the estate. They too had travelled hot foot to the big house. Lady Saye and Sele's husband had cut his throat with his own razor in 1788 before stabbing himself with his sword. She told Jane and Cassandra tales of how, following her husband's suicide, she ate only boiled chicken for two weeks and had never eaten it since: 'Poor Lady Saye and Sele', wrote Jane's mother, 'to be sure is rather tormenting, tho' sometimes amusing and affords Jane many a good laugh.'[9] She later amused them by asking with grave importance 'if the macaroni was made with Parmesan'. There was a deathly silence before the servant replied 'Yes, my lady.'

According to her niece Caroline, Jane Austen made a conquest at Stoneleigh in the person of a visitor called Robert Holt-Leigh, a Member of Parliament from Wigan. Mrs Austen said that he was 'a single man, the wrong side of forty; chatty and well bred and has a large estate'.[10] Jane herself left no account of the visit (there are no surviving letters for the whole of 1806), so we have no way of knowing whether the little group discussed cousin Cassandra Hawke's sentimental novel or cousin Cassandra Cooke's Gothic thriller, but many details from Stoneleigh Abbey found their way into Austen's novels. It is possible that the idea of a newly modernized neo-classical house retaining its Gothic name of Abbey gave her some ideas for Northanger Abbey – we have no idea what the name or the character of the big house was in the early version of that novel, which by this time Austen had already sent to a publisher. What is much more certain is that the geography and architectural detail of Stoneleigh Abbey bear a strong resemblance to the description of Sotherton Court in *Mansfield Park*.

At Sotherton Court the view from the west front 'looked across a lawn to the beginning of the avenue', exactly as at Stoneleigh. Both houses have a wood, a stream and a 'wilderness'. The Abbey is situated far away enough from the church so that residents and visitors would not be disturbed by hearing the bells ringing, just as the village of Stoneleigh is at some distance from the great house. It has an ostentatious excess of windows – 'more', as Henry Crawford puts it, 'than could be supposed to be of any use than to contribute to the window tax'.[11] Under the guidance of Mrs Rushworth, the party are given a tour of Sotherton Court whose rooms are described as 'all lofty, and many large, and amply furnished in the taste of fifty years back, with shining floors, solid mahogany, rich damask, marble, gilding and carving'[12] – all reminiscent of Stoneleigh. Family portraits line the walls, including a woman called Elizabeth Wentworth, whose romantic story mirrors that of Anne Elliot in *Persuasion*.[13]

Above all, Jane Austen uses the details of Stoneleigh Chapel to flesh out the important scene in *Mansfield Park* where Mary Crawford discovers that Edmund is to be a clergyman. Mrs Rushworth takes her guests to the Sotherton family chapel via the servants' entrance, below the overhanging family gallery furnished with those 'crimson velvet cushions' peeping over the ledge. Sotherton Chapel is a 'spacious, oblong room ... nothing awful here, nothing melancholy, nothing grand ... no arches, no inscriptions, no banners'.[14] Edmund Bertram points out that the family ancestors are not buried here but in a local church, just as the Leigh ancestors were buried in the local church. All of these details are taken from the Stoneleigh visit.

And then of course there is Pemberley:

It was a large, handsome, stone building, standing well on rising ground, and backed by a ridge of high woody hills; – and in front, a stream of some natural importance was swelled into greater, but without any artificial appearance. Its banks were neither formal, nor falsely adorned. Elizabeth was delighted. She had never seen a place for which nature had done more, or where natural beauty had been so little counteracted by an awkward taste.[15]

Mr Darcy's Pemberley and Mr Knightley's significantly named Donwell Abbey in *Emma* seem organically connected to the surrounding country-side. They appear to have evolved naturally and gradually rather than to have been designed to display the taste of a particular person. Donwell has 'ample gardens stretching down to meadows washed by a stream, of which the Abbey, with all the old neglect of prospect, had scarcely a sight – and its abundance of timber in rows and avenues, which neither fashion nor extravagance had rooted up'.[16]

It would appear that the Reverend Thomas Leigh did the right thing in pressing his claim with the Austen women at his side. He became tenant of Stoneleigh for life. He moved in and, as at Adlestrop, but on a much grander scale, Humphry Repton was hired to make improvements. To help clients visualize his designs, Repton produced 'Red Books' (so called for their binding) in which he proposed an idealized view with explanatory text and watercolours to show 'before' and 'after' views. The Stoneleigh Abbey Red Book is one of his finest and largest, although not all of the improvements he suggested were implemented. Still, he did widen the River Avon in front of the house to form a lake. A picturesque stone bridge was built, based on a design of Inigo Jones, and an inspirational reflective pool was created to mirror in its stillness the south façade. Repton regarded the estate as one of his more important commissions. It is tempting to think that he was discussed by the family during the Stoneleigh visit, as he is mooted as the right man to undertake the improvements at Sotherton in *Mansfield Park*: 'I should be most thankful to any Mr Repton who would undertake it, and give me as much beauty as he could for my money.'[17]

Humphry Repton (with umbrella) personally
supervises the widening of the Avon as one of his
'improvements' at Stoneleigh

The unmarried Reverend Thomas Leigh died in 1813, at which point his nephew James Henry Leigh took the life tenancy. He and his wife Julia (Twiselton), a beautiful and forceful woman, made further improvements to the landscape and oversaw extensive interior redecoration. Their son Chandos then inherited. He would eventually be made Baron Leigh of the second creation. At the time of Jane Austen's visit to Stoneleigh he was Lord Byron's fag at Harrow.

As for Mr Leigh-Perrot, Jane Austen's uncle, he resigned his claim in favour of a large lump sum and an annuity. Jane Austen perhaps hoped that he might have pressed further. She does not appear to have been a fan of James Henry Leigh. She referred to the Reverend Thomas Leigh on his death in 1813 as 'the respectable, worthy, clever, agreeable Mr Tho. Leigh [who] died the possessor of one of the finest Estates in England and of more worthless Nephews and Nieces than any other private Man in the united Kingdoms'. In the next breath she turns to her aunt, Mrs Leigh-Perrot: 'There is another female sufferer on the occasion to be pitied. Poor Mrs L. P. – who would now have been Mistress of Stonleigh had there been none of that vile compromise, which in good truth has never been allowed to be of much use to them. – It will be a hard trial.'[18] Just for a moment, she would have allowed herself the fantasy of her brother James, the Leigh-Perrots' heir, becoming the eventual owner of Stoneleigh.

Her wealthiest family relations, the Leigh-Perrots and the Knights, were childless and thus without heirs to their elegant estates. In *Sense and Sensibility*, *Pride and Prejudice*, *Emma* and *Persuasion*, the absence of a male heir is an important plot-line. The Dashwood sisters are forced out of Norland Park, Mrs Bennet bewails the entailment that will leave her (and her daughters) homeless. Anne and Elizabeth Elliot are exiled from Kellynch and forced into lodgings at Bath.

Furthermore, Austen returns again and again to the theme of irresponsible custodians. While none of them is mad, like her relation Edward Leigh, several of them (General Tilney, Sir Thomas Bertram, Sir Walter Elliot) are incompetent or uninvolved landlords. Often the worthy housekeeper is portrayed in a better light than the owners. Thus at Sotherton, the dowager mistress 'had been at great pains to learn all that the housekeeper could teach, and was now almost equally well qualified to show the house'.[19] Elizabeth Bennet begins to alter her opinion of Mr Darcy when his housekeeper praises him as a worthy landlord, who looks after his estate, his workers and his family: "'He is the best landlord, and the best master," said she, "that ever lived. Not like the wild young men now-a-days, who think of nothing but themselves. There is not one of his tenants or servants but what will give him a good name.'" For Elizabeth this is praise in the highest degree: 'The commendation bestowed on him by Mrs Reynolds was of no trifling nature. What praise is more valuable than the praise of an intelligent servant?'[20] The visit to Stoneleigh, where there were more servants than at any other place she ever stayed in, focused Austen's thoughts on many questions regarding the importance of the good stewardship of a great estate.

Charlotte Brontë in a letter to G. H. Lewes famously calls Jane Austen's houses 'elegant but confined', describing the country house in her novels as 'an accurate daguerreotyped portrait of a commonplace face; a carefully fenced, highly cultivated garden, with neat borders and delicate flowers but no glance of a bright, vivid physiognomy, no open country, no fresh air, no blue hill, no bonny beck. I should hardly like to live with her ladies and gentlemen.'[21] This reductive and essentially unfair description plays on both a north/south and a class divide: Austen country is 'neat' and 'highly cultivated' whereas Brontë country is 'open country' with its 'fresh air' and 'bonny becks'. But at least Brontë saw that the country house was a character in Austen's novels every bit as important as Wuthering Heights, Thornfield Hall and Thrushcross Grange in hers and her sister's. Jane Austen was indeed one of the first novelists to emphasize the symbolic importance of the English ancestral home. Northanger Abbey, Norland Park, Pemberley Court, Combe Magna, Rosings Park, Sotherton Court, Donwell Abbey, Mansfield Park, Kellynch Hall: the question of who will inherit them, and who cannot, is at the centre of the novels. As a visitor Jane Austen knew many English country homes well, such as Godmersham, Rowling, Goodnestone Park, Hurstbourne Park, Kempshott Park, The Vyne, Laverstock House, Scarlets and Chawton House. But the greatest of them all was Stoneleigh and the visit there in the summer of 1806 was the moment when she was most vividly forced to confront her own status. As the Leighs descended upon Stoneleigh from north and south, competing for their inheritance, she watched in semi-detachment. She was an outsider.

In early September, lawyer Hill sorted out the minor details of Mary Leigh's will. All that Jane Austen received from Stoneleigh was a 'Single Brilliant Centre Ring'.[22]

workers and his family.' 'He is the best landlord, and the best master,' said she, 'that ever lived. Not like the wild young men now-a-days, who think of nothing but themselves. There is not one of his tenants or servants but what will give him a good name.' For Elizabeth this is praise in the highest degree. The commendation bestowed on him by Mrs Reynolds was of no trifling nature. What praise is more valuable than the praise of an intelligent servant?' The visit to Sonedeigh, where there were more servants than at any other place she ever visited, focused Austen's thoughts on a great estate.

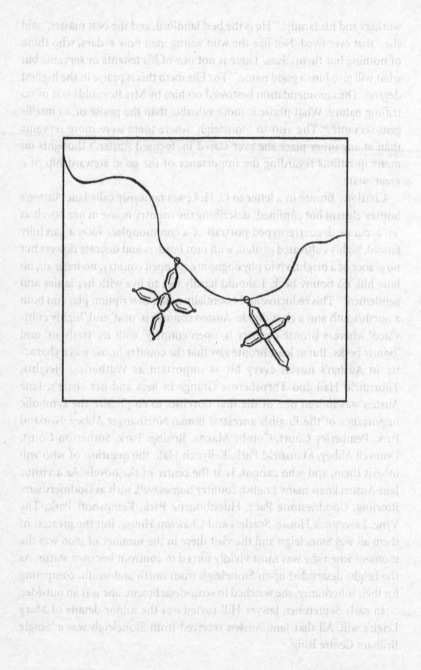

Charlotte Brontë in a letter to G. H. Lewes famously called Jane Austen's domain but confined describing the country house in her novels as an 'accurately clipped portrait of a commonplace face; a carefully fenced, highly cultivated garden, with neat borders and delicate flowers; but no glance of a bright vivid physiognomy, no open country, no fresh air, no blue hill, no bonny beck. I should hardly like to live with her ladies and gentlemen.' This reductive — essentially a prescription placed on both a comely stuith and a vision of the Austen country, neat and highly culti-vated, whereas Brontë's country is open country, with its 'fresh air' and 'bonny becks.' But it is Brontë now that the country house was a charac-ter in Austen's novels every bit as important as Wuthering Heights, Thornfield Hall and Thrushcross Grange in hers and her sister's. Jane Austen was indeed one of the first novelists to emphasise the symbolic importance of the English ancestral home: Northanger Abbey, Norland Park, Pemberley Court, Combe Magna, Rosings Park, Sotherton Court, Donwell Abbey, Mansfield Park, Kellynch Hall. The question of who will inherit them, and who who cannot, is at the centre of the novels. As a visitor Jane Austen knew many English country homes well, such as Godmersham, Rowling, Goodnestone Park, Hurstbourne Park, Kempshott Park, The Vyne, Laverstock House, Seaford, and Chawton House. But the greatest of them all was Stoneleigh and the visit there in the summer of 1806 was the moment when she was most vividly forced to confront her own status. As the heiress descended upon Stoneleigh from north and south, competing for their inheritance, and watched in some-detachment, she was an outsider. In early September, lawyer Hill sorted out the minor details of Mary Leigh's will. All that Jane Austen received from Stoneleigh was a single brilliant Centre Ring.

14

The Topaz Crosses

In May 1801, just as the Austens were settling in Bath, there was a daring capture of a French privateer, *Le Scipio*, by the British frigate *Endymion* in the choppy waters of the war-torn Mediterranean. The French ship was newly built and very fast. There followed an 'arduous chase', reported the *Endymion*'s Captain, Sir Thomas Williams. A junior officer, despite a fierce gale, left his own vessel in an open boat with only four men. He boarded the *Scipio* and held it until reinforcements arrived the next day. He was Second Lieutenant Charles Austen, and his distinguished and courageous action earned him a share in the prize money bestowed for the capture of the privateer.

Captain Tom Williams was both friend and patron to Charles. He was also a relation by marriage, as he had married Charles's first cousin Jane Cooper in 1792. Tom and Jane had been married at the Austen home at Steventon after a whirlwind courtship, and the marriage was extremely happy until Jane was tragically killed in a road accident on the Isle of Wight in 1798. Charles Austen and Tom Williams were drawn even closer. Tom must have been delighted by the brave conduct of his cousin. Charles was given £30 in prize money, and expected a further ten. In his delight and good fortune, he made a purchase of two gold chains and beautiful amber crosses, made out of topaz. They were for his sisters, Cassandra and Jane. The crosses are not identical: one is in the traditional crucifix shape, the other with the symmetry of a saltire. We do not know which went to Cassandra and which to Jane.

Jane was delighted by the present and wrote to Cassandra of her joy and pride, but with characteristic irony: 'of what avail is it to take prizes if he lays out the produce in presents for his Sisters. He has been buying Gold chains and Topaze Crosses for us; – he must be well scolded ... I shall write again by this post to thank and reproach him. – We shall be unbearably fine.'[1]

Cassandra and Jane treasured the crosses and they can be seen today at Chawton Cottage. Topaz was all the rage, but the fact that Charles chose crosses rather than lockets is significant, alluding as it does to his sisters' deep Christian faith as well as marking their delight in fashion. Jane repaid the gesture by using the crosses as a present sent by another sailor brother, the fictional William Price in *Mansfield Park*.

The 'how she should be dressed' was a point of painful solicitude; and the almost solitary ornament in her possession, a very pretty amber cross which William had brought her from Sicily, was the greatest distress of all, for she had nothing but a bit of ribbon to fasten it to; and though she had worn it in that manner once, would it be allowable at such a time in the midst of all the rich ornaments which she supposed all the other young ladies would appear in? And yet not to wear it! William had wanted to buy her a gold chain too, but the purchase had been beyond his means, and therefore not to wear the cross might be mortifying him.[2]

Jane Austen's sailor brothers were an important influence on her work. In *Mansfield Park* and *Persuasion* she pays tribute to Frank and Charles Austen. While writing *Mansfield Park* she asked Frank's permission to include the name of his ship, the *Elephant*.[3] Lieutenant Price's naval jargon perfectly captures the voice of 'Jack Tar', the affectionate nickname given to sailors:

Have you heard the news? The Thrush went out of harbour this morning. Sharp is the word, you see. By G—, you are just in time ... I have been to Turner's about your mess; it is all in a way to be done. I should not wonder if you had your orders tomorrow; but you cannot sail in this wind, if you are to cruise to the westward ... with the Elephant. By G—, I wish you may. But old Scholey was saying, just now, that he thought you would be sent first by Texel. Well, well, we are ready, whatever happens.[4]

Midshipman William Price owes not a little to Charles Austen, 'our own particular little brother'. Charles was a brave and plucky sailor, who longed for serious action and promotion (and prize money, of course). In the absence of a sweetheart to buy presents for, Charles (like William) buys for his sisters. Charles Austen, like William Price, loved dancing. His navy report for 1793–4 noted 'Dances very well'.[5] The ballroom was the place to be when on leave, particularly a ballroom with pretty girls in it. Jane remembered how on one leave Charles 'danced the whole Evening, and to day is no more tired than a gentleman ought to be'.[6]

Later in the war Charles was 'charged with the regulation of all the men raised for the navy in the river Thames and eastern ports, as also with the detail of manning the ships of war fitted out in the Thames and Medway'.[7] He was then given command of a thirty-two-gun frigate called the *Phoenix* and in the brief period of renewed hostilities in 1815 following Napoleon's escape from Elba he did valuable work mopping up the remnants of the French fleet in the Mediterranean. He eventually rose to the rank of rear-admiral and commanded the British expedition during the Second Anglo-Burmese War. He died of cholera aboard ship on the Irrawaddy river in Burma on 7 October 1852, at the age of seventy-three – quite a contrast to his brother Edward, the adopted gentleman, who died in his sleep, aged eighty-five, in the big house at Godmersham a few weeks later.

Jane Austen also used details from her other naval brother, Frank, to flesh out William Price's back-story. As we have seen, Francis, nicknamed Fly, was described by his sister as 'Fearless of danger' with 'warmth, nay insolence of spirit', a boy of 'saucy words and fiery ways'.[8] He was small of stature, but had great energy. Like his brother Charles, he was enrolled in the Royal Naval Academy at Portsmouth.

Two days before Christmas in 1789, the fifteen-year-old Frank set sail for the East Indies on board the *Perseverance*. The voyage took seven months and the men were plagued with scurvy. There were so many rats aboard their sister ship, the *Crown*, that the sailors caught them with fish hooks, stabbed them with forks and ate them. Frank stayed for four years and arrived back home at Steventon in November 1793, summoned back by the

The naval brothers: Captain Charles Austen in
1809 (left) and Captain Francis Austen in 1806
(right, with his decoration as Companion of the
Bath, awarded 1814, painted in at a later date)

Lords of the Admiralty to assume war duties. Jane Austen accordingly did
not see the brother closest in age to her from her fourteenth birthday until
a few weeks before her eighteenth. There still survives a moving and beautifully written advice letter to Frank from his father, a letter he treasured for
all of his long life. We have no way of knowing Jane's feelings, since her
earliest surviving letter dates from 1796, but we can gauge them from Fanny
Price's feelings in *Mansfield Park* when William Price returns from the West
Indies after an absence of five years. The sister waits impatiently for the
moment to arrive: 'watching in the hall, in the lobby, on the stairs, for the
first sounds of the carriage which was to bring her a brother'.[9]

William Price keeps the family enthralled with his stories of naval life:
'Young as he was, William had already seen a great deal. He had been in the
Mediterreanean – in the West Indies – in the Mediterranean again ... and
in the course of seven years had known every variety of danger, which sea
and war together could offer.' The details of sea and war – 'such horrors' –
even move to action the lethargic Lady Bertram: 'Dear me! how disagree-
able. – I wonder anybody can ever go to sea.'[10]

For the rich, idle rake Henry Crawford, William's tales 'gave a different feeling. He longed to have been at sea, and seen and done and suffered as much.' His 'heart was warmed, his fancy fired, and he felt a great respect for a lad who, before he was twenty, had gone through such bodily hardships, and given such proofs of mind'. It is William who inspires in Henry an attack of conscience and self-knowledge: 'The glory of heroism, of usefulness, of exertion, of endurance, made his own habits of selfish indulgence appear in shameful contrast; and he wished he had been a William Price, distinguishing himself and working his way to fortune and consequence with so much self-respect and happy ardour, instead of what he was!'[11]

William's only complaint is that as a lowly midshipman the young girls won't give him a second look: 'The Portsmouth girls turn up their noses at anybody who has not a commission. One might as well be nothing as a midshipman.'[12] Charles and Frank Austen may well have suffered the same romantic indignities, though it wasn't long before Frank obtained his lieutenant's commission. He was just eighteen.

In some cases, early promotion led to discontent among the crews, particularly when over-enthusiastic young officers meted out punishments to their inferiors. Logbooks taken from Frank's ships show the severity of the punishments. Forty-nine lashes would be given for theft and a hundred for insolence to a superior officer. One midshipman was punished by having his uniform stripped and his head shaved in full view of the crew. Mrs Lefroy was embarrassed when a lad called Bob Simmons whom she got into the navy through Charles Austen and Tom Williams turned out to be a thief. The boy was punished by the severest whipping Captain Williams had ever inflicted on a man under his command. It seems that she was corresponding with Charles Austen, as she later told her son that Charles had informed her that Prince Augustus had witnessed the lashing. On another occasion she recalled that Charles had leave of absence from his ship in order to appear as a character witness in a trial at Winchester for a Lieutenant Lutwich, who was accused of murder as a result of striking a sailor with the tiller of the boat, which fractured his skull.[13]

There were other transgressions, too. Wherever males live in close quarters for extended periods (prison, ship and boarding school) consensual and non-consensual homosexual behaviour will occur. Naval sodomy was a hanging offence. Article 28 of the Royal Navy's Articles of War (1757) stated the facts clearly: 'If any person in the fleet shall commit the unnatural and detestable sin of buggery and sodomy with man or beast, he shall be punished with death by the sentence of the court martial.' Of course it is difficult to judge the number of incidences in the Royal Navy during the Napoleonic wars. Some officers turned a blind eye, others punished men for the less serious crime of 'uncleanness'. Captain George Moore, brother to Sir John Moore, who was known to the Austen family,[14] kept a journal in which he wrote of having to flog a man 'who had acted in a manner disgraceful to the character of an Englishman'.[15] But some were indeed given a court martial and hanged. Officers were not exempt. Captain Henry Allen of the *Rattler* was executed for sodomy in 1797. Perhaps the most notorious case, which reached the press, was that of Lieutenant William Berry, who was hanged in 1807 for sodomizing a young boy. Berry, the press reported, was a handsome young lieutenant aged twenty-two and over six feet in height (this in an age when average heights were well below what they are now). His affair with Thomas Gibbs, a young tar, was reported in the eyewitness account of a young girl called Elizabeth Bowden, who had peeped through a keyhole. She had apparently been on board for eight months, disguised as a boy. Berry, who was due to be married, acted with great honour and dignity in the days leading up to his death. He accepted his punishment and endured a horrific death by hanging as the rope slipped over his chin, and he had to be weighed down to finish the job. It took more than fifteen minutes before he died.

In 1798, men on Frank's ship, the *London*, were flogged for 'insolence, mutiny and an unnatural crime of sodomy': the sentence was recorded in the ship's log.[16] Given this context, it is perfectly plausible that Jane Austen showed her awareness of the issue when she allows her anti-heroine, Mary Crawford, to make her most shocking pun.

'Miss Price has a brother at sea,' said Edmund, 'whose excellence as a correspondent makes her think you too severe upon us.'
'At sea, has she? – In the king's service of course?'

Fanny would rather have had Edmund tell the story, but his 'determined silence' obliges her to relate her brother's situation: 'her voice was animated in speaking of his profession, and the foreign stations he had been on; but she could not mention the number of years that he had been absent

9. The Card of Lace

The Form of an Entry of Publication of Banns.

The Banns of Marriage between *A. B.* of
and *C. D.* of   were duly published in this

Church for the {first / second / third} Time, on Sunday the

Day of   in the Year One Thousand Seven
Hundred and

J. J. {Rector / Vicar / Curate}

The Form of an Entry of a Marriage.

A. B. of   and *C. D.* of
were married in this Church by {Banns / Licence} this

Day of   in the Year One Thousand Seven
Hundred and   by me

J. J. {Rector / Vicar / Curate}

This Marriage was solemnized between us *A. B. C. B.* late *C. D.*
in the Presence of *E. F. G. H.*

* Infert thefe Words, viz. with Confent of {Parents / Guardians} where both, or either
of the Parties to be married *by Licence*, are under Age.

10. The Marriage Banns

Died Dec.r 16. 1804

11. The Ivory Miniature

12. The Daughter of Mansfield

13. The Crimson Velvet Cushions

without tears in her eyes'. Miss Crawford civilly wishes him an early promotion:

'Do you know anything of my cousin's captain?' said Edmund; 'Captain Marshall? You have a large acquaintance in the navy, I conclude?'

'Among Admirals, large enough; but,' with an air of grandeur, 'we know very little of the inferior ranks. Post captains may be very good sort of men, but they do not belong to *us*. Of various admirals, I could tell you a great deal; of them and their flags, and the gradation of their pay, and their bickerings and jealousies. But, in general, I can assure you that they are all passed over, and all very ill used. Certainly, my home at my uncle's brought me acquainted with a circle of admirals. Of *Rears*, and *Vices*, I saw enough. Now, do not be suspecting me of a pun, I entreat.'

Edmund again felt grave, and only replied, 'It is a noble profession.'[17]

Edmund's shock and his defence of the nobility of the profession show that he is deeply offended. The fact that Mary draws explicit attention to her crude pun by pretending not to have made it does make it seem that she is referring to sexual vices involving rears. But the 'I saw enough' is interesting. Mary's cynicism is given context – what exactly did she see at her home with Admiral Crawford? What has made her so jaded about the navy? We know that Admiral Crawford has brought a mistress under his roof, but Mary hints at 'seeing' evidence of particularly shocking sexual behaviour. It is worth remembering that in *Mansfield Park* flogging is directly connected with sexual misbehaviour when ex-marine Lieutenant Price suggests 'giving the rope's end' to Maria Bertram for her adultery.

Frank, the most pious of the brothers, was known for lacking a sense of humour. He was a ponderous and serious-minded sailor. In the Austen family his letters were famous for their length and their mundane detail. A family anecdote recalled his character perfectly. A naval colleague went swimming in the tropics. Frank observed calmly and slowly, 'Mr Pakenham you are in danger of a shark – a shark of the blue species.' The captain thought it was a joke, but was told by Frank, 'I am not given to joking. If you do not return immediately, soon the shark will eat you.'[18] Jane, who lived for jokes, continued to tease him in her own letters, 'I hope you

The *Peterel* (under Captain Francis Austen)
engages with *La Ligurienne*

continue beautiful and brush your hair, but not all off.'[19] Given his lack of
humour, it is remarkable that – as noted in my prologue – he seems to have
recalled the 'Rears, and Vices' joke nearly forty years after his sister wrote it.

Frank had a distinguished war record. Among his many triumphs was
the capture of the French brig *La Ligurienne* just off the Mediterranean
coast, close to Marseilles, in March 1800. Frank reported the very satisfactory outcome: '*Peterel*: Killed, none; wounded, none. *La Ligurienne*: Killed,
the captain and one seaman; wounded, one gardemarin and one seaman.'[20]

Frank missed the Battle of Trafalgar in 1805 by a hair's-breadth. He was
dispatched by Lord Nelson to Gibraltar for supplies and missed the great
victory. This twist of fate caused him serious mental anguish. However in
1806 he was present at the Battle of San Domingo. Jane acknowledged this
victory in *Persuasion* by having Captain Wentworth 'made commander in
consequence of action off St. Domingo'.[21]

When the Austen women – Jane, Cassandra and their mother, the 'dear
trio' as brother Henry called them – fell on hard times, they were reliant
upon the financial assistance of the brothers. Frank offered twice as much
money as he needed to, asking that the full amount be kept a secret. He
then concocted a plan to have them live with his wife-to-be Mary Gibson
in Southampton. Jane also wanted Martha Lloyd, whom she had once

hoped would marry Frank, to be part of the new family arrangement: 'With Martha ... who will be so happy as we?'[22]

Though she summered at Godmersham, Southampton was Jane Austen's primary home for two years, from March 1807 until the summer of 1809. This large town, another popular spa, with an assembly room for dancing, a theatre, circulating libraries and a tree-lined beach walk, had many associations. It was the place where as a girl she had contracted typhus and almost died; then she had returned in 1793 to help a cousin with the birth of a new baby. Southampton was fixed upon as a suitable town, due to its proximity to Portsmouth, which was necessary for Frank.

Their leased home in Southampton was a 'commodious old fashioned house' in a corner of Castle Square. It hugged the old city walls and, according to Jane, contained the best garden in the town. Just as important, it had extensive views across Southampton Water. The Isle of Wight could be seen in the distance. Living in such close proximity to the sea must have felt a blessing after the confinement of Bath, the city that they had left 'with happy feelings of escape'.[23] She sometimes complained of 'Castle Square weather', as it was breezy, but they enjoyed living there.

The Austens made family excursions by ferryboat on the River Itchen. They saw naval sights and the Gothic ruins of Netley Abbey. Jane continued her long walks when she was in Southampton, rambling through the lovely countryside surrounding the town, beside Southampton Water and along the banks of the Itchen and Test rivers. A surviving fragment from a pocket diary belonging to her during this time notes her expenditure, which included 'waterparties and plays', which cost 17s 9d, and the hire of a piano, which cost £2 13s 6d.

Mary Gibson, now Frank's wife, was in the early stages of pregnancy and suffered badly from morning sickness. It was the first time that Jane would live in such close proximity to a pregnant woman and she observed her well. Frank was away for the birth, which was painful and long, and there were some initial fears for the mother who was 'most alarmingly ill'.[24] She did recover, however, and called her baby Mary-Jane. Jane's phobia about childbirth was not helped by Mary's distressing confinement.

Naval matters were of course much on her mind. She was living in a place that was a hive of wartime activity and she came into close contact with Frank's sailor friends. There's no knowing if she read the press accounts of the court martial of Lieutenant William Berry, but she was certainly aware of another naval court martial in that same year of 1807, that of Home Popham. In protest at what she considered gross injustice, she fired off a terse satirical poem 'On Sir Home Popham's Sentence'. Popham was charged with having withdrawn troops and carried out a military expedition without orders from the Admiralty. It is a remarkable poem, a satire on a public event, but revealing a depth of anger and 'spite' that suggests her fierce interest in the conduct of the war:

> Of a Ministry pitiful, angry, mean,
> A gallant commander the victim is seen.
> For promptitude, vigour, success, does he stand
> Condemn'd to receive a severe reprimand!
> To his foes I could wish a resemblance in fate:
> That they, too, may suffer themselves, soon or late,
> The injustice they warrant. But vain is my spite,
> *They* cannot *so* suffer who never do right.[25]

She kept a close eye on news in the papers regarding the campaign in the Iberian peninsula against Napoleon. On 10 January 1809 she wrote to Cassandra, 'The St Albans perhaps may soon be off to help bring home what may remain by this time of our poor army, whose state seems dreadfully critical.'[26] She was referring to the notorious Battle of Corunna.

The British army had been sent into Spain under the command of General Sir John Moore to aid the locals in expelling the French. The British were forced to retreat through the mountains of northern Spain in the depths of winter. The forced march wreaked havoc on health and morale, resulting in the army degenerating into a rabble. Moore finally reached Corunna. His army expected to find a fleet to evacuate them but they discovered that the transport vessels that had been ordered had not arrived. The *St Albans* mentioned by Jane was one of the ships sent to evacuate the wounded. The British losses were terrible and Sir John Moore was fatally wounded. Jane kept up to date with the latest dispatches and upon hearing of the General's death wrote, 'grievous news from Spain. – It was well that Dr Moore [a family friend] was spared the knowledge of such a Son's death.'[27]

Back in Britain there was much talk of Moore's mishandling of the campaign. *The Times* reported it as a shameful disaster. Moore's dignity in

'Mr B. Promoted to Lieut and first putting on his
Uniform' by George Cruikshank

death was praised by most, though not by Jane Austen. His last words were
reportedly 'I hope the people of England will be satisfied! I hope my country will do me justice!' Austen disapproved, as there was no reference to
God and the afterlife: 'I wish Sir John had united something of the Christian
with the Hero in his death,' she remarked. She then added, 'Thank Heaven!
we have had no one to care for particularly among the Troops.'[28] With
brothers in the navy and Henry in the militia she had good reason to be
thankful that no one close to her had been involved. Frank Austen was in
charge of the disembarkation of Moore's troops at Spithead, and would
have seen many of the wounded at first hand.

* * *

Early in the final volume of *Mansfield Park*, Fanny Price's brother William
is promoted to the rank of lieutenant. He visits his sister at the big house,
but is not allowed to show off his new uniform to her there, because 'cruel
custom prohibited its appearance except on duty'. So the uniform remains

at Portsmouth, and Edmund worries whether Fanny will have any chance of seeing it before 'all its own freshness, and all the freshness of its wearer's feelings, must be worn away'. But then his father, Sir Thomas, tells him of 'a scheme which placed Fanny's chance of seeing the 2d lieutenant of H. M. S. Thrush in all his glory, in another light': she is to go to Portsmouth herself.[29]

But Sir Thomas also has a darker purpose. Fanny has defied his wish for her to marry the unprincipled Henry Crawford, so she is sent 'home' to Portsmouth as an 'experiment', a 'medicinal project' upon her understanding. Sir Thomas Bertram's hope is that 'a little abstinence from the elegancies and wealth of Mansfield Park, would bring her mind into a sober state'. 'Her Father's house would, in all probability, teach her the value of a good income.'[30]

Portsmouth comes alive as a bustling, busy seaport. Fanny and William arrive and are driven through the spectacular moated drawbridge. There is the High Street with its good shops, the beautiful ramparts, the sea views to Spithead and the Isle of Wight, the Crown Inn where Henry Crawford stays, the Garrison Chapel where the Price family worship on a Sunday. In the famous Portsmouth Dockyard, which resembled a small town, with dwelling-houses, offices, store-houses and lofts employing more than two thousand men, Fanny and Henry sit upon 'timbers in the yard' and chat. They wander aboard a stationary sloop. There is a strikingly evocative passage describing the Portsmouth seascape:

> The day was uncommonly lovely. It was really March; but it was April in its mild air, brisk soft wind, and bright sun, occasionally clouded for a minute; and every thing looked so beautiful under the influence of such a sky, the effects of the shadows pursuing each other, on the ships at Spithead and the island beyond, with the ever-varying hues of the sea now at high water, dancing in its glee and dashing against the ramparts with so fine a sound.[31]

However, once inside the Price family home, we are given a very different picture. Jane Austen wanders into previously uncharted territory in her depiction of the lower-middle-class Price family, and her depiction of this, her first naval family, is not wholly flattering.

As seen through the eyes of Fanny Price, who has been reared in luxury at Mansfield Park, the tiny, terraced house is cramped and dirty. The walls are marked with greasy hair oil, 'half-cleaned plates, and not half-cleaned knives and forks', dust motes circle in the glare of the sunshine, china is 'wiped in streaks', 'the milk a mixture of motes floating in thin blue'.[32]

Fanny's father, Lieutenant Price, 'disabled for active service', is presented as little more than a thug: 'he read only the newspaper and the navy-list; he talked only of the dock-yard, the harbour, Spithead, and the Motherbank; he swore and he drank, he was dirty and gross'. His home, where he drinks grog with his sailor friends and makes his daughter the object of 'coarse jokes', epitomizes the life of the vulgar tar: 'it was the abode of noise, disorder, and impropriety'.[33] Fanny's mother is a slattern who cannot control her many children and her useless maid. Other than the depiction of midshipman William Price, who is drawn with great charm, the navy in *Mansfield Park* has little to recommend it.

Interestingly, Jane Austen's sailor brothers did not mention the Portsmouth scenes in their responses to *Mansfield Park*, unlike James and Edward who singled them out for special praise. Jane wrote that Admiral Foote (a close friend of Frank's) was 'surprised that I had the power of drawing the Portsmouth-Scenes so well',[34] but one wonders if her sailor brothers were offended by her depiction of the navy. Her portrayal of naval families in *Persuasion* was drawn with a kindlier and more respectful eye perhaps as a form of atonement.

Captain Harville, living in his rented rooms in Lyme Regis, is the master of a tiny, cramped home, but it is cosy, tidy and clean. Here Harville and his wife have made the best of 'the deficiencies of lodging-house furniture'. He has barricaded the windows and doors against the winter storms, and his treasures from the West Indies furnish the room. Unlike Fanny Price, who compares her father's house unfavourably to Mansfield Park, Anne has no such views: 'how much more interesting to her was the home and friendship of the Harvilles and Captain Benwick, than her own father's house'.[35]

When Anne returns to Kellynch Hall she realizes that Admiral and Mrs Croft are worthy tenants in comparison to her father: 'she could not but in conscience feel that they were gone who deserved not to stay, and that Kellynch-hall had passed into better hands than its owners'.[36] They have respected the spirit of the place and the only substantial change they have made is the removal of the vain Sir Walter's many looking-glasses. She knows that the 'strangers' who have made their own way by hard work and courage are far more worthy of Kellynch than her own 'ancient family'.

Anne rejoices in this: she is happy to enter the 'wooden world' that comes with being a naval wife and to escape Sir Walter and his obsession with the baronetage.

In *Mansfield Park*, the well-bred but selfish Bertram children fare much less well than the Price children who have endured the squalor and alcohol fumes of the little house in Portsmouth:

> In her [Susan Price's] usefulness, in Fanny's excellence, in William's continued good conduct, and rising fame, and in the general well-doing and success of the other members of the family, all assisting to advance each other, and doing credit to his countenance and aid, Sir Thomas saw repeated, and for ever repeated, reason to rejoice in what he had done for them all, and acknowledge the advantages of early hardship and discipline, and the consciousness of being born to struggle and endure.[37]

Jane Austen admired the discipline of the navy because of its bracing effect on character formation.

For all his merits, William Price is not the hero of *Mansfield Park*. But in the portrayal of Captain Wentworth, we see Jane Austen's most deserving self-made hero. He is indeed her only truly romantic hero. He has risen in society not through inheritance but by hard work, courage and enterprise. If Sir Walter represents 'old money' and the decaying gentry, Wentworth is the embodiment of the new, the confident and the professional:

> Captain Wentworth had no fortune. He had been lucky in his profession, but spending freely, what had come freely, had realized nothing. But, he was confident that he should soon be rich; – full of life and ardour, he knew that he should soon have a ship, and soon be on a station that would lead to everything he wanted. He had always been lucky; he knew he should be so still.[38]

If you had a commission and the right luck, there was money to be made on the high seas in both the West and the East.

There is a moment in *Mansfield Park* when Edmund Bertram says that his cousin Fanny 'will be taking a trip into China'. 'How does Lord Macartney go on?' he asks.[39] Fanny is obviously reading a recently published 'great book', John Barrow's two-volume *Some Account of the Public Life and a Selection from the Unpublished Writings of the Earl of Macartney* (1807), which included the text of Lord Macartney's *Journal of the Embassy to China*. This was a key moment in the history of trade relations with China. More specifically, it was the period when opium was being shipped by the ton from Bengal to China.

In the early spring of 1809, Captain Frank Austen said goodbye to his wife, his mother and his sisters. He set sail on the *St Albans*. His destination was China, in support of a convoy of East Indiamen. He ended up on Canton river, engaged in a very tricky encounter in the pirate-infested islands known as the Ladrones. Having negotiated a satisfactory settlement with the local Mandarin authorities, he negotiated his way back across the China Seas to Madras. By July he was on his way home, sending Chinese presents to his brother Charles from aboard ship. He safely sailed the *St Albans* back to London, where his cargo was unloaded: ninety-three chests of treasure 'said to contain 470,000 Dollars or Bullion to that amount' (the dollar was the coin adopted by traders in the Dutch East Indies). For his pains, Frank Austen was rewarded with over £500 for the escorting of the convoy and offered freight money of just over a thousand pounds – a sum that he negotiated up to £1,500 by claiming a percentage on the value of the treasure.[40] The modern equivalent for his total earnings from the voyage would be about £100,000 or $150,000. There can be little doubt that this was opium money.

There is no explicit reference to opium in *Persuasion*, but Captain Wentworth, like Jane Austen's sailor brothers, successfully reconciles duty – the 'national importance' of the navy in time of war, as the last sentence of the novel has it – with material success. Frank Austen later served in the North America and West Indies Station in 1844 and was promoted an Admiral of the Red in 1855. He died in his fine house, Portsdown Lodge, above his beloved Portsmouth, ten years later. His sister would have wished analogous prosperity and longevity upon that most deserving fictional naval couple, Frederick and Anne Wentworth.

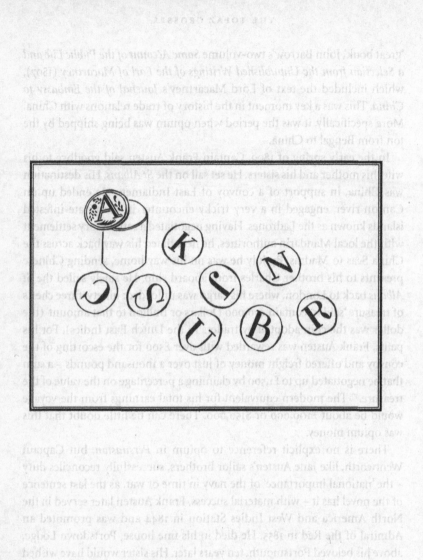

15

The Box of Letters

'Miss Woodhouse,' said Frank Churchill, after examining a table behind him, which he could reach as he sat, 'have your nephews taken away their alphabets – their box of letters? It used to stand here. Where is it? This is a sort of dull-looking evening, that ought to be treated rather as winter than summer. We had great amusement with those letters one morning. I want to puzzle you again.'

Emma, VOL. 3, CH. 5

It is an educational toy, but also a popular game among adults, to while away the time in a world without television and computers. Any number of people can play. The hand-painted bone or ivory counters are marked with capital letters on one side and lower case on the reverse. The aim is to mix up the letters and make as many words from them as possible, or as long a word as possible. It was a simple version of Scrabble. Sometimes the ivory squares or circles were bought blank and the purchaser would draw letters on them, as Emma Woodhouse does in a beautifully elegant hand. Equally well, the box of letters could be used to teach a child to spell and to broaden her vocabulary.[1]

Frank Churchill placed a word before Miss Fairfax. She gave a slight glance round the table, and applied herself to it ... The word was discovered, and with a faint smile pushed away ... The word was *blunder*; and as Harriet exultingly proclaimed it, there was a blush on Jane's cheek which gave it a meaning not otherwise ostensible ... These letters were but the vehicle for gallantry and trick. It was a child's play, chosen to conceal a deeper game on Frank Churchill's part.[2]

The adults in this scene are playing with children's toys, which uncover a deeply unpleasant adult psychological game. Most of them, in particular Frank Churchill, are behaving like children. The same could be said of Emma's behaviour in the scene at Box Hill when she insults Miss Bates. *Emma* is the novel most interested in games, especially mind-games and manipulation.

Jane Austen's vision of how human beings behave in society is built on disguise and role-play, equivocation and mystery. She was one of the first authors to use games – riddles, conundrums, play at cards – to reveal (often) dubious social conduct. In *Mansfield Park*, she uses the gambling card game Speculation, one of her own favourites, in an important scene involving the main characters. The scene is loaded with symbolism. The object of the game is to hold the highest trump card, when all cards in play have been revealed. Cards can be bought or sold with other cards. The game, of course, is played on more than one level. Jane Austen played Speculation with her nephew George, and pretended to be cross when her nephews showed a preference for another card game, Bragg: 'it mortifies me deeply, because Speculation was under my patronage'.[3]

In *Emma*, Jane Austen fully explores the importance of silence, plain-speaking and non-verbal communication, offset against verbal ambiguities, equivocations, comic misunderstandings, riddles and word-games. Riddles and puns are used with great effect to exploit the comic misunderstandings between Emma and Mr Elton (his riddle on 'woodhouse' is blithely misinterpreted by Emma), but with the arrival of Frank Churchill we see a master game-player.

From the outset, the Knightley brothers are associated with a lack of gallantry and a love of plain-speaking, which Austen described as 'the true English manner', whereas Frank's gallantry and charm are manifested by his love and mastery of word-play. He plays a flirtatious double-game with Emma and the woman he is secretly engaged to, Jane Fairfax. He makes love to Jane, but uses Emma as a blind.

In the memorable 'Blunder' scene Frank uses the alphabet game to communicate with Jane and to deceive Emma. He is, of course, apologizing for his blunder in divulging the gossip about Mr Perry's carriage, which reveals to the attentive reader that he is communicating in secret with Jane. Mr Knightley, who is a close observer of people, perceives that Frank and Jane are playing a game. Emma is oblivious to the real state of play. Even worse, Frank uses the word-game to taunt Jane and please Emma, by placing the word DIXON close to Jane. The final word, which as readers we are not privy to, but which Jane Austen later revealed to her nieces and nephews, is PARDON.

Emma is also a good and clever player, more in the mould of Mary Crawford than Fanny Price. But her wit and verbal dexterity are shown to be heartless and hollow when she mocks Miss Bates on Box Hill. After all the wearying games and verbal acrobatics she has indulged in, Emma plays backgammon all evening with her father to soothe her great distress after the distressing incident, 'giving up the sweetest hours of the twenty-four to his [her father's] comfort'.[4]

Mr Knightley, the reserved and sincere Englishman, abhors subterfuge and game-playing, telling Emma at the end of the novel, 'Mystery; Finesse – how they pervert the understanding! My Emma, does not every thing serve to prove more and more the beauty of truth and sincerity in all our dealings with each other?'[5] It's a noble sentiment but is ironically undercut by Emma's 'blush of sensibility on Harriet's account' – for she is withholding the full truth of Harriet's love for him. Jane Austen warns us in *Emma*: 'Seldom, very seldom, does complete truth belong to any human disclosure; seldom can it happen that something is not a little disguised, or a little mistaken.'[6] We are left wondering if Emma will ever fully disclose the truth to her future husband. The acknowledgement of the incompleteness of human disclosure strikes at the very heart of Jane Austen's creative vision.

Jane Austen and her family loved charades, puzzles, conundrums and riddles. Her nieces and nephews left accounts of all the games they played together with their beloved aunt. There were physical games such as battledore, shuttlecock and bilbocatch (Cup and Ball) and those of skill such as spillikins (pick-up-sticks), which Austen considered 'a very valuable part of our Household furniture'.[7] She loved playing card games with children: Cribbage, Loo, Commerce, Casino, Speculation, Bragg and Nines. As we have seen, she also liked dressing-up games and private theatricals.

With no children of her own, she took her duties as aunt and godmother seriously. Austen seems to have been asked to be godmother to Anne 'Nanny' Littleworth's daughter Eliza-Jane in 1789, when she was only thirteen. Anne was married to John Littleworth, who was coachman to James Austen. Jane was also witness to the marriage of John's brother and clearly adored the extended family of the woman who had fostered the Austen children in their infancy. Later, Jane became godmother to her cousin Elizabeth's daughter Elizabeth-Matilda Butler Harrison, and to her niece Louisa. After her death her gold chains were bequeathed to her godchildren. Coming from a large, loving family, she was used to having children around. Of the Austen brothers, only Henry and disabled George remained childless. James had three children, Edward eleven, Frank eleven, and Charles had eight.

Austen's letters reveal her great love of children's company.[8] In 1805, she played shuttlecock with William Knight and reported that with practice they kept the shuttlecock in the air six times. She was good with children who were not related to her. There is a glimpse in the letters of her playing Cribbage with little Daniel Finch-Hatton, son of Lord Mansfield's adopted daughter. Another small child, a daughter of one of her brother's naval friends, took a fancy to her, and sat at her side while she wrote her daily letters:

> She is now talking away at my side and examining the Treasures of my Writing-desk drawer; – very happy I beleive; – not at all shy of course … What is become of all the Shyness in the World? … she is a nice, natural, openhearted, affectionate girl, with all the ready civility which one sees in the best Children of the present day; – so unlike anything that I was myself at her age, that I am often all astonishment and shame.[9]

As a maiden aunt, she was expected to give practical help and emotional support to her female relations. Families of half-siblings and step-parents were not at all unusual with such high rates of maternal mortality. Aunts, grandmothers and sisters were depended upon to be available to motherless children. After Anna Austen's mother died when she was a toddler, the little girl was constantly crying for 'mama' and was sent to Steventon to be looked after by Jane and Cassandra.

Jane knew and understood children, without being at all sentimental about them. When Elizabeth Knight died in childbed, leaving eleven grieving children behind, Jane sent for the two elder boys to stay with her at her home in Southampton. She distracted the boys with games and day trips, taking them to see a real man of war and to row on the Itchen. They played 'spillikins, paper ships, riddles, conundrums, and cards, with watching the flow and ebb of the river'.[10]

What made her very special was her capacity to enter into the world of children. She observed their ways and understood them. She sympathized with a niece's acne 'breakouts', a nephew's prowess in skipping ('I hope he will continue to send me word of his improvement in the art'),[11] and another's ingenuity in pulling faces and throwing her fan in the river. She was amused at her niece Cassy's interest in her much older cousin Anna's romance with Benjamin Lefroy: 'She asked a thousand questions, in her usual way – What he said to you? and what you said to him?'[12]

All this resonates with the knowledge of children's behaviour she shows in *Emma* when the children want to be told every small detail of the Gypsies

Drawing of Jane Austen's cup and ball by Ellen Hill
in her sister Constance Hill's book *Jane Austen:
Her Homes and her Friends* (1902)

incident: 'Henry and John were still asking every day for the story of Harriet and the gipsies, and still tenaciously setting her right if she varied in the slightest particular from the original recital.'[13]

* * *

Austen's peripatetic life came to an end in 1809. Her wealthy brother Edward was now in possession of the 'Great House' at Chawton. He rented it out but arranged for his mother and sisters to take a house on his estate. It was at the junction of the two roads that went through the village, the front door opening directly on to the road, though there was a narrow enclosure to protect the house 'from the possible shock of any runaway vehicle'.[14] There were two parlours, called the dining and the drawing room, both intended originally to look out on the road. The large drawing-room window was blocked up by a bookcase when the Austen women took possession, and another was opened at the side, giving a view out on to turf and trees. The property had a reasonably sized garden with a gravel walk, long grass for mowing, an orchard, a kitchen garden and many outbuildings, which children loved to play in. The extended family, children included, often came to visit – there were enough bedrooms, albeit some of them very small. Another pleasure for the nephews and nieces was the thrill of the traffic thundering by, right outside the door: 'Collyer's daily coach with six horses was a sight to see! and most delightful was it to a child to have the awful stillness of night so frequently broken by the noise of passing carriages, which seemed sometimes, even to shake the bed.'[15]

The house at Chawton gave Jane Austen a secure home for the first time since her departure from Steventon eight years before. A sturdy bookcase, a green view at the side, the sound of the road to remind her of life and the city, her beloved sister at her side, room for visiting nephews and nieces. This was the stable environment that enabled her to revise *Pride and Prejudice* for publication, then to write *Mansfield Park*, *Emma*, *Persuasion* and the beginning of *Sanditon*. Chawton remained Jane Austen's home – though one from which she frequently departed for trips to London – for eight years, until she was removed to Winchester in the last months of her life.

One of the best descriptions of Jane Austen was given by someone who knew her well in her Chawton years, Charlotte Maria Middleton. She stayed at Chawton Manor as a little girl and remembered Austen as having a 'keen sense of humour' that 'oozed out very much in Mr. Bennett's Style': 'She was a most kind and enjoyable person *to Children* but somewhat stiff and cold to strangers ... my remembrance of Jane is that of her entering into all Childrens Games and liking her extremely. – We were often asked to meet her young nephews and nieces.'[16]

She liked children's blunt honesty and their openness; she was amused by their malapropisms and the way they created a private language. In one letter she wrote, 'Nunna Hat's Love to George. – A great many People wanted to mo up in the Poach as well as me.' George Knight was a particularly sweet toddler to whom she wrote fondly, 'I flatter myself that *itty Dordy* will not forget me at least under a week. Kiss him for me.' 'Itty Dordy' (Little Georgy) was how he pronounced his own name. This was the same boy who as a grown-up schoolboy came to Jane Austen to be comforted after his mother's death, and whom she describes making and naming paper ships as his elder brother is deep in a novel, 'twisting himself about in one of our great chairs'.[17] That phrase describes so perfectly the motions of this bereaved fidgety boy and brings him alive.

To her niece Caroline she wrote: 'Only think of your lost Dormouse being brought back to you!' To little Cassy Esten she wrote mirror letters, 'Ym raed Yssac, I hsiw uoy a yppah wen raey.' She encouraged their games, advised on romances and told good jokes – 'Send my love to Cassy, – I hope she found my bed comfortable last night and has not filled it with fleas.'[18]

She refused to patronize children. When they became older, she wrote sensible letters that treated them as grown-ups. 'I have always maintained the importance of Aunts,' she wrote to her niece Fanny. To ten-year-old Caroline, she wrote, 'Now that you are become an Aunt, you are a person of some consequence.'[19] When Jane Austen thought she had gone too far in her criticisms of her nephews and nieces, she was quick to make amends, 'As I wrote of my nephews with a little bitterness in my last, I think it particularly incumbent on me to do them justice now.' As she said in another letter, 'After having much praised or much blamed anybody, one is generally sensible of something just the reverse soon afterwards.'[20]

In 1983 a scrap of a letter by Jane Austen was unearthed in a library in America and published for the first time. The letter was written to her niece, Jane-Anna (known as Anna), who was very close to her aunt, having lost her own mother at the age of two. She was also struggling with being the stepsister of two younger siblings. Jane Austen tells her: 'from the first, being *born* older, is a very good thing. – I wish you perseverance and success with all my heart.'[21] On the reverse of the letter she writes about another child, little Charles Lefroy, 'we thought him a very fine boy, but terribly in want of Discipline. – I hope he gets a wholesome thump, or two, whenever it is necessary.'[22] The fragment is a revealing snapshot of the author and her attitude towards the younger generation. The voice is surprisingly modern and fresh, comforting one moment, teasing the other. It is not the voice of a querulous spinster, embittered by her own childlessness, which is how Jane Austen has sometimes been misrepresented.

She didn't idealize children, and she expected good behaviour and good manners. Nor did she like being treated by her brothers as an unpaid nanny. She had great sympathy with the plight of governesses, and befriended Fanny Knight's governess Anne Sharp. Anne was, according to Fanny, 'good-natured' and 'pretty'.[23] She was well educated and devoted to the Knight children, though poor health meant that she left Godmersham after only two years. Jane Austen considered her to be a close friend; she was a visitor to Chawton and they regularly corresponded. She sought Anne's opinions of her novels: 'Oh! I have more of such sweet flattery from Miss Sharp,' she told Cassandra after the publication of *Pride and Prejudice*, which was Anne's favourite. 'She is an excellent kind friend.' When Jane asked her opinion of *Mansfield Park* she implored her friend to be 'perfectly honest'.[24]

Jane worried about her friend and cherished fantasies that one of her employers would fall in love with her: 'I do so want him to marry her! ... Oh! Sir W[illia]m – Sir Wm – how I will love you, if you will love Miss Sharp,' she wrote in 1814.[25] Her next novel, *Emma*, indulged that fantasy when Miss Taylor, Emma's governess, marries widowed Mr Weston.

After Jane's death, Cassandra sent Anne a lock of her hair and a bodkin from her sewing kit. In 2008 a presentation copy of *Emma* to 'Anne Sharp' from 'The Author' was discovered (it came up for auction at Bonhams). Austen was allowed only twelve presentation copies and this was the only one given to a personal friend. Anne later established a school for girls in Liverpool.[26]

When another governess came to take charge of the large motherless brood of Knight children, Jane showed her empathy: 'By this time I suppose she is hard at it, governing away – poor creature! I pity her, tho' they *are* my nieces.'[27] Jane was often on babysitting duties herself. She took care of

Charles's two small daughters for a month. She wrote to Frank telling him that she was 'quite sorry' to see them go. She was pleased that time away from their doting parents had improved them: 'Harriet in health – Cassy in manners', and of the latter she added, 'She will really be a very pleasing child, if they will only exert themselves a little.'[28] Lack of firmness in parents was not to be admired.

Charles adored his children, and this aspect of his character is given to Captain Harville in *Persuasion*, who talks movingly of how it feels to leave children behind and then be reunited with them:

'Ah!' cried Captain Harville, in a tone of strong feeling, 'if I could but make you comprehend what a man suffers when he takes a last look at his wife and children, and watches the boat that he has sent them off in, as long as it is in sight, and then turns away and says, "God knows whether we ever meet again!" And then, if I could convey to you the glow of his soul when he does see them again; when, coming back after a twelvemonth's absence perhaps, and obliged to put into another port, he calculates how soon it be possible to get them there, pretending to deceive himself, and saying, "They cannot be here till such a day," but all the while hoping for them twelve hours sooner, and seeing them arrive at last, as if Heaven had given them wings, by many hours sooner still! If I could explain to you all this, and all that a man can bear and do, and glories to do for the sake of these treasures of his existence! I speak, you know, only of such men as have hearts!' pressing his own with emotion.[29]

Though in this passage Austen indulges her character's strong paternal feeling, when it came to mothers she admired love that was rational and just rather than doting: 'Harriot's fondness for her [small daughter] seems just what is amiable and natural, and not foolish.'[30]

Jane Austen was as keen not to idealize children in her novels as she was in real life. In *Sense and Sensibility* she deflates one of the conventions of sensibility: the idealization of childhood innocence. She presents children as they really are, refusing to venerate them as Rousseauistic free spirits. The Steele sisters know that the way to make themselves agreeable to Lady Middleton is through courting her odious and very spoilt children. When they first arrive at Barton Park the Steeles come with a coachful of toys, and they indulge every whim of Anna Maria: "'I have a notion," said Lucy, "you think the little Middletons rather too much indulged … I love to see children full of life and spirits; I cannot bear them if they are tame and quiet.'" With cool irony, Elinor replies with the confession 'that while I am at Barton Park, I never think of tame and quiet children with any abhorrence'.[31]

Austen was of the opinion that doting mothers could be a harmful influence. Anne Elliot in *Persuasion* is respected and loved by her nieces, though they clearly do not respect their own mother. Mrs Weston in *Emma* is described as 'Standing in a mother's place but without the mother's affection to blind her'. A child can also be a plaything to a mother, as in *Sense and Sensibility*: 'Mrs Parker had her child, and Mrs Jennings her carpet work.'[32]

Love of children is often a guide to character in the novels. Mr Knightley forgives Emma's wrongdoing against Mr Martin when he sees her holding her baby niece in her arms: 'though he began with grave looks and short questions, he was soon led on to talk of them all in the usual way, and to take the child out of her arms with all the unceremoniousness of perfect amity'. Mr Knightley then says, 'If you were as much guided by nature in your estimate of men and women, and as little under the power of fancy and whim in your dealings with them, as you are where these children are concerned, we might always think alike.'[33] By contrast, Edmund Bertram says of Mrs Norris, with lethal understatement, '[she] never knew how to be pleasant to children' – a chilling indictment of her character.[34]

Many moments of emotional intensity in the novels are mediated through the witnessing presence of small children. In *Emma*, when Mr Knightley's emotional distress overwhelms him at Brunswick Square, one of his brother's children observes that 'Uncle seems always tired now.'[35]

Two especially memorable scenes centre upon small children. Few can forget the emotional impact of the moment in *Persuasion* when Captain Wentworth silently removes the troublesome toddler from Anne's back. In a scene of excruciating comic embarrassment and high emotion, he enters Uppercross Cottage to find not the Miss Musgroves whom he expects, but Anne, alone except for little Charles Musgrove resting on a sofa nursing a broken collar-bone. She is unable to leave the room because the little boy requires her help, and she kneels to assist him. Wentworth is embarrassed and silent until he gathers his thoughts to enquire coldly after the little boy's health. The high discomfort is compounded when Charles Hayter enters, displeased to see Wentworth. He takes up his newspaper in silence. The door opens again and a stout two-year-old boy enters:

> There being nothing to eat, he could only have some play; and as his aunt would not let him teaze his sick brother, he began to fasten himself upon her, as she knelt, in such a way that, busy as she was about Charles, she could not shake him off. She spoke to him – ordered, intreated, and insisted in vain. Once she did contrive to push him away, but the boy had the greater pleasure in getting upon her back again directly.
>
> 'Walter,' said she, 'get down this moment. You are extremely troublesome. I am very angry with you' … In another moment, however, she found herself in the state of being released from him; some one was taking him from her, though he had bent down her head so much, that his sturdy little hands were unfastened from around her neck, and he was resolutely borne away, before she knew that Captain Wentworth had done it.[36]

The emotion between the former lovers is beautifully depicted. Anne is unable to speak her thanks, but her internal 'disordered feelings' are rendered by Austen's innovative device of free indirect speech (third-person narrative that is written as if from within the mind of a character): 'His kindness in stepping forward to her relief – the manner – the silence in which it had passed – the little particulars of the circumstance – with the conviction soon forced on her by the noise he was studiously making with the child, that he meant to avoid hearing her thanks … produced such a confusion of varying, but very painful agitation, as she could not recover from.'[37]

To the reader, of course, other things are at play: Charles Hayter's barely concealed jealousy of Wentworth, Anne's intense but silent emotion, Wentworth's icy formality towards her as he hides his pain and anger about the past. The point is that Wentworth doesn't realize that he still loves Anne: he tries to punish her with his indifference and coldness but he is betrayed by his actions.[38] Her guilt and sorrow are suggested in her bowing head and kneeling posture, his 'angry pride' in refusing her thanks. These details and the child's 'sturdy hands', determined not to be shaken off, all show great delicacy of touch in this powerfully rendered and exceptionally tender scene.

Perhaps the most vividly drawn child in Jane Austen's novels is the charming and true-to-life Charles Blake in the fragment *The Watsons*. The ten-year-old boy is drawn in great detail at a ball where he is waiting to dance the first two dances with Miss Osborne: 'Oh yes, we have been engaged this week … and we are to dance down every couple.' But Miss Osborne casually breaks her engagement to Charles and the child's humiliation is acutely drawn:

> He stood the picture of disappointment, with crimson'd cheeks, quivering lips, and eyes bent on the floor. His mother, stifling her own mortification, tried to soothe his with the prospect of Miss Osborne's second promise; – but tho' he contrived to utter with an effort of Boyish Bravery 'Oh! I do not mind it' – it was very evident by the unceasing agitation of his features that he minded it as much as ever.[39]

As with the scene in *Persuasion*, the child's action is a turning point in the novel. The boy is trying not to cry. A child trying not to cry is always more moving than a child who is crying. The heroine Emma Watson comes to his rescue, an action that brings her to the notice of the wealthy family who have hitherto ignored her:

> Emma did not think, or reflect; – she felt and acted –. 'I shall be very happy to dance with you Sir, if you like it', said she, holding out her hand with most unaffected good humour. – The Boy in one moment restored to all his first delight – looked joyfully at his Mother and stepping forwards with an honest and simple Thank you Maam was instantly ready to attend to his new acquaintance.[40]

Charles invites Emma to Osborne Castle: 'there is a monstrous curious stuff'd Fox there, and a Badger – anybody would think they were alive. It is a pity you should not see them.'[41] This is a wonderful example of the way children believe that their own passions must be of interest to any right-thinking adult.

Jane Austen gets children right because the children in her life and in the life of the novels are realistic portraits, pleasant and unpleasant. They can be brats like Anna Maria Middleton in *Sense and Sensibility* (surely the best depiction of a vile spoilt child in all of the novels), or as adorable as Charles Blake or Henry and John Knightley, who sit and count raindrops until there are too many to count. This lovely detail is based on a real-life observation. Following their mother's death in childbed, Lizzy and Marianne Knight were sent away to boarding school in Essex. Their journey was undertaken in wet weather and Jane advised them to 'amuse themselves with watching the raindrops down the Windows'.[42]

She knew perfectly well that, as with adults, some children were nice and some were not. So with Anna Lefroy's girls: 'Jemima has a very irritable bad Temper (her Mother says so) – and Julia a very sweet one, always pleased and happy.'[43] Jane Austen lived in the age of Rousseau and Wordsworth, when writers were more fascinated by children than ever before. She was no Romantic – *Northanger Abbey*, *Sense and Sensibility* and *Sanditon* all cast an ironic eye on the excesses of Romantic feeling – but she shared with the Romantics a belief that the inner child never really leaves us. When she was ill from the slow painful disease from which she never recovered, she wrote, 'tell [William] I often play at *Nines* and think of him'.[44] On her deathbed she played cards and wrote comic verses.

16

The Laptop

It is a wooden box that can be placed on a table. Or on a writer's lap. It can be used as a book rest. It opens to reveal a sloped leather-inlaid writing surface and storage space for inkpot and writing implements. There is a long drawer for paper. It is surprisingly small, about the size of a portable typewriter. Small, light and easily transportable, it can go anywhere. It has a lock and key, so its contents are private, rather like a diary. Like any portable device, it can be easily misplaced or even stolen.

This particular writing box or 'slope' was bought at Ring Brothers, a shopping emporium in Basingstoke. The Reverend George Austen recorded the purchase in his pocket book: 'A Small Mahogany Writing desk with 1 Long Drawer and Glass Ink Stand Compleat. 12 s[hillings]. December 5, 1794'.[1] Given the timing, it is probable that it was intended as a present for his daughter Jane's nineteenth birthday.

The descendants of Jane Austen's eldest brother James, the Austen-Leigh family, were in possession of this box until the end of the twentieth century. Joan Austen-Leigh kept it safe in an old suitcase in a closet in her home in Canada. In 1999, she and her eldest daughter travelled to London and donated it to the British Library, where it is now exhibited to the public along with various other literary treasures.[2]

Throughout Jane Austen's lifetime writing boxes were to be found on military expeditions and on travels in pursuit of pleasure or knowledge, as well as in libraries and drawing rooms. Great literature was created on them. At the same time, dispatches, contracts, letters and postcards were written on their simple but practical sloping surfaces. The writing box allowed for the swift transaction of both business and personal activity in an age when communication was vastly speeded up by huge improvements in the postal system. In a time of global voyaging and emergent empire, letters were of immense importance. Pages and pages penned on Jane Austen's writing box found their way to her naval brothers as they served their country in the East Indies and the West, in the Mediterranean and off the African coast.

Writing boxes such as Jane Austen's were highly desirable items, a form of state-of-the-art equipment in a world where the improvement of roads and carriages meant that people were travelling more than ever before. A piece of kit that holds precious and private information, that can be locked away safely and that can be taken along with you on your travels: this is the Georgian forerunner of the laptop computer. The device was actually sometimes known as a 'lap-desk'. Unlike the full-size writing desk or for that matter the little round drawing-room table at which we usually imagine Jane Austen sitting with her quill, this was a personal and not a household possession. It was the place to keep your most intimate correspondence. Or the manuscript of your latest novel.

The nineteenth-birthday present was highly significant to Jane Austen. It was a symbol of her father's faith in her and his encouragement of her writing. More than this, as a particularly well-travelled young woman, who often spent time away from home, it allowed her to carry on with her scribbling wherever she happened to be.

It wasn't long before she nearly lost it. At the end of October 1798 Jane and her parents had left Godmersham, where they had been on an extended visit to Edward and his family.

Edward's carriage had taken them as far as Sittingbourne. From there they travelled in a post-chaise. Jane joked that 'we had a famous pair of horses, which took us to Rochester in an hour and a quarter; the postboy seemed determined to show my mother that Kentish drivers were not always tedious'.[3] Their stopping post was an inn at Dartford, the Bull and George, where they took rooms for the night. Jane's mother was not a good traveller and took some bitters to calm her nerves – bitters were used for stomach complaints and helped with insomnia. Jane noted, grimly, that her mother's stomach complaints included excessive diarrhoea, 'that particular kind of evacuation which has generally preceded her Illnesses'.[4] She and her father, meanwhile, had a dinner of beefsteak and boiled fowl, though, to her disappointment, there was no oyster sauce.

She administered laudanum to her mother while her father sat by the fire reading a Gothic thriller called *The Midnight Bell* and she wrote to Cassandra about a near-miss when her portable desk, along with her dressing box, had accidentally been taken to a chaise that was just packing off as they came in. It was 'driven away towards Gravesend in their way to the West Indies'.[5] To her great relief, someone gave chase and her boxes were safely returned. She made a joke of the incident, but it had shaken her up. In the box was seven pounds ('all my worldly wealth') and a deputation for a friend, Harry Digweed, giving him permission to shoot game on Steventon land, and signed by Edward Austen. We shall never know what other precious items might have been inadvertently shipped to the West Indies.

The late 1790s were crucial years for both Austen's travels and her writings. The laptop desk was her constant companion. According to a memorandum of Cassandra's, 'First Impressions' (the lost original version of *Pride and Prejudice*) was begun in October 1796 and finished in August 1797. In 1797 she was also transforming 'Elinor and Marianne' into *Sense and Sensibility*. And *Northanger Abbey*, or 'Susan' as it was then called, was written between 1798 and 1799.

She now learnt how to write on the hoof – and this explains why once at Chawton (with relative peace) she was able to write fluently despite the disturbances of family and visitors. At Godmersham, she remarked that 'In this House there is a constant succession of small events, somebody is always going or coming.'[6] She was expected to join in expeditions about the countryside, which interfered with her time for writing.

The fact that Jane Austen had many distractions from her work does not, however, mean that, as is sometimes said, she 'fell silent' or endured a 'barren period' between leaving for Bath in 1801 and settling down at Chawton in 1809.[7] Admittedly it wasn't as fertile a time as the two periods of intense creativity at Steventon in the 1790s and Chawton between 1809 and her death, but it was hardly a decade of literary inactivity. She spent the first decade of the nineteenth century polishing, revising and making fair copies of manuscripts for publication. In addition, it was a time when two further novels were developed, though aborted.

In the autumn of 1797, the completed manuscript of 'First Impressions' was sent to Thomas Cadell, perhaps the leading literary publishing house in London. The Cadell list included an array of impressive titles from the poetry of Robert Burns to Dr Johnson's *Lives of the English Poets* to Edward Gibbon's *Decline and Fall of the Roman Empire*. More to the point from Jane Austen's point of view, Thomas Cadell the younger, who had taken over the business following his father's retirement in 1793, had shown a strong interest in fiction. Following a rival's huge success with Mrs Radcliffe's *The Mysteries of Udolpho*, he had snapped up her next title, *The Italian*. And he was the co-publisher of Fanny Burney's *Camilla*. Austen could not have been in better company. George Austen sent the manuscript on his daughter's behalf. It was rejected by return of post.

Jane Austen was not deterred. She got on with her revision of 'Elinor and Marianne', and she started her new work, 'Susan'. It was a parody of the Gothic novel, that genre to which the younger Cadell had committed himself. Perhaps some part of her was having a dig at Cadell: if he was willing to pay the large sum of £800 (£75,000 or more than $100,000 in modern terms) for the successor to *The Mysteries of Udolpho* but then to reject her own book without even reading it, she would show him just how foolish a genre the Gothic was. Just over a year later, she would take 'First Impressions' with her in the writing box on her first trip to Bath. Presumably, she was intending to do some further work on it, in the hope of finding an alternative publisher.

By 1803, halfway through her period of residence in Bath, 'Susan' – embellished with many details of life in the fashionable spa – was ready for publication. Henry Austen's business associate Mr Seymour sold the manuscript on Jane's behalf to a London publishing house called Crosby and Co. of Stationer's Court, for £10, with a stipulation for early publication. How delighted she must have been to have the ten pounds in her pocket book. For the first time, she had made some money from her writing.

Crosby, who had a long list of historical and Gothic novels on his roster, liked to advertise forthcoming publications in his annual review *Flowers of Literature*. Within a short time of his receiving Austen's manuscript from Seymour, he duly announced that among the 'NEW and USEFUL BOOKS; *Published by B. Crosby and Co. Stationers' Court, London*', the following were '*In the Press*': '15. SUSAN; a Novel, in 2 vols. 16. DICTIONARY OF CELEBRATED WOMEN. By Miss Beetham, in one volume.'[8] The dictionary of female historical celebrities by Matilda Betham, a friend of Coleridge and Charles Lamb, was duly published the following year, but 'Susan' never appeared. The story in the Austen family was that as a publisher of 'Gothic Romances' Crosby got cold feet about being associated with a satire on the kind of books that filled his list.

The William Seymour who made the sale to Crosby was a lawyer and bachelor friend of Henry Austen. He lived in Cavendish Square. Jane Austen socialized with him when she was in London. On one occasion they dined 'tete a tete', much to Jane's amusement, as Seymour seems to have had a crush on her.[9] He even visited her at Chawton in 1816. He later told a story of how he spent a whole carriage ride in Jane Austen's company, from London to Chawton in a post-chaise, trying to decide whether to ask her to marry him or not. In the event, he did not.

After her success in selling 'Susan' to a well-regarded London publisher, Austen set to work on two further stories: a new novel about a family called the Watsons and an epistolary novella about a charismatic villain called Lady Susan.

Imagine an alternative scenario in which Crosby stuck to his word and published 'Susan' in 1803 or 1804. Many of Crosby's novels by women were published anonymously, as 'Susan' would have been. But the identity of female authors was often an open secret within the literary world. Jane Austen's name would have begun to circulate among the people who mattered. She would have become known as a witty Bath author, a gifted satirist of both literary fashion and spa-town life. Buoyed by her success, she might have completed *The Watsons* and *Lady Susan*, then polished up 'First Impressions' and 'Elinor and Marianne'. She could have had five published novels by 1810 instead of none before 1811.

These two transitional works, *Lady Susan* and *The Watsons* (both titles were provided by her family after her death), reveal a lot about the development of Jane Austen's art.

Some scholars believe that *Lady Susan* was drafted in 1794 or 1795, after the completion of the vellum notebooks, then revised in fair copy, with a new conclusion, in about 1805. The surviving manuscript, now in the Pierpont Morgan Library in New York, is on paper with a watermark of that date. But there is no definitive evidence for an early date: other Austen scholars believe that *Lady Susan* was an entirely new work belonging to the years following the submission of 'Susan' to Crosby. Either way, it is curious that, while waiting for the proofs of 'Susan' to arrive, she should have made a fair copy of a story about an anti-heroine with the same name.

Lady Susan is Austen's only extant epistolary novel of substance. It was an important transitional work – a serious trial of the 'novel in letters' form that had been pioneered by Richardson and adopted by Burney in her debut fiction, *Evelina*. As with Richardson's *Clarissa* and *Sir Charles Grandison* it has multiple letter-writers, allowing Austen to experiment with a variety of male and female voices, ranging from the cruel wit of Lady Susan to the kindly words of her morally superior sister-in-law Mrs Vernon. Unusually for Jane Austen, she also gets inside the head of an intelligent, strong hero, Reginald de Courcy, who, against his judgement and principles, falls in love with the sexually dominant widow.

Early in the story Reginald warns his sister Mrs Vernon that Lady Susan is 'the most accomplished Coquette in England'.[10] But she is no mere flirt. She is Jane Austen's most unscrupulous, even sadistic, female character. She is a woman of 'perverted abilities', almost a feminine version of the notorious Lovelace of Richardson's *Clarissa*. Her response to Reginald's admonitions against her is to make him fall in love with her: 'There is exquisite pleasure in subduing an insolent spirit, in making a person predetermined to dislike, acknowledge one's superiority.'[11] Reginald de Courcy cannot resist the prospect of enjoying 'the conversation of a Woman of high mental powers'.[12] He is twelve years her junior. She is an older woman, an experienced temptress who manipulates men by her sexual charisma. In modern parlance, she is not so much a coquette as a 'cougar', one of the first in English literature.

Lady Susan Vernon is charming, clever, beautiful, vicious, witty and morally corrupt. She is also a bad mother. She is utterly lacking in maternal feeling and heartily dislikes her guileless daughter, Frederica. She wreaks revenge on all who cross her. 'There is something agreable in feelings so easily worked on,' she says of Reginald.[13] We are not far from the world of that most infamous eighteenth-century epistolary novel, Choderlos de Laclos' *Les Liaisons dangereuses* (1782).

Lady Susan is a character firmly rooted in city life. 'London will always be the fairest field of action,' she says.[14] As in Richardson and Burney, the metropolis is the immoral centre of corrupt society. It is only when Lady Susan is buried alive in the country that she makes mischief: she is bored and she can't help herself. She boldly enters into an adulterous affair with her friend's husband, Manwaring, and continues the affair despite being secretely engaged to Reginald. When she is caught red-handed and Reginald breaks off the engagement, she shows no remorse and duly marries a rich and dull baronet. Reginald is 'talked, flattered and finessed' into marrying the dull, pious daughter, Frederica. For all Lady Susan's villainy, she is utterly fascinating. Her language gives her energy and charm that make her letters fizz with life. She refuses to repent, and she is not punished by the author.

The *femme fatale* is a character type that clearly fascinated Jane Austen. We have seen that following a visit to the theatre she spoke of Don Juan as a 'fascinating compound of cruelty and lust', and there are similar characteristics in Willoughby and Wickham. Lady Susan is their feminine counterpart. The only woman to approach her in Austen's published fiction is Mary Crawford in *Mansfield Park*, though she is more of a coquette than an outright seductress. In each case, what really intrigues Austen is the power of language. 'If I am vain of anything, it is of my eloquence,' writes Lady Susan Vernon. 'Consideration and Esteem as surely follow command of Language, as Admiration waits on Beauty.'[15] This might just tell us something about Lady Susan's creator as well: the reason why so many men esteemed Jane Austen and considered proposing marriage to her was her eloquence and wit.

It might be imagined that Austen held back from developing *Lady Susan* into a full-length novel and seeking to publish it because the subject matter was too risqué. But that would not necessarily have deterred her. In 1794 the actress turned novelist Mary Robinson had published a brilliant epistolary novel called *The Widow*, in which there is both an unprincipled widow of the *ton* (fashionable world) named Amelia Vernon and a scheming but lively and charismatic anti-heroine called Lady Seymour who bears a strong resemblance to Lady Susan (Austen's choice of the name Vernon is perhaps a nod of gratitude to Mrs Robinson). Again, Madame de Staël's international epistolary bestseller of 1802, *Delphine*, had included closely analogous plot elements: a young widow, a man tricked into marrying the daughter when he really loves the widow, a scheming woman (this one called Sophie de Vernon). Austen would not have been ashamed to be counted in the company of Robinson and de Staël.

The more likely reason for Austen's setting aside of *Lady Susan* was discontent with its epistolary form. Though the device of composing a novel in the form of letters gave her the opportunity to write from the point of view of more than half a dozen different characters, the structure does not quite work because the counter-balancing voices are insufficiently strong. Lady Susan dominates the narrative. The epistolary form did not give Austen the authorial control that she required. From this point on, she wrote in the form of third-person narrative, where she could be the one in control.

The epistolary experiment gave Austen the chance to find voices for particular character types, but some of the most lively sequences in *Lady Susan* are those in which extended passages of dialogue are transcribed into the letters.[16] Austen was beginning to see that her true forte was the spoken voice and the immediate social encounter, as opposed to the reflection and retrospection of the character sitting writing a letter. Her frequent theatre-going in the Bath years intensified her love for dialogue and witty exchange. According to family tradition, 'Elinor and Marianne' was originally an epistolary novel. Its rewriting as *Sense and Sensibility* would have involved major surgery, the reworking of letters between parted sisters into dialogue between sisters who are nearly always together.

The direction in which Austen's art was moving is made clear by her other project in the period when the manuscript of 'Susan' was gathering dust in Crosby's office in Stationer's Court. Fun as it was to create a character with Lady Susan's excesses and transgression, Austen's more serious ambition as a novelist was to explore the real emotional lives of women constrained by their social and financial circumstances.

Mr Watson is a widowed clergyman with two sons and four daughters. The youngest daughter, Emma, has been brought up by a rich aunt and is consequently better educated and more refined than her sisters. But when her aunt contracts a foolish second marriage, Emma Watson is obliged to return to her father's house. As suggested earlier, this plot-line is a striking reversal of the conventional adoption narrative.

Living near the Watsons are the Osbornes, a great titled family. Emma attracts attention from the boorish Lord Osborne, while one of her husband-hunting sisters, Mary, pursues Lord Osborne's arrogant, social-climbing friend Tom Musgrave. The plan was that Emma would decline a marriage proposal from Lord Osborne, and would eventually marry Osborne's virtuous ex-tutor, Mr Howard.

The father, Mr Watson, is seriously ill in the opening chapters. Austen confided to her sister Cassandra that the intention was that he should die in the course of the work. According to family tradition, Jane abandoned the novel upon the sudden and unexpected death of her own father. Its plot-line had become too uncomfortably close to her own. Elizabeth Jenkins, among the best of Austen's twentieth-century biographers, wrote of the story's 'painful realism', suggesting that its depiction of daughters who are a burden upon their family was just too much for Austen to go on contemplating at a time when she was herself dependent on her brothers.[17]

Yet the plot-line of the plight of (impoverished) unmarried daughters was one that Jane Austen never abandoned. She mined this vein to its full extent. The novel sitting at Crosby's was about a very ordinary girl of limited means who is mistaken for being an heiress. And it was not so very long after George Austen's death that his daughter was returning to, and seeking to publish, a novel that begins with a father's death leaving three sisters in reduced circumstances: *Sense and Sensibility*.

It may simply have been that Jane Austen thought that the Emma Watson novel wasn't terribly good. It ends after five chapters, suggesting that she just ran out of steam. She was not always a finisher – the rapidity of movement from subject to subject in so many of her letters reveals that with the quickness of her mind came a low boredom threshold. If a story wasn't working, she would leave it and go on to another one.

The interesting thing about Cassandra's description of the plot of the novel, recorded many years later, is what it reveals about her sister's compositional method: Jane Austen sketched out the entire plot of the novel first. She knew from the beginning how each of her novels was going to end. The work was not in the plotting, but in the execution. With rigorous self-criticism, she saw that the writing in *The Watsons* was not flowing and that the characters were failing to come to life. The aristocratic Osborne household was beyond her experience and she knew it. Emma Watson herself, and the character of the little boy called Charles Blake, are nicely rendered, but there is no sparkle to the prose. Notably lacking is the sophisticated Austen device of seeming to be both inside and outside her characters, with the author sympathetically animating their thought processes while simultaneously directing her irony against them.

Jane Austen was a worker. She revised and improved and honed. We know that she made late changes to her juvenile writings, as late as 1809, and these were changes made to stories intended for private use, not public consumption. Artistic perfectionism was the only reason for continuing to work on them. As for the published novels, the revisions to the first three would have been substantial, going far beyond the changes to their titles.

Henry Austen, who knew her books better than anyone apart from Cassandra, commented on her compositional methods: 'For though in composition she was equally rapid and correct, yet an invincible distrust of her own judgement induced her to withhold her works from the public, till time and many perusals had satisfied her that the charm of recent composition was dissolved.'[18] This is absolutely right with regard to the 'time and many perusals' his sister devoted to her drafts, but perhaps wrong in the phrase 'invincible distrust of her own judgement': it was rather that she trusted the considered judgement that came with rewriting. Just as it takes her heroines time to make the right choice of a husband, so it took her time to perfect the right words for each sentence of each novel.

In the meantime, she was still waiting for Crosby to publish 'Susan'. By the spring of 1809, she realized that the case was hopeless. Determined to know once and for all whether he intended to honour his contract, she wrote to Crosby. Her letter was polite, but extremely firm. If he had lost the manuscript, she could send another. If he had decided not to publish, then she would find another publisher. Unable to resist a closing barb of wit, she signed off the letter 'I am Gentlemen etc. etc. MAD.' The reply, she

Jane Austen's brother Frank with his laptop
open and ready for use

instructed, was to be directed to Mrs Ashton Dennis at the Southampton Post Office. MAD: Mrs Ashton Dennis. Not Austen but Ashton.

Richard Crosby[19] replied promptly and curtly, saying that they had purchased the manuscript outright with no legal obligation to publish it and no firm stipulation as to time. If she or anyone else sought to publish it elsewhere, they would sue. She could, however, buy it back for the original sum of £10. Tellingly, she did not buy back the manuscript. She probably could not afford to at this time. The very best bit of this sad and annoying story is that she had the money to buy back the rights in 1816, at which point she added the 'Advertisement' which duly appeared when the novel was published posthumously:

This little work was finished in the year 1803, and intended for immediate publication. It was disposed of to a bookseller, it was even advertised, and why the business proceeded no farther, the author has never been able to learn. That any bookseller should think it worth while to purchase what he did not think it worth while to publish seems extraordinary. But with this, neither the author nor the public have any other concern than as some observation is necessary upon those parts of the work which thirteen years have made comparatively obsolete. The public are entreated to bear in mind that thirteen years have passed since it was finished, many more since it was begun, and that during that period, places, manners, books, and opinions have undergone considerable changes.[20]

Only then was Crosby told that 'Susan' had been written by the author of four novels, including the highly successful *Pride and Prejudice*.

Humiliated as she must have felt in 1809, she set about finding another publisher. With 'Susan' temporarily on the shelf, she returned to the two other full-length manuscripts that she had drafted back in the late 1790s. After the letter to Crosby of April 1809, there is a huge gap in her surviving correspondence. We jump two years to April 1811.[21] This two-year gap is extremely frustrating for a biographer as this was the time that she found her first publisher. In the absence of letters, we have no idea how or why she turned to Thomas Egerton of Whitehall. Nor do we know if she – or Henry Austen or William Seymour acting on her behalf – approached, and was rejected by, other more famous and more literary houses. Fanny Burney's publisher Cadell and Davies had rejected her, Crosby had let her down. Did she try Joseph Johnson, who had published Mary Wollstonecraft and Maria Edgeworth's *Belinda*? Or G. G. Robinson, who published Elizabeth Inchbald? We simply don't know, but the choice of Egerton's Military Library has the feel of a last resort.

But when he accepted *Sense and Sensibility* she was delighted. The surviving correspondence picks up after the long gap of two years with Jane Austen back in London, in extremely high spirits. She wrote from Sloane Street in April 1811, full of news of 'pleasant little parties', theatre-visits, trips to museums and exhibitions, and shopping. 'I am sorry to tell you', she wrote to Cassandra, 'that I am getting very extravagant and spending all my Money; and what is worse for you, I have been spending yours too.'[22] The high spirits were in no small way connected to the fact that she was deep in proof-correcting for *Sense and Sensibility*. Her excitement is evident:

> No indeed, I am never too busy to think of S. and S. I can no more forget it, than a mother can forget her sucking child ... I have had two sheets to correct, but the last only brings us to W.s. [Willoughby's] first appearance. Mrs. K.[night] regrets in the most flattering manner that she must wait *till* May, but I have scarcely a hope of its being out in June. – Henry does not neglect it; he *has* hurried the Printer, and says he will see him again today. – It will not stand still during his absence, it will be sent to Eliza.[23]

Any writer who has had a book published will recognize the special thrill of seeing one's words in proof for the first time. As if by magic, words written in one's own hand – the labour of quill and ink on blank paper – have reappeared in the permanent form of print on a publisher's sheets. It is the moment of transition from the dream of professional authorship to the reality.

The method of publication does not, however, suggest great faith in the author on Egerton's part. He did not offer to buy the copyright, but chose the method which presented the least risk to him. He accepted *Sense and Sensibility* on a commission basis. This meant that the main risk was to the author. The author was expected to pay initial printing costs (this could be several hundred pounds, depending on the size of the print run) and the expenses for advertisement, which might be as much as £50. The profit on sales (if all went well) would then be shared between the publisher and the author. On the title page of *Sense and Sensibility* it says 'PRINTED FOR THE AUTHOR'. To a degree, this is the early nineteenth-century equivalent of vanity publishing.

So who put up the money for the initial publishing costs? When Jane Austen sold 'Susan' to Crosby, she received £10 for the copyright and if he had gone ahead the rest of the costs would have been his. This time it was different. The initial costs for a print run of 750 copies would have been about £180.[24] 'Printed for the Author' clearly indicates that Egerton did not front the money himself. Jane Austen's own allowance was meagre: in her father's lifetime she was given £20 a year for personal expenses. After George Austen's death, Mrs Austen had receipts of little more than £40 per quarter from her late husband's Old South Sea Annuities, from which she had to meet all her own expenses and those of her two unmarried daughters.[25] In January 1807 Mrs Austen began the new year with just £99 in hand.[26] There was some additional support from her sons, especially Frank, and occasional small gifts of money from wealthier relatives, but £180 was a huge sum for such a speculative endeavour as the publication of a first novel by an unknown lady.

One possibility is that Henry's bank advanced the money, but there is no record of this. Another intriguing possibility is that the money was fronted by a generous benefactor. In the course of those remarks about the printing and proofing of *Sense and Sensibility*, Jane Austen wrote, 'I am very much gratified by Mrs K.'s interest in it; and whatever may be the event of it *as to my credit with her* [my italics], sincerely wish her curiosity could be satisfied sooner than is now probable. I think she will like my Elinor, but cannot build on any thing else.'[27]

Why was Mrs Knight, her brother Edward's adoptive mother, involved in the process? What was the 'credit' that Jane Austen mentions in relation to her liking the novel? The word could mean 'good faith' or 'reputation', but it could also have been meant in the financial sense. In the past Mrs Knight had regularly given Jane small sums of money.[28] What did Austen mean by 'Mrs. K. regrets in the most flattering manner that she must wait *till* May' in the passage quoted above regarding the publication of *Sense and Sensibility*? Merely that Mrs Knight was looking forward to the book's appearance? Or that she was hoping for her credit to be repaid? Could it be that she was Austen's literary patron in a larger capacity than has hitherto been assumed, that she was determined to help see her become a published author?

Catherine Knight died in October 1812. Jane Austen is not mentioned in her will: perhaps she thought she had done enough for her. When it came to a second edition of *Sense and Sensibility* the following year, it was Henry to whom Jane owed 'a great deal for printing etc'.[29]

Whether the benefactor was Henry Austen or Catherine Knight, the important point is that there was a lot at stake for Jane Austen. If *Sense and Sensibility* failed to sell well, she would have to cover the high costs of printing and advertising. In his retrospective account, Henry Austen insisted that Jane was so concerned about the book not meeting the 'expense of publication' that she 'made a reserve from her very moderate income to meet the expected loss'.[30] But at the very time that her first novel was being printed, she was dashing around London spending her money on two new hats, 'silk stockings' (three pairs), yards and yards of checked muslin for new dresses, pelisses with 'expensive buttons' and 'bugle trimming'.[31] This is not the conduct of an author who thinks that her book won't sell. Jane Austen had far more confidence in her own ability than her brother would have us believe.

Eighteen-eleven was a busy and happy year. She was correcting proofs for *Sense and Sensibility*, preparing *Pride and Prejudice* for publication and beginning a new novel, *Mansfield Park*. She spent much of the year in London, staying with Henry and Eliza. This of course ensured that she was close to her publisher and printer, able to keep a close eye on progress and costs. She wasn't going to allow a repeat of the Crosby experience.

Sense and Sensibility finally appeared in October as a three-volume set, priced at fifteen shillings. The reviews were favourable: 'pleasant and entertaining', 'well-written', 'incidents are probable, and highly pleasing', 'better than most' – though this was hardly praise to set the world alight.[32]

Most reviews of the time were written for the benefit of those making library lists, so a plot summary was essential and often a short excerpt to give the flavour of the novel. Library sales were important to publishers, who could take chances on unknown authors and make a small profit. *Sense and Sensibility* appeared in the Alton library, as we know from a family anecdote. Jane, Cassandra and their niece Anna were browsing through the new novels at their local library, when Anna picked up *Sense and Sensibility* 'with careless contempt, little imagining who had written it, exclaiming to the great amusement of her Aunts who stood by "Oh that must be rubbish I am sure from the title".[33]

Jane could not know, and possibly wouldn't especially care, that other, more aristocratic readers were enjoying the novel. Lady Bessborough, sister to the notorious Georgiana, Duchess of Devonshire, commented on *Sense and Sensibility* in a letter to a friend: 'it is a clever novel ... tho' it ends stupidly, I was much amused by it'. The fifteen-year-old daughter of the Prince Regent, Princess Charlotte Augusta, compared herself to one of the book's heroines: 'it certainly is interesting, and you feel quite one of the company. I think Maryanne and me are very like in *disposition*, that certainly I am not so good, the same imprudence etc., however remain very like.'[34]

In the event, the novel sold out by July 1813 and the remaining profit, after the payment of the upfront costs, was £140.[35] A second edition was published by Egerton the following autumn, with some corrections and changes, but also a number of textual errors, and it sold only slowly.

SENSE

AND

SENSIBILITY:

A NOVEL.

IN THREE VOLUMES.

BY A LADY.

VOL. I.

London:

PRINTED FOR THE AUTHOR,
By C. Roworth, Bell-yard, Temple-bar,
AND PUBLISHED BY T. EGERTON, WHITEHALL.
1811.

By November 1812 Jane Austen had negotiated a new deal with Egerton to publish *Pride and Prejudice*. This time he had sufficient confidence to buy the copyright for £110. She had asked for more: 'I would rather have had £150, but we could not both be pleased, and I am not at all surprised that he should not chuse to hazard so much.' One of the reasons she sold the copyright of *Pride and Prejudice* was to save Henry the problems associated with commission publishing: 'Its being sold will I hope be a great saving of Trouble to Henry, and therefore must be welcome to me – The Money is to be paid at the end of the twelvemonth.'[36]

Pride and Prejudice was duly published in January of 1813, also in three volumes by Egerton, in a print run that was probably of fifteen hundred copies. Five copies were sent to the author, and on 29 January she wrote that 'I have got my own darling child from London.' She couldn't have known it at the time, but selling the copyright of what would be her most popular novel was a mistake. The risk and the profit were all Egerton's and the novel was a success.[37]

The reviews for Austen's second novel were much more favourable than for her first. The *British Critic* remarked that *Pride and Prejudice* was 'very far superior to almost all the publications of the kind which have lately come before us'. Elizabeth Bennet as a character was 'supported with great spirit and consistency throughout'.[38] The *Critical Review* noted the depiction of a large and various cast of characters:

A whole family, every individual of which excites the interest … very superior to any novel we have lately met with in the delineation of domestic scenes. Nor is there one character which appears flat, or obtrudes itself upon the notice of the reader with troublesome impertinence. There is not one person in the drama with whom we could readily dispense; – they have all their proper places; and fill their several stations, with great credit to themselves, and much satisfaction to the reader.[39]

It is clear from reading the contemporary reviews that there was a subdued but strong sense that Austen – still an unnamed 'Lady' – was pioneering a new kind of novel of 'domestic scenes' peopled with 'probable' characters.

Pride and Prejudice was also creating a stir among the rich and famous: Richard Sheridan, playwright, theatre manager and politician, advised a friend, Miss Shirreff, to 'buy it immediately', for it 'was one of the cleverest things' he had ever read. Annabella Milbanke, future wife of the poet Lord Byron, wrote that 'I have finished the Novel called *Pride and Prejudice*, which I think a very superior work. It depends not on any of the common resources of novel writers, no drownings, no conflagrations, nor runaway horses, nor lap-dogs and parrots, nor chambermaids and milliners, nor rencontres and disguises. I really think it the *most probable* fiction I have ever read.' It had, she reported, become 'at present the fashionable novel'.[40]

A partner in the prestigious publishing house of Longman wrote to one of his female authors, 'we are particularly interested for the success of the Austen and we sincerely regret that her works have not met with the encouragement we could wish'.[41] The clear implication is that they would have done a much better job than Egerton, if only they had been given the opportunity. Warren Hastings, meanwhile, sent a letter of praise to Jane, saying that he particularly admired the character of Elizabeth Bennet. It is clear that Elizabeth was perceived as a new kind of heroine, a spirited, witty and feisty young woman who without money, family or connections wins the hand of the proud Mr Darcy and becomes mistress of Pemberley.

Jane Austen read *Pride and Prejudice* aloud at home, in an all-female reading circle, as she knew that Fanny Burney had done with *Evelina* all those years ago. On the very day that the books arrived a local friend Miss Benn came to dine, and the family gave a reading to her. The idea was not to tell her that the new novel was by Jane, but Miss Benn seems to have guessed the truth from the general excitement in the household. Austen was especially pleased that 'she really does seem to admire Elizabeth. I must confess that *I* think her as delightful a creature as ever appeared in print, and how I shall be able to tolerate those who do not like *her* at least, I do not know.'[42] It went so well that Miss Benn was invited back for a second evening. Jane wrote to Cassandra:

> I am much obliged to you for all your praise; it came at a right time, for I had had some fits of disgust; our second evening's reading to Miss Benn had not pleased me so well, but I beleive something must be attributed to my Mother's too rapid way of getting on – and tho' she perfectly understands the Characters herself, she cannot speak as they ought.

For Austen, reading her own novels aloud in the correct way – in the manner of a dramatic performance – was a particular skill and a special joy. She was, though, as critical of her own literary performance as she was of her mother's inferior recitation: 'The work is rather too light and bright, and sparkling; it wants shade.' But then, as ever, she turns the self-criticism into a joke at the expense of more pedantic, digressive novels:

> It wants to be stretched out here and there with a long Chapter – of sense if it could be had, if not of solemn specious nonsense – about something unconnected with the story; an Essay on Writing, a critique on Walter Scott, or the history of Buonaparte – or anything that would form a contrast and bring the reader with increased delight to the playfulness and Epigrammatism of the general stile.

She was equally attuned to the deficiencies of her printer: 'The greatest blunder in the Printing that I have met with is in Page 220 – Vol. 3. where two speeches are made into one. – There might as well have been no suppers at Longbourn, but I suppose it was the remains of Mrs. Bennet's old Meryton habits.'[43]

She was anxious to hear the opinions of those who were in on the secret of her authorship: 'Fanny's praise is very gratifying ... Her liking Darcy and Eliz[abeth] is enough. She might hate all the others, if she would.'[44] Fanny's diary for 5 June 1813 records that 'A[un]t Jane spent the morning with me and read P and P to me.' The younger Knight sisters were not allowed to listen. One of them later remembered: 'I and the younger ones used to hear peals of laughter through the door, and thought it very hard that we should be shut out from what was so delightful.'[45]

Jane was brimming with pride and confidence about *Pride and Prejudice*: 'Oh! I have more of such sweet flattery from Miss Sharp ... I am read and admired in Ireland too.'[46] To her amusement she had heard that she had an obsessive Irish fan: 'There is a Mrs Fletcher, the wife of a Judge, an old Lady and very good and very clever, who is all curiosity to know about me – what I am like and so forth. I am not known to her by *name* however.' She was keen to know whether Mrs Fletcher had read *Sense and Sensibility* as well. She asked Cassandra to find out and let her know while she was in London.[47]

As for the Miss Shirreff whom Sheridan advised to secure a copy of *Pride and Prejudice* at the earliest possible opportunity, she told Mary Gibson

(Jane's sister-in-law), who passed word on to Cassandra, that she was a huge admirer of Jane Austen. Indeed, every time her carriage rode past Chawton Cottage, she wished it would break down so that she could be introduced to the author. She was not far short of becoming Jane Austen's stalker.

Though the posthumous family memoir emphasized the desire for anonymity, Jane herself was relaxed about people discovering that she was an author. She asked Cassandra to let their niece Anna in on the secret: 'if you see her and do not dislike the commission, you may tell her for me'.[48] She also told her that the secret was not really a secret in Chawton: 'you must be prepared for the Neighbourhood being perhaps already informed of there being such a Work in the World, and in the Chawton World!'[49] Now that the reviews were out and the book was such a big hit with the family, she didn't seem to care who knew about it. She even imagined herself becoming a celebrity: 'I do not despair of having my picture in the Exhibition at last – all white and red, with my Head on one Side.'[50]

Once again she spent time in London, driving around in Henry's barouche, amusing herself by picking out portraits of fine ladies at the Exhibition and pretending they were characters from *Pride and Prejudice*. 'Mrs Bingley's is exactly herself, size, shaped face, features and sweetness; there never was a greater likeness.'[51] She couldn't find a likeness of Mrs Darcy, whom she imagined in yellow.

By October 1813 Egerton was advertising second editions of both novels. 'I have now therefore written myself into £250,' Jane Austen proudly told her brother Frank, who was as usual away at sea, 'which only makes me long for more. – I have something in hand.'[52]

The 'something in hand' was *Mansfield Park*, begun in 1811 and finished in the summer of 1813, to be published in three volumes by Egerton in May 1814. This time she got her best deal yet. She neither had to sell the copyright nor bear the printing costs. The novel was printed 'for T. Egerton', not 'for the author'. The print run was, however, only 1,250 copies. Rival publisher John Murray later expressed 'astonishment that so small an edition of such a work should have been sent into the world'.[53] Even so, Jane Austen made her biggest profit from this novel, clearing over £300 (about £20,000 or $30,000 in today's terms).

She read *Mansfield Park* on the journey to London with Henry. 'We did not begin reading till Bentley Green. Henry's approbation hitherto is even equal to my wishes; he says it is very different from the other two, but does not appear to think it at all inferior.'[54] He particularly admired Lady Bertram and Mrs Norris; 'likes Fanny and I think foresees how it will all be'. Later she reported, 'Henry is going on with Mansfield Park; he admires H. Crawford – I mean properly – as a clever, pleasant Man.'[55]

Jane Austen herself seems to have been particularly pleased with her third published novel, though many did not share her feelings. There were few reviews, which was disappointing. Perhaps to make up for this, she decided to take down her own notes of the opinions of her friends and families, in a sense anticipating the modern phenomenon of brief reader reviews on book websites. The fact that she copied down all the opinions of her family on *Mansfield Park* suggests that she thought it an especially important work. On the whole, it wasn't a great favourite with them. Fanny was praised but Edmund deemed a failure. Mrs Norris was universally admired. Most preferred *Pride and Prejudice*.

But she was now looking beyond her family. The views of outsiders were highly encouraging. Mr Egerton the publisher 'praised it for it's Morality, and for being so equal a Composition. – No weak parts'. The Scottish Lady Kerr, who had greatly admired her previous novels, told her that *Mansfield Park* was 'Universally admired in Edinburgh, by all the *wise ones*. – Indeed, I have not heard a single fault given to it.' Best of all was a comment from a Mrs Carrick: 'All who think deeply and feel much will give the Preference to Mansfield Park.'[56]

She had truly arrived as a professional writer, and she was loving it. Her simple pleasure in the act of writing is brought vividly alive by two of her Godmersham nieces, who recalled her at work. Louisa: 'She was very absent indeed. She would sit awhile, then rub her hands, laugh to herself and run up to her room.' And Marianne: 'I … remember how Aunt Jane would sit quietly working beside the fire in the library, saying nothing for a good while, and then would suddenly burst out laughing, jump up and run across the room where pens and paper were lying, write something down, and then come back to the fire and go on quietly working as before.'[57]

Louisa also remembered Cassandra begging Jane Austen to change the ending of *Mansfield Park* and allow Henry Crawford to marry Fanny, but Aunt Jane stood firm and would not allow the change. This again suggests, as we know from *The Watsons*, that she planned the novels in her head beforehand. Much as she gave way to Cassandra in most things, she would not be swayed when it came to her novels. She knew how the book had to end, but she also knew that a good story will keep the reader guessing. Reporting to Cassandra on her brother Henry's first reading of the manuscript, she noted with pleasure that he 'has changed his mind as to foreseeing the end; – he said yesterday at least, that he defied anybody to say whether H.C. would be reformed, or would forget Fanny in a fortnight'.[58]

The little laptop desk had seen some heavy duty by now. From the small girl who had circulated manuscripts of her short stories, Jane Austen had grown up and begun to cut a figure in the literary world. But she was increasingly unhappy with Egerton. He had not given the opportunity to correct errors before bringing out the second edition of *Pride and Prejudice*. He was pricing her books too highly. The lack of reviews of *Mansfield Park* indicated his weakness in the marketing department. He was reluctant to publish a second edition of *Mansfield Park*. The Military Library of Whitehall would no longer do. She decided to cast her net a little wider.

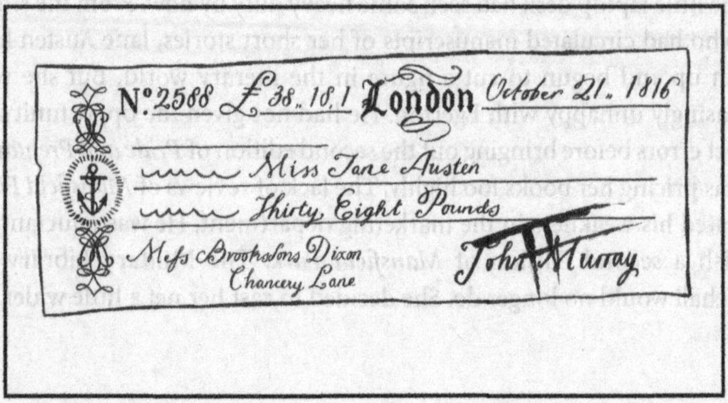

No. 2588 £ 38 „ 18 „ 1 London October 21 „ 1816
Miss Jane Austen
Thirty Eight Pounds
Mess Brooks & Sons Dixon
Chancery Lane
John Murray

The Royalty Cheque

It is the most ordinary but perhaps the most revealing of objects: a cheque for £38 18s 1d. According to the Bank of England's historic inflation calculator, the modern equivalent would be about £3,200 or nearly $5,000. From the eighteenth century until the end of the twentieth, the signed cheque was the principal basis for the transfer of funds between the bank accounts of businesses and individuals. This one, dated 21 October 1816, bears two very famous names: the account holder is John Murray the second of Albemarle Street, publisher of Lord Byron, and the payee is 'Miss Jane Austin' (the spelling of names was casual in those days – the Austens were frequently referred to as Austins). This is a business transaction: between a prestigious publisher and a professional woman writer.[1]

At the start of 1814, with two published novels and one forthcoming (and one still with the publisher Crosby), Jane Austen began working on what would be her fourth published novel, *Emma*. She had written to her brother Frank the previous year to tell him that she no longer cared about keeping the secret of her authorship: 'the truth is that the Secret has spread so far as to be scarcely the Shadow of a secret now – and that I beleive whenever the third [novel] appears, I shall not even attempt to tell Lies about it. – I shall rather try to make all the Money than all the Mystery I can of it. People shall pay for their Knowledge if I can make them.'[2] As so often, her tongue is in her cheek. But her comment underlines how deadly serious she was to make as much money as possible from her books. She now established a routine for writing and was freed from much of the burden of housekeeping by her mother and sister – it was the least they could do, given the income her writing contributed to the Chawton household.

By November 1814, the first edition of *Mansfield Park* was sold out. Austen wrote to Fanny Knight:

> You will be glad to hear that the first Edit[ion] of M.P. is all sold. Your Uncle Henry is rather wanting me to come to Town to settle about a second Edit[ion]:—but as I could not very conveniently leave home now, I have written him my Will and pleasure, and, unless he still urges it, shall not go. I am very greedy and want to make the most of it; but as you are much above caring about money, I shall not plague you with any particulars. The pleasures of Vanity are more within your comprehension, and you will enter into mine at receiving the *praise* which every now and then comes to me, through some channel or other.[3]

She wanted money and approbation: that is only human, though it is not how the family represented her in the posthumous memoir.

Every scrap of praise was important to her. 'Make everybody at Hendon admire Mansfield Park,' she told Anna.[4] She had heard that *Sense and Sensibility* was 'much admired at Cheltenham' and that it had been given to the author Elizabeth Hamilton: 'It is pleasant to have such a respectable writer named.'[5] But plaudits were not enough. She was also writing for cash. She told Fanny that Egerton was havering over a second edition: 'People are more ready to borrow and praise, than to buy ... but tho I like praise as well as anybody, I like what Edward calls *Pewter* too.'[6] She was encouraged that she had made more than £300 from *Mansfield Park* even though she had always felt that it would not be as popular as *Pride and Prejudice*. If Egerton was going to mess her around, Henry would be dispatched to find a better publisher.

Despite her own success, she still made time to encourage the literary endeavours of her nieces and nephews. Caroline, Anna and Edward all fancied themselves as authors, and asked the advice of the expert: their aunt. Her letters to them, regarding the novels they were reading as well as those they were writing, shed valuable light on her own high literary standards: 'there are a thousand improbabilities in the story', she complained of Laetitia Hawkins's *Rosanne*, when Anna asked her opinion of it.[7]

Anna Austen was writing a novel called *Which is the Heroine?* She sent it to Aunt Jane, who read it aloud to Cassandra and her mother, then conveyed back comments. Anna, in a fit of despondency, later destroyed her novel, along with her aunt's annotations. The key advice was to keep things 'natural' – characters should not be 'very Good or very Bad'. Aunt Jane was also punctilious about solecisms: 'There is no such Title as Desborough,' 'As Lady H is Cecilia's superior, it would not be correct to talk of *her* being introduced.' A little scene was 'scratched out' for being unrealistic: 'I think it can be so little usual as to *appear* unnatural in the book.' But many of her comments (she sent four long letters of detailed analysis and criticism) were supportive: 'we are all very much amused and like the work as well as ever ... St Julien is the delight of one's Life.' Cassandra joined in with the task: 'Your Aunt C. and I both recommend your making a little alteration in the last scene ... We think they press him too much – more than sensible Women or well-bred Women would do.'[8]

It was in reference to Anna's novel that Jane Austen made her much quoted observation: 'You are now collecting your People delightfully, getting them exactly into such a spot as is the delight of my life; – 3 or 4 families in a Country Village is the very thing to work on.'[9] This has been taken as a manifesto for Jane Austen's own oeuvre but it should be remembered in its context. She is referring to Anna's novel and not her own. It is important to remember, too, that at this time Jane Austen was working on *Emma*, her only novel set in one location and with a cast confined to '3 or 4 families in a Country Village'. In the other novels there are important scenes set in the cities of London, Bath and Portsmouth. Before *Emma* there had been *Mansfield Park*, in which the village and neighbouring families play a minimal part. After *Emma*, she would return to the city of Bath in *Persuasion*, where she also tried her hand at a seaside setting, a location she then moved centre-stage in *Sanditon*. The point of her remark was to support young Anna: three or four families in a country village was the right subject matter for the girl because that was what she knew. Jane Austen herself knew much more: the city, naval life, families with plantations in the West Indies or relatives in the East, great houses such as Godmersham and even greater ones such as Stoneleigh, scandal in high places and women eking out a living in service as governesses.

To Caroline Austen, who also sent her own novel for approval, she noted drily: 'I wish I could finish Stories as fast as you can.'[10] Likewise, her comments regarding her nephew's novel point to his over-hasty composition in contrast to her own painstaking work. It was here that Austen compared her art to that of the portrait miniaturist. The phrase about her 'little bit of ivory' is often quoted, but its context is usually neglected. It comes in a letter to her nephew James Edward Austen-Leigh, in a passage that begins by referring to the literary skills of Henry Austen:

> Uncle Henry writes very superior Sermons. You and I must try to get hold of one or two, and put them into our Novels; it would be a fine help to a volume; and we could make our Heroine read it aloud on a Sunday Evening, just as well as Isabella Wardour, in the Antiquary, is made to read the 'History of the Hartz Demon' in the ruins of St Ruth, though I beleive, on recollection, Lovell is the Reader. By the bye, my dear Edward, I am quite concerned for the loss your Mother mentions in her Letter. Two Chapters and a half to be missing is monstrous! It is well that *I* have not been at Steventon lately, and therefore cannot be suspected of purloining them; two strong twigs and a half towards a Nest of my own would have been something. I do not think however, that any theft of that sort would be really very useful to me. What should I do with your strong, manly, spirited Sketches, full of Variety and Glow? How could I possibly join them on to the little bit (two Inches wide) of Ivory on which I work with so fine a Brush, as produces little effect after much labour?[11]

Putting the quotation back in context puts Jane Austen back into her literary context. Brother Henry's sermons are in their way literary works of art. Nephew James Edward is writing a novel: Aunt Jane jokily asks if he has thought of inserting one of his uncle's sermons into the story. After all, in the most recent fashionable novel of the day – Sir Walter Scott's *The Antiquary*, which Austen devoured as soon as it was published – there is a digressive insertion read aloud by one of the characters. Austen then turns to the news that two and a half chapters of her nephew's novel have gone missing. Perhaps they had been used by a maid to light a fire. Or could they have been stolen? Kleptomania was, as has been seen, far from a joking matter in the Austen family, but here she is unquestionably making a joke:

John Murray II, whom Jane Austen called
'a Rogue of course, but a civil one'

her nephew's 'manly' style – something akin, no doubt, to what Sir Walter
Scott called his own 'bow-wow strain' – could never be stitched together
with hers. It would be like trying to paste a bold landscape sketch to a finely
executed portrait miniature.

* * *

Her new novel, with a heroine most unlike the dispossessed and sickly
Fanny Price, was another literary gamble of the kind Jane Austen hugely
enjoyed. 'I am going to take a heroine whom no one but myself will much
like,' she announced.[12] Despite the fact that Emma is indeed irritatingly
meddlesome, pleased with herself, misguided, spoilt, manipulative, the
novel takes for its theme, kindness. Kindness especially to neighbours, and
to dispossessed single women, such as Miss Bates, is crucial.

Jane Austen, who often joked about spotting real-life characters in
novels, was amused when others started imagining that they were the

models for characters in hers. There was, for example, a Miss Dusautoy whom she met at Godmersham: 'Miss D. has a great idea of being Fanny Price, she and her younger sister together, who is named Fanny.'[13]

One of her neighbours at Chawton was Mary Benn, a spinster living in greatly reduced circumstances. She was the sister of the Reverend John Benn, rector of nearby Farringdon. It was Miss Benn who had greatly admired Elizabeth Bennet when in attendance at the first family reading of the published copy of *Pride and Prejudice*. The Chawton women were extremely kind to Mary, inviting her to tea and supper, buying presents, offering hospitality frequently. Jane is never tart when she is speaking of 'Poor Miss Benn'. Martha Lloyd wanted to give her a present and because her cottage was so cold and had been lashed by recent storms, Jane suggested a warm shawl 'to wear over her Shoulders within doors in very cold weather … but it must not be very handsome or she would not use it. Her long Fur tippet is almost worn out.'[14]

She was the worry of the neighbourhood. Jane reassured Miss Benn's friends that she 'is not being neglected by her neighbours … Miss B dined last Wednesday at Mr Papillons, on Thursday with Capt and Mrs Clement – friday here – saturday with Mr Digweed and Sunday with the Papillons again.'[15] But then, to Jane Austen's dismay, Miss Benn was evicted from her cottage (or in Austen's words, her 'wretched abode') and had to find new lodgings: 'Poor Creature! You may imagine how full of cares she must be, and how anxious all Chawton will feel to get her decently settled somewhere.'[16] Another time she wrote that though Miss Benn had been ill, 'her Spirits are good and she will be most happy I beleive to accept any Invitation'.[17]

Following the spinster's death in 1816, Jane sent *Emma* to her friend Catherine Prowting: 'Had our poor friend lived these volumes would have been at her service, and as I know you were in the habit of reading together and have had the gratification of hearing that the *Works of the same hand* had given you pleasure.'[18] Miss Benn and Catherine Prowting, like so many others in Austen's wide circle of acquaintance, clearly knew the secret of her authorship. Sadly, it was too late for poor Miss Benn to read about poor Miss Bates.

One wonders how she would have reacted had she lived. Was the mischievous part of Jane Austen risking offence, like Emma at Box Hill? Or was the kindly part of her performing an act of good neighbourliness by giving a little bit of immortality to a woman who had lived a hard life?

She finished *Emma* in March 1815, and was keen to see it in print. By October she had had an offer from John Murray, who as well as publishing *Emma* was happy to release a second edition of *Mansfield Park*. Both books appeared in early 1816.[19] This was probably a commercial error: they competed with one another, reducing the number of copies sold and forcing Murray to remainder 539 of the two thousand copies of *Emma*.

The scholar Kathryn Sutherland has argued convincingly that John Murray's interest in Austen's novels dates from earlier than hitherto assumed.[20] Having scoured the Murray archive, she has redated to November 1814 an important letter from Murray's reader, William Gifford, drawing his attention to Austen's work. 'I have, for the first time, looked into "Pride and Prejudice;" and it is really a very pretty thing. No dark passages – no secret chambers, no wind-howling in long galleries, no drops of blood upon a rusty dagger – things that should now be left to lady's maids, and sentimental washerwomen.'[21] Murray was a publisher of modern poetry – Byron, pre-eminently – and of travel books and history. He kept away from novels, the 'trash of the circulating library'. But here Gifford, one of the most astute editors and critics of the age, is implying that Murray might consider taking a punt on Austen because of the power of her realism. Another letter unearthed by Sutherland reveals that he also read, and thought highly of, *Mansfield Park*.

So it was timely when John Murray was approached with the manuscript of *Emma*. Gifford read it for him, and expressed great enthusiasm. 'Of *Emma*, I have nothing but *good* to say,' he reports on the manuscript, strongly advising publication: 'I was sure of the writer before you mentioned her. The M.S., though plainly written has yet some, indeed many little omissions, and an expression may now and then be amended in passing through the press. I will readily undertake the revision.'[22] Murray was thinking of offering the generous sum of £500, presumably for *Emma* together with the copyright of *Mansfield Park*. Gifford replies: 'Five hundred pounds seems a good deal for a novel ... Cannot you get the third novel thrown in, Pride and Prejudice? I have lately read it again – tis very good.'[23]

In the event, Murray offered just under five hundred for the copyright of *Sense and Sensibility*, *Mansfield Park* and *Emma*. 'Mr Murray's letter has come,' Jane wrote to Cassandra from Henry's new home in Hans Place, London, on 17 October 1815, 'he is a Rogue of course, but a civil one. He offers £450 – but wants to have the copyright of MP and SandS included.

It will end in my publishing for myself I daresay.'[24] Henry Austen rejected the offer – 'the Terms you offer are so very inferior to what we had expected, that I am apprehensive of having made some great Error in my Arithmetical Calculation'[25] – but illness prevented him from continuing negotiations and Jane took over herself. Her reluctance to part with her copyrights for the sum proposed meant that they fell back on a commission arrangement. In hindsight, Jane Austen would have done better to accept Murray's offer for the copyright. All her profits from *Emma* were offset against the losses incurred on the reprint of *Mansfield Park*, which meant that her only profit was the cheque for £38 18s 1d. However, she could say with pride that she was the first female novelist to be published by the same house as Lord Byron, the most famous poet since Shakespeare.

Murray had moved premises in 1812 to the fashionable Mayfair address of 50 Albemarle Street. It was the centre of a literary circle, fostered by Murray's tradition of 'Four o'clock friends' – writers who came to afternoon tea. We have no surviving evidence of Austen's attendance at any of his salons – she once passed up the opportunity to meet the famous Madame de Staël – but she did engage directly with Murray. While nursing Henry back to health, Jane sought a meeting with her new publisher: 'desirous of coming to some decision on the affair in question, I must beg the favour of you to call on me here any day that may suit you best … A short conversation may perhaps do more than much Writing.'[26]

In the meantime she told Cassandra that she was pleased with Murray's opinion of *Emma*: 'He sends more praise however than I expected. It is an amusing letter. You shall see it.'[27] Once terms were agreed, Jane Austen went full speed ahead in urging immediate publication. Her letters hint at her frustration at the dilatoriness of the printers. Henry wrote to the printer, Roworth, to complain. Jane wrote to Murray to complain. The blame in the meantime was thrown on the stationer: 'The Printers have been waiting for Paper' and the stationer 'gives his word that I shall have no further cause for dissatisfaction'.[28] Cassandra was kept informed of all the problems of proof-reading: 'A *Sheet* come in this moment. 1st and 3rd vol. are now at 144. – 2nd at 48. – I am sure you will like Particulars. We are not to have the trouble of returning the Sheets to Mr Murray any longer, the Printer's boys bring and carry.'[29] Hans Place was becoming a professional literary household, couriers knocking at the door with regular deliveries of proof packages.

'The "ne plus ultra" of Life in London – Kate, Sue, Tom,
Jerry and Logic viewing the throne room at Carlton
Palace', from Pierce Egan's *Life in London* (1822). Jane
Austen achieved the 'ne plus ultra' of a viewing, thanks
to the Prince Regent's librarian

In her frustration, Austen cunningly used the news of a potential dedi-
catee as a bargaining tool to hurry things along. 'Is it likely that the Printers
will be influenced to greater Dispatch and Punctuality by knowing that the
Work is to be dedicated, by Permission, to the Prince Regent?'[30] (In 1811, the
madness of King George had been deemed so severe that the Prince of
Wales had formally become Prince Regent.)

According to the memory of Caroline Austen, Henry Austen shared a
doctor with the Prince. This was probably Sir Henry Halford, who was
brought in to minister to Henry when his illness took a sharp turn for the
worse. As Henry recovered, Halford continued to visit, met Jane Austen,
was informed that she was the author of *Pride and Prejudice* and let drop
the information that the Prince was a great admirer of her novels, 'that he
had often read them, and had a set in each of his residences'.[31] Perhaps his
friend Sheridan had recommended them.

The doctor told the Prince that Jane Austen was in London and the
Prince advised his librarian to wait upon her. The librarian, the Reverend
James Stanier Clarke, called on her at Hans Place and invited her, at the

Prince's request, to visit Carlton House, the Regent's London residence. She duly visited on 13 November 1815, where Clarke gave her a guided tour. The Prince himself was away at a shoot in Staffordshire.

Carlton House was huge and spectacular, with a frontage in excess of two hundred feet. Visitors entered the house through a portico of Corinthian columns that led to a foyer flanked on either side by anterooms. From there, one proceeded to a double-storey top-lit Great Hall decorated with Ionic columns of yellow marble scagliola. Beyond the hall was an octagonal room that was also top lit. The octagon room was flanked on the right by the grand staircase and on the left by a courtyard, while straight ahead was the main anteroom. Once in the anteroom, the visitor either turned left into the private apartments of the Prince of Wales or right into the formal reception rooms: Throne Room, Drawing Room, Music Room, Dining Room. Decor and furnishings were in the grand French style and the walls were hung with a superb collection of paintings, ranging from Old Masters to modern portraits.

The library, on the basement floor, was a beautiful room with Gothic-style open bookcases, furnished with Buhl furniture and Tudor ebony chairs. Miss Jane Austen from Chawton must have felt quite the important literary figure as she was shown around the opulent room with its shelves and shelves of fine bindings. On the visit, Stanier Clarke suggested that Austen should dedicate her latest novel to the Prince.

She was horrified. Her dislike of the Prince Regent went back a long way. From 1788 to 1795, he rented Kempshott Park near Steventon, where he ensconced Mrs Fitzherbert, the mistress whom he had secretly (and illegally) married. He humiliated his legal wife, Princess Caroline, by taking her to Kempshott for their honeymoon. Lord Minto, who was a close friend of the Princess and was there during the honeymoon, remarked that the scene at Kempshott resembled that of Eastcheap in *Henry IV Part One*, Shakespeare's play about an unruly Prince of Wales.[32] Jane Austen's brother James sometimes rode to hounds with the Prince and there was much gossip in the neighbourhood about the wild parties at Kempshott, and the huge debts that the Prince had incurred, so she had no illusions about his lifestyle.

One of the strongest expressions of dislike in all her surviving letters is directed against the Regent. The whole of England had become caught up in the war of the Waleses, which had reached epic proportions in 1813 when the Princess of Wales leaked a private letter to the press, which aimed to present her husband in the worst possible light for refusing access to their daughter, Princess Charlotte. Jane Austen knew which side she was on: 'I suppose all the World is sitting in Judgement upon the Princess of Wales's Letter. Poor Woman, I shall support her as long as I can, because she *is* a Woman, and because I hate her Husband.' The blame, she felt, could be firmly laid upon the Regent: 'I am resolved at least always to think that she would have been respectable, if the Prince had behaved only tolerably by her at first.'[33]

Now, the man she 'hated' was showing the greatest respect for her novels and expecting an obsequious dedication. Caroline Austen remembered, 'My Aunt made all proper acknowledgments at the moment, but had no intention of accepting the honor offered – until she was avised by some of her friends that she must consider the permission as a command.'[34] Jane Austen wrote to Stanier Clarke to clarify the matter:

Sir

I must take the liberty of asking You a question – Among the many flattering attentions which I recd from you at Carlton House, on Monday last, was the Information of my being at liberty to dedicate any future Work to HRH the P. R. without the necessity of any Solicitation on my part. Such at least, I beleived to be your words; but as I am very anxious to be quite certain of what was intended, I intreat you to have the goodness to inform me how such a Permission is to be understood, and whether it is incumbent on me to shew my sense of the Honour, by inscribing the Work now in the Press, to H.R.H. – I shd be equally concerned to appear either presumptuous or Ungrateful.[35]

Clarke took the hint: 'it is certainly not *incumbent* on you to dedicate your work ... The Regent has read and admired all your publications.'[36] He continued with some praise of his own, especially of *Mansfield Park*, and suggested that they might meet again when he returned from an upcoming trip to Sevenoaks.

Jane Austen swallowed her moral principles and went for the promotional opportunity, realizing that she could use the patronage of the Regent to her advantage to hurry along John Murray. She confessed to Cassandra:

'I *did* mention the P.R. in my note to Mr Murray, it brought me a fine compliment in return; whether it has done any other good I do not know, but Henry thought it worth trying.' She worried about what the principled Martha Lloyd would think of her: 'I hope you have told Martha of my first resolution of letting nobody know that I *might* dedicate etc – for fear of being obliged to do it – and that she is thoroughly convinced of my being influenced now by nothing but the most mercenary motives.'[37]

So she made her dedication for marketing reasons and suggested a brief perfunctory acknowledgement: 'Dedicated by Permission to H.R.H. The Prince Regent'.[38] Murray, however, was quick to suggest an expanded dedication, moved to a separate page: 'To His Royal Highness The Prince Regent, This Work Is, BY His Royal Highness's Permission, Most Respectfully Dedicated, by his Royal Highness's Dutiful and Obedient Humble Servant, The Author.' She allowed this and expressed her gratitude to Murray for putting her right, but she was clearly irritated by having to spend her own hard-earned money on a presentation copy: 'It strikes me that I have no business to give the P.R a Binding, but we will take Counsel upon the question.'[39] She ended up arranging to have the three volumes bound in handsome crimson leather with gold tooling, including the

Emma, specially bound for the Prince, at Jane
Austen's expense

three-feather heraldic badge of the Prince of Wales at the top of the spine. This cost her almost two pounds. The copy is still in the Royal Collection.

The dedication was not acknowledged in person by the Prince, and it did nothing for sales or publicity. But Murray had other tools of the trade of which Jane Austen was a beneficiary. His *Quarterly Review*, the leading literary periodical of the day (the equivalent of the *Times Literary Supplement* or *New York Review of Books*), provided a lengthy review of her novels by no less an authority than Sir Walter Scott. 'Have you any fancy to dash off an article on Emma?' Murray asked Scott.[40] He granted that the book 'wants incident and romance', but suggested that a review-essay reflecting on Austen's career to date would be of great value, especially given the brilliance of *Pride and Prejudice*.

Scott perceived that Jane Austen's novels were exemplars of a notable departure from Gothic and sentimental fiction, 'neither alarming our credulity nor amusing our imagination by wild variety of incident', but perfecting instead 'the art of copying from nature as she really exists in the common walks of life, and presenting to the reader, instead of the splendid scenes of an imaginary world, a correct and striking representation of that which is daily taking place around him'.[41]

Murray sent the review to Jane Austen, who was pleased, though unhappy that Scott had failed to register that she was the author of *Mansfield Park*. This was important to her as the second edition of *Mansfield Park* was about to be published, and was in need of publicity, particularly as it was the only one of her novels which had not been reviewed elsewhere. 'I cannot but be sorry that so clever a Man as the reveiwer of *Emma*, should consider [*Mansfield Park*] so unworthy of being noticed,' she complained to Murray.[42]

Scott's review drew attention to the new kind of 'middling class' characters that Jane Austen depicted:

By keeping close to common incidents, and to such characters as occupy the ordinary walks of life, she has produced sketches of such spirit and originality, that we never miss the excitation which depends upon a narrative of uncommon events, arising from the consideration of minds, manners and sentiments, greatly above our own ... The author of *Emma* confines herself chiefly to the middling classes of society; her most distinguished characters do not rise greatly above well-bred country gentlemen and ladies; and those which are sketched with most originality and precision, belong to a class rather below that standard.

Scott perceived that Austen's characters are instantly recognizable as 'real' people: 'A friend of ours, whom the author never saw or heard of, was at once recognized by his own family as the original of Mr. Bennet, and we do not know if he has yet got rid of the nickname.' He was thus the first to pinpoint in print one of the greatest qualities of Austen's characters: the fact that we can all identify people like them among our own acquaintance.

Scott was clever enough to see what was pioneering and ground-breaking in the novels, unlike the Reverend James Stanier Clarke, librarian to the Prince, who advised her to write a novel about 'an English Clergyman ... Fond of and entirely engaged in Literature – carry your Clergyman to sea as the Friend of some distinguished Naval Character about a Court'. Clarke, whose letters to Austen make him sound like a real-life incarnation of the pompous and self-serving Mr Collins, seems to have been more than a little in love with Jane Austen. But when he offered her a bed at 37 Golden Square – 'if you can make the Cell render you any service as a sort of Half-way House, when you come to Town' – he was stepping a little too far.[43]

Clarke also sought to offer her the patronage of his new boss, Prince Leopold of Saxe-Coburg, who was to be married to Princess Charlotte: 'Perhaps when you again appear in print you may chuse to dedicate your Volumes to Prince Leopold: any Historical Romance illustrative of the History of the august house of Cobourg, would just now be very interesting.'[44] In firmly rejecting this idea, Jane Austen gives a perfect illustration of her own literary concerns:

You are very, very kind in your hints as to the sort of Composition which might recommend me at present, and I am fully sensible that an Historical Romance, founded on the House of Saxe Cobourg might be much more to the purpose of Profit or Popularity ... but I could no more write a Romance than an Epic Poem. – I could not sit seriously down to write a serious Romance under any other motive than to save my Life, and if it were indispensable for me to keep it up and never relax into laughing at myself or other people, I am sure I should be hung before I had finished the first Chapter. – No – I must keep to my own style and go on in my own Way.[45]

What comes across so vividly here is her confidence. She goes on in her own way. Far from being intimidated by the clergyman with royal connections, she gently teases and firmly rebuffs him. She also – as Scott saw – rebuffs 'Romance' as opposed to realism. She makes absolutely clear that she is a comic, not an historical novelist: she will never give up on books that 'relax into laughing at myself or other people'. This is perhaps her most wonderfully self-revelatory phrase.

The correspondence with the absurd Stanier Clarke, which she gleefully passed on to friends and family, encouraged her to write a short and mischievous satire at Clarke's expense, 'Plan of a Novel, according to some hints from various quarters'. In a style reminiscent of the vellum notebooks, it was a return to parody of all that was absurd in the fiction of her day. The heroine is a 'faultless character', the hero 'all perfection'. The 'Plan' also shows her commitment to her own style of novel. It slyly digs at the well-meaning but irritating views of friends and family and acquaintances, even her publisher's reader Mr Gifford. But the joke is really on Stanier Clarke who had the temerity to suggest the topic of her next novel – 'his going to sea as Chaplain to a distinguished naval character about the Court, his going afterwards to Court himself, which introduced him to a great variety of Characters and involved him in many interesting situations, concluding with his opinions on the Benefits to result from Tithes being done away, and his having buried his own Mother (Heroine's lamented Grandmother) in consequence of the High Priest of the Parish in which she died refusing to pay her Remains the respect due to them'.[46]

By now she was writing *Persuasion* and this was probably the time when she bought back the rights to 'Susan'. Henry Austen, who recovered fully from his potentially fatal illness, emphasized that she envisaged a long and successful career for herself: 'The natural constitution [the Austens were all in rude health with a good track record of longevity], the regular habits, the quiet and happy occupations of our authoress, seemed to promise a long succession of amusement to the public, and a gradual increase of reputation to herself.'[47]

* * *

The Reverend George Austen, Henry Austen,
Frank Austen, 'Miss Jane Austin', Charles Austen

What did Jane Austen look like at this time? In the brief biographical memoir prefixed to the posthumously published *Northanger Abbey* and *Persuasion*, Henry Austen said that his sister 'possessed a considerable share' of personal attractions:

> Her stature was that of true elegance. It could not have been increased without exceeding the middle height. Her carriage and deportment were quiet, yet graceful. Her features were separately good. Their assemblage produced an unrivalled expression of that cheerfulness, sensibility, and benevolence, which were her real characteristics.[48]

These words are designed to create a flattering image. They do not tell us much about Jane Austen's actual appearance, other than to hint that she was tall. Her niece Anna Lefroy fleshes out the picture: 'figure tall and slender not drooping ... The complexion of that rather rare sort which seems limited to the light Brunette – a mottled skin, not fair, but perfectly clear and healthy in its hue: the fine naturally curling hair; neither light nor dark – the bright hazel eyes to match – the rather small but well shaped nose.' Another niece, Caroline Austen, recalled that 'her face was rather round than long – she had a bright, but not pink colour – a clear brown complexion and very good hazle eyes … Her hair, a darkish brown, curled naturally – it was in short curls around the face (for then ringlets were not.) She always wore a cap – Such was the custom with ladies who were not quite young.'[49]

Actually, Austen was still quite young – twenty-two – when she revealed her penchant for caps. In 1798 she wrote to Cassandra, 'I have made myself two or three caps to wear of evenings since I came home, and they save me a world of torment as to hair-dressing, which at present gives me no trouble beyond washing and brushing, for my long hair is always plaited up out of sight, and my short hair curls well enough to want no papering.'[50]

Another recollection came from Charlotte-Maria Beckford, a cousin of William Beckford, who was frequently in Austen's company as a girl, and recalled her vividly. She lived to see the image published in the 1870 family memoir and said that it certainly wasn't a good likeness. 'I remember her as a tall thin spare person, with very high cheek bones, great colour, sparkling Eyes not large but joyous and intelligent. The face by no means so broad and plump as represented.'[51] And perhaps the best account of her at the time when she made her mark as a professional author is that of a fellow-writer, Mary Russell Mitford, noted down in April 1815:

> À propos to novels, I have discovered that our great favourite, Miss Austen, is my countrywoman; that mamma knew all her family very intimately; and that she herself is an old maid (I beg her pardon – I mean a young lady) … a friend of mine, who visits her now, says that she has stiffened into the most perpendicular, precise, taciturn piece of 'single blessedness' that ever existed, and that, till *Pride and Prejudice* showed what a precious gem was hidden in that unbending case, she was no more regarded in society than a poker or a fire-screen, or any other thin upright piece of wood or iron that fills its corner in peace and quietness. The case is very different now; she is still a poker – but a poker of whom every one is afraid.[52]

Thin, upright and just a little intimidating, Jane Austen was poised in her skin and firm in her gaze.

She was a dedicated follower of fashion. In London in the mid-Regency period, having made some money from her books, she started splashing out on her wardrobe. In September 1813, she wrote to Cassandra from London as follows: 'Miss Hare had some pretty caps, and is to make me one like one of them, only white satin instead of blue. It will be white satin and lace, and a little white flower perking out of the left ear, like Harriot Byron's feather [in Richardson's *Sir Charles Grandison*]. I have allowed her to go as far as £1 16s.' That was a lot of money to spend on a single cap. The letter continues with delight in the nicer points of couture: 'My Gown is to be trimmed everywhere with white ribbon plaited on somehow or other. She says it will look well. I am not sanguine. They trim with white very much.'[53]

She kept up with fashion with all the avidity of a modern woman reading *Vogue* or *Elle*. In 1814, she hesitated about wearing long sleeves, but the following year she went out in London and noted, 'Long sleeves appear universal, even as Dress.'[54] We should imagine the London Austen, preparing for her meetings with John Murray, as a woman in a finely finished cap fastened with ribbons beneath the chin and a long-sleeved dress with a high waistline, perhaps trimmed with white lace.

Her whereabouts during much of 1815 are unknown. She intended to go to London in March, but nobody knows whether or not she did. She was certainly there, staying with Henry, for two months between October and December. This was the period when she was potentially beginning to cut a figure in society. She would certainly have needed a fashionable dress for the visit to Carlton House – she wasn't to know whether the Prince or some other person of note might have been there in person. If ever there was a moment in her career when she would have sat for her portrait, pen in hand (whether in the studio of a professional or the drawing room of a friend or relation with artistic pretensions), this would have been it.

The woman in this small Regency portrait sketch appears to be on the point of erasing or revising the line of prose she has just written. There is a spare pen at the ready and a sheaf of paper on the table – rather than a single letter sheet. The intense thoughtfulness in the gaze bespeaks an encounter with the Muse. This does not seem to be any genteel lady writing a letter. It looks like a portrait of a writer at work. On the verso is written,

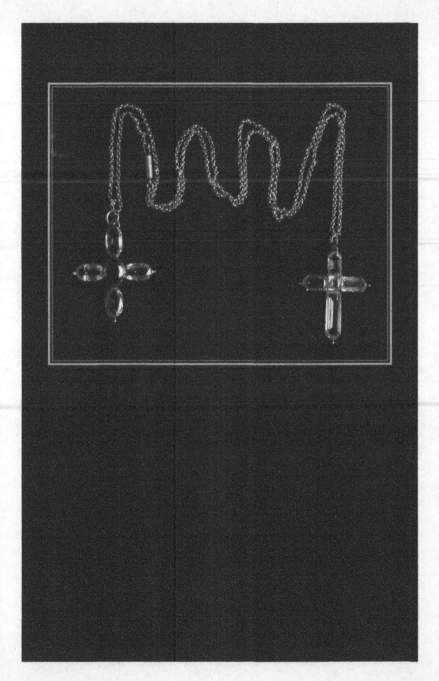

14. The Topaz Crosses

15. The Box of Letters

16. The Laptop

No. 2500   £30.10.1   **London**   October 21ˢᵗ 1816
120   Four   Months after date I promise to pay to
Miss Jane Austin   or Order the Sum of
Thirty Eight Pounds 18/1
for Value received in Account to Self & hrst
At Messʳˢ Brooks Son & Dixon
Bankers Chancery Lane.   John Murray

17. The Royalty Cheque

18. The Bathing Machine

in what seems to be an early nineteenth-century hand, the name 'Miss Jane Austin'.

There is a great deal of uncertainty about the portrait.[55] Forensic, architectural and art historical evidence reveals that it is unquestionably authentic to the mid-Regency. The inscription on the back might have been an erroneous later addition, either wishful or deceitful, but until we find another potential sitter who was middle-aged in about 1815, who had a taste for long sleeves and a cap, who was tall and spare, straight-backed, with dark curly hair and facial features bearing an uncanny resemblance to Jane Austen's brothers, we must keep open the possibility that this truly is a lifetime portrait of the woman who signed her name on the back of John Murray's royalty cheque for *Emma* as 'Miss Jane Austin'.

It is an intriguing image, one that was lost to view for over a hundred years. It purports to show Jane Austen as a mature woman, a self-assured professional writer, at work on a manuscript, in a London setting, within a stone's throw of Westminster Abbey and Poets' Corner, the shrine to the literary genius of the British Isles. Its provenance prior to the twentieth century remains shrouded in mystery and it is by no means certain that the face is really Austen's, but there is firm evidence that by the end of the nineteenth century someone had identified it as the novelist, framed it and hung it with a label reading 'JANE AUSTEN B. 1775 – D. 1817'.

Who was that someone? Certainly not a member of the family. But certainly someone who knew and loved the novels. Perhaps they should be identified as 'the unknown reader'. Readers sometimes know the true spirit of a great writer more profoundly than the writer's own family and descendants do. The unknown reader who cherished this as their image of Jane Austen intuited what this biography has sought to prove: that she was the consummate professional, the woman prepared to devote her life, and to sacrifice her prospects of marriage, to her art as a novelist. She coped with rejection from successive publishers not by giving up, but by carrying on: rewriting old material and starting afresh with new. She was prepared to take the risk of publishing at her own expense in the unlikely stable of Egerton's Military Library. Having succeeded in her gamble, she went on to negotiate her own terms with the prestigious house of John Murray. She won the acclaim of readers ranging from the Prince Regent to Sir Walter Scott, the giant of European literature. It is fitting, therefore, that there should be an image of her not as the shrinking violet of family lore but as a Regency writer of genius, confident in her gaze and steady in her grasp of the novelist's pen.

And yet the pale, sickly appearance of the woman gives the portrait an aura of melancholy. To some observers, her thinness and the oddly distended bone-structure suggest the onset of an attritional disease such as Addison's.

18

The Bathing Machine

It looks like a beach hut on wheels, a small roofed and walled wooden or canvas cart with four wheels. The bather entered in her street clothes, changed into her swimming costume and put her outdoor clothes on a high shelf. The bathing machine would be wheeled down to the water, and the bather would descend the small steps and enter the sea, completely concealed from the public view. Female bathers would wear a cotton or flannel dress of the kind seen in this evocative caricature 'Mermaids at Brighton', executed by William Heath, one of the leading satirical cartoonists of the 1820s.

As shown here, most seaside resorts employed 'dippers', burly local females who would push the lady bathers into the water and then help them out again.[1] It could be a bumpy ride to the water's edge if the beach was of pebbles. If the bather could not swim, the dipper would tie a strong rope around her waist and lower her into the water. After ten or fifteen minutes of splashing and paddling, the dipper would haul the client back and perhaps earn a gratuity for their pains.

The best literary description of a bathing machine is given by Tobias Smollett in his epistolary road novel *The Expedition of Humphry Clinker*, published in 1771 when the contraption was very new-fangled:

Image to yourself a small, snug, wooden chamber, fixed upon a wheel-carriage, having a door at each end, and on each side a little window above, a bench below. The bather, ascending into this apartment by wooden steps, shuts himself in, and begins to undress, while the attendant yokes a horse to the end next the sea, and draws the carriage forwards, till the surface of the water is on a level with the floor of the dressing-room, then he moves and fixes the horse to the other end. – The person within being stripped, opens the door to the sea-ward, where he finds the guide ready, and plunges headlong into the water. – After having bathed, he re-ascends into the apartment, by the steps which had been shifted for that purpose, and puts on his clothes at his leisure, while the carriage is drawn back again upon the dry land; so that he has nothing further to do, but to open the door, and come down as he went up. – Should he be so weak or ill as to require a servant to put off and on his clothes, there is room enough in the apartment for half a dozen people.[2]

Though Smollett writes here of 'he', bathing machines were designed primarily for women. At the seaside it was acceptable for men's bodies to be seen.

If you bathed for health reasons, many doctors believed the winter months were the most beneficial time of year. Eliza de Feuillide and her son Hastings spent December 1790 through to January 1791 in Margate, one of the most popular south-eastern resorts. The poor little boy was forced to endure bathing in the severe conditions of frost and snow:

I had fixed on going to London the end of this Month, but to shew You how much I am attached to my maternal duties, on being told by one of the faculty whose Skill I have much opinion of that one month's bathing at this time of the Year was more efficacious than six at any other and that consequently my little Boy would receive the utmost benefit from my prolonging my stay here beyond the time proposed, like a most exemplary parent I resolved on foregoing the fascinating delights of the great City for one month longer ... Was not this heroic? ... Hastings grows much and begins to lisp english tolerably well, his education is likewise begun, his Grandmamma having succeeded in teaching him his letters. The Sea has strengthened him wonderfully and I think has likewise been of great service to myself, I still continue bathing notwithstanding the severity of the Weather and Frost and Snow which is I think somewhat courageous.[3]

The doughty Scottish lady Elizabeth Grant gives an account of the sensation of being immersed in the cold North Sea water of Margate and Ramsgate:

> The shock of a dip was always an agony: that over, we would have ducked about much longer than the woman let us. It was rather frightful bathing when the waves were high, at least to the timid ones. Some people went into the sea when they really might have been carried away by it, when they and the women had to keep hold of the ropes while the waves went over them.[4]

Sea-bathing in combination with the drinking of sea water became fashionable as the cure for many and varied diseases. It was also a source of relaxation and entertainment. In *Pride and Prejudice*, Mrs Bennet longs to visit Brighton: 'A little sea-bathing would set me up for ever,' she says in anticipation of the sea, using imagined ill-health (her poor nerves) to achieve her real aim of novelty and pleasure.[5]

Before long, most seaside resorts boasted rows of brightly coloured bathing machines. Royalty were responsible for popularizing the devices. George III holidayed in Weymouth, and Fanny Burney recorded in her diary an amusing account of his being dipped into the sea:

> The bathing-machines make it ['God Save the King'] their motto over all their windows; and those bathers that belong to the royal dippers wear it in bandeaus on their bonnets, to go into the sea; and have it again, in large letters, round their waists, to encounter the waves. Flannel dresses, tucked up, and no shoes or stockings, with bandeaus and girdles, have a most singular appearance; and when first I surveyed these loyal nymphs it was with some difficulty I kept my features in order.
>
> Nor is this all. Think but of the surprise of His Majesty when, the first time of his bathing, he had no sooner popped his royal head under water than a band of music, concealed in a neighbouring machine, struck up 'God save great George our King'.[6]

THE REAL JANE AUSTEN

Some of the dippers became quite famous, particularly if they had dipped members of royalty. Two of the most famous were at Brighton, Martha Gunn and Old Smoaker. One imagines them looking very like the burly figure on the left of Heath's caricature. In August 1806 the *Morning Herald* reported:

The Beach this morning was thronged with ladies, all anxious to make interest for a dip. The machines, of course, were in very great request, though none could be run into the ocean in consequence of the heavy swell, but remained stationary at the water's edge, from which Martha Gunn and her robust female assistants took their fair charges, closely enveloped in their partly coloured dresses, and gently held them to the breakers, which not quite so gently passed over them.[7]

Both Martha Gunn and Old Smoaker dipped the Prince Regent. On one occasion Old Smoaker had to persuade him not to bathe because the sea was too dangerous:

'I shall bathe this morning, Smoaker.'
'No, no, Your Royal Highness, its too dangerous.'
'But I will.'
'Come, come, this won't do … I'll be damned if you shall bathe. What do you think your royal father would think of me if you were drowned?'
'He would say, "this is all owing to you, Smoaker. If you had taken proper care of him, poor George would still be alive."'[8]

In the late summer of 1804, Jane Austen and her family visited Lyme Regis with her family. They were undertaking an extensive tour of Devon and Dorset. While at Lyme, Jane caught a fever – 'it has been all the fashion this week in Lyme' – and as part of her recovery she took to the bathing machines. 'I continue quite well,' she told Cassandra, who had taken off to Weymouth with Henry and Eliza, 'in proof of which I have bathed again this morning.'

Jane Austen enjoyed the experience of being dipped so much that she continued to take advantage: 'The Bathing was so delightful this morning and Molly so pressing with me to enjoy myself that I believe I staid in rather too long, as since the middle of the day I have felt unreasonably tired. I shall be more careful another time, and shall not bathe tomorrow, as I had before intended.'[9] Molly appears to have been her dipper.

Emma Woodhouse, for all her privileges, has never seen the sea, but her honeymoon is two weeks by the sea. Jane Austen herself was never happier than when beside the sea, or even in it. We have seen that one of the compensations of her removal to Bath in 1801 was the prospect of summer holidays by the sea. Then the Southampton years gave a period of residence in a seaside town. She had got to know Lyme, Dawlish and Colyton and also Teignmouth, Sidmouth and Charmouth. Her nieces recalled that she even went as far as Wales, staying at Tenby and Barmouth.

Barmouth's location on the west coast of North Wales, on the mouth of the River Mawddach, lying between a mountain range and the sea, is one of the most beautiful in a land of beauties. It has a glorious sandy beach. William Wordsworth described it thus: 'With a fine sea view in front, the mountains behind, the glorious estuary running eight miles inland, and Cadair Idris within compass of a day's walk, Barmouth can always hold its own against any rival.'[10] Assuming that the nieces' memories did not fail them, this was the most sublime country that Jane Austen ever saw.

The holiday in Sidmouth was probably in the summer of 1801. 'Sidmouth', she had written in a letter to Cassandra in January of that year, 'is now talked of as our summer abode.'[11] Following a visit from the King in 1791, this small, secluded East Devon seaside village suddenly and unexpectedly found itself a place of minor fashion. Though Cassandra later recalled a young clergyman falling in love with Jane there, the real story is that Jane fell in love with the sea.

Sidmouth is a lovely unspoilt seaside town nestling beneath majestic red cliffs and the green hills of the glorious Sid Valley. Austen, always a keen walker, could climb up Peak Hill and see the panoramic views of Sidmouth's two beaches, Clifton and Jacob's Ladder. The latter stretches for a mile and is set in a beautiful sheltered bay. The sea at Sidmouth is a shimmering blue and pink, a peculiar effect of the red sand. The inns and lodging houses were set on the wide sweeping esplanade to command the finest sea views.

The soft, clear air at Sidmouth, and its warm climate, added to its attractions, as noted in a contemporary guide: 'The inhabitants are remarkable for their healthy appearance and for their longevity. Such, indeed, might be naturally expected from the suitability of the air, the fine dry soil and a situation most delicious, open to the ocean yet not subject to fogs, and screened from all but the southern winds.'[12]

Thanks to its newly fashionable status, the town had a good library, public rooms, an elegant ballroom and bathing machines lining the beach. According to a guide of 1803 it was a particularly good place to enjoy the 'fashionable rage for bathing'.[13] It was only a few miles from Lyme Regis – in *Persuasion* William Elliot travels to Lyme via Sidmouth.

The Austens were invited to East Devon at the request of Richard Buller, one of George Austen's Steventon pupils, who was now married and settled in the village of Colyton where he was vicar. Colyton, with its magnificent rural views, nestles between Sidmouth in Devonshire and Lyme Regis and Charmouth in Dorsetshire, making it an ideal location from which to make a tour of the seaside.

Jane Austen also hoped that visiting the Bullers would 'assist with the Dawlish scheme'.[14] They may have discovered that Dawlish, on the south coast of Devon, was too far to travel on that occasion, but they spent a holiday there in 1802, when they also visited Teignmouth. Teignmouth was a quaint fishing port, which became a fashionable resort around the turn of the century. A major attraction, apart from the mild climate, were the 'Amazons of Shaldon' – muscular women who pulled fishing nets while 'naked to the knee'. Shaldon was a small village on the opposite bank of the river. Teignmouth also boasted a theatre, a tea house and public rooms. Balls were held, usually once a fortnight, and there was an excellent local market.[15] Fanny Burney, a regular visitor, took her first dip in the sea here, and John Keats would stay for several weeks, completing his long poem *Endymion* ('A thing of beauty is a joy for ever'). According to family tradition, the Austens stayed at a house called Great Bella Vista.[16]

Dawlish was Teignmouth's smaller neighbour, its name derived from 'Devil's water' because the water that ran from the red cliffs into the water looked like blood. It was known for its pure air and its long sandy beach, lined with bathing machines.[17] In 1800 John Nash built Luscombe Castle here for the banker Charles Hoare, with grounds laid out by Humphry Repton, commanding fine coastal views. Odious Robert Ferrars in *Sense and Sensibility* loves Dawlish and chooses it for his honeymoon destination. He mistakenly believes that the Dashwoods' cottage is located there: 'it seemed rather surprising to him that anybody could live in Devonshire without living near Dawlish'. Jane Austen clearly knew it well, as her niece

Anna, who set her novel there, asked her aunt to fact check for her. 'I am not sensible of any Blunders about Dawlish,' Jane wrote reassuringly, before adding, 'The Library was particularly pitiful and wretched 12 years ago and not likely to have had anybody's publication.'[18]

It was, of course, Lyme Regis, 'the pearl of Dorset', that truly captured Jane Austen's imagination, as we know from *Persuasion*. Strikingly, she sets her Lyme episode off season, in November, the very month in which she first visited Lyme in 1803: 'the rooms were shut up, the lodgers almost all gone, scarcely any family but of the residents left'; the beach is not as in the summer 'animated with bathing machines', but it is perhaps even more beautiful out of season; it is a 'very strange stranger', she tells us, 'who does not see charms in the immediate environs of Lyme, to make him wish to know it better'.[19]

Lyme had Assembly Rooms, where Jane Austen danced, and her mother played cards. The principal inns were the Three Cups and the Royal Lion, but there were many lodging houses to accommodate the tourists.

A great fire broke out in November 1803, which Jane Austen and her family witnessed.[20] It began at Crossman's, the bakers, near the George Inn on the evening of 5 November. A little boy had called at the bakers in the hope of buying furze for his bonfire. A female servant took a candle to the attic in search of the furze, but to her horror the flame made contact with the dry furze and a fire broke out. Instead of calling for help, she panicked, left the fire and ran off to fetch water. In the meantime, the roof went up. Unluckily, a gale was blowing and the house next door was soon ablaze. At that point chaos broke out, the flames quickly spread as far as Mill Green and a clothing manufactory, which was burnt down. Efforts were made to save the chapel, but forty-two houses were destroyed.[21]

The destroyed houses belonged to the poor, so a subscription was started to help feed them. A soup kitchen was set up in the chapel. The fire did not put the Austens off, as they returned to Lyme Regis the following year with Henry and Eliza Austen. They may have stayed on Broad Street at Mr Pyne's Lodgings House before moving to Hiscott's Boarding House.

After Cassandra, Henry and Eliza had gone on to Weymouth, Jane wrote to tell Cassandra that she had been bathing and dancing at the Assembly Rooms, where a young man was 'eyeing' her:

The Ball last night was pleasant, but not full for Thursday. My Father staid contentedly till half-past nine – we went a little after eight – and then walked home with James and a Lanthorn, tho' I beleive the Lanthorn was not lit, as the Moon was up. But this Lanthorn may sometimes be a great convenience to him. My Mother and I staid about an hour later. Nobody asked me the two first dances; the next two I danced with Mr Crawford, and had I chosen to stay longer might have danced with Mr Granville, Mrs Granville's son, whom my dear friend Miss Armstrong offered to introduce to me, or with a new odd-looking Man who had been eyeing me for some time, and at last, without any introduction asked me if I meant to dance again. I think he must be Irish by his ease, and because I imagine him to belong to the Hon Barnwells, who are the son, and son's wife of an Irish Viscount, bold queer-looking people, just fit to be Quality at Lyme.[22]

Her remark about the ease of the Irish is interesting, given her experience with Tom Lefroy.

Constance Hill, the early twentieth-century biographer who went on a pilgrimage to all the places associated with Jane Austen, saw the Assembly Rooms before they were destroyed:

The ball-room is little changed since Miss Austen danced in it that September evening nearly a hundred years ago. It has lost its three glass chandeliers which used to hang from the arched ceiling, but these may still be seen in a private house in the neighbourhood. The orchestra consisted, we are told, of three violins and a violoncello. We visited the room by day-light, and felt almost as if it were afloat, for nothing but blue sea and sky was to be seen from its many windows. From the wide recessed window at the end, however, we got a glimpse of the sands and of the harbour and Cobb beyond.[23]

This is an image to cherish: Jane Austen dancing with nothing but blue sky and sea visible through the high Georgian windows.

* * *

The Cobb at Lyme, as drawn in Constance Hill's
Jane Austen: Her Homes and her Friends

It is in *Persuasion* that she brings together her literary art and the lure of the sea, with its mesmerizing charm – 'lingering only, as all must linger and gaze on a first return to the sea'.[24] Her picture of Captain Harville's cottage – a disabled sailor, living so close to the sea – is poignant. Anne wakes early to walk by the sea before breakfast. She is joined by Henrietta: 'they went to the sands, to watch the flowing of the tide, which a fine south-easterly breeze was bringing in with all the grandeur so flat a shore admitted. They praised the morning; gloried in the sea; sympathized in the delight of the fresh-feeling breeze.'[25]

While Henrietta rattles away about the health benefits of the sea and air, Anne shows quiet amusement at her passion, but as she ascends the steps 'leading upwards from the beach' she is openly admired by William Walter Elliot. The point here is that we see through his eyes the veracity of the clichés that Henrietta has been spouting, for the sea air has benefited Anne: 'She was looking remarkably well; her very regular, very pretty features, having the bloom and freshness of youth restored by the fine wind which had been blowing on her complexion, and by the animation of eye which it had also produced.'[26]

It is also at the sea's edge, and as a backdrop to Louisa's fall from the Cobb, that Anne and Captain Benwick discuss poetry. In a detail to appeal to her publisher John Murray, Austen says that Lord Byron's 'dark blue seas' from *The Corsair* 'could not fail of being brought forward by their present view':

> O'er the glad waters of the dark blue sea,
> Our thoughts as boundless, and our soul's as free
> Far as the breeze can bear, the billows foam,
> Survey our empire, and behold our home![27]

Most famously, Lyme is the scene of the sickening accident which almost kills Louisa Musgrove, the fall from the precipitous steps of the Cobb – the old stone jetty – when she is jumped by Wentworth. The fall, foreshadowed by the 'bad fall' suffered by little Charles Musgrove earlier in the novel, causes a serious head injury, and is a turning point in the plot.

Persuasion is full of damaged characters. There are those who have been deeply affected and afflicted by life's events, such as the invalid Mrs Smith, Captain Benwick, even Anne. There are physical accidents, ranging from the commonplace to the serious. Admiral Croft suffers from gout. Captain Harville has been injured at sea and is lame. Charles Musgrove breaks his collar-bone and his family fear spinal damage. Louisa suffers that head injury. Then there are those who are spiritually damaged, such as William Walter Elliot, 'black of heart, hollow and black'.[28]

Jane Austen moves the action from the spa town to the seaside, reflecting an important trend in the health and leisure industries. Weymouth became one of the first modern tourist destinations after King George III's brother the Duke of Gloucester built a grand residence there, Gloucester Lodge, to pass the winters in the mild climate. The King himself made Weymouth his summer-holiday residence on fourteen occasions between 1789 and 1805. When Henry, Eliza and Cassandra left Lyme for Weymouth, hoping to see the royal family, Jane wrote, 'I was in some measure prepared; and particularly for your disappointment in not seeing the Royal Family go on board Tuesday'[29] – the Austens had arrived too late to see the King board the Royal Yacht. Jane professed to show little interest in Weymouth or the royals: 'Weymouth is altogether a shocking place I perceive, without recommendations of any kind and worthy only of being frequented by the inhabitants of Gloucester.'[30]

Brighton was the seaside destination of choice for the Prince Regent. He had commissioned the Royal Pavilion, which was transformed by Nash in the exotic oriental style beloved of the Prince. Brighton is the dissipated backdrop for the sexually active Lydia Bennet: 'that gay bathing place' is where she elopes with Wickham.

In Jane Austen's novels, the raffish seaside resorts associated with the royal family and their hangers-on are the places offstage where meetings with unfortunate consequences take place. In *Mansfield Park* Weymouth is the backdrop for Tom Bertram's disastrous meeting with John Yates, who later elopes with Tom's sister, and it is the place where Frank Churchill meets and becomes engaged to Jane Fairfax in *Emma*. 'I am really very glad that we did not go there,' Austen says of the Weymouth excursion in 1804, and indeed we do not go there in the novels.

'Bathing Place, Morning Dresses' from *The Gallery of Fashion* (September 1797): rear view of ladies in bonnets, on a clifftop looking out to sea, with bathing machines below.

The diversion to Lyme in *Persuasion* clearly whetted her appetite for writing about the seaside. As soon as she finished *Persuasion* she began a new novel that she thought she would call 'The Brothers'. The action is set in a fictional resort on the Sussex coast, somewhere between Hastings and Eastbourne (Bexhill, as it might now be?). It is called Sanditon, and that was the title given to the unfinished novel by the scholar R. W. Chapman when he published the manuscript in full for the first time in the 1920s.

Sanditon is a brilliant and evocative depiction of a newly emerging seaside community, replete with property developers encouraging tourism by transforming fishermen's cottages into boarding houses and constructing modern houses on the hillside overlooking the sea. The new-builds have modish names such as Trafalgar House and there are plans for the construction of a crescent, to be named after Waterloo. There are shops (Whitby's, Jebb's and Heeley's, displaying 'blue shoes and nankin boots in the shop window') and a garden centre, Stringer's, where tourists can buy fruit and vegetables. Further away from the village, up on The Hill, where Mr Parker has built his new house, is a cluster of new shops and facilities, a library containing its own smaller shopping mall, a terrace for walking, a milliner's for acquiring the latest headwear and a hotel and billiard room. From here it's an easy walk to the beach 'and to the bathing machines' that colourfully line the shore's edge.

The heroine, newly arrived in Sanditon, is invigorated by the energy of the place as she stands at her 'ample Venetian window' looking over the 'miscellaneous foreground of unfinished Buildings, waving Linen, and tops of Houses, to the Sea, dancing and sparkling in Sunshine and Freshness'.[31] The surviving fragment is full of such pacy prose. It reads like an early Victorian novel, bursting with a range of fascinating characters and exuding vitality, a mix of delight in and scorn for the march of progress. There is a myth that *Persuasion* was Jane Austen's autumnal valedictory novel, that she knew she was dying, but *Sanditon* suggests otherwise.

The 'Brothers' are Tom, Sidney and Arthur Parker. Tom, open-hearted and gregarious, is the man dedicated to popularizing Sanditon. Though he is happily married, 'Sanditon was a second Wife and four Children to him – hardly less Dear – and certainly more engrossing – He could talk of it forever.'[32] Part of the reason he loves the seaside is that he belongs to a family of hypochondriacs, in particular his two sisters, who are 'sad invalids', and his youngest brother, Arthur, who is described as delicate but is in fact a lazy glutton. Sanditon is Tom Parker's 'Lottery, his Speculation and his Hobby-Horse'. Austen's gift for free indirect discourse – animating the voices of her characters while keeping her own narrative voice coolly detached from them – is given free rein here. Tom Parker talks like a promotional advertisement:

> The Sea air and Sea Bathing together were nearly infallible, one or other of them being a match for every Disorder, of the Stomach, the Lungs or the Blood; They were anti-spasmodic, anti-pulmonary, anti-sceptic, anti-bilious and anti-rheumatic. Nobody could catch cold by the Sea, Nobody wanted Appetite by the Sea, Nobody wanted Spirits, Nobody wanted Strength ... if the Sea breeze failed, the Sea-Bath was the certain corrective, and where Bathing disagreed, the Sea Breeze alone was evidently designed by Nature for the cure.[33]

The Parker sisters, Diana and Susan, are intriguing characters. When we meet Diana, she is indeed obsessed with health but is disillusioned with conventional medicine: 'We have entirely done with the whole Medical tribe.' The sisters now physic themselves ('self-doctoring') homeopathically with herbal teas and home-made tonics or 'bitters'. Their relationship to food is particularly interesting: 'Susan never eats,' says Diana, and 'I never eat for about a week after a Journey.'[34]

Charlotte, the novel's clear-eyed heroine, decides that 'Some natural delicacy of Constitution ... with an unfortunate turn for Medecine, especially quack Medecine', has indeed harmed the sisters' physical health, but 'the rest of their suffering was from Fancy'.[35] When she first meets them her eyes are drawn to the numerous bottles of salts and drops which line the mantelpiece. Tea is served in several different pots, since they have a large selection of 'herb-tea'. They eat only dry toast and sip dishes of strong green tea. The seaside always attracts people drawn to an alternative lifestyle, as well as the elderly, the sick and the transient.

The Parkers diagnose their own ill-health as being psychologically linked to nerves and hysteria. Charlotte, all good sense and the picture of 'Youth and bloom', advises, 'As far as I can understand what nervous complaints are, I have a great idea of the efficacy of air and exercise for them, daily, regular Exercise.'[36]

Diana Parker is drawn to other invalids, such as the delicate girl from the West Indies, Miss Lambe. On Miss Lambe's behalf she secures lodgings in

Sanditon and makes deals with the dippers for sea-bathing. She vows that she will accompany Miss Lambe in 'taking her first Dip. She is so frightened, poor Thing, that I promised to come and keep up her Spirits, and go in the Machine with her if she wished it.'[37] A mixed-race girl and a woman with batty views on medicine and diet, together in a bathing machine on a Sussex beach: this is not our usual image of Jane Austen's novels.

The other main plot-line in *Sanditon* involves the heirs of a rich dowager, Lady Denham, a brother–sister duo who have come to the resort to ingratiate themselves with her. At the time when Jane was writing the novel, the Austen family were anxiously awaiting news of their own inheritance from Mr Leigh-Perrot. The subject was very much on Jane Austen's mind. She was also concerned about a lawsuit that someone was bringing against Edward Austen, challenging his Knight inheritance. The Austen women were very much aware that they could lose their home. Much of their future security depended upon their uncle's will. Jane's health was declining, and the stress did not help.

In *Sanditon* there are two factions in the battle for Lady Denham's inheritance. Sir Edward Denham and his sister stand in one corner and in the other is the lovely but poor Clara Brereton. Sir Edward is one of Jane Austen's most interesting rakes. He plans to seduce his rival Clara. His other more extreme plan, should she fail to respond to his charms, is to abduct and presumably force himself upon her. Sir Edward self-consciously models himself on Samuel Richardson's wicked monster Lovelace, who abducts and rapes Clarissa Harlowe. He reads Richardson, and specifically *Clarissa*, to inflame his ardour and add an 'incentive to Vice': 'His fancy had been early caught by all the impassioned and most exceptionable parts of Richardson ... so far as Man's determined pursuit of Woman in defiance of every opposition of feeling and convenience.'

His 'great object in life', we are told, 'is to be seductive ... he felt that he was formed to be a dangerous Man – quite in the line of the Lovelaces ... it was Clara whom he meant to seduce. Her seduction was quite determined upon ... if she could not be won by affection, he must carry her off. He knew his business.'[38] He plans 'ruin and disgrace for the object of his affections'. That Clara is a version of Clarissa 'young, lovely and dependant' is made clear. That her fate may be the same is suggested in the final pages of *Sanditon* when Charlotte discovers them alone in the outer boundaries of Sanditon House.

But we will never know if Sir Edward abducted and raped Clara, or if he was all talk and no action. Nor will we know whether or not Charlotte married Sidney Parker. Anna Austen recalled having conversations about *Sanditon* with Jane in her final months, but was not told how the novel would end. Austen had began *Sanditon* in January 1817, but had a serious relapse in early March. She had not been well since July 1816. The two plotlines of *Sanditon*, inheritance and health, intruded into her own life. Her interest in the relationship between physical and psychological health became all too real when she heard the news of her uncle's will.

Mr Leigh-Perrot died on 28 March 1817, and left everything to his wife. The Austens were expecting an inheritance, particularly Jane's mother and James Austen, who was the childless Leigh-Perrot's heir. They would now have to wait until the death of Mrs Leigh-Perrot to receive a penny of their legacy. The news caused Jane to collapse. She begged Cassandra, who was away, to return home: 'I am ashamed to say that the shock of my Uncle's Will brought on a relapse, and I was so ill ... that I could not but press for Cassandra's return ... I am the only one of the Legatees who has been so silly, but a weak Body must excuse weak nerves.'[39] This has an added poignancy given her remarks in *Sanditon* about the connection between 'weak bodies' and 'nerves'. She would have had no way of knowing that Addison's Disease, from which she was probably suffering, appears to be linked specifically to stress.[40] In Addison's Disease, or hypocortisolism, the adrenal glands, located just above the kidneys, don't make enough of a hormone called cortisol. Cortisol's most important function is to help the body respond to stress. Today the disease is treated successfully with hydrocortisone, a steroid hormone. Extra doses are given at times of stress known as an 'Addisonial crisis'.

The first shock she experienced was in March 1816, when her brother Henry's bank collapsed. This seems to have precipitated her Addison's. If her second Addisonial crisis was the family's exclusion from the will, it is particularly poignant that women's financial insecurity, of which she wrote so brilliantly in her novels, undermined her health so badly. Henry's financial disaster coupled with those of the Leigh-Perrot will and her uncertainty about Edward's ongoing lawsuit most certainly exacerbated her condition. Fresh sea air and exercise could no longer save her. On 24 May 1817, Cassandra took her fast-fading sister to Winchester for better medical treatment than that available at Chawton. Jane died eight weeks later.

EPILOGUE

She is sitting on the ground out of doors dressed in light blue, shaded by a tree and looking into an empty space. She is drawn from behind, so we cannot see her face. We will never know what was concealed beneath the elegant bonnet. What we do know is that this is the only incontestably authentic surviving portrait of Jane Austen.[1]

It is a watercolour drawing signed C.E.A., the initials of her beloved sister, Cassandra Elizabeth Austen, and dated 1804, when Jane would have been twenty-eight. Its origin was described over half a century later in a letter from Jane and Cassandra's niece Anna Lefroy, written to James Edward Austen-Leigh in 1862, when he was gathering material for his memoir: 'a sketch which Aunt Cassandra made of her in one of their expeditions – sitting down out of doors on a hot day, with her bonnet strings untied'.[2] This is not Aunt Jane sitting in a quiet room, concealing her writing upon hearing the creak of a door. It is a woman out on an *expedition*, in company with the person she loves more than anyone else in the world. The image is wonderfully evocative of the outdoor Austen, of such scenes in the novels as the strawberry-picking party or the trip to Box Hill in *Emma*. However, by not revealing her face it creates a sense of mystery as to the novelist's true appearance.

Her face was unknown to her original public. There was no engraving of her in the press at the time of her death, no frontispiece to the brief biographical notice that her brother published in 1818 with *Northanger Abbey* and *Persuasion*. Fifteen years after Austen's death, a publisher of popular classics called Richard Bentley decided to reprint *Sense and Sensibility* in his collection of Standard Novels. He asked the family if there was an image of her that he could use as a frontispiece. A letter from Henry Austen to Bentley, dated 4 October 1832, gives a very interesting answer: 'When I saw you in London, I mentioned that a sketch of her had been taken – on further enquiry, and inspection, I find that it was merely the figure and attitude – The countenance was concealed by a veil – nor was there any resemblance of features intended – it was a "Study". Henry presumably consulted his sister Cassandra and she may well have shown him the sketch drawn from behind.

Jane Austen remains the most elusive of all our great writers with the exception of Shakespeare – the one author to whom, according to her admiring early reviewers, she stands second, and another figure whose image, like Austen's, is a matter of fierce controversy. Austen left no intimate diaries or revelatory notebooks. The vast majority of her letters are lost. Correspondence is infuriatingly lacking in so many key periods – residence in Bath, the two years leading up to her first appearance in print, the moment of her move from Egerton to Murray. Besides, the novels and the letters are so full of irony and playfulness that her real feelings and beliefs can never be fully pinned down. She keeps her face turned away from us.

In the end, then, it is fitting that the only irrefutably authentic image of the real Jane Austen is Cassandra's sketch of her back. Yet this sketch reveals more than has been realized by previous biographers. The context in which Anna Lefroy described its origin was a question about Jane Austen's travels. '*She* was once I think at Tenby – and once they went as far north as Barmouth – I would give a good deal, that is as much as I could afford, for a sketch which Aunt Cassandra made of her in one of their expeditions – sitting down out of doors on a hot day, with her bonnet strings untied.' This is not any expedition, but a very specific one: a trip to the seaside on one of those family holidays during the Bath years.

Charmouth was especially favoured by sea-bathers. Warmed by the Gulf Stream, the sea is relatively temperate. In *Persuasion*, Mary Musgrove bathes there. Charmouth did not boast fashionable pleasures, but was a place for lovers of nature. Its elevated position meant that it commanded particularly good views. Rising steeply above the golden sands are Stonebarrow Hill and Golden Cap, whose cliffs are the highest point on the south coast of Great Britain. From the green and golden cliffs the views stretching out over Lyme Bay are spectacular. Walkers are encouraged to ascend the cliffs and to sit and contemplate the expanse of sea below.

In *Persuasion*, Austen is deeply moved by Charmouth, 'with its high grounds and extensive sweeps of country, and still more its sweet, retired bay, backed by dark cliffs, where fragments of low rock among the sands make it the happiest spot for watching the flow of the tide, for sitting in unwearied contemplation'.[3] If we had to hazard a guess as to which of Jane and Cassandra's 'expeditions' they were on when the drawing was sketched, as good an answer as any would be one to Charmouth in August 1804, before Cassandra went on to Weymouth.

Austen is clearly sitting in an elevated position. Could a light wind from the sea be gently lifting the ribbons of her unloosened bonnet? Is she 'watching the flow of the tide ... in unwearied contemplation'? The blankness of the view beyond suggests that this is indeed a sea, not a country, view.

Two women, sisters and best of friends, are walking on the cliff tops on a hot summer's day on the south coast of England. They sit down to rest. It is the year before Trafalgar. They have talked, as they do every day, about their two brothers who are away fighting the fiercest maritime war in history, risking their lives for the preservation of their nation. The elder sister takes out the watercolours that she has brought with her. Painting *en plein air* was a new fashion. She sketches her companion from behind. The bonnet of the beloved younger sister is untied, the strings blowing in the salty breeze. Jane Austen is looking out to sea.

NOTES

PROLOGUE: CAPTAIN HARVILLE'S CARPENTRY

1 The image is one of a series of delicate watercolour and pencil drawings of Lyme Regis and its environment, executed by Copleston Warre Bampfylde on a tour in 1784, now in the Victoria and Albert Museum.

2 *Persuasion*, 1.11.

3 *Jane Austen's Letters*, ed. Deirdre Le Faye (3rd edn, 1995), Letter 104, Aug 1814. All letters cited by month and Le Faye's letter number.

4 Mary Lloyd to Anna Lefroy, 9 July 1829, quoted in William Austen-Leigh and Richard Arthur Austen-Leigh, revised by Deirdre Le Faye, *Jane Austen: A Family Record* (1989), p. 237. Cited hereafter as *Family Record*.

5 *Persuasion*, 1.11.

6 Quoted, M. A. DeWolfe Howe, 'A Jane Austen Letter, with Other "Janeana" from an Old Book of Autographs', *Yale Review*, 15 (1925–6), pp. 319–35. All subsequent quotations from this correspondence are cited from the same source.

7 Letter 91, Oct 1813.

8 Letter 4, Sept 1796.

9 Henry Austen, 'Biographical Notice of the Author' (1818), repr. in *J. E. Austen-Leigh: A Memoir of Jane Austen and Other Family Recollections*, ed. Kathryn Sutherland (2002), pp. 137–43. Cited hereafter as *Memoir*.

10 Almost every known fact has been gathered by the indefatigable Deirdre Le Faye in *A Chronology of Jane Austen and her Family 1700–2000* (2006), a work to which I am much indebted. Cited hereafter as *Chronology*.

11 The most thorough, reliable and judicious cradle-to-grave biography is Park Honan, *Jane Austen: Her Life* (1987). *Family Record* also remains indispensable.

12 Kingsley Amis, *Memoirs* (1992), p. 15.

13 *The Letters of Jane Austen*, ed. Edward, Lord Brabourne (1884), p. x.

14 Ibid., p. xi.

15 *Quarterly Review*, Oct 1815, repr. in *Jane Austen: The Critical Heritage*, ed. B. C. Southam (1968), pp. 58–69.

16 Edward Orme, *An Essay on Transparent Prints and Transparencies in General* (1807), quoted in *British Critic*, vol. 30 (Dec 1807), p. 688.

CHAPTER ONE: THE FAMILY PROFILE

1 Mary Augusta Austen Leigh, *James Edward Austen Leigh: A Memoir by his Daughter* (1911), p. 11. See also Sophia Hillan, *May, Lou and Cass: Jane Austen's Nieces in Ireland* (2011), p. 56. On Wellings, Lavater and the art of the silhouette, see http://www.wigsonthegreen.co.uk/silhouettes_guide.html (accessed 16 June 2012).

2 *Emma*, 1.11.

3 This account was given by Anna Austen in her memoir 'Recollections of Aunt Jane' (1864), quoted from *J. E. Austen-Leigh: A Memoir of Jane Austen and Other Family Recollections*, ed. Kathryn Sutherland (2002), p. 160. Cited hereafter as *Memoir*.

4 Richard Arthur Austen-Leigh, *Austen Papers, 1704–1856* (1940), pp. 32–3.

5 Letter 18, Jan 1799, adapting a phrase from Burney's *Camilla* (1796), 'my own particular little niece' (vol. 4, p. 30), where the context is family separation.

6 *Family Record*, p. 20.

7 Austen-Leigh, *Austen Papers*, p. 27.

8 Letter of 23 Sept to 7 Nov 1772, ibid., pp. 64–8.

9 'I have all four at home': Austen-Leigh, *Austen Papers*, pp. 27–8 (8 November 1772).

10 Another letter from Mrs Austen, dated 6 June 1773, mentions all the children in the house but not George, suggesting that he was boarded out earlier that year, at precisely the time when the Reverend George Austen began taking in boys.

11 See Thomas Bewley, *Madness to Mental Illness: A History of the Royal College of Psychiatrists* (2008).

12 Letter 95, Nov 1813.

13 Letter 69, 26 July 1809.

14 See the excellent Linda Robinson Walker, 'Why Was Jane Austen Sent Away to School at Seven? An Empirical Look at a Vexing Question', *Persuasions On-Line* 26.1 (Winter 2005).

15 Austen-Leigh, *Austen Papers*, p. 28.

16 Letter 99, Mar 1814.

17 Thomas Moore, *Letters and Journals of Lord Byron* (1830), vol. 1, pp. 364–5.

18 Letter 24, Nov 1800.

19 Letter 25, Nov 1800.

20 An early form of baseball was a popular game, especially for girls, in the late eighteenth century (compare modern rounders).

21 *Memoir*, p. 18.

22 *Family Record*, p. 46.

23 See Constance Hill, *Jane Austen: Her Homes and her Friends* (1902), p. 23.

24 William and Richard Arthur Austen-Leigh, *Jane Austen: Her Life and Letters: A Family Record* (1913), p. 25.

25 *Emma*, 1.3.

26 Letter 4, Sept 1796.

27 Henry Fielding had got under the skin of a boy in *Tom Jones*, a novel well known to Austen.

28 *Mansfield Park*, 1.2.

29 Ibid., 3.14.

30 William Cowper, *Poetical Works with Notes and a Memoir* (1785), vol. 2, p. 217.

31 'An inclination for the Country is a venial fault. – He [her brother Henry's servant William] has more of Cowper than of Johnson in him, fonder of Tame Hares and Blank verse than of the full tide of existence at Charing Cross': Letter 95, Nov 1813. Cowper wrote an epitaph on a pet hare.

32 *Mansfield Park*, 3.17.

33 Letter 53, June 1808.

CHAPTER TWO: THE EAST INDIAN SHAWL

1 Austen-Leigh, *Austen Papers*, pp. 57–8; *Chronology*, p. 51.

2 Letter of personal testamentary dispositions made at the same time as her will, Pierpont Morgan Library, New York, MA4500; *Chronology*, p. 664.

3 Letter 15, Dec 1798; Letter 121, Oct 1815; Letter 19, May 1799.

4 *Mansfield Park*, 2.13.

5 'Catharine, or the Bower', in *Volume the Third*, in *Juvenilia*, ed. Peter Sabor (2006), pp. 256–7. The Sabor edition, to which I am much indebted, is cited hereafter as *Juvenilia*.

6 Letter 153, Mar 1817.

7 *Family Record*, p. 3.

8 Quoted, Mark Bence-Jones, *Clive of India* (1974), p. 34.

9 'Catharine', in *Juvenilia*, p. 257.

10 For further local colour, see *Birds of Passage: Henrietta Clive's Travels in South India 1798–1801*, ed. Nancy K. Shields (2009).

11 Tysoe Hancock letterbook in Warren Hastings papers, British Library; quoted in *Jane Austen's 'Outlandish Cousin': The Life and Letters of Eliza de Feuillide*, ed. Deirdre Le Faye (2002), p. 31. Cited hereafter as *Eliza Letters*.

12 Quoted, Bence-Jones, *Clive of India*, p. 220.

13 Quoted, *Eliza Letters*, p. 30.

14 Letter 87, Sept 1813.

15 *Juvenilia*, pp. 6, 92, 156.

16 Quoted, *Eliza Letters*, p. 29.

17 Quoted, ibid., p. 23.

18 Quoted, ibid., p. 26.

19 Ibid., p. 46.

20 Quoted in letters from John Woodman to Warren Hastings in India: Hastings Papers, British Library Add. MSS 29150, fo. 23; 29152, fo. 150.

21 *Sense and Sensibility*, 1.10.
22 *Eliza Letters*, p. 142.
23 Ibid., p. 62.
24 Ibid., pp. 88–9.
25 *Family Record*, p. 57.
26 *Eliza Letters*, p. 102.
27 Ibid., p. 112.
28 Ibid., p. 113.
29 See William Holland's print 'Prelude to Riots in Mount Street', June 1792 (Department of Prints and Drawings, British Museum).
30 *Eliza Letters*, p. 116.
31 Ibid., p. 118.
32 *The Times*, 10 Sept 1792.
33 *Family Record*, p. 53.
34 Quoted, *Eliza Letters*, pp. 85–6.
35 Quoted, ibid., p. 125.
36 Ibid., pp. 90, 95, 102, 119.
37 Warren Hastings pocketbook, 15 Mar 1794, BL Add. MSS 39882.
38 That is, 23 February 1794. Le Faye, in *Eliza Letters* and *Chronology*, mistakes the day of condemnation for that of execution: see *Liste générale et très-exacte de tous ceux qui ont été condamnés à mort par le Tribunal révolutionnaire*, vol. 2 (1795), prisoner no. 396.
39 Louis Prudhomme, *Révolutions de Paris, dédiées à la nation* (1794), p. 540, my translation.
40 See her biography in Prosper Jean Levot, *Biographie Bretonne* (1857).
41 *Juvenilia*, p. 278.
42 Ibid., p. 251.
43 Spelt 'Catharine' in the title, but nearly always 'Catherine' in the text.
44 *Juvenilia*, pp. 286–7.
45 Years later, Austen inserted here a reference to Hannah More's moralistic novel *Coelebs in Search of a Wife*, published in 1809: this is evidence of the mature Austen's continuing interest in her own early works.
46 *Northanger Abbey*, 1.14. Subsequent quotations from same chapter.
47 Cited in *Jane Austen: The Critical Heritage*, vol. 2: *1870–1940*, ed. Brian Southam (1996), pp. 87–8.

CHAPTER THREE: THE VELLUM NOTEBOOKS

1 MS Don.e.7, Bodleian Library, Oxford; Add. MSS 59874 and 65381, British Library, London. Detailed bibliographic description, facsimile and diplomatic transcription, ed. Kathryn Sutherland et al., at www.janeausten.ac.uk (accessed 11 July 2012), on which my account of the three volumes is based.
2 Virginia Woolf, 'Jane Austen', in *The Common Reader* (1925), pp. 168–72.

3 *Juvenilia*, p. 131.

4 Caroline Austen, 'My Aunt Jane Austen', in *Memoir*, p. 174.

5 The latest amendment was probably made in 1811, when she substituted 'Regency Dress' and 'Regency Bonnet'.

6 Henry Fielding, *Shamela* (1741), Letter 2.

7 *Juvenilia*, p. 6.

8 Ibid.

9 The *Oxford English Dictionary* records instances going back to 1699.

10 *Juvenilia*, pp. 7, 12.

11 Ibid., p. 16.

12 Ibid., p. 18.

13 Ibid., p. 16.

14 Ibid., p. 38.

15 *All's Well that Ends Well*, 4.3.70. One of the favourite Shakespearean quotations of Austen's contemporary William Hazlitt.

16 *Juvenilia*, p. 150.

17 Ibid., p. 190.

18 In Peter Sabor's superb Cambridge edition of the *Juvenilia*.

19 Ibid., p. 306.

20 Annotations to Goldsmith quoted from ibid., pp. 318–51.

21 'History of England' quotations from ibid., pp. 176–89.

22 Ibid., pp. 353–5.

23 I owe this suggestion to ibid., p. 467.

24 James fell in love with Carr, when the latter was just seventeen. They remained close until their estrangement in 1615. James wrote a letter in which he complained that Carr had been 'creeping back and withdrawing yourself from lying in my chamber, notwithstanding my many hundred times earnest soliciting you to the contrary'. See Louis Crompton, *Homosexuality and Civilization* (2003), p. 387.

25 'The Generous Curate', *Juvenilia*, p. 94.

26 *Juvenilia*, pp. 59–60.

27 See the most ingenious *Jane Austen's 'The History of England' and Cassandra's Portraits*, ed. Annette Upfal and Christine Alexander (2009).

28 *Juvenilia*, p. 133.

29 Ibid., p. 28.

30 Ibid., pp. 37, 92–3.

31 *Loiterer*, no. 29. Full text available online at www.theloiterer/org/loiterer (accessed 15 July 2012).

32 *Loiterer*, no. 47, by James Austen.

33 *Loiterer*, no. 27.

34 The case was first made by Zachary Cope, 'Who was Sophia Sentiment? Was She Jane Austen?', *Book Collector*, 15 (1966), pp. 143–51. Strong supporting evidence (e.g. the source in Hayley) has been provided by Deirdre Le Faye

and the case is reviewed, with the conclusion broadly in favour of the ascription, by Sabor in *Juvenilia*, pp. 356–61. Sceptics suppose that Sophia Sentiment is Henry Austen writing with a female voice, but it is worth noting that where imaginary letters to the *Loiterer* are 'ventriloquized' by James or Henry, this is signalled with their initials, but that is not the case here.

35 See further, Margaret Rogers, 'Jane Austen's First Publisher', http://ibooknet-books4all.blogspot.co.uk/2009/12/jane-austens-first-publisher.html (accessed 15 July 2012).
36 *Juvenilia*, p. 142.
37 Ibid., p. 126.
38 Cassandra Hawke, *Julia de Gramont*, 2 vols (1788), vol. 1, p. 200.
39 *Juvenilia*, pp. 127–8.
40 Coleridge, 'Lecture on the Slave Trade', Bristol, 16 June 1795.

CHAPTER FOUR: THE SUBSCRIPTION LIST

1 Fanny Burney, *Camilla, or the Picture of Youth*, ed. Edward Alan Bloom and Lillian D. Bloom (1999), p. xvii.
2 Austen annotation in her copy of *Camilla*, Bodleian Library, Oxford.
3 See David Allen, *A Nation of Readers: The Lending Library in Georgian England* (2008) and Katie Halsey, *Jane Austen and her Readers* (2011).
4 *Pride and Prejudice*, 1.14.
5 *Sanditon*, ch. 6, quoted from Oxford World's Classics edition of *Northanger Abbey, Lady Susan, The Watsons, and Sanditon*, ed. John Davie (1990).
6 Ibid.
7 *Pride and Prejudice*, 2.19.
8 *Memoir*, p. 16.
9 *Spectator* (1709), no. 365.
10 Letter 14, Dec 1798.
11 Letter 54, June 1808.
12 *Sanditon*, ch. 8.
13 Fanny Burney, Preface to *The Wanderer* (1814), vol. 1, p. xx.
14 *Sanditon*, ch. 8; *Northanger Abbey*, 1.14.
15 *Northanger Abbey*, 1.5.
16 Ibid., 1.7.
17 Ibid., 1.5.
18 Journal, 6 Apr 1782, in *The Early Journals and Letters of Fanny Burney*, vol. 5: *1782–1783* ed. Lars E. Troide and Stewart J. Cooke (2012), p. 44.
19 Fanny Burney, *Cecilia*, ed. Peter Sabor and Margaret Anne Doody (1988), p. 930.
20 *Diary and Letters of Madame D'Arblay*, ed. Charlotte Barrett, 7 vols (1904), vol. 2, pp. 72, 154.
21 See Pat Rogers, 'Sposi in Surrey', *Times Literary Supplement*, 23 Aug 1996.

22 Letter 10, Sat 27–Sun 28 Oct 1798.

23 See further, Claire Harman's excellent essay 'Partiality and Prejudice', www. claireharman.com/documents/Austenmarginalia_001.docx (accessed 11 July 2012).

24 See www.chawton.org/library/files/Hawke2.pdf (accessed 11 July 2012).

25 *Diary and Letters of Madame D'Arblay*, vol. 3, pp. 500–1.

26 *Early Journals and Letters of Fanny Burney*, vol. 5, p. 24.

27 Ibid., vol. 2, pp. 5–7.

28 'Among those who sooner or later were neighbours of the Leigh-Perrots were Maria Edgeworth's father Richard Lovell Edgeworth (who speaks of the help he received from Mr Perrot in his experiments of telegraphing from Hare Hatch to Nettlebed by means of windmills)': Austen-Leigh, *Jane Austen: Her Life and Letters*, ch. 9.

29 *The Life and Letters of Maria Edgeworth*, ed. Augustus Hare (2 vols, 1895), vol. 1, p. 131.

30 Letter to her half-brother Charles Sneyd Edgeworth, quoted, *Family Record*, p. 208.

31 Maria Edgeworth, *Belinda* (1801), ch. 17.

32 Letter 65, Jan 1809.

33 Quoted, Lisa Wood, *Modes of Discipline: Women, Conservatism, and the Novel after the French Revolution* (2003), p. 121.

34 Letter 108, Sept 1814. The best account of the differences between Jane Austen and Jane West, and their political consequences, remains Claudia L. Johnson's *Jane Austen: Women, Politics and the Novel* (1988).

35 Letter 43, Apr 1805.

36 *Memoir*, p. 71.

37 Anne Elliot's phrase in *Persuasion*, when she tries to move closer to Captain Wentworth.

38 Praised by Austen to her nephew Edward – see David Gilson, *A Bibliography of Jane Austen* (1982), p. 89.

39 Letter 66, Jan 1809.

40 Letter 5, Sept 1796.

41 Letter 108, Sept 1814.

CHAPTER FIVE: THE SISTERS

1 English Provincial School (artist unknown), *The Trevanion Sisters*, c.1805, private collection.

2 *West Briton*, 27 Mar 1840.

3 I have been unable to trace Charles Leigh's parentage, but the fact that he rose to the rank of general, became a governor in the West Indies and a groom of the chamber of the Prince Regent shows that he was well connected – there were many branches of the Leigh family, going back to Sir Thomas

Leigh, the Elizabethan Mayor of London. A further Byronic connection is that Jane Austen's cousin Chandos Leigh, whose father was to inherit Stoneleigh some years after Jane's visit there (discussed in a later chapter) was a Harrow schoolmate and close friend of Lord Byron. They dined together on the evening before Byron left England for ever in April 1816.

4 Letter 98.

5 Letter of 30 Nov 1796, *Family Record*, p. 92. Different scholars assign the date of Cassandra's engagement to various times between 1792 and 1795.

6 Letter 1, Jan 1796.

7 Letter 2, Jan 1796.

8 *Pride and Prejudice*, 3.19.

9 Jane and Cassandra's mother, Cassandra Leigh, was the granddaughter of Theophilus Leigh (1643–1725) and his second wife Mary Brydges (sister of the Duke of Chandos). Tom Fowle's mother was a Jane Craven, from a family that intermarried with the Leighs.

10 Dr Johnson's *Dictionary* gives the correct usage: 1. Accurate in judgement to minute exactness; superfluously exact, 2. Delicate; scrupulously and minutely cautious.

11 Letter 58, Oct 1808.

12 Letter 2, Jan 1796.

13 *Eliza Letters*, p. 138.

14 Letter 89, Sept 1813.

15 Letter 84, May 1813.

16 Letter 12, Sun 25 Nov 1798.

17 *Memoir*, p. 175.

18 Letter 4, Sept 1796.

19 Letter 10, Oct 1798.

20 Letter 92, Oct 1813.

21 Letter 39, Sept 1804.

22 Christopher Ricks, 'The Business of Mothering', *Essays in Appreciation* (2004).

23 Letter 53, June 1808.

24 Letter 1, Jan 1796.

25 Ibid.; and Letter 85, May 1813.

26 Letter 27, Nov 1800.

27 Letter 92, Oct 1813.

28 *Memoir*, p. 159.

29 Letter 74, May 1811.

30 Letter 10, Oct 1798.

31 Letter 89, Sept 1813.

32 Letter 159, May 1817.

33 *Family Record*, p. 177.

34 *Sense and Sensibility*, 1.2.

35 *Memoir*, p. 158.
36 Letter 55, June/July 1808.
37 Letter 58, Oct 1808.
38 Austen, Mrs Charles-John (Fanny Palmer), Letters 1810–14: Gordon N. Ray Collection, Morgan Library and Museum, New York (MA 4500).
39 *Persuasion*, 1.8.
40 Fanny Palmer Letters, Morgan Library.
41 Letter 93, Oct 1813.
42 Letter 92, Oct 1813.
43 *Family Record*, p. 194.
44 Charles Austen pocketbook, *Chronology*, p. 501.
45 Ibid., p. 506.
46 Quoted, Brian Southam, *Jane Austen and the Navy* (2000), p. 255.
47 Fanny-Caroline Lefroy (daughter of Austen's niece Anna and Mrs Lefroy's son Ben), 'Family History', quoted, *Memoir*, p. 198.
48 *Juvenilia*, pp. 75, 223.
49 *Memoir*, p. 158.
50 Letter 17, Jan 1799.
51 *Pride and Prejudice*, 2.1.
52 *Family Record*, p. 76.
53 *Sense and Sensibility*, 3.14.
54 Letter 109, Nov 1814.
55 *Sense and Sensibility*, 3.10.
56 *Persuasion*, 1.4.
57 *Family Record*, p. 241.
58 Quoted, Hillan, *May, Lou and Cass*, p. 70.
59 Ibid., p. 71.
60 *Memoir*, p. 157.
61 Ibid., p. 160.
62 Letter CEA/1, Sun 20 July 1817.

CHAPTER SIX: THE BAROUCHE

1 Quoted, George Athelstane Thrupp, *The History of Coaches* (1877), p. 84.
2 *Juvenilia*, p. 51.
3 Letter 87, Sept 1813.
4 Letter 6, Sept 1796.
5 Letter 28, Dec 1800.
6 *Pride and Prejudice*, 2.14.
7 *Chronology*, p. 211.
8 Letter 7, Sept 1796.
9 *Persuasion*, 2.12.
10 *Pride and Prejudice*, 3.10.

11 Letter 7, Sept 1796. The reference is to Richardson's heroine Clarissa Harlowe. Carriages hurtling along the road – taking a young man to adventure in the city, a young woman to a dangerous destination or a family on a tour – are essential features in the novels of Fielding, Richardson and Smollett which so decisively shaped the development of English fiction.

12 'Love and Freindship', Letter 13.

13 *Eliza Letters*, p. 25.

14 *Northanger Abbey*, 2.14.

15 Ibid.

16 *Emma*, 1.15.

17 *Northanger Abbey*, 2.1.

18 Ibid., 1.7.

19 Ibid., 2.5.

20 Letter 142, July 1816.

21 See William Curtis, *A Short History and Description of the Town of Alton* (1896).

22 Letter 90, Sept 1813.

23 Letter 105, Aug 1814.

24 *Juvenilia*, p. 133.

25 Ibid., p. 134.

26 Ibid., p. 136.

27 *Gilpin on the Wye*, ed. T. D. Fosbroke (1822), p. 44.

28 George Colman, *The Plays*, ed. Peter Tasch, 2 vols (1983), p. 38.

29 *Juvenilia*, p. 181.

30 *Pride and Prejudice*, 1.10.

31 *Mansfield Park*, 1.8.

32 Ibid.

33 *Family Record*, p. 226.

34 Letter 85, May 1813.

CHAPTER SEVEN: THE COCKED HAT

1 Object OBLI:5673 in the Soldiers of Oxfordshire Museum, Woodstock.

2 *Mansfield Park*, 1.13.

3 *Mansfield Park*, 1.11.

4 *Pride and Prejudice*, 1.16.

5 Mary Wollstonecraft, *A Vindication of the Rights of Woman* (1792), p. 26.

6 *Pride and Prejudice*, 2.18.

7 Ibid., 1.15.

8 *Family Record*, p. 52.

9 Letter 102, June 1814.

10 Clive Caplan, 'Jane Austen's Soldier Brother: The Military Career of Captain Henry Thomas Austen of the Oxfordshire Regiment of Militia, 1793–1801',

Persuasions, 18 (1996), pp. 122–43 (p. 124). This chapter is most indebted to Caplan's admirable original research.

11 Ibid., p. 130.

12 Quoted, Chris Koening, *Oxford Times*, 10 Nov 2010.

13 Ibid.

14 Caplan, 'Jane Austen's Soldier Brother', pp. 130–1.

15 In 1768 King George III bestowed the title of the 12th (Prince of Wales's) Regiment of (Light) Dragoons, and the regiment was given the Prince's badge of three ostrich feathers and his motto 'Ich Dien'. For the quotation, see *Northanger Abbey*, 1.14.

16 Ibid., 2.12.

17 *Pride and Prejudice*, 3.8.

18 Letter 1, Jan 1796.

19 *Eliza Letters*, p. 139.

20 *Mansfield Park*, 1.9.

21 *Eliza Letters*, p. 151.

22 Ibid., p. 154.

23 Ibid., p. 153.

24 Ibid., p.155.

25 WO17/960, Public Record Office, Kew, quoted, Caplan, 'Jane Austen's Soldier Brother', p. 142.

26 Clive Caplan, 'Jane Austen's Banker Brother: Henry Thomas Austen of Austen and Co., 1801–1816', *Persuasions*, 20 (1998), pp. 69–90 (p. 71). For Charles James, see further, David Gilson, 'Henry Austen, Banker', *Jane Austen Society Report for 2006*, pp. 43–6.

27 Title page to 4th edition, 1816. The earliest edition I have seen is the 2nd (1805), 'Printed for T. Egerton, at the Military Library, near Whitehall'.

28 In 1802, Henry and Eliza actually visited France during the brief Peace of Amiens to try to recover some of her first husband's sequestered estates.

29 *Eliza Letters*, p. 159.

30 He had undertaken some literary publishing, but usually only as part of large consortia of booksellers producing editions of Shakespeare, collections of classic English poets and so forth; he had very little prior experience of publishing and marketing novels. Further connections between Henry Austen and Thomas Egerton include the fact that Egerton had, years before, been London distributor for the *Loiterer* and their sharing of a printer: the bank of Austen, Maunde and Austen availed themselves of the services of the same Charles Roworth of Bell Yard, Temple Bar, who printed Egerton's books, including *Sense and Sensibility*. The second 'Austen' in the title of the bank seems to have been the result of one of the sailor brothers becoming a sleeping partner.

31 Letter 70, April 1811.

32 Letter 71, April 1811.

33 Ibid.

CHAPTER EIGHT: THE THEATRICAL SCENES

1 *The Collected Poems of James Austen*, ed. David Selwyn (2003), p. 8.
2 From their listing among the barrels and hops, it seems likely that the 'theatrical scenes' are indeed stage flats, but it is just possible that the reference is to a set of engravings of dramatic scenes analogous to the 'Curious collection, consisting of 627 prints of theatrical scenes and portraits of the performers, engraved from different masters. Many of them proofs, in 3 large vols, folio' that appears in the *Catalogue of the Library of the late John, Duke of Roxburghe* (1812), no. 4034. Either way, the testimony to the Austen family's theatrical interests remains vivid.
3 *Mansfield Park*, 1.13.
4 Ibid., 3.3.
5 This chapter draws heavily on my full-length study *Jane Austen and the Theatre* (2002), but also includes new research and analysis.
6 *The Works of Jane Austen* (Oxford Jane Austen), ed. R. W. Chapman, vol. 6: *Minor Works*, revised by B. C. Southam (1975), p. 65. Cited hereafter as *Minor Works*.
7 *Mansfield Park*, 1.13.
8 *Family Record*, p. 58.
9 Ibid., p. 47.
10 *Eliza Letters*, p. 83.
11 *Poems of James Austen*, p. 20.
12 *The Wonder*, quoted from *The Modern British Drama*, ed. Walter Scott (1811), vol. 4, p. 264.
13 Letter 31, Jan 1801.
14 See my *Jane Austen and the Theatre*, p. 27.
15 See Hillan, *May, Lou and Cass*, p. 18.
16 See my *Jane Austen and the Theatre*, p. 25.
17 Gisborne, *An Enquiry into the Duties of the Female Sex* (1797), p. 175.
18 Letter 30, Aug 1805.
19 Letter 3, Aug 1796.
20 Quoted, Byrne, *Jane Austen and the Theatre*, p. 35.
21 *Pride and Prejudice*, 3.9.
22 Byrne, *Jane Austen and the Theatre*, pp. 45–6.
23 Letter 70, Apr 1811.
24 Letters 71, Apr 1811.
25 Letter 114, Nov 1814.
26 Siddons actually retired, returned and retired again several times over.
27 Letter 112, Nov 1814.
28 Letter 99, Mar 1814.
29 Letter 98, Mar 1814.
30 Letter 71, Apr 1811.

31 Letter 87, Sept 1813.

32 Ibid.

33 Letter 30, Jan 1801.

34 Letter 71, Apr 1811.

35 Letter 51, Feb 1807.

36 *Lovers' Vows* was performed at least seventeen times in Bath from 1801 to 1806.

37 See Belville Penley, *The Bath Stage* (1892).

38 Letter 98, Mar 1814.

39 *Lovers' Vows*, script reprinted in *Mansfield Park*, ed. R. W. Chapman (Oxford Jane Austen, 1923), p. 462.

40 *Mansfield Park*, 1.18.

41 Ibid., 1.17.

42 Ibid., 3.5.

43 Ibid.

44 Ibid., 1.18.

45 Ibid.

46 *Mansfield Park*, 2.2.

CHAPTER NINE: THE CARD OF LACE

1 From a private collection.

2 *Pride and Prejudice*, 1.7.

3 *Northanger Abbey*, 1.6.

4 Ibid., 1.14.

5 *Sense and Sensibility*, 2.11.

6 *Emma*, 3.19.

7 Letter 88, Sept 1813.

8 Southey, 'Shops', in his *Letters from England* (1808), vol. 1, p. 39.

9 *Sophie in London, 1786, being the diary of Sophie v. La Roche*, translated from the German with an introductory essay by Clare Williams (1933), p. 28.

10 Jane Austen, 'Love and Freindship', Letter 4.

11 *Bath Chronicle*, 23 Nov 1797. It is possible that Austen had made an earlier visit, though no record of it survives. The novelette 'Evelyn' in the vellum notebooks includes a letter dated from 'Westgate Buildings' (at that time a more fashionable address than it was by the time of *Persuasion*, where it is the down-at-heel residence of poor Mrs Smith). Austen may have been familiar with the name as the result of a childhood visit to her aunt Jane Cooper (Mrs Austen's sister, who married Dr Edward Cooper, who resided in Bath despite being a prebendary of Wells Cathedral).

12 Letter 19, May 1799.

13 Letter 21, June 1799.

14 Letter 21, June 1799.

15 Christopher Anstey, *New Bath Guide* (1799), p. 26.

16 Letters 19 and 20, May 1799.

17 Letter 22, June 1799.

18 Letters 20 and 21, June 1799.

19 Letter 21, June 1799.

20 *Family Record*, p. 113.

21 *Chronology*, p. 249.

22 *Family Record*, p. 107.

23 Ibid., pp. 106–10.

24 Ibid., p. 109.

25 See Elia Aboujaoude and Lorrin M. Koran, *Impulse Control Disorders* (2010), ch. 3: 'Kleptomania: Clinical Aspects'.

26 *Mansfield Park*, 2.2.

27 Letter 31, Jan 1801.

28 Letter 29, Jan 1801.

29 Letter 32, Jan 1801.

30 Letter 29, Jan 1801.

31 Letter 37, May 1801.

32 *Family Record*, p. 120.

33 Claire Tomalin, *Jane Austen: A Life* (1997), pp. 167–9.

34 Cassandra remembered 'Susan' as being written in 1798, but various allusions indicate redrafting in the Bath years – for instance the reference to Maria Edgeworth's novel *Belinda*, which was only published in 1801.

35 Letter 3, Aug 1796.

36 *Northanger Abbey*, 1.10.

37 Anstey, *New Bath Guide*, p. 26.

38 *Northanger Abbey*, 1.3.

39 Ibid.

40 Letter 36, May 1801.

41 Ibid.

42 Letter 37, May 1801.

43 *Northanger Abbey*, 1.10, 1.11.

44 *Emma*, 2.14.

45 *Northanger Abbey*, 1.10.

46 Setting aside the possibility that she was Sophia Sentiment.

47 *Northanger Abbey*, 1.1.

48 Ibid., 2.9.

49 Ibid., 2.15.

CHAPTER TEN: THE MARRIAGE BANNS

1 Hampshire Archives and Local Studies, 71M82/PR3.

2 *Memoir*, p. 133.

3 Letter 1, Jan 1796; Letter 25, Nov 1800.

4 Letter 1, Jan 1796.

5 Ibid.

6 Letter 2, Jan 1796.

7 *Family Record*, pp. 251–2.

8 *Memoir*, p. 186.

9 *Pride and Prejudice*, 2.1.

10 Letter 2, Jan 1796.

11 Letter 11, Nov 1798.

12 Letter 15, Dec 1798.

13 Letter 46, Aug 1805.

14 Letter 55, June/July 1808.

15 Letter 57, Oct 1808.

16 Letter 61, Nov 1808.

17 Letter 90, Sept 1813.

18 Letter 94, Oct 1813.

19 Letter 14, Dec 1798.

20 Quoted from Francis Austen's autobiographical memoir by Honan, *Jane Austen: Her Life*, p. 156.

21 Letter 11, Nov 1798.

22 Ibid.

23 Letter 155, Mar 1817.

24 Letter 86, July 1813.

25 *Memoir*, p. 188.

26 Quoted, R. W. Chapman, *Jane Austen: A Study of Facts and Problems* (1948), pp. 67–8.

27 *Family Record*, p. 122.

28 Catherine Hubback (Frank's daughter), reporting on a letter – presumably to Frank – that is no longer extant (ibid.).

29 Ibid.

30 Letter 114, Nov 1814.

31 Letter 25, Nov 1800. In 1802 Mrs Lefroy wrote that Harris Wither's hand 'is still very lame and I now fear he will never recover the use of it' – *Letters of Mrs Lefroy: Jane Austen's Beloved Friend*, ed. Helen Lefroy and Gavin Turner (2007), p. 69.

32 Letter 18, Jan 1799.

33 http://addictedtojaneausten.blogspot.co.uk/ (accessed 25 July 2012).

34 *Pride and Prejudice*, 1.22.

35 Wollstonecraft, *A Vindication of the Rights of Woman* (1792), ch. 9, 'Of the Pernicious Effects which arise from the Unnatural Distinctions established in Society'.

36 *Pride and Prejudice*, 3.4.

37 Ibid., 3.10.

38 *Mansfield Park*, 1.10.

39 *Pride and Prejudice*, 3.5.

40 Ibid., 3.14.

41 Ibid., 3.6.

42 Letter 13, Dec 1798.

43 Letter 56, Oct 1808.

44 Letter 155, Mar 1817.

45 Ibid.

46 Letter 153, Mar 1817.

47 Letter 109, Nov 1814.

48 *Memoir*, p. 188.

49 Burney's draft introduction to *Cecilia*, ed. Peter Sabor (1992), p. 945.

50 Letter 109, Nov 1814.

51 Letter 151, Feb 1817.

52 See Glenda Hudson, *Sibling Love and Incest in Jane Austen's Fiction* (1992). The classic examples are Byron's *The Bride of Abydos* and Shelley's *Laon and Cythna*.

53 *Emma*, 3.13.

54 *Mansfield Park*, 3.17.

55 *Persuasion*, 2.11.

56 Cancelled chapter of *Persuasion*.

57 Caroline Austen to Anna Lefroy, quoted, Constance Hill, *Jane Austen*, p. 236; *Memoir*, p. 188; *Emma*, 1.8.

58 *Juvenilia*, p. 142.

59 Quoted, Chapman, *Facts and Problems*, p. 67.

60 Letter 135, ?Dec 1815/Jan 1816.

CHAPTER ELEVEN: THE IVORY MINIATURE

1 Ledger of Richard Crosse, transcribed *Walpole Society*, vol. XVII (1929), p. 72, quoted http://www.historicalportraits.com/Gallery.asp?Page=ItemandItemID=1483andDesc=Anne-Lefroy,-by-Richard-Crosse-|-Richard-Crosse (accessed 27 Sept 2012).

2 *The Autobiography, Times, Opinions, and Contemporaries of Sir Egerton Brydges*, 2 vols (1834), 1.137.

3 Ibid., 1.5.

4 Ibid., 1.137.

5 'On seeing some school-boys', 'Poetical Epistle to Miss KB', 'Poem to Miss D.B.', in *The Poetical Register and Repository of Fugitive Poetry* (1801); *Carmina Domestica; or Poems on Several Occasions (The Majority Written in the Early Part of Life)*, edited by her son Christopher Edward Lefroy (1812).

6 Brydges, *Autobiography*, 1.137.

7 Ibid., 1.11.

8 Quoted, *Letters of Mrs Lefroy*, p. 20.

9 Ibid., p. 8.

10 The admiration did not extend from Jane to Egerton: she later professed disdain for his writings, particularly his novel *Arthur Fitz-Albini*, which she read with her father in November 1798: 'We have neither of us yet finished the first volume. My father is disappointed – I am not, for I expected nothing better.' She added, 'Never did any book carry more internal evidence of its author. Every sentiment is completely Egerton's' (Letter 12, Nov 1798). Here is Austen, not yet twenty-three but fully confident in her own literary judgement, even if it means speaking bluntly of her mentor's brother. She knows already what makes a good novel: balance, elements of impersonality, the voicing of different sentiments for different characters.

11 *Letters of Mrs Lefroy*, p. 44.

12 Ibid., pp. 139–40.

13 Ibid., p. 114.

14 *Gentleman's Magazine*, vol. 96 (1804), p. 1179.

15 *Minor Works*, pp. 440–2.

16 Ibid.

17 Letter 40, Jan 1805.

18 Letter 41, Jan 1805.

19 There are three prayers in all, copied in two different hands, probably Cassandra's and Henry's. Two of Charles's granddaughters sold them, along with other Austen papers and memorabilia, in 1927. They are now in the Heller Rare Book Room of the F. W. Olin Library at Mills College, Oakland, California. See Bruce Stovel, '"A Nation Improving in Religion": Jane Austen's Prayers and their Place in her Life and Art', *Persuasions*, 16 (1994), pp. 185–96.

20 Letter 60, Oct 1808.

21 *Mansfield Park*, 1.9.

22 Letter 106, Sept 1814.

23 Letter 53, June 1808.

24 *Memoir*, p. 141.

25 *Juvenilia*, p. 186.

26 Evangelical Joseph Milner, decrying Locke, quoted by Irene Collins in her excellent *Jane Austen and the Clergy* (2003), p. 44.

27 Letter 145, Sept 1816.

28 Edward Cooper, *Two Sermons Preached in Wolverhampton* (1816), p. 15.

29 Letter 67, Jan 1809.

30 Letter 55, Oct 1808.

31 Letter 65, Jan 1809.

32 Letter 67, Jan 1809.

33 Letter 109, Nov 1814.

34 Letter 114, Nov 1814.

35 Quoted, *Jane Austen: The Critical Heritage*, ed. Brian Southam (1968), p. 95.

36 *The Watsons*, quoted from Oxford World's Classics edition of *Northanger Abbey, Lady Susan, The Watsons, and Sanditon*, ed. John Davie (1990), p. 301.

37 *Minor Works*, p. 439.

38 Letter 108, Sept 1814.

39 Gilson, *Bibliography*, p. 445.

40 Ibid.

41 *Pride and Prejudice*, 2.13.

42 *Sense and Sensibility*, 3.10.

43 *Mansfield Park*, 3.5.

44 Ibid., 1.9.

45 Ibid., 1.11.

46 For an excellent account of Austen and the 'reasoned' religion of the eighteenth century, see Peter Knox-Shaw, *Jane Austen and the Enlightenment* (2004), which persuasively places her in a very English religious and political 'middle road'.

47 'Opinions of *Mansfield Park*', in *Minor Works*, pp. 431–5.

48 *Mansfield Park*, 1.11, 1.9.

49 Ibid., 1.9.

50 Ibid., 3.16.

51 Letter 79, Jan 1813.

52 *Mansfield Park*, 3.17.

53 'Opinions of *Mansfield Park*', in *Minor Works*, pp. 431–5.

54 *Mansfield Park*, 3.13.

55 *Sense and Sensibility*, 2.6; *Pride and Prejudice*, 2.4; *Persuasion*, 1.12.

56 *Persuasion*, 1.11.

57 *Memoir*, p. 178.

58 Letter 159, May 1817.

59 Letter CEA/1, Sun 20 July 1817.

60 Charles Austen's weather note in his pocketbook (*Chronology*, p. 577) – he was at Eastbourne, but the *Gentleman's Magazine* weather report for the day records heavy rain across southern England.

61 'When Winchester races', in *Minor Works*, pp. 451–2.

CHAPTER TWELVE: THE DAUGHTER OF MANSFIELD

1 *The Diary and Letters of His Excellency Thomas Hutchinson*, 2 vols (1884–6), vol. 2, p. 277, entry for August 1779.

2 Letter 45, Aug 1805.

3 *Sanditon*, ch. 11.

4 *Somersett v Stewart*, King's Bench, 22 June 1772.

5 William Cowper, *The Task* (1785), Book 2.

6 *Emma*, 2.17.

7 Though to be fair to Mr Suckling, the name 'Maple Grove' does have abolitionist overtones: the anti-slavery lobby advocated maple as an alternative to the sugar produced on the West Indian slave plantations.

8 See Gabrielle White, *Jane Austen in the Context of the Abolition* (2006), p. 149.

9 Southam, *Navy*, p. 189.

10 Letter 78, Jan 1813.

11 Thomas Clarkson, *History of the Rise, Progress and Accomplishment of the Abolition of the African Slave-Trade*, 2 vols (1808), vol. 1, ch. 7.

12 Ibid., vol. 2, p. 154.

13 *Family Record*, p. 54.

14 For a copy of the map, see 'Jane Austen and the Antigua Connection' on the website of the Jane Austen Society of Australia, http://www.jasa.net.au/antigua.htm (accessed 21 Aug 2012).

15 Austen-Leigh, *Austen Papers*, pp. 26–7.

16 *Persuasion*, 1.8.

17 *Emma*, 2.4.

18 See Eric Williams, *Capitalism and Slavery* (1944), p. 151.

19 See Robert Blackburn, *The Overthrow of Colonial Slavery* (1998), pp. 303–4.

20 *Mansfield Park*, 3.17.

21 Clarkson, *History*, vol. 2, ch. 2.

22 *Mansfield Park*, 2.3.

CHAPTER THIRTEEN: THE CRIMSON VELVET CUSHIONS

1 *Mansfield Park*, 1.9.

2 *Family Record*, p. 138.

3 See Mairi Macdonald, 'Not Unmarked by Some Eccentricities: The Leigh Family of Stoneleigh Abbey', in Robert Bearman, ed., *Stoneleigh Abbey: The House, its Owners, its Lands* (2004), p. 151.

4 Stoneleigh archive (Shakespeare Birthplace Trust Records Office, Stratford-upon-Avon), DR 18/17/27/171.

5 It was rebuilt in the tradition of Chatsworth, with all four ranges around a courtyard on the model of Hampton Court. See Andor Gomme, 'Abbey into Palace: A Lesser Wilton', in Bearman, ed., *Stoneleigh Abbey*, p. 82.

6 'Epistle to Joseph Hill', line 62 (1785).

7 Part of this letter is printed in *Family Record*, pp. 139–40.

8 Ibid.

9 Austen-Leigh, *Austen Papers*, p. 247.

10 See the excellent essay by Gaye King, 'The Jane Austen Connection', in Bearman, ed., *Stoneleigh Abbey*, p. 173.

11 *Mansfield Park*, 1.9.

12 Ibid., 1.9.

13 Elizabeth 'Betty' Lord secretly married a poor Lieutenant Wentworth who went on to make a fortune in the navy and was finally accepted into the family. See King, 'The Jane Austen Connection', pp. 174–5.

14 *Mansfield Park*, 1.9.

15 *Pride and Prejudice*, 3.1.

16 *Emma*, 3.6.

17 *Mansfield Park*, 1.5.

18 Letter 86, July 1813.

19 *Mansfield Park*, 1.9.

20 *Pride and Prejudice*, 3.1.

21 Letter of 12 Jan 1848 to George Lewes, *The Letters of Charlotte Brontë*, ed. Margaret Smith, vol. 2: *1848–1851* (2000), p. 10 – though in the same letter Charlotte Brontë gave high praise to Austen's style: 'with infinitely more relish can I sympathise with Miss Austen's clear common sense and subtle shrewdness. If you find no inspiration in Miss Austen's page, neither do you find mere windy wordiness; to use your words over again, she exquisitely adapts her means to her end; both are very subdued, a little contracted, but never absurd.'

22 Stoneleigh archive (Shakespeare Birthplace Trust Records Office, Stratford-upon-Avon), DR/18/17/32.

CHAPTER FOURTEEN: THE TOPAZ CROSSES

1 Letter 38, May 1801.

2 *Mansfield Park*, 2.8.

3 'And by the bye – shall you object to my mentioning the Elephant in it, and two or three other of your old Ships?' Letter 86, July 1813.

4 *Mansfield Park*, 3.7.

5 See Southam, *Navy*, p. 32.

6 Letter 27, Nov 1800.

7 John Marshall, *Royal Naval Biography* (1828), p. 74.

8 Letter 69(D), July 1809.

9 *Mansfield Park*, 2.6.

10 Ibid.

11 Ibid.

12 *Mansfield Park*, 2.7.

13 *Lefroy Letters*, pp. 30, 63.

14 Jane Austen mentions a connection to Sir J. Moore. Her godfather's physician was Sir John's father, who was also a novelist. See Southam, *Navy*, p. 69.

15 Robert Gardiner, *Memoir of Admiral Sir George Moore* (1912).

16 See Honan, *Jane Austen: Her Life*, p. 160, Mss Nat. Mar. Mus., log of *London*, 27 Aug 1798.

17 *Mansfield Park*, 1.6.

18 *Letters of Jane Austen*, ed. Brabourne, vol. 1, p. 37.
19 Letter 86, July 1813.
20 Quoted, J. H. and Edith C. Hubback, *Jane Austen's Sailor Brothers* (1906), p. 85.
21 *Persuasion*, 1.4.
22 Letter 18, Jan 1799.
23 Letter 55, June/July 1808.
24 *Family Record*, p. 143.
25 Verses, in *Minor Works*, p. 446.
26 Letter 64, Jan 1809.
27 Letter 66, Jan 1809.
28 Letter 67, Jan 1809.
29 *Mansfield Park*, 3.6.
30 Ibid.
31 Ibid.
32 Ibid., 3.15.
33 Ibid., 3.7–3.8.
34 *Minor Works*, p. 435.
35 *Persuasion*, 2.1.
36 Ibid.
37 *Mansfield Park*, 3.17.
38 *Persuasion*, 1.4.
39 *Mansfield Park*, 1.16.
40 India Office Library, Ms. EUR B151, quoted Southam, *Navy*, p. 98.

CHAPTER FIFTEEN: THE BOX OF LETTERS

1 Alphabet blocks, English, 1800–40, Victoria and Albert Museum, ref.
E.1739–1954.
2 *Emma*, 3.5.
3 Letter 64, Jan 1809.
4 *Emma*, 3.8.
5 Ibid., 3.15.
6 Ibid., 3.13.
7 Letter 50, Feb 1807.
8 The best account of this subject is David Selwyn's excellent book *Jane Austen and Children* (2010).
9 Ibid.
10 Letter 60, Oct 1808.
11 Letter 30, Jan 1810.
12 Letter 112, Nov 1814.
13 *Emma*, 3.3.
14 Caroline Austen, 'My Aunt Jane Austen', in *Memoir*, p. 167.
15 Ibid., p. 168.

16 Quoted, *Family Record*, p. 178.
17 Letter 105, Aug 1814; Letter 9, Oct 1798; Letter 60, Oct 1808.
18 Letter 148, Jan 1817; Letter 97, Mar 1814.
19 Letter 123, Oct 1815.
20 Letter 91, Oct 1813.
21 Letter 117, July 1815.
22 Ibid.
23 Quoted in Deirdre Le Faye, *Fanny Knight's Diaries: Jane Austen through her Niece's Eyes* (2000), p. 6.
24 *Minor Works*, p. 434.
25 Letter 102, June 1814.
26 See 1851 census, Parish of Everton. Her school was at 124 York Terrace.
27 Letter 72, Apr 1811.
28 Letter 86, July 1813.
29 *Persuasion*, 2.11.
30 Letter 53, June 1808.
31 *Sense and Sensibility*, 1.21.
32 *Emma*, 1.18; *Sense and Sensibility*, 3.6.
33 *Emma*, 1.12.
34 *Mansfield Park*, 1.3.
35 *Emma*, 3.17.
36 *Persuasion*, 1.9.
37 Ibid.
38 He later admits 'he had imagined himself indifferent, when he had only been angry', ibid., 2.11.
39 *The Watsons*, quoted from Oxford World's Classics edition of *Northanger Abbey, Lady Susan, The Watsons, and Sanditon*, ed. John Davie (1990), p. 289.
40 Ibid., pp. 289–90.
41 Ibid., p. 291.
42 Letter 67, Jan 1809.
43 Letter 153, Mar 1817.
44 Letter 155, Mar 1817.

CHAPTER SIXTEEN: THE LAPTOP

1 *Chronology*, p. 171.
2 George Austen also recorded a second purchase of a writing box at another time, so we cannot be absolutely certain that the one in the British Library is Jane's.
3 Letter 9, Oct 1798.
4 Letter 10, Oct 1798.
5 Letter 9, Oct 1798.
6 Letter 89, Sept 1813.

7 This myth springs from the family memoir (*Memoir*, p. 81). Tomalin goes even further. 'For ten years she produced almost nothing,' she claims (p. 167), hinting at writer's block and even clinical depression.

8 *Flowers of Literature 1801–1802* (1803), p. 462. On Crosby's record of novel publishing, see Anthony Mandal, *Jane Austen and the Popular Novel: The Determined Author* (2007).

9 Letter 121, Oct 1815.

10 *Lady Susan*, Letter 4.

11 Ibid., Letter 7.

12 Ibid., Letter 14.

13 Ibid., Letter 25.

14 Ibid.

15 Ibid., Letter 16.

16 For example ibid., Letter 24.

17 Elizabeth Jenkins, *Jane Austen: A Biography* (1938, repr. 1949), p. 156.

18 'Biographical Notice', in *Memoir*, p. 138.

19 Biographers write of the manuscript being sold to Richard Crosby in 1803, but at that time the firm was 'B. Crosby' – Richard had taken over the family business in the intervening years.

20 Advertisement 'by the Authoress' to *Northanger Abbey* (1818).

21 Save for a verse letter to Frank, congratulating him on the birth of a son in July 1809.

22 Letter 70, Apr 1811.

23 Letter 71, Apr 1811.

24 See Jan Fergus, *Jane Austen: A Literary Life* (1991), p. 131. Fergus offers an exceptionally good account of Austen's professional career.

25 *Chronology*, pp. 324, 328. Though Cassandra also had her legacy from her late fiancé.

26 Letter 49, Jan 1807.

27 Letter 71, Apr 1811.

28 'This morning brought me a letter from Mrs Knight, containing the usual Fee, and all the usual Kindness' (Letter 53, June 1808).

29 Letter 95, Nov 1813.

30 1818 'Biographical Notice', in *Memoir*, p. 140.

31 Letter 70, Apr 1811.

32 *Critical Review*, Feb 1812; *British Critic*, May 1812.

33 *Family Record*, p. 171.

34 Ibid., p. 168.

35 Jane to Frank: 'You will be glad to hear that every Copy of S and S is sold and that it has brought me £140' (Letter 86, July 1813).

36 Letter 77, Nov 1812.

37 Jan Fergus has calculated that Egerton made around £450 from the first two editions of *Pride and Prejudice*.

38 *British Critic*, Feb 1813, and see also the *New Review or Monthly Analysis of General Literature*, Apr 1813, pp. 393–6.

39 *Critical Review*, Mar 1813, pp. 318–24.

40 See Gilson, *Bibliography*, pp. 25–7.

41 To Amelia Opie, 11 Oct 1813, quoted, Fergus, *Jane Austen: A Literary Life*, p. 188.

42 Letter 79, Jan 1813.

43 All quotations from Letter 80, Feb 1813.

44 Letter 81, Feb 1813.

45 See Hillan, *May, Lou and Cass*, p. 37.

46 Letter 95, Nov 1813.

47 Ibid.; the information about Mrs Fletcher reached Austen via a Mrs Carrick.

48 Letter 81, Feb 1813.

49 Letter 80, Feb 1813.

50 Letter 95, Nov 1813.

51 Letter 85, May 1813.

52 Letter 86, July 1813.

53 Gilson, *Bibliography*, p. 49.

54 Letter 97, Mar 1814.

55 Ibid.

56 'Opinions of *Mansfield Park*', pp. 431–5.

57 *Family Record*, p. 184.

58 Letter 98, Mar 1814.

CHAPTER SEVENTEEN: THE ROYALTY CHEQUE

1 It is now in the John Murray Archive, National Library of Scotland.

2 Letter 90, Sept 1813. The 'third' novel is *Mansfield Park*.

3 Letter 109, Nov 1814.

4 Letter 110, Nov 1814.

5 Letter 96, Nov 1813.

6 Letter 114, Nov 1814.

7 Letter 118, Feb/Mar 1815.

8 Letter 104, Aug 1814.

9 Letter 107, Sept 1814.

10 Letter 115, Dec 1814.

11 Letter 146, Dec 1816.

12 *Memoir*, p. 119.

13 Letter 102, June 1814.

14 Letter 77, Nov 1812.

15 Letter 78, Jan 1813.

16 Letter 82, Feb 1813.

17 Letter 102, June 1814.

18 Letter 136, 1816.

19 *Emma* was actually published in December 1815, though the title page says 1816. The second edition of *Mansfield Park* was published in February 1816.

20 See Kathryn Sutherland, 'Jane Austen's Dealings with John Murray and his Firm', *Review of English Studies*, Mar 2012, http://res.oxfordjournals.org/content/early/2012/03/31/res.hgs020.full.

21 The letter has been known since the publication of a Victorian biography of John Murray II, but there it is incorrectly dated a year later. The Murray–Gifford correspondence is in the John Murray Archive in the National Library of Scotland. I quote the letters from Sutherland's article.

22 29 Sept 1815. Another version of this letter also survives in the Murray Archive; dated 21 Sept 1815, it is probably an unsent draft: 'I have read the Novel, and like it much – I was sure, before I rec'd your letter, that the writer was the author of P. and Prejudice etc. I know not its value, but if you can procure it, it will certainly sell well. It is very carelessly copied, though the hand-writing is excellently plain, and there are many short omissions which must be inserted. I will readily correct the proof for you, and may do it a little good here and there, though there is not much to do, it must be confessed.' Gifford did indeed make 'improvements' to the manuscript of *Emma*, as Sutherland has shown.

23 Undated, but almost certainly early Oct 1815.

24 Letter 121, Oct 1815.

25 Letter 122(A), Henry Austen to John Murray, Oct 1815.

26 Letter 124, Nov 1815.

27 Letter 121, Oct 1815.

28 Letter 127, Nov 1815.

29 Ibid.

30 Jane Austen to John Murray, Letter 126, Nov 1815.

31 Caroline Austen, 'My Aunt Jane Austen', in *Memoir*, p. 176.

32 See Lewis Melville, *The First Gentleman of Europe* (1906), p. 30 and A. M. W. Stirling, ed., *The Diaries of Dummer* (1934), p. 80.

33 To Martha Lloyd, Letter 82, Feb 1813.

34 Caroline Austen, 'My Aunt Jane Austen', in *Memoir*, p. 176.

35 Letter 125, Nov 1815.

36 James Stanier Clarke to Jane Austen, Letter 125(A), Nov 1815.

37 Letter 128, Nov 1815.

38 To John Murray, Letter 130, Dec 1815.

39 Letter 129, Dec 1815.

40 Murray to Scott, 25 Dec 1815.

41 Scott, *Quarterly Review*, Oct 1815, repr. in *Jane Austen: The Critical Heritage*, ed. B. C. Southam (1968), pp. 58–69. Subsequent quotations from same source.

42 Letter 139, Apr 1816.

43 Letter 132(A), Stanier Clarke to Austen, Dec 1815.

44 Letter 138(A), Stanier Clarke to Austen, Mar 1816.

45 Letter 138(D), Apr 1816.

46 'Plan of a Novel', in *Minor Works*, pp. 428–30.

47 1818 'Biographical Notice', in *Memoir*, p. 138.

48 Ibid., p. 139.

49 Ibid., p. 169.

50 Letter 13, Dec 1798.

51 *Family Record*, p. 254.

52 Ibid., pp. 198–9.

53 Letter 87, Sept 1813.

54 Letter 106, Sept 1814.

55 See my 'Who was Miss Jane Austin? A possible alternative to Aunt Jane: the professional writer at work', *Times Literary Supplement*, 13 Apr 2012, and Deirdre Le Faye's response (14 May). Also Deborah Kaplan's judicious account, '"There She is at Last": The Byrne Portrait Controversy', *Persuasions*, issue 34 (2012).

CHAPTER EIGHTEEN: THE BATHING MACHINE

1 See Andrea Richards's excellent online article for the Jane Austen Society of Australia, '"The Bathing was so delightful this morning": The bathing experience of Jane Austen and others', http://www.jasa.net.au/seaside/ Bathing.htm (accessed 1 Sept 2012), to which I also owe the references to Smollett, Grant and Burney.

2 Tobias Smollett, *The Expedition of Humphry Clinker* (1771, repr. 2 vols, 1793), 1.245.

3 *Eliza Letters*, pp. 97–9.

4 Elizabeth Grant, *Memoirs of a Highland Lady* (1950), pp. 106–7.

5 *Pride and Prejudice*, 2.18.

6 *Diary and Letters of Madame D'Arblay*, vol. 5, pp. 35–6.

7 Clifford Musgrave, *Life in Brighton* (1970), p. 199.

8 James Walvin, *Beside the Seaside: Social History of the Popular Seaside Holiday* (1978), p. 25.

9 Letter 39, Sept 1804.

10 *The Prose Works of William Wordsworth* (2005), p. 246.

11 *Chronology*, p. 261.

12 John Feltham, *Guide to all Watering and Sea-Bathing Places* (1803), p. 366.

13 Ibid., p. 365.

14 Letter 25, Nov 1800.

15 Feltham, *Guide to all Watering and Sea-Bathing Places*, p. 418.

16 *Chronology*, p. 272.

17 Feltham, *Guide to all Watering and Sea-Bathing Places*, p. 420.

NOTES

18 *Sense and Sensibility*, 2.14; Letter 104, Aug 1814.
19 *Persuasion*, 1.11.
20 Letter 57, Oct 1808.
21 See George Roberts, *The History and Antiquities of the borough of Lyme Regis and Charmouth* (1834), pp. 171–2.
22 Letter 39, Sept 1804.
23 Hill, *Jane Austen: Her Homes and her Friends*, pp. 142–4.
24 *Persuasion*, 1.11.
25 Ibid., 1.12.
26 Ibid.
27 *The Works of Lord Byron*, 6 vols (1831), vol. 2, p. 68.
28 *Persuasion*, 2.9.
29 Letter 39, Sept 1804.
30 Ibid.
31 *Sanditon*, ch. 4.
32 Ibid., ch. 2.
33 Ibid., ch. 2.
34 Ibid., ch. 9.
35 Ibid., ch. 10.
36 Ibid., ch. 10.
37 Ibid., ch. 12.
38 Ibid., ch. 8.
39 Letter 157, Apr 1817.
40 Sir Zachary Cope was the first to suggest that she was suffering from Addison's. See 'Jane Austen's Final Illness', *British Medical Journal*, 18 July 1964.

EPILOGUE

1 The often reproduced (and often reworked) sketch, assumed to be by Cassandra and now in the National Portrait Gallery, is not signed or identified on the back. Though it almost certainly is Jane, it is unfinished, was regarded by family members as unlike, and may even be best construed, as Kathryn Sutherland brilliantly suggests in her *Jane Austen's Textual Lives: From Aeschylus to Bollywood* (2007), as a caricature rather than a portrait (p. 115).
2 Quoted, R. W. Chapman, *Jane Austen: Facts and Problems* (1948), p. 213. My reproduction is of a black and white photograph of the sketch, published as the frontispiece to Chapman's edition of *Jane Austen's Letters to her sister Cassandra and others* (1932, repr. 1952). According to Chapman's note to his 'List of Illustrations', the original drawing was inserted by Anna Lefroy into her manuscript volume of family history and at least two copies of it exist in other family collections.
3 *Persuasion*, 1.11.

PICTURE CREDITS

Copyright Victoria and Albert Museum, London: Copleston Warre Bampfylde's watercolour of 'Lyme Regis and the Dorsetshire Coast'; Bone Spelling Alphabet, English c.1800.

Courtesy of the David Collection, Copenhagen: square woollen shawl, made in Kashmir, c.1800 (inventory no. 26/1992), photo: Pernille Klemp.

Copyright Science Museum/Science and Society Picture Library: high-perch sociable barouche carriage, from a collection of engravings of carriages published by R. Ackermann, 1816.

Courtesy of a private collector: card of French lace, probably manufactured in the English midlands.

Courtesy of The Pierpont Morgan Library, New York (MA 977.4). Photography by Schecter Lee: part of a letter from Jane to Cassandra Austen, 2 June 1799, with sketch of lace design.

Courtesy of Hampshire Record Office (71M82/PR3): Jane Austen's 'marriage' entries in Steventon parish register.

From a private collection, copyright Philip Mould and Company: miniature of Mrs Lefroy by Richard Crosse.

From the collection of the Earl of Mansfield, Scone Palace: portrait of Dido Belle and Lady Elizabeth Murray, attributed to Zoffany.

Courtesy of the Board of Stoneleigh Abbey Limited: crimson velvet cushion in the family chapel at Stoneleigh; letter from Thomas Leigh to Thomas Hill; watercolour by Humphry Repton from his Stoneleigh Red Book. Photos: Tom Bate.

From a private collection, photograph copyright Sotheby's: title page of presentation copy of *Emma* sent by Jane Austen to Maria Edgeworth.

Copyright The British Library Board: Jane Austen's writing box; vellum notebook *Volume the Second*.

Courtesy of The National Library of Scotland (from the John Murray Archive): front and back of John Murray's royalty cheque for *Emma*, countersigned by Jane Austen.

Courtesy of the Jane Austen Memorial Trust (Jane Austen's House Museum): Anna (Austen) Lefroy's sketch of the rear of Steventon rectory; miniature of Phila Hancock; watercolour of Fanny Knight writing; topaz crosses owned by Jane and Cassandra Austen; miniatures of George Austen and Henry Austen.

Courtesy of the Soldiers of Oxfordshire Museum, Woodstock: cocked hat worn by Captain John Meadows of the Oxfordshire Militia.

Copyright Georgios Kollidas/Dreamstime.com: John Murray II (1778–1843), engraved by E. Finden and published in London by A. Fullarton.

Courtesy of The Royal Collection Trust, copyright HM Queen Elizabeth II, 2012: presentation set of *Emma* given to the Prince Regent.

Courtesy of Royal Pavilion and Museums, Brighton: William Heath's caricature 'Mermaids at Brighton' (1829).

Illustrations from J. H. and E. C. Hubback's *Jane Austen's Sailor Brothers* (1905), in the author's personal collection: drawing of a ship by Herbert Austen; silhouette of Cassandra Austen; miniature of Captain Charles Austen; '*Peterel* in action with the French brig *La Ligurienne*, after driving two others on the rocks near Marseilles, on 21 March 1800' sketched by Herbert Austen; miniature of Captain Francis Austen; 'Vice-Admiral Sir Francis Austen KCB's writing desk' sketched by his daughter Cassandra.

Illustrations from Constance Hill's *Jane Austen: Her Homes and her Friends* (1902), in the author's personal collection: silhouette of 'Rev George Austen presenting his son Edward to Mr and Mrs Thomas Knight'; sketch of hallway of Godmersham House; portrait miniature of Eliza de Feuillide; sketch of Jane Austen's cup and ball; sketch of steps on the Cobb, Lyme Regis (sketches by Ellen G. Hill).

Illustrations from Jane Austen, *Love and Freindship and other early works now first printed from the original manuscripts* (1922), in the author's personal collection: wording of dedication to 'Love and Freindship'; Cassandra Austen's sketches in Jane Austen's 'A History of England'.

Frontispiece to R. W. Chapman's *Jane Austen's Letters to Her Sister Cassandra and Others* (1932, repr. 1952), in the author's personal collection: photograph, courtesy of Oxford University Press, of Cassandra Austen's watercolour sketch of the back view of Jane Austen.

Original works in the author's personal collection: first edition of Fanny Burney's *Camilla* (1796) and engraving of Fanny Burney; portrait of the Trevanion Sisters (c.1803) by unknown artist; George Cruikshank's caricature 'Travelling in England, or a peep from the White Horse cellar' (1819); photograph of Steventon auction advertisement from the *Reading Mercury* (27 April 1801); Cruikshank engraving of 'The Honourable Tom Dashall and his Cousin Bob, in the Lobby at the Drury Lane Theatre' from Pierce Egan's *Real Life in London* (1821); engraving by C. Heath after a painting by Howard of a scene in *Lovers' Vows* (1816); engraving of Mrs Leigh Perrot; engraving of Bath Street (from *Nattes's Bath*, 1806); title page of pamphlet *The Trial of Jane Leigh Perrot* (Taunton, 1800); caricatures by George Cruikshank of 'Mr B on the Middle Watch' and 'Mr B Promoted to Lieut and first putting on his Uniform' (1835); Cruikshank engraving of 'The "ne plus ultra" of Life in London – Kate, Sue, Tom, Jerry and Logic viewing the throne room at Carlton Palace' from *Life in London* (1822); graphite on vellum drawing of 'Miss Jane Austin', c.1815; photograph of engraving 'Bathing Place, Morning Dresses' from *The Gallery of Fashion* (September 1797).

All photographs from the author's personal collection © Tom Bate.

Images in the public domain: title page of Byrne and Jones's Dublin edition of *The Loiterer* (1792); title pages of *Sense and Sensibility* (1811) and *Pride and Prejudice* (1813); engraving of Harris Bigg-Wither (released into the public domain from the family archive).

The publisher has made every effort to trace copyright holders of images reproduced in this book, but will be glad to rectify any omissions in future editions.

ACKNOWLEDGMENTS

The writing of this biography would not have been possible without the work of other Jane Austen scholars, past and present. Many local debts are acknowledged in the endnotes. I owe most to the editions of Jane Austen's letters by Lord Brabourne (1884), R. W. Chapman (1932 and 1952) and Deirdre Le Faye (1995 and 2011), and to *A Family Record* by Richard and William Austen-Leigh (1913) and its revision by Le Faye (1989). Deirdre Le Faye's extraordinarily detailed *A Chronology of Jane Austen and her Family* (2006) has been my constant companion. It is now the definitive day-to-day record of the life of Austen, and perhaps the book that makes unnecessary any further chronological cradle-to-grave biography. Barring a miracle such as the discovery of a cache of lost letters, if future biographers are to say anything new they will have to be innovative in their methods, as I have tried to be here. But innovation often has a way of looking back as well as forward, and so it has been for me: I have drawn particular inspiration from Constance Hill's *Jane Austen: Her Homes and her Friends* (1902), which was based on a pilgrimage to the places where Austen lived and which included illustrations by Constance's sister, Ellen: this created a pioneering combination of 'footsteps' (a technique I already knew from Richard Holmes, the living biographer whom I most admire) and 'things' (among Ellen Hill's sketches are the steps on the Cobb and Jane Austen's ivory cup and ball).

The other innovation that has been of enormous assistance in my research is the internet: what previous biographer has had access at the click of a mouse to the full text of, say, the novels of Jane Austen's cousins or the now obscure books mentioned in her letters? Constance Hill's first chapter was called 'An Arrival in Austen-land': a hundred years later, Austen-land is a teeming virtual world of online journals and blogs where remarkably fresh scholarship co-exists with unashamedly 'Janeite' sentiment: my special thanks to pemberley.com, austenprose.com, austenonly. com and many more.

Back in the world visited by Constance Hill, I have had enormous help from Louise West and all the staff at Jane Austen's House Museum.

Professor Kathryn Sutherland has been generous with both warm friendship and exemplary scholarship, and since my arrival in Oxford I have been lucky enough to enter a sisterly circle of Austen scholars, including Fiona Stafford, Mary Favret, Freya Johnston and Nicola Trott. My thanks to Kelvin Everest and Edward Burns for their help with my early thoughts on Austen when I was at the University of Liverpool, and to the great Austen scholar Claudia L. Johnson, who has been a valued supporter ever since she examined my doctorate.

The jury remains out on the plumbago drawing of 'Miss Jane Austin', but thanks to the research that went into the television documentary 'Jane Austen: The Unseen Portrait?' we can be sure that it is authentic to the Regency period, and for this I am deeply grateful to Liz Hartford, Neil Crombie, all the team at Seneca Productions and all the expert contributors, especially Roy Davids, Hilary Davidson of the Museum of London and Nicholas Eastaugh of Art Access and Research; also to Janice Hadlow and Mark Bell at BBC2.

For particular help with the sourcing of images, my thanks to Mette Korsholm of the David Collection, Copenhagen; Marcie Knowles, lace collector in Alabama; David Rymill and Nicola Pink at the Hampshire Record Office; Marilyn Palmeri at the Morgan Library, New York; Sara Denham and Emma Rutherford at Philip Mould and Company; Daniel Bell at the Royal Collection; Beverley Green at the Royal Pavilion and Museums, Brighton; Bernard Robinson and Kevin Tobin at the Soldiers of Oxfordshire Museum, Woodstock; Katherine Marshall at Sotheby's; Paula Cornwell and Gretchen Ames at Stoneleigh Abbey; Olivia Stroud at the Victoria and Albert Museum.

Bob Bearman drew my attention to the importance of the Stoneleigh archive in the Shakespeare Birthplace Trust Records Office in Stratford-upon-Avon and David McClay, Curator of the John Murray Archive, was generous with his time. Richard Ovenden provided wonderful support from the Bodleian Library. Claire Johnstone of Mansfield College, Oxford, checked and corrected references for me at amazing speed, despite being in the process of moving house.

For the opportunity to try out material in advance of publication, I am grateful to James Runcie of the Bath Literature Festival, Vicky Bennett of the Chipping Campden Literature Festival and Tim Hipperson and Juliette Coles of Oundle School.

At HarperPress, Arabella Pike is the best of all possible commissioning editors – massively enthusiastic in her support for my books but also rigorous and imaginative in her line-by-line editing. The same goes for her counterpart, Terry Karten in New York. Kate Tolley saw the book through the press in record time, an achievement all the more remarkable because of the number of illustrations, and Peter James was an amazing copy editor, making invaluable suggestions and saving me from crass errors.

As the life of Jane Austen shows, it has never been easy for a woman to earn her living by the pen, but in our own very difficult time for the economics of authorship no professional biographer could wish for better agents than Andrew Wylie and Sarah Chalfant.

Tom Bate took superb photographs of both documents and places. Following in Jane Austen's footsteps with him, and on other occasions with my parents Tim and Clare Byrne, has been one of the great pleasures of the research. My niece Sarah Bate helped with references. Many thanks to Agnieszka Kuzminska, without whose hard work and help with the children I would have been lost. Ecclesiastical minutiae were furnished by my dear friends the Reverends Matthew Catterick and Paul Edmondson.

During the hectic process of completing the book in time for the bicentenary of the publication of *Pride and Prejudice*, while also settling three children into new schools and taking on the busy role of 'Mrs Provost', my sanity was preserved by Northwick Park (where Warren Hastings came over from Daylesford to visit) and by all my friends there, especially Betina Goodall, Fiona Laidlaw and Katy Whyard.

Above all, my deepest gratitude is reserved for my dearest husband Jonathan Bate. I could not have written this book without his faith, love and support. I am thankful to have him in my life.

INDEX

ABOUT THE AUTHOR

PAULA BYRNE's first book, *Jane Austen and the Theatre*, was shortlisted for the Theatre Book Prize and has been described by Paul Johnson as "the best book on Jane Austen." Her second, *Perdita*, was a much-praised biography of the eighteenth-century actress, poet, novelist, feminist, celebrity and royal mistress Mary Robinson; and her third book, *Mad World*, was a highly acclaimed and brilliantly original biography of Evelyn Waugh. In 2011 Paula Byrne made a BBC documentary about her discovery of a portrait of Jane Austen, thought by many experts to be the only professional portrait of the novelist painted from life. She is married to the critic and biographer Jonathan Bate and lives in Oxford.

BOOKS BY PAULA BYRNE

DIDO BELLE
Available in Paperback and eBook

Based on a painting that shocked 18th century England, Paula Byrne's biography and the forthcoming film, "Belle," tell the tale of one of the most powerful men of the 18th century and his controversial adoption of a mixed race girl. The portrait was commissioned by Lord Mansfield, whose name was synonymous with the campaign against slavery, and the presentation of a black girl, expensively dressed and on equal footing with her white sibling, was a stunning statement for society.

MAD WORLD
Evelyn Waugh and the Secrets of Brideshead

Available in Paperback

This brilliantly original biography unlocks for the first time the extent to which Waugh's great novel encoded and transformed his own experiences. In so doing, it illuminates the loves and obsessions that shaped his life, and brings us inevitably to the great writer's own tragic secret.

THE REAL JANE AUSTEN
A Life in Small Things

Available in Paperback and eBook

This new biography explores the forces that shaped one of our most beloved novelists: her father's religious faith; her mother's pedigree; her eldest brother's adoption; her other brothers' military experiences; her relatives in the East and West Indies; her cousin who lived through the French Revolution; the amateur theatricals; her love of the seaside; and her determination to become a published author.